T0320205

European Union Trade Politics and Development

The 'Everything but Arms' (EBA) regulation of the European Union (EU) has been hailed as a groundbreaking initiative for developing countries. Since 2001, EBA grants almost completely liberalized access to the European market for products from the least developed countries (LDCs). It quickly became the most symbolic European trade initiative towards the Third World since the first Lomé Convention in the 1970s.

Given its central position in EU discourse and its continuing relevance for the European and international trade agenda, this book attempts to present a thorough analysis of EBA. *European Union Trade Politics and Development* contains contributions from a diverse range of scholars who collectively present a comprehensive picture of EBA. This volume also contains a broader analysis of EU trade politics towards the South, focusing on agricultural policy reform and Europe's evolving relationship with ACP countries (ex-colonies from Africa, the Caribbean and the Pacific). It also links EBA with Europe's negotiating position within the World Trade Organization. Contributions to this volume also consider the continuing negotiation leverage of EBA within the Doha Development Agenda, make comparisons with United States trade policy vis-à-vis the LDCs, and focus on the economic effectiveness of EBA in terms of its stated objectives as well as on the institutional skirmishing within the EU.

This volume demonstrates that EBA has had a significant influence on internal and external EU politics. This impact is likely to continue in the coming years. As such, the book is useful reading for those who study the relationship between trade and development as well as all those with an interest in the politics and economics of the EU.

Gerrit Faber is Associate Professor of International Economics at Utrecht University, the Netherlands.

Jan Orbie is Assistant Professor in EU Politics at Ghent University, Belgium.

Routledge Studies in Development Economics

European Union Trade Politics and Development

'Everything but Arms' unravelled

**Edited by Gerrit Faber
and Jan Orbie**

Routledge
Taylor & Francis Group

LONDON AND NEW YORK

First published 2007
by Routledge
2 Park Square, Milton Park, Abingdon, Oxon OX14 4RN

Simultaneously published in the USA and Canada
by Routledge
270 Madison Ave, New York, NY 10016

Routledge is an imprint of the Taylor & Francis Group, an informa business

British Library Cataloguing in Publication Data
A catalogue record for this book is available from the British Library

Library of Congress Cataloging in Publication Data
European Union trade politics and development : 'Everything but Arms'
unravelled/edited by Gerrit Faber and Jan Orbie.
p. cm.
Includes bibliographical references and index.
ISBN-13: 978–0–415–42627–5 (hb)
1. Free trade–European Union countries. 2. Free trade–Developing countries.
3. Tariff preferences–Law and legislation–European Union countries.
4. Developing countries–Economic conditions. I. Faber, G. J. II. Orbie, Jan, 1978–
HF2036.E875 2007
382'.9142–dc22   2006031335

ISBN10: 0–415–42627–8
ISBN13: 978–0–415–42627–5

Contents

Illustrations

Tables

Notes on the contributors

Olufemi Babarinde is Academic Director for MBA and Associate Professor, Europe and Africa Studies, at Thunderbird, the Garvin School of International Management in Glendale AZ. His research and publications have focused on African integration and regionalism, African enterprises, Nigeria, the euro, external relations of the EU, and ACP–EU relations.

Sanoussi Bilal is Programme Coordinator of the ACP–EU Economic and Trade Cooperation Programme at the European Centre for Development Policy Management, Maastricht, the Netherlands.

Paul Brenton works at the International Trade Department (PRMTR) of the World Bank, Washington DC.

Michael Brüntrup works at the German Development Institute in Bonn in the areas of agricultural trade and trade policies, with a focus on sub-Saharan Africa.

Maurizio Carbone is lecturer in the Department of Politics, University of Glasgow.

Gerrit Faber is Associate Professor, International Economics, at the Utrecht School of Economics, Utrecht University, the Netherlands.

Jacques Gallezot is Director of Research at INRA, UMR Economie Publique INRA-INAPG, Paris, and associate researcher at CEPII (Centre d'études prospectives et d'informations internationales).

Adrian van den Hoven worked as a Schuman Researcher at the European University Institute before joining the Confederation of European Business (UNICE), where he is International Relations Director.

Bart Kerremans is Associate Professor of International Relations at the University of Leuven (KU Leuven) in Belgium.

Dries Lesage is a Postdoctoral Fellow of the National Fund for Scientific Research (Belgium), Department of Political Science, Ghent University, Belgium.

Alan Matthews is Jean Monnet Professor of European Agricultural Policy in the Department of Economics and a Research Associate of the Institute for International Integration Studies, Trinity College Dublin, Ireland.

Jan Orbie is Assistant Professor in the Centre for EU Studies, Department of Political Science, Ghent University, Belgium.

Çaglar Özden is affiliated to the Development Research Group (DECRG) of the World Bank, Washington DC.

Jess Pilegaard works at the Danish Ministry of Foreign Affairs/Embassy of Denmark in Lusaka, Zambia.

Preface

Trade is the most powerful external policy domain of the European Union (EU). It also constitutes a major avenue for Europe's relations with developing countries. Whereas most research has focused on Europe's multilateral and bilateral trade policies vis-à-vis the South, this book departs from the unilateral dimension. It looks more specifically at the 'Everything but Arms' (EBA) initiative, which has granted the least developed countries almost completely liberalized access to the European market since 2001. EBA quickly became the most symbolic and politicized EU trade initiative towards developing countries since the first Lomé Convention in the 1970s.

Five years after the inception of EBA, we organized a symposium with the provocative question '"Everything but Arms": All about Nothing?' at Ghent University in December 2005. Thanks to the participation of people from different academic backgrounds and with different professional affiliations – economists and political scientists, scholars in development, agriculture, international relations, trade policies and EU studies – we gradually gained insight into the peculiarities and the wide-ranging consequences of EBA.

The first aim of this book is to present a thorough and comprehensive analysis of EBA. Given its central position in EU discourse and its continuing relevance for the European and international trade agenda, we attempt to provide an in-depth examination of EBA. Second, as the title of this book suggests, the EBA theme is used as the occasion for a broader analysis of EU trade politics towards the South. Therefore the book is more than a case study: it deals with EU agricultural policy reform, it looks at Europe's evolving relationship with ACP countries, it links EBA with Europe's negotiating position in the World Trade Organization, it considers the continuing negotiation leverage of EBA within the Doha Development Agenda, it makes comparisons with US trade policy vis-à-vis the least developed countries, it focuses on the economic effectiveness of EBA in terms of its stated objectives as well as on the institutional skirmishing within the EU. Indeed, the general conclusion reads that, although EBA may have had a very modest impact on development, its influence on internal and external EU politics has been significant, and is expected to become more so in the coming years.

All the chapters in this volume were first presented at the symposium and subsequently revised. We are very grateful to the participants for their contribution to the unravelment of EBA, and for their diligence in meeting our (rather tough) deadlines. We would also like to thank the Jean Monnet European Centre of Excellence and the Department of Political Science at Ghent University, whose funding made it possible to organize the workshop. A special note of thanks goes to Professor Hendrik Vos, Director of the Centre for EU Studies of Ghent University, for his enthusiastic encouragement of the project. The task of the editors was facilitated by a grant of the Tjalling C. Koopmans Institute of the Utrecht School of Economics, which is gratefully acknowledged. We also owe special thanks to two external referees commissioned by Routledge, and to Terry Clague, Taiba Batool and the editorial staff at Routledge for their support and their efficient handling of the manuscript.

Gerrit Faber
Utrecht School of Economics

Jan Orbie
Centre for EU Studies,
Department of Political Science,
Ghent University

Abbreviations

ACP	Africa Caribbean and Pacific group
AGOA	African Growth and Opportunity Act
AoA	Agreement on Agriculture
APEC	Asia–Pacific Economic Cooperation
ASEAN	Association of South East Asian Nations
BLNS	Botswana, Lesotho, Namibia, Swaziland
CACM	Central American Common Market
CAFTA	Central American Free Trade Agreement
CAP	Common Agricultural Policy
CARIFORM	Caribbean Forum of ACP States
CBI	Caribbean Basin Initiative
CEMAC	Central African Economic and Monetary Community
COMESA	Common Market for Eastern and Southern Africa
DDA	Doha Development Agenda
DFQF	Duty-free and Quota-free
DRC	Democratic Republic of Congo
EBA	Everything but Arms
ECOWAS	Economic Community of West African States
EPA	Economic Partnership Agreement
ESA	Eastern and Southern Africa
EU	European Union
FDI	foreign direct investment
FTA	Free Trade Agreement
GAC	General Affairs Council
GAERC	General Affairs and External Relations Council
GATS	General Agreement on Trade in Services
GATT	General Agreement on Tariffs and Trade
GDP	gross domestic product
GNP	gross national product
GSP	Generalized System of Preferences
GTAP	Global Trade Analysis Project
HIPC	Heavily Indebted Poor Countries
IMF	International Monetary Fund

LDC	least developed country
MAT	Mozambique, Angola, Tanzania
MFN	most favoured nation
MGA	Maximum Guaranteed Area
MNC	multinational company
NAFTA	North American Free Trade Agreement
NAMA	Non-agricultural Market Access
NDTPF	National Development and Trade Policy Forum
NIEO	New International Economic Order
NTE	non-traditional exports
ODA	Official Development Assistance
OECD	Organization for Economic Cooperation and Development
SAARC	South Asian Association for Regional Cooperation
SACU	Southern African Customs Union
SADC	Southern African Development Community
SPS	Sanitary and Phytosanitary Standards
SSA	sub-Saharan Africa
TBT	technical barriers to trade
TDCA	Trade, Development and Cooperation Agreement
TIFA	Trade and Investment Framework Agreements
UNCTAD	United Nations Conference on Trade and Development
UNECA	United Nations Economic Commission for Africa
USTR	United States Trade Representative
WAEMU	West African Economic and Monetary Union
WTO	World Trade Organization

1 The least developed countries, international trade and the European Union

What about 'Everything but Arms'?

Gerrit Faber and Jan Orbie

EBA and harnessing globalization

The basic features of the 'Everything but Arms' (EBA) initiative by the European Union[1] are simple: provide the least developed countries (LDCs) with a fully liberalized access to the market of the EU in order to boost their exports and development. Box 1.1 gives an outline of EBA. Although EBA is a straightforward arrangement at first glance, it also is probably the most symbolic and politicized trade initiative of the EU since the conclusion of the first Lomé Convention in 1975. For the EU, EBA is much more than a technical regulation (EU 2001):

> It's a worldwide first. At the end of the day, we will have 100 per cent access, with no exclusions, except of course for arms. We have delivered on our fine words. This sends a signal to the rest of the world that we are serious about getting the most disadvantaged to share in the fruits of trade liberalization.

Pascal Lamy, then EU Trade Commissioner and currently Director General of the World Trade Organization (WTO), highlighted the importance of EBA as a crucial step in the development of the poorest countries.

BOX 1.1 'EVERYTHING BUT ARMS' IN A NUTSHELL

- Granting duty-free and quota-free (DFQF) market access for all products originating from the 50 least developed countries (LDCs)
- But transition period for sensitive agricultural products: bananas (2006), rice and sugar (2009)

---

continued

- Commission proposal in 2000, Council decision in February 2001
- A unilateral regulation under European Community law (trade policy, article 133 Treaty of the European Community)
- Special application of the Generalized System of Preferences (GSP) in favour of LDCs, legitimized under WTO law (Enabling Clause, article 2d)

A remarkably broad audience recognized the value of EBA. It was welcomed by the European political spectrum at large. Some criticized the transition periods for the sensitive products bananas, rice and sugar, others feared the consequences for European farmers. These different evaluations also emerged within the EU institutions such as the Council of Ministers, the European Commission and the European Parliament. But the fundamental desirability of the objective of duty-free and quota-free (DFQF) market access for the LDCs was out of question. EBA was widely considered as a step in the right direction – be it a huge or a small step.

Oxfam wrote a letter to the *Financial Times* in support of Lamy's EBA proposal (FT 14 December 2001), and in its preface of an early impact assessment the Director of Oxfam describes the Commission proposal as a 'small but welcome step towards fairer trade in the world' and an 'important step towards achieving internationally agreed targets to reduce poverty' (Stevens and Kennan 2001). United Nations (UN) Secretary General Kofi Annan wrote a letter to the President of the EU Council of Ministers to urge a quick approval of EBA (Lamy 2002a: 79–80). Former chief economist of the World Bank and winner of the 2001 Nobel Prize in Economics Joseph Stiglitz considered EBA as 'a big step in the right direction' (Stiglitz 2002: 246). In its review of the EU development policies, the Development Assistance Committee of the Organization for Economic Cooperation and Development called EBA 'a major success with policy coherence' (OECD/DAC 2002: I-22).

EBA quickly became the showpiece of the development-friendly nature of EU trade policy. In speeches and documents, the EU presented it as groundbreaking and did not fail to point out that other WTO members should follow its lead. Since 2001 the initiative has occupied a central place in the discourse about 'harnessing globalization' – Pascal Lamy's favourite motto, and European policy makers' dominant conception of the much contested globalization phenomenon. The trade policy objective of harnessing globalization basically implies a commitment to sustainable development (social and ecological considerations; development of the Third World) and global rules (rule-based multilateralism). It is seen as the external projection of the post-war integration project on the European continent. The international pursuit of such normative objectives or 'milieu goals' (cf. Smith 2003: 13, 200–1) reflects a more general trend in EU policy makers' discourse, as well as in the academic literature, to emphasize the normative dimension of Europe's action on the world scene (cf. Manners 2002; Diez 2005).

Constituting its most powerful external policy domain, EU trade policy has also incorporated this 'normative power Europe' strand. The overarching aim of harnessing globalization indicates that in EU trade policy it 'is no longer only economic interests that are in question, but also values' (Lamy in *Agence Europe* 1999). These include a commitment to development of the South. The following citation shows how Europe's normative world role, the harnessing of globalization through trade and ultimately the EBA initiative are closely interlinked in EU discourse (Lamy 2002b):

> The ambition of the Convention [to produce a draft constitution for the EU] should be to give Europe a clearer place in the world – a project that reflects the values we hold dear. While this will eventually have to encompass all fields of foreign and security policy, we should start with a common roadmap on the governance of globalisation, notably in North–South relations. This is a long-standing concern of the EU, as various existing instruments show: EU/ACP agreements, the Generalised System of Preferences for developing countries, regional trade agreements, the 'Everything but Arms' initiative which grants duty-free and quota-free access to the EU market to the 49 poorest countries. But we now need to devote all tools of external policy (trade, development, diplomacy) to harnessing globalisation, towards sustainable development and a global partnership with Developing Countries.

The result of this European Convention also witnesses the increased normative bias of trade policy objectives. The text of the EU Constitutional Treaty strengthens the consistency requirement of trade policy by explicitly stating that commercial policy 'shall be conducted in the context of the principles and objectives of the Union's external action' (Article III-315). Furthermore, in Article I-3(4) about the Union's objectives in the world, the goal of 'free and fair trade' is mentioned. Although it is unclear what the new 'fair trade' provision exactly means, it cannot be seen as a veiled reference to protectionism (Eeckhout 2004: 53); it rather illustrates Europe's augmented attention for the trade and development nexus.

This sketches the broader political context of the EBA initiative. But for the rest, many questions emerge. How successful has the EU been in promoting LDC export performance through EBA? What about the political debate among EU actors in the decision-making process towards this regulation? How and to what extent does this much discussed initiative signal a break from the past in Europe's approach towards developing countries? What are the consequences of EBA for agricultural markets inside the EU and for Europe's traditional partners in Africa, the Caribbean and the Pacific (ACP)? How does this initiative relate to the WTO and to Europe's position in the Doha Development Round of trade negotiations? How unique is the EBA formula compared with other developed countries' trade initiatives – in particular the US? And in general, more than five years after its inception, the main question of this volume reads: is EBA all about nothing, or has it somehow a political and economic relevance?

This chapter introduces the issues that will be elaborated in the next chapters. In the next sections we will first discuss the group of beneficiary countries: the history of the LDC group as well as their current position in international trade. Then the trade and development nexus will be considered, giving a brief review of the literature on the effectiveness of non-reciprocal preferences. Finally, the composition of the volume will be presented.

The least developed countries

For a long time, developing countries have tried to operate as a unified group, often under the flag of 'the Group of 77' (e.g. during the negotiations for a New International Economic Order in the 1970s). More recently, there is the emergence of developing country groups in the context of the WTO negotiations, such as the G-20, the G-33 and the G-90. Nevertheless, very poor – or least or lesser-developed – countries were recognized as a special category rather early in the history of development cooperation. This section will present the history of this special category of countries and their position in world trade.

History of the LDC group and the demand for DFQF market access

The idea that the concept of developing countries is too broad and hides large differences between sub-groups dates back to the second half of the 1960s. In 1968 the United Nations Conference on Trade and Development (UNCTAD) adopted the first resolution on the subject of the LDCs. The first list of LDCs was established by the UN General Assembly in 1971 (UN, n.d.). After the identification of the group, special measures and plans were designed and agreed in order to stimulate their development. Their lagging growth led to an intensification of these efforts by the end of the 1970s.

The Tokyo Round (1973–79) of the General Agreement on Tariffs and Trade (GATT) established the 'Enabling Clause'. This forms the legal basis for the Generalized System of Preferences (GSP). Under the GSP system, essentially an exception to the Most Favoured Nation (MFN) principle of the GATT/WTO, developed countries can unilaterally determine which products benefit from more favourable and non-reciprocal access to their markets. The Enabling Clause – officially the Decision on Differential and More Favourable Treatment, Reciprocity and Fuller Participation of Developing Countries – gave the temporary GATT waiver of 1971 permanent status. Interestingly, paragraph 2(d) enables further tariff reductions for countries belonging to the group of LDCs. EBA can be seen as a radical application of this provision: it basically constitutes a more generous form of Europe's 'standard' GSP, specifically targeted at the LDCs.

This differentiation among developing countries is thus allowed under WTO rules. But another 'special' GSP regime of the EU, the so-called GSP drugs regime, was found illegal by the WTO. Following the inclusion of Pakistan in Europe's

GSP drug arrangement in November 2001, India went to the WTO dispute settlement mechanism. In 2004 the WTO Appelate Body ruled that the Enabling Clause allows discrimination among developing countries, albeit that the selection has to be based on objective and transparent criteria (cf. Charnovitz *et al.* 2004). In response the EU transformed its special GSP drugs regime, together with a similar arrangement for countries respecting core labour standards, into a 'GSP-plus' regime. Since 2006, to be eligible for additional GSP preferences, developing countries have to ratify and effectively implement a number of international conventions relating to sustainable development and good governance (e.g. Kyoto Protocol, ILO core conventions, UN convention against corruption). The application of this GSP-plus regime is limited to vulnerable developing countries (not necessarily LDCs) and it is less generous than EBA (no DFQF market access) (Orbie *et al.* 2005).

This shows that EBA is not the only game in town. Europe has used its available preferential margin – between standard GSP and zero tariffs – for other (normative) foreign policy goals as well. The same is true for the Free Trade Agreements that the EU has concluded with a number of developing countries (e.g. Mexico, Chile) in recent years, establishing free (albeit reciprocal) market access for 'substantially all' products, in addition to a number of 'WTO-plus' provisions about services, investment, labour standards, etc. Yet EBA is the only European trade initiative that has granted DFQF market access for almost all products since 2001 and for all imports from 2009 onwards.

Besides the GSP as a legitimized exception to the MFN principle, the Tokyo Round also resulted in the establishment of a special 'Sub-committee on Trade of LDCs' within the GATT system. This committee would monitor, *inter alia*, the trade problems of the LDCs, and keep under review the special treatment (e.g. GSP preferences) accorded to these countries. Its activities (see e.g. GATT 1985) were given impetus by the GATT Ministerial Declaration of 1982, which explicitly refers to LDCs. It calls for special treatment of LDCs and in annex it enumerates a number of actions for LDCs that are strikingly similar to the LDC provisions in the Doha Development Agenda (DDA) 20 years later: the improvement of market access for LDCs with the objective of 'providing fullest possible duty-free access', eliminating or reducing non-tariff barriers for LDCs, more flexible rules of origin, technical assistance for LDCs, strengthening trade promotion activities, facilitating participation of LDCs in international negotiations, and considering the interests of LDCs in other trade policy issues (GATT 1982). Four years later the Ministerial Declaration of Punta del Este, launching the Uruguay Round of trade negotiations, stated that the 'expeditious implementation' of these LDC provisions would 'be given appropriate attention'. The conclusion of the Uruguay Round also included a 'decision on measures in favour of LDCs', *inter alia* calling for special and differential treatment, but without mentioning the issue of DFQF market access. Neither did the DFQF demand emerge from the meetings of the LDC Sub-committee in 1995–96, which emphasize the importance of trade-related issues such as financial and technical assistance for LDCs, rather than market access.[2]

Also within the UN institutions, the situation of LDCs gained significance by the end of the 1970s. In 1981 this led to the first UN Conference on the LDCs, held in Paris. The conference adopted a Substantial New Programme of Action for the 1980s for the LDCs. Every ten years a UN conference on the LDCs would be convened. The last one was hosted by the European Commission in Brussels in May 2001, shortly after the adoption of EBA. This was the first time that the EU hosted a major UN conference.

In 1979 the GSP scheme of the European Community, for the first time, started to apply special tariff treatment to LDCs. Through the 1980s, each revision of Europe's GSP extended the number of LDC products that were granted duty-free and/or quota-free access to the European market. This illustrates the gradual 'globalization' of EU trade policies,[3] away from an exclusive focus on the ACP group. Yet GSP preferences for LDCs continued to be less generous than trade preferences for the ACP countries under the successive Lomé Conventions. Although the European Community had started its own GSP system as early as 1971, legitimized by a temporary GATT waiver (see above), its beneficiaries still had 'second class' status compared with Europe's preferential treatment under the Yaoundé and Lomé agreements. This was also the case for a number of non-ACP LDCs, mainly in Asia. EBA heralds a much more radical distinction in EU trade policy between LDCs on the one hand and non-LDCs on the other – whether or not belonging to the ACP group.

Similarly, on the international trade level, the importance of the LDC group as a dominant category is relatively recent. Although the situation of LDCs had gained prominence on the international trade agenda since the 1970s, the international community's focus on the LDC category was still largely related to development strategies and financial support. For a long time, the LDC category was primarily used by donor agencies for the distribution of development aid and other measures of development cooperation. The DFQF market access demand for LDCs was scarcely raised and not politicized during the Uruguay Round. As explained above, this issue was not addressed during the first three meetings of the Sub-committee on LDCs in 1995–96.

This changed in the second half of 1996, with the initiative of WTO Director General Renato Ruggiero and the subsequent Ministerial Conference in Singapore. The Action Plan for the LDCs, adopted at the Singapore Conference, promises a 'comprehensive approach' to the trade problems of LDCs by combining assistance for capacity building and duty-free market access. In October 1997 the Integrated Framework was established by the WTO and other multilateral organizations such as UNCTAD, to support LDC governments in trade capacity building and integrating trade issues into overall national development strategies. The Sub-committee on LDCs monitors the support for LDCs provided by the Integrated Framework, and discusses issues such as market access of LDCs, implementation of WTO agreements and technical assistance.

The role of the LDC group also changed in the second half of the 1990s. After the conclusion of the Uruguay Round, the LDCs started to formulate an independent course and became more active in the WTO negotiations (Jess Pilegaard,

Chapter 8 of this volume). Technical assistance to participate more actively in the WTO negotiations and support by the Integrated Framework will have contributed to this more active participation. In 2001, the LDCs convened a meeting of trade ministers of the group in Zanzibar (Tanzania) and decided to have such a meeting every two years, preceding WTO Ministerials. The demand for DFQF market access held a prominent position in all declarations issued by these LDC trade conferences.

At the start of the DDA in 2001, WTO members confirmed their commitment to take special measures for the LDCs. DFQF treatment for their exports would be the main initiative. In the Sub-committee on LDCs, members will identify and examine all market access barriers confronting LDC exports, will annually review all market access improvements and will examine additional measures to improve market access for these countries. Technical assistance and support for export diversification for LDCs are promised as well in the Doha Declaration. The Doha Work Programme as adopted in August 2004 points out that the LDCs will not be required to undertake reduction commitments in agriculture while 'they are expected to substantially increase their level of binding commitments' in non-agricultural products (WTO 2004). The commitment to DFQF treatment of LDC exports by industrialized countries is repeated with the addition of the words 'and developing members in a position to do so'. One of the results of the sixth Ministerial Meeting in Hong Kong was to implement this commitment 'on a lasting basis . . . by 2008 or no later than the start of the implementation period' (WTO 2005). However, members that face difficulties in the implementation of this are allowed to keep 3 per cent of the products out of the arrangement and will bring these under the arrangement on a later date. Developing countries have much freedom in the phasing in of their preferential system in favour of LDCs. During the Hong Kong meeting, India and Brazil said that they would introduce a preferential system for the LDCs.

The position of LDCs in international trade

Who are the LDCs?

The UN General Assembly decides on the list of LDCs on a recommendation of the UN Economic and Social Council. The list is reviewed every three years. There are three criteria used to determine the status of a country. First, the GNP *per capita* should be below a certain level. This was US$750 in the 2003 review, while the graduation level was US$900. The second criterion is the Human Assets Index, a composite index based on variables that measure the *per capita* calorie intake, child mortality rate, secondary school enrolment and adult literacy rate. The Economic Vulnerability Index is the third criterion. It is based on instability in agricultural production, the share of the population displaced by natural disasters, instability in exports of goods and services, economic importance of non-traditional activities in gross domestic product (GDP), export concentration and economic smallness. For inclusion in the list, a country should satisfy all three criteria and should have a population of less than 75 million. Senegal was added in 2000, and Timor-Leste was put on the list in 2003, bringing the total number to 50. A country qualifies for graduation if it surpasses the maximum values of the criteria in at least two consecutive triennial reviews. In 1994 Botswana graduated and disappeared from the LDC list. In the 2003, both Cape Verde and Maldives met the benchmarks for graduation. As the two countries still have very high vulnerability indexes, they were not graduated (Simonis 2003). Appendix 1.1 to this chapter provides a list of the 50 LDCs, and indicates their status in the preferential schemes of the EU and the US. The majority of LDCs – 34 – are in sub-Saharan Africa (SSA) and are members of the ACP group of countries that signed the Lomé and Cotonou Agreements with the EU. Haiti in the Caribbean and five countries in the Pacific also belong to both the LDC and the ACP groups. Thus, 40 of the 50 LDCs enjoyed non-reciprocal preferential access to the EU market long before EBA was introduced. The other ten LDC are in Asia, and came under the standard EU GSP before EBA. For these countries, EBA in 2001 – and 'EBA *avant la lettre*'[4] in 1998 – constituted an increase of preferential margins for a larger number of goods. Myanmar is an exceptional case as the GSP preferences of this country were withdrawn since 1997 – and consequently also its eligibility for EBA market access since 2001 – because of serious violations of core labour standards (practices of forced labour). In several chapters of this book, a comparative analysis is made of EBA and the US preferential system for African countries, the African Growth and Opportunity ACT (AGOA). Appendix 1.1 shows that the list of AGOA beneficiaries is quite different from the list of SSA LDCs, as 15 of the 36 AGOA beneficiaries are not on the LDC list.

Living conditions in LDCs

In 2004, more than 11 per cent of the world population was living in LDCs. Their share in world GDP was much lower: 0.6 per cent (UNCTAD 2005). Living conditions of the average LDC citizen are harsh, whatever the yardstick. UNCTAD reviews the basic data for these countries in the series of 'The Least Developed Countries Report' (data in this section from UNCTAD 2004). Life expectancy in the LDCs is much lower than in the developing world at large (50 against 63 years). Child mortality under five years is estimated to be 160 per 1,000 live births (eighty-nine for all developing countries). Daily calorie intake is substantially lower in LDCs compared with other developing countries. Of the total number of people in developing countries living with HIV/AIDS, 37.5 million in 2001, more than one-third live in LDCs. The adult literacy rate is estimated at 56 per cent in the LDCs in 2005, this being 77 per cent for all developing countries. The general welfare level, as reflected in the GDP *per capita*, stood at US$281 in 2002, against US$1,195 for all developing countries. About half of the LDC population lives on less than US$1 a day.

How LDCs trade

For the LDCs as a group, international trade is just as important as for most other groups of countries. Around the year 2000, trade constituted 50.7 per cent of their GDP. For all economies of the world, this was 51.7 per cent, and 43 per cent for the high-income countries. The LDC share in world trade was 0.63 per cent in 2001, down by almost one-third compared with 1980. However, the downward trend was reversed in 1994 as a result of increasing exports of manufactures and services by some LDCs. Merchandise exports are more or less equally distributed over oil exports, non-oil commodity exports and manufactured exports. Services are significant as well, accounting for 17 per cent of total exports of goods and services. However, for 31 LDCs, commodities are the main export item. Textiles and garments constituted 61 per cent of the exports of Asian LDCs (mainly Bangladesh and Cambodia), and only 2 per cent of the exports of African LDCs (mainly Lesotho and Madagascar). The export structure of all LDCs shows high concentration on a few products only. For the group as a whole, the three largest export items summed to 76 per cent of total exports (UNCTAD 2004). The combination of high openness and concentration on a few products tends to make these countries vulnerable for export shocks and for declining markets. On the import side, it is a striking fact that LDC economies are very 'import sensitive' as they lack a diversified industrial base. The high openness of these economies is the result of the extremely limited capacity to produce manufactured products – and food in some of them. A large share of the capital goods and services to enlarge the productive capacity, and components to keep the existing capacity in good repair, has to be imported.

The destinations of LDC exports are presented in Figure 1.1. The share of exports going to developing countries shows a steady rise, while the share of the EU and the US has been falling. There is no interruption of this steady decline in 2001 when EBA and AGOA were introduced. Still, the EU is the single most important market for LDCs. The rise of the share of developing countries and the fall in the share of the EU show up for the exports of manufactures by LDCs as well. The destination of fuel exports has changed most. The US receives a much lower share of these exports, while China is largely responsible for the rising share of developing countries as destinations of LDC fuel exports.

Given the commodity composition of LDC exports, it is interesting to know whether there is room for more preferential treatment. Taking all exports by LDCs (excluding arms), more than three-quarters entered the markets of developed countries duty-free in 2001. However, excluding oil, this proportion falls to 69.1 per cent, down from 81.1 per cent in 1996. There has been a significant rise in the dutiable imports from LDCs (WTO 2003: 126), thus creating room for preferential treatment.[5] Despite the introduction of 'EBA *avant la lettre*' in 1998, and Lomé preferences, many LDC products faced a tariff on importation in the EU, mainly of agricultural origin: meat, dairy products, flour, sugar, cereals, etc. EBA extended DFQF market access for more than 900 tariff lines (Cernat *et al.* 2003). In a simulation study using a general equilibrium framework and taking into

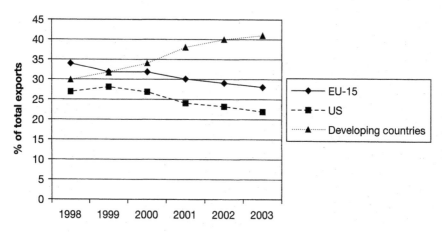

Figure 1.1 Destination of LDC total exports, 1998–2003, as a percentage of total exports.
Source of data: UNCTAD (2005)

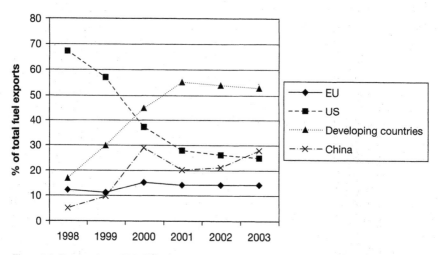

Figure 1.2 Destination of LDC fuel exports, 1998–2003, as a percentage of total fuel exports.

Source of data: UNCTAD (2005)

account pre-existing preferences on LDC exports to the EU, Cernat *et al.* (2003) draw the conclusion that export increases will be concentrated in paddy rice, sugar cane and processed rice. Total LDC exports are expected to increase by US$300 million US dollars annually, almost 0.5 per cent of the base line value. Much depends on the assumption whether the LDCs will be able to grasp the extra market opening for 900 tariff lines.

In short, despite continuing tariff erosion, there was still scope for improvement of LDC tariff preferences at the time of the adoption of EBA. The lowering of average tariffs disguises tariff peaks for some 'sensitive' LDC export products. In addition, the 'dirty tarification' of agricultural variable levies after the Uruguay Round has resulted in relatively high tariffs for a number of agricultural imports to the EU, thus creating large potential preferential margins for the products concerned.

Trade, trade preferences and development

EBA has been introduced in order to stimulate growth and diversification of exports. The underlying expectation is that export development constitutes a stimulus for economic and social development. International trade and exploiting comparative advantages hold the promise of a more efficient use of the economy's resources, which brings the economy on a higher level of welfare, necessary to alleviate poverty. These conclusions follow from the classical and neoclassical trade theories of comparative advantage. Although these theories may be criticized for their assumptions and the lack of attention to the distribution of the gains from trade, their value for the understanding of international trade and for trade policy is substantial (Bhagwati 2002). A problem is that trade theory generally prescribes free trade, not export development by non-reciprocal trade preferences. We will return to this below. One may argue that more exports will give LDCs more room for imports, as these countries generally have severe balance of payments problems. An enlargement of the import capacity as a result of more exports will facilitate investment and maintenance of the productive capacity.

However, the link with sustained economic development is rather complex. In the 1990s many studies were published by economists that found a positive relationship between the 'openness' of an economy, mainly measured by the trade to GDP ratio or by levels of trade barriers. Later studies questioned the reliability of these outcomes on the argument that openness is a poor measure of trade policy and may also represent a proxy for other causes of economic performance (Rodriguez and Rodrik 2000). This is not to say that trade is not important for development. A good summary is given in World Bank (2002: 38): 'since 1980 the global integration of markets in merchandise has enabled those developing countries with reasonable locations, policies, institutions, and infrastructure to harness their abundant labor to give themselves a competitive advantage in some manufactures and services.' Trade is a stimulus for development if a number of other conditions have been fulfilled (Winters 2004). Financial resources have to be available for viable private and public investment projects. This also requires entrepreneurial capacity, institutional quality and macro-economic stability. One does not need many arguments to see that it is difficult in a very poor country to create the right conditions for sustained economic development, as Pilegaard shows for Zambia in Chapter 8 of this volume.

It is a different question whether trade preferences, such as EBA, constitute an effective and efficient instrument to produce the gains from trade in developing countries. It has been pointed out that a country's own policies largely determine its gains from trade, although the policies of export markets' governments will have an impact as well (Bhagwati 2002; Hoekman *et al.* 2006). From the second half of the 1960s, much energy has been invested in creating non-reciprocal preferential systems that would give developing countries a more favourable than MFN treatment. EBA is one of the most recent initiatives in this area. Despite the applause that the introduction of EBA got from a large number of people and organizations, one should not overlook the studies that point out that non-reciprocal preferential systems are rather ineffective or even counterproductive. As a result of low and zero MFN tariffs, exclusion of particular ('sensitive') products, burdensome formalities and rules of origin that exclude many manufactured products, a large share of developing countries' exports are not imported into developed countries under these preferential systems. Nevertheless, many empirical studies find some effectiveness of preferential systems (e.g. Babarinde and Faber in Chapter 6 of this volume). It is also clear these effects come at a cost. Özden and Reinhardt (2003) show that eligibility for the US GSP makes a country less likely to liberalize its own trade policy. The main reason for this result is that preferences weaken the incentive for the domestic export sector to lobby for trade liberalization in order to improve its competitiveness. This was pointed out earlier by Hudec (1987). In addition, to the extent that exports grow under the preferences, there is a threat of a safeguard by the preference donor. This creates an incentive to implement more protectionist policies by the beneficiary country. Limão and Olarreaga (2006) investigate the question whether there is a link between the granting of preferences by large countries to small developing countries and MFN liberalization by the large preference donor. They elaborate on the finding that MFN tariff cuts by the EU and the US for goods exported by preferential partners are about half the average tariff cut. A plausible explanation for this is that preference donors get a return for the preferences, in terms of, e.g., political influence or regulatory standards applied in the beneficiary country. As far as this is the case, preference erosion will also lower the returns for the donor.

Thus, it may be concluded that trade as such has a stimulating effect on development if a number of other conditions have been met. However, non-reciprocal preferences tend to have a low direct effectiveness and diminish progress in MFN liberalization of those products that figure prominently in developing-country exports.

Overview of the book

The basic hypothesis of this book is, that although DFQF treatment of exports from the LDCs may have been proposed with the development needs of the poorest countries in mind, in the process of the introduction of EBA many factors have had an impact and many effects have surfaced far beyond the trade relations between the LDCs and the EU. This hypothesis stems from the consideration that EBA has had broader implications for a number of actors in a number of domains – inside the EU and internationally – although it is unclear where, how and why this is the

Table 1.1 Analytical overview of research themes (chapter numbers in parentheses)

	Internal (inside EU)	External (outside EU)	Comparison US
Realization of EBA *(motives)*	EU actors/ institutions (3, 4) EU lobbies (3, 4, 10)	WTO: Ruggiero (2, 8) LDC economic marginalization (1, 8)	Political dynamics behind EBA/ AGOA (5)
Impact of EBA *(effects)*	EU CAP reform (9, 10) EU civil society (4, 12)	Development LDC (6, 7, 8) EU–ACP (2, 3, 4, 11) Normative power (1) WTO Doha Development Agenda (2, 12)	Effects of EBA/ AGOA (6, 7)

case. Table 1.1 gives a starting point to structure the different research questions relating to this hypothesis. It makes an analytical distinction between the intra-EU and international dimension on the one hand, and the materialization and conse-quences of EBA on the other. In addition, it suggests comparing these different facets of EBA with US policy vis-à-vis these developing countries. Each of the chapters can be situated into this internal/external and realization/impact scheme; some of them fit into several boxes. In general the matrix illustrates the compre-hensive approach of this book to Europe's EBA initiative and indicates that it is broader than an EBA case study.

The composition of the book is as follows. In Chapter 2, Jan Orbie undertakes a detailed process-tracing analysis of the development of EBA. He examines two hypotheses that shed light on the political dynamics behind the realization of EBA: (1) the Doha hypothesis, stating that EBA was necessary to get the Doha Development Agenda off the ground in 2001, and (2) the EU–ACP hypothesis, suggesting that the EU used EBA to split the ACP group. Together these two explanatory perspectives cover the bulk of Europe's external trade agenda in the past ten years: (1) launching and negotiating a new trade round within the WTO and (2) elaborating a successor to the EU–ACP Lomé trade regime. How does EBA relate to these trade agendas?

Two subsequent chapters focus on explanations for institutional skirmish-ing within the EU about EBA, focusing on the North–South dimension within the EU and on competing games between 'trade' and 'agriculture' bureaucracies. In Chapter 3, Maurizio Carbone analyses intra-European conflicts over EBA from the perspective of the perceived North–South cleavage among EU member states in trade and development politics (diverging preferences for globalist/liberal versus regionalist/protectionist measures). The second part of this chapter looks more specifically at the role of two actors that seem to be marginalized in the decision-making process about EBA: DG Development (the traditional advocate of the ACP group within the EU) and the ACP group (Europe's erstwhile most preferred development partner). In contrast with the 'vertical' approach of the previous chapter, Adrian van den Hoven presents a 'horizontal' conceptualization of conflicts over EBA. After explaining the competing two-level game model for examining EU external trade policy, the chapter illustrates how EBA seems to be driven by two contradictory strategies – one directed by the Trade Commissioner and the other directed by the Agriculture Commissioner, operating in an environment of lobbies and civil society organizations.

These 'EU' accounts are followed by a comparison between Europe's EBA scheme and the American equivalent, namely AGOA. In Chapter 5, Dries Lesage and Bart Kerremans investigate the political dynamics behind the two trade initiatives towards LDCs, and present a comparison on the basis of their main similarities and differences and offer an explanation from a political point of view. This political science contribution is the stepping stone for two economic accounts that compare the impact of EBA and AGOA on developing country export performances. Olufemi Babarinde and Gerrit Faber analyse the effectiveness of the two systems while taking into account that the groups of beneficiary countries are different, and that institutional, infrastructural and geographical factors play a role as well. The impact of rules of origin is the subject of Chapter 7 by Paul Brenton and Çaglar Özden. By concentrating on the differences in these rules for EBA and AGOA for clothing, they investigate whether the effectiveness of preferences is determined by these often overlooked technicalities.

Confronted with a rather limited impact of EBA in terms of increased export figures, in Chapter 8 Jess Pilegaard raises the question why the LDCs continue to support initiatives for DFQF market access. By discussing the bottlenecks that hamper the export performance of Zambia, he puts the relevance of preferences to a practical test. This chapter also looks more closely at the impact of EBA on Zambia's sugar exports to the EU.

Sugar is indeed one of the few agricultural products where LDCs have the potential to export sizable quantities to the EU. The Common Agricultural Policy (CAP) has a profound impact on the internal EU markets for these products. The CAP is under reform, and EBA is interlinked with the reforms. In Chapter 9, Alan Matthews and Jacques Gallezot analyse these linkages by charting the agricultural trade flows from LDCs with the EU, and by investigating the preferential effects and the impact that these enlarged trade flows may have on the EU agricultural markets and on CAP reform. The following chapter by Michael Brüntrup focuses on sugar, as this is an important export product for the LDCs where a large part of the effects of EBA on export growth and welfare are concentrated. The author describes the effects of EBA on the highly segmented sugar markets, the cost structures of the suppliers and the link with the CAP. He also addresses the 'Trojan horse' hypothesis: was the motivation for including sugar in EBA to destabilize the EU sugar market system?

As Appendix 1.1 shows, 40 of 50 LDCs are members of the ACP group that has concluded the Cotonou Agreement with the EU. Under this agreement, regional groups of ACP countries are negotiating Economic Partnership

Agreements (EPAs) with the EU, which include Free Trade Agreements. In Chapter 11, Sanoussi Bilal looks into the interaction between the two sets of trade preferences (EBA and EPAs) and how EBA may impact upon these negotiations and the process of regional integration among ACP countries.

The final chapter wraps up the most important conclusions of the preceding chapters and addresses the basic hypothesis of the book: does the main function of EBA lie in promoting the development of LDCs or elsewhere? Did EBA indeed have broader ramifications, inside the EU as well as internationally, beyond the export of LDC products to the European market? And what about the future relevance of EBA for the multilateral trading system and for Europe's regional integration schemes with developing countries?

Appendix 1.1

LDCs and their status in EBA, AGOA and Cotonou, and non-LDCs under AGOA and Cotonou, as of 2005

Country	LDC – EBA	ACP – EPA	AGOA[a]		Sugar Protocol
Africa					
Angola	•	•	•	in: 2004	o
Benin	•	•	••		o
Botswana	o	•	••		o
Burkina Faso	•	•	o		o
Burundi	•	•	o		o
Cameroon	o	•	••		o
Cape Verde	•	•	••		o
Central African Republic	•	•	o	out: 2004	o
Chad	•	•	•		o
Comoros	•	•	o		o
Congo	o	•	•		o
Democratic Republic of Congo	•	•	•	in: 2004	•
Djibouti	•	•	•		o
Equatorial Guinea	•	•	o		o
Eritrea	•	•	o	out: 2004	o
Ethiopia	•	•	••		o
Gabon	o	•	•		o
Gambia	•	•	•		o
Ghana	o	•	••		o
Guinea	•	•	•		o
Guinea Bissau	•	•	•		o
Côte d'Ivoire	o	•	o	out: 2005	•
Kenya	o	•	••		•
Lesotho	•	•	••		o
Liberia	•	•	o		o
Madagascar	•	•	••		•
Malawi	•	•	••		•

continued

Appendix 1.1 (continued)

Country	LDC – EBA	ACP – EPA	AGOA[a]	Sugar Protocol
Mali	•	•	••	○
Mauritania	•	•	•	•
Mauritius	○	•	••	○
Mozambique	•	•	••	○
Namibia	○	•	••	○
Niger	•	•	••	○
Nigeria	○	•	•	○
Rwanda	•	•	••	○
São Tomé and Príncipe	•	•	•	○
Senegal	•	•	••	○
Seychelles	○	•	•	○
Sierra Leone	•	•	• in: 2003	○
Somalia	•	•	○	○
South Africa[b]	○	•	••	○
Sudan	•	•	○	○
Swaziland	○	•	••	•
Tanzania	•	•	••	•
Togo	•	•	○	○
Uganda	•	•	••	•
Zambia	•	•	••	•
Zimbabwe	○	•	○	•
Caribbean				
Antigua and Barbuda	○	•	○	○
Bahamas	○	•	○	○
Barbados	○	•	○	○
Belize	○	•	○	○
(Cuba)	○	•	○	○
Dominica	○	•	○	○
Dominican Republic	○	•	○	○
Grenada	○	•	○	○
Guyana	○	•	○	○
Haiti	•	•	○	○
Jamaica	○	•	○	•
St Kitts and Nevis	○	•	○	•
St Lucia	○	•	○	•
St Vincent and the Grenadines	○	•	○	•
Seychelles	○	•	○	○
Suriname	○	•	○	•
Trinidad and Tobago	○	•	○	•
Pacific				
Cook Islands	○	•	○	○
Timor-Leste	•	•	○	○
Fiji	○	•	○	•
Kiribati	•	•	○	○
Marshall Islands	○	•	○	○

Appendix 1.1 (continued)

Country	LDC – EBA	ACP – EPA	AGOA[a]	Sugar Protocol
Micronesia	○	•	○	○
Nauru	○	•	○	○
Niue	○	•	○	○
Palau	○	•	○	○
Papua New Guinea	○	•	○	○
Samoa	•	•	○	○
Solomon Islands	•	•	○	○
Tonga	○	•	○	○
Tuvalu	•	•	○	○
Vunuatu	•	•	○	○
Asia				
Afghanistan	•	○	○	○
Bangladesh	•	○	○	○
Bhutan	•	○	○	○
Cambodia	•	○	○	○
Laos	•	○	○	○
Maldives	•	○	○	○
Myanmar[c]	○	○	○	○
Nepal	•	○	○	○
Yemen	•	○	○	○
India	○	○	○	•
Total	49	80	36	20

Notes
a • is eligible for AGOA preferences, •• is also eligible for Textiles and Clothing (T&C) preferential access.
b South Africa has a special Free Trade Agreement with the EU since 1999.
c Myanmar is an LDC, but GSP (EBA) preferences are withdrawn because of violation of core labour standards (forced labour).

Notes

1   Throughout this volume, the terms 'European Union' (EU), 'Union' and 'Europe' are used interchangeably. The terms 'European Economic Community' or 'European Community' are used only when emphasizing the historical dimension (pre-Maastricht era) or the legal basis (common commercial policy under the first pillar of the Treaty, viz. Article 133).

2   See the notes of the proceedings of the first three meetings of the LDC Sub-committee after the Uruguay Round: WT/COMTD/LLDC/1-2 and 3.

3   Another indication is the establishment of COMPEX in 1985, a stabilization fund for export earnings similar to STABEX but eligible for non-ACP LDCs. However, the COMPEX scheme proved 'largely symbolic' and in the 1990s it ended 'without fanfare' (Page and Hewitt 2001: 38).

4   In 1998, all LDCs were offered ACP preferences. Orbie discusses this decision ('EBA *avant la lettre*') in Chapter 2.

5   For dutiable products, the MFN tariff is positive.

References

Agence Europe (1999) No. 7590, 10 November.

Bhagwati, J. (2002) *Free Trade Today*, Princeton NJ: Princeton University Press.

Cernat, L., Laird, S., Monge-Roffarello, L. and Turrini, A. (2003) 'The EU's Everything but Arms Initiative and the Least-developed Countries', Discussion Paper No. 2003/47, Wider, United Nations University. Available online at http://www.wider.unu.edu/publications/dps/dps2003/dp2003-047.pdf (accessed 8 May 2006).

Charnovitz, S., Bartels, L., Howse, R. and Bradley, J. (2004) 'The appellate body's GSP decision', *World Trade Review*, 2, 3: 239–65.

Diez, T. (2005) 'Constructing the self and changing others: reconsidering "normative power Europe"', *Millennium: Journal of International Studies*, 33, 3: 613–36.

Eeckhout, P. (2004) *External Relations of the European Union: Legal and Constitutional Foundation*, Oxford: Oxford University Press.

EU (2001) 'EU approves "Everything but Arms" trade access for Least Developed Countries'. Press Release IP/01/261, 26 February.

GATT (1982) 'Ministerial Declaration'. L/5424, 29 November.

GATT (1985) 'Proposals for action in favour of the least developed countries', Note by the Secretariat, Sub-committee on Trade of Least Developed Countries, COM.TC/LLDC/W/27, 25 July.

Hoekman, B., Michalopoulos, C. and Winters, L.A. (2006) 'Improving special and differential treatment: some proposals' in P. van Dijck and G. Faber (eds) *Developing Countries and the Doha Development Agenda of the WTO*, Abingdon and New York: Routledge.

Hudec, R.E. (1987) *Developing Countries in the GATT Legal System*, London: Gower.

Lamy, P. (2002a) *L'Europe en première ligne*, Paris: Éditions du Seuil.

Lamy, P. (2002b) 'Europe's role in global governance. The way ahead', Speech delivered at Humboldt University, Berlin, 6 May.

Limão, N. and Olarreaga, M. (2006) 'Trade preferences to small developing countries and the welfare costs of lost multilateral liberalization', *World Bank Economic Review*, advance access, published 17 May, pp. 1–24

Manners, I. (2002) 'Normative power Europe: a contradiction in terms?', *Journal of Common Market Studies*, 40, 2: 235–58.

OECD/DAC (2002) *Development Co-operation Review. European Community*, Paris: OECD.

Orbie, J., Vos, H. and Taverniers, L. (2005) 'EU Trade policy and a social clause: a question of competences?', *Politique Européenne*, 17: 159–87.

Özden, C. and Reinhardt, E. (2003) 'The Perversity of Preferences. The Generalized System of Preferences and Developing Country Trade Policies, 1976–2000', Policy Research Working Paper No. 2995, Washington DC: World Bank.

Page, S. and Hewitt, A. (2001) 'World Commodity Prices: still a problem for developing countries?', ODI Special Report, London: Overseas Development Institute.

Rodriguez, F. and Rodrik, D. (2000) 'Trade Policy and Economic Growth: A Skeptic's Guide to the Cross-national Evidence', mimeo, University of Maryland and Harvard University.

Simonis, U.E. (ed.) (2003) 'Review of the List of LDCs', Discussion Paper No. FS-II 02-408, Berlin: Science Center Berlin.

Smith, K. (2003) *European Union Foreign Policy in a Changing World*, Cambridge: Polity.

Stevens, C. and Kennan, J. (2001) *The impact of the EU's 'Everything but Arms' proposal: a report to Oxfam*, Brighton: Institute of Development Studies.

Stiglitz, J.E. (2002) *Globalization and its Discontents*, New York and London: Norton.

UN (n.d.) *The Least Developed Countries: Historical Background.* http://www.un.org/events/ldc3/prepcom/history.htm (accessed 17 March 2006).

UNCTAD (2004) *The Least Developed Countries Report 2004. Linking International Trade with Poverty Reduction*, Geneva: UNCTAD.

UNCTAD (2005) *Handbook of Statistics 2005*, Geneva: UNCTAD.

Winters, L.A. (2004) 'Trade liberalisation and economic performance: an overview', *Economic Journal*, 114: 4–21

World Bank (2002) *Globalization, Growth, and Poverty: Building an Inclusive World Economy*, Oxford and Washington DC: Oxford University Press and the World Bank.

WTO (2003) *World Trade Report 2003*, Geneva: World Trade Organization.

WTO (2004) *Doha Work Programme. Decision Adopted by the General Council on 1 August 2004*, Geneva: World Trade Organization WT/L/579.

WTO (2005) *Doha Work Programme. Draft Ministerial Declaration. Revision*, Hong Kong: World Trade Organization WT/MIN(05)/3/Rev.2.

2 The development of EBA

Jan Orbie

EBA's role in Europe's international trade agenda

What is the role of 'Everything but Arms' (EBA) in Europe's international trade agenda? From the perspective of political science, EBA has two striking aspects. On the one hand, since EBA's impact is limited in terms of trade flows, we should look at the broader political framework. On the other hand, EBA constitutes the showpiece of the normative trade policy of the European Union (EU), occupying a central place in the 'trade and development' discourse of European policy makers (see Chapter 1).

This chapter elaborates on two possible avenues of research. Together these two approaches cover the bulk of Europe's external trade agenda in the past ten years: the negotiations concerning the World Trade Organization (launching and negotiating a new WTO trade round) and the relationship between the EU and the ACP group (launching and negotiating a successor to the Lomé trade regime with former colonies in Africa, the Caribbean and the Pacific). We hypothesize that, each time, the apparently limited EBA initiative plays a crucial role in the realization of Europe's external trade objectives.

First, EBA can be seen as a strategic attempt to show Europe's goodwill towards developing countries and to gain their approval for launching a new WTO trade round in Doha. Although this 'Doha hypothesis' clarifies some parts of the puzzle, we argue that EBA's role in the post-Lomé reform process offers a complementary line of approach. This observation is based on a process-tracing analysis of the development of EBA. Going back to the EBA *avant la lettre* decisions in 1997 and 1998, some remarkable parallels with the post-Lomé reform process can be noticed. Our analysis indicates that Europe's EBA initiative plays a catalyzing role in two key aspects of the newly established Cotonou regime: the break-up of the ACP group and the abolition of interventionist Lomé remnants.

This account is structured in three parts. The first section starts with this process-tracing analysis. Although Europe's EBA initiative has often been highlighted by policy makers and academics, its antecedents since 1996 are usually overlooked. The second part then situates the EBA Regulation in the context of the Doha negotiations. Finally, we look at EBA's role in the shift from Lomé to Cotonou. In line with historical-institutionalist theorizing (Pierson 1996), it is illustrated that the EBA *avant la lettre* initiative as well as the EBA Regulation created a path-dependent process, narrowing down the range of options in EU–ACP trade negotiations until today.

The development of EBA: process-tracing

The EU in 1996: low-profile

As explained in Chapter 1 of this volume, the idea of preferential market access for the least developed countries is far from new. The GATT Enabling Clause of 1979 (para. 2d) already allowed special treatment for the Least Developed Country (LDC) group. In 1986 Ravenhill suggested: 'The obvious ideal solution to the trade needs of the least developed is to grant access for all their current and future exports completely free of tariff and non-tariff barriers.' But whereas such proposals were then considered as 'naïve' and 'quixotic' (Ravenhill 1986: 472, 483), during the past decade most industrialized countries have started to launch concrete LDC initiatives (UNCTAD 2003a).

In May 1996 the WTO Director General Ruggiero stirred the debate, making the tentative suggestion that 'a commitment to bind all tariffs that they [the LDCs] face at zero and eliminate all remaining quantitative restrictions on their exports by a firm date would be one useful initiative' (Ruggiero 1996). Ruggiero managed to put this proposal on the international trade agenda. Subsequent meetings of the G-7 (Lyon, June 1996) and the Quad (Seattle, September 1996) agreed on the desirability of greater market access for LDCs, albeit less far-reaching than Ruggiero's original suggestion to set (1) 'a firm date' to (2) 'eliminate all' barriers on LDC exports. The ensuing Plan of Action for the LDCs adopted at the WTO Singapore Ministerial of December 1996 is not much more ambitious than this new G-7/Quad consensus. Developed and developing country members 'would explore the possibilities' of 'granting preferential duty-free access' for LDC exports, but with the explicit qualification that 'exceptions could be provided for' and that members decide 'on an autonomous basis' (WTO 1996).

What about Europe's role in this new consensus? The low-profile position of the EU in the run-up to Singapore strongly contrasts with its later initiatives and discourse. Two elements of Europe's attitude towards the Ruggiero initiative are worth mentioning. First, it took the Council of Ministers until the beginning of December 1996 to finish an EU position on the LDC issue. This indicates that the topic was certainly not a priority on Europe's trade agenda. An analysis of official documents, Council conclusions and reporting in newsletters such as *Agence Europe* also makes clear that the LDC issue is hardly (and at best superficially) mentioned. Instead, the emphasis lies on the 'new issues' (investment, competition policy, labour standards and the environment) and on sectors such as telecoms and shipping.[1] In the first meeting of the WTO Sub-committee on LDCs where the demand for duty-free and quota-free (DFQF) market access comes up (September 1996), in contrast with previous meetings, there is no intervention by the EU.[2] Second, the eventual EU position 'on the involvement of the LDCs in the WTO system' largely reflects the existing G-7/Quad consensus. While the Union wants to make commitments with a view to 'opening further' its markets to imports from all LDCs, this should be in parallel with similar initiatives by other developed and more advanced developing countries in the context of the Action Plan (EU 1996b: 1).

EBA avant la lettre: *the Council's LDC strategy of June 1997*

But not all EU member states wanted to maintain a low profile on this topic. Their position gained weight in the course of 1997, when the 'LDC issue' gained momentum on Europe's trade agenda, crystallizing into the decision of the General Affairs Council on 2 June. In retrospect, these conclusions by the European Ministers of Foreign Affairs determined the lines of EU policy towards the LDCs for the years to come. Table 2.1 gives a broad outline of Europe's June 1997 LDC strategy and indicates how this scheme was translated into policy decisions during the following years.

The General Affairs Council (GAC) conclusions specify two kinds of measures. In the short term, the nine non-ACP LDCs (Afghanistan, Bangladesh, Bhutan, Cambodia, Laos, Maldives, Myanmar/Burma,[3] Nepal and Yemen) should be granted equivalent market access as the 40 ACP LDCs, which enjoy tariff preferences through the Lomé Convention. In the medium term, the EU intends to provide duty-free market access for 'essentially all' LDC imports. This is a much more extensive commitment than Europe's 1996 position, albeit less radical ('essentially all' products and safeguard measures for 'sensitive sectors') than the Ruggiero initiative.

This medium-term commitment basically reflects the later EBA Regulation. Therefore we argue that the fundamental breakthrough in the EBA initiative occurred in 1997, rather than in the five-month period between the Commission's EBA proposal and the adoption of the Council Regulation in February 2001. From the second half of 1997 the exact wording of the medium-term option (duty-free

Table 2.1 Europe's LDC strategy of June 1997

1 Short-term: bringing all LDC market access into line
   • Equivalent market access for all LDCs: ACP LDCs and non-ACP LDCs (cf. Lomé)
   • By January 1998

2 Medium-term: EBA *avant la lettre*
   • Duty-free access for essentially all LDC products; an appropriate mechanism to defend sensitive sectors
   • Cf. Cotonou mandate (June 1998), *'Everything but Arms'* initiative (2000–1)

3 Long-term: export of EBA
   • Multilateralizing EBA: tariff scheme with all WTO members
   • Cf. Seattle (1999), Doha (2001), Cancun (2003) and commitment in Hong Kong (2005)

access for essentially all products from LDCs) would regularly recur in speeches of EU trade officials and in Council minutes. As explained below, it also appears in the Council's negotiation mandate for a new EU–ACP trade agreement.

This LDC strategy is much more ambitious than Europe's position in the run-up to Singapore. The Union intends to take *autonomous* measures to increase LDC import, apart from possible commitments by other WTO members. The 2 June orientations unambiguously indicate that more generous LDC access to the European market is no longer conditional on similar decisions by other countries. These countries are instead asked to follow the Union's example. Trade Commissioner Sir Leon Brittan declares that 'the Union will proceed with these initiatives, whatever our partners do. Nevertheless we call on them to open their markets for LDCs in a similar way' (*Agence Europe* 1997). Likewise, the absence of a multilateral WTO tariff scheme for LDCs – a long-term objective – does not prevent the EU from taking autonomous measures. And contrary to the Union's low profile on the LDC issue in 1996, henceforth the EU discourse did not fail to emphasize the 'leading' role of the Union in the fight for the development of the poorest countries (especially since the High-level Meeting on LDCs in October 1997).

Another indication of this acceleration can be found in the General Report on the Activities of the European Union. While the review of the Singapore Conference in the 1996 report refers to all kinds of trade-related topics without mentioning a word about the LDC issue, the 1997 report reminds us of the fact that 'the integration of LDCs into the world economy was one of the Community's priorities at the Singapore Conference'.

As pointed out by Van den Hoven in Chapter 4 of this volume, the far-reaching consequences of this package of LDC measures relate to the fact that these discussions were ignored by the Agricultural Commissioner and Council. Indeed, DG Trade and the General Affairs Council took the lead in this dossier. Below, however, we will elaborate on a complementary explanation, looking at interactions between the 2 June 1997 decisions and the simultaneous reform process of the EU–ACP Lomé trade regime. But first this chapter gives an account of the materialization of the EBA Regulation in 2001 and of the 'Doha hypothesis'.

Towards 'Everything but Arms': radicalization and consolidation

Although the EU stipulated this EBA *avant la lettre* in 1997, the Commission waited until October 2000 – three months after the conclusion of the Cotonou Agreement and one year before the Doha conference – to publish a specific proposal for regulation. Interestingly, this 'Everything but Arms' proposal is more radical than the medium-term option of 1997. The Commission deviates from the standard 'essentially all' phrasing, stating that 'the Community can go beyond its undertakings by granting all products (except arms and munitions) from all LDCs duty-free access without quantitative restrictions immediately' (EU 2000). After a three-year transition period, even the most sensitive agricultural products (rice, bananas, sugar) would benefit from duty-free access to the European market. Although the safeguard provisions were more restrictive in the proposed EBA than in the existing GSP and Lomé trade regimes,[4] the Commission's document resembled the Ruggiero initiative, rather than Europe's LDC strategy.

This more radical departure from the 1997 consensus opened a Pandora's box and sparked off fierce intra-European debates. Disagreements within the Council of Ministers and within the Commission on Commissioner Lamy's proposal broadly reflected the traditional European 'trade culture' dichotomy of 'southern protectionists' (including DG Agriculture) versus 'northern free traders' (including DG Trade) (Smith 1999: 279–80). Particularly noticeable is the publication of an impact study on the website of DG Agriculture in November 2000, highlighting the 'potentially disruptive consequences' of EBA for the European agricultural sector (DG Agriculture 2000: 4). Running counter to DG Trade's more moderate appraisal, this assessment largely supported the arguments of the southern member states and of the agricultural (especially sugar) lobbies.

To cut a long story short:[5] five months of debate resulted in a weakening of the original Commission proposal. Although the principle of EBA was not contested, considerable divergences on the timetable and on the possibility to use safeguard measures emerged. Table 2.2 summarizes the amendments in three phases.

Back to square one? The tenor of the final EBA Regulation indeed bears much resemblance to the European LDC consensus since 1997. Although it is true that 'at the end of the day, we will have 100 per cent access, with no exceptions, except of course for arms' (Lamy 2001), this liberalization is spread over a much longer period than anticipated (2006 for bananas, 2009 for sugar and rice). Moreover, the safeguard provisions in the EBA Regulation are even more stringent than those in the Commission proposal, and the ultimate compromise includes a rather restrictive Commission statement about the application of rules of origin and safeguard measures.

One provisional conclusion is thus that the effects of this modified EBA on LDC exports are probably limited. This question is elaborated by Babarinde and Faber in Chapter 6 and by Özden and Brenton in Chapter 7 of this volume. Another remarkable conclusion from this historical overview is that the decision to grant non-ACP LDCs equivalent market access as the Lomé beneficiaries from 1998 may be more relevant than the 2001 EBA Regulation. Although the latter was much more politicized and received a captivating label, the effects of Europe's EBA *avant la lettre* initiative could be equally important.

The Doha hypothesis: EBA as catalyst for a new WTO trade round?

The persuasion power of EBA

Many observers have highlighted the explanatory value of the Doha hypothesis. As *The Economist* (3 March 2001) reported, 'the biggest benefit [of EBA] may accrue

Table 2.2 From Commission proposal to EBA regulation: three-phased weakening

Commission proposal (September 2000)	EBA Regulation (February 2001)
Transition period	
Art. 6 : three years	Cf. *fine-tuning* Commission proposal (January 2001)
	art. 6(2)–(6): longer transition period for:
	• Bananas (gradual tariff reduction of 20% per year from 2002; 0-tariff in 2006)
	• Rice (gradual quota increase from 2001; 0-tariff between July 2006 and September 2009)
	• Sugar (gradual quota increase from 2001; 0-tariff between 9/2006 and 9/2009)
Safeguard measures	
Consideration 13 and art. 4 :	Cf. compromise Swedish presidency (February 2001)
stricter safeguard provisions than GSP: in case of 'massive increases in imports' (also fraud and lack of administrative cooperation)	Ibid. + two additional provisions :
	• Art. 2(7): suspension: Commission and Member States 'carefully monitor imports of rice, bananas and sugar . . . Where the Commission finds that there is sufficient evidence . . . all appropriate measures will be taken as quickly as possible'.
	• Art. 5: suspension of banana/rice/sugar import from LDCs 'if imports of these products cause serious disturbance to the Community markets and their regulatory mechanisms'
Additional guarantees	
	Cf. Commission statement (26 February 2001)
	• Rules of origin: 'strict compliance' and 'supplement existing rules of origin'
	• Safeguard provisions for rice/sugar/bananas: Commission will 'automatically examine' if imports rise by > 25%
	• Commission Report to the Council in 2005: 'appropriate proposals if necessary'

to Mr Lamy. He can bank any goodwill arising from the new policy and cash it later, when trying to launch a new round of multilateral trade talks.' There are indeed indications that the prospect of the WTO conference in Doha in November 2001 influenced Europe's EBA initiative.

First, since the WTO conference in Geneva in 1998, the EU has been the most outspoken supporter of a new round of multilateral trade negotiations. From the perspective of the Doha hypothesis, this could explain why EBA is more radical than the LDC initiatives of other industrialized countries. Second, this line of approach sheds light on the timing of EBA (cf. Page and Hewitt 2002: 99), namely after the failure of Seattle but before Doha, and more specifically on the pro-activeness of DG Trade within the European Commission. Acting as the 'agent' of the member states within the European institutional framework, DG Trade has a distinct interest in negotiating a new round of WTO talks. In this respect it is important to notice that the above-mentioned radicalization of the Commission – arguing for the liberalization of 'all' instead of 'essentially all' LDC imports – already became clear shortly after the debacle of Seattle. Before the European Parliament, Trade Commissioner Lamy (2000a) emphasized that:

> first of all, it is necessary to address the questions which concern developing countries, in particular the least developed countries, which are those, who feel most frustrated by the failure in Seattle. This means that in parallel with the work on the built-in agenda, it is necessary to push forward our initiative on duty and quota exemptions for the least developed countries.

Shortly afterwards Lamy asked the question of 'how long we will be able to restrict the exemption to "essentially" all goods' (Lamy 2000b). The explanatory memorandum of the Commission's EBA proposal stresses the importance of 'genuine efforts to take on board the needs and concerns' of LDCs after Seattle (EU 2000: 3); and in their statements at the Doha conference six EU member states refer to EBA.[6]

Apart from Europe's possible motives in designing EBA, it is fair to say that this initiative did increase the legitimacy of Europe's call for a WTO 'Development Round' in Doha. Research indicates that the EBA initiative is one of the trade areas where Europe is perceived to play a leadership role by non-EU actors (Chaban *et al.* 2006: 253). In spite of the limited expected effects of EBA, as pointed out in an early impact assessment (Stevens and Kennan 2001), the EU did manage to give EBA a crucial symbolic place in its 'trade and development' discourse. Van Den Hoven emphasizes that the political relevance of the Trade Commissioner's 'development discourse', both externally *and* within the EU, cannot be underestimated. Regarding EBA, he states that it 'enabled the EU to hold the high moral ground in the WTO' compared with the US and other industrialized countries (Van den Hoven 2004: 264). EBA could indeed be considered as another instance of the 'competition for generosity' between EU and US development discourses (Orbie 2003: 404).[7]

Until today EBA continues to hold a notable power of persuasion within the WTO. The commitment to establish a worldwide EBA constitutes an important element of the WTO Ministerial Declaration in Hong Kong (December 2005). Therefore Europe's EBA did not only stimulate the *launching* of the Doha Round in 2001, but the 'multilateralization' of EBA also increases the chances of the Round's successful conclusion, as we will argue in Chapter 12 of this volume.

Remaining question marks

Broadly speaking, two kinds of objections to this Doha hypothesis can be raised. First, it seems to use a distorted view of power relations: on the one hand the importance of LDCs in the WTO decision-making system is overestimated; on the other hand it neglects the resistance of other and more powerful trade actors. Although member-driven in principle, the WTO decision-making system can be conceptualized as a system of concentric circles (Moon 2004: 31). It is not surprising that the least developed countries – besides, 18 LDCs were not even members of the WTO in 2001 – find themselves in the exterior circle.

In addition, EBA may harm the economic interests of a larger group of more powerful developing countries. Here we can discern two categories: non-LDC ACP countries and other (non-LDC non-ACP) developing countries. Since about half of the ACP countries do not belong to the LDC group, they were outstripped by the EBA beneficiaries on Europe's preferential pyramid. Among them are relatively large countries who lose market access to the benefit of LDCs (e.g. Nigeria, Kenya, Senegal) as well as small and vulnerable island or landlocked countries that (to their own dissatisfaction, e.g. St Kitts and Nevis) do not belong to the UN-defined LDC category. As explained below, EBA also hinders the export opportunities of the Sugar Protocol beneficiaries (e.g. Fiji and Mauritius) among the ACP countries. Non-LDC ACP countries also have to engage in reciprocal trade liberalization in order to reach a similar level of access to the European market as LDCs. These ACP countries expressed their fear of losing market access to the EU, disapproved of the Union's decision to exclude vulnerable island and landlocked states from the EBA beneficiaries, and criticized the Commission for breaching the consultation requirement of the Cotonou Agreement (cf. Page and Hewitt 2002: 94; *Financial Times* 21 March 2001).

EBA could also damage the export interests of the most powerful non-ACP countries, such as India, Brazil or Egypt (Page and Hewitt 2002: 100–1). Having moved closer to the core of the informal decision-making system of concentric circles, these countries (often members of the G-20) have played a crucial role in WTO negotiations during the past decade. From this perspective, EBA would hinder rather than facilitate the launching of a new trade round in Doha.

Although these considerations somewhat put the explanatory value of the Doha hypothesis into perspective, they should in turn be qualified. The EU did take other initiatives than EBA to get developing on board of the Doha Round. Obvious examples are Europe's role in the TRIPS declaration (on compulsory licensing for trade in generic medicines), the negotiation of the Cotonou waiver (extending the Lomé trade preferences until 2008) and the abandonment of labour standards of the trade agenda (referring this issue to the International Labour Organization) (Kerremans 2004: 373–5).

The second point is more important for the purposes of this chapter. Going back to the process-tracing analysis in the previous section, we could say that the prospect of Doha largely explains the radicalization of the Commission (DG Trade). It also sheds light on the timing of the EBA proposal, although the signing of the Cotonou Agreement is an equally important factor here (see below). However, the

Doha hypothesis fails to account for the 'acceleration' of Europe's LDC position in the first half of 1997. At the time when the EU departed from its low-profile position and elaborated a comprehensive LDC strategy – including the medium-term objective of EBA *avant la lettre* – there was no talk of a new WTO round. An EU consensus on the desirability of such a round materialized only at the end of March 1998.

In short, the Doha hypothesis explains why 'EBA' remained on the European agenda during the years after the 1997 LDC strategy and why it was effectively implemented at the beginning of 2001, albeit less ambitiously than the Commission proposals of 2000. Its explanatory value thus corresponds with the 'radicalization' and 'consolidation' phases in the process tracing (Table 2.3). However, we need an additional line of approach to account for the preceding phase, namely the acceleration of 1997. Since the reform of the Lomé regime dominated Europe's trade and development agenda at that time, it is obvious to look at the EU–ACP trade relationship.

Lock-in effects: EBA as catalyst for reforming the Lomé trade regime

The development of EBA and the reform of Lomé

If we extend the process-tracing analysis and look at the position of LDCs in the reform of the Lomé trade regime, some remarkable parallels emerge. Since the EU–ACP negotiations are typically asymmetrical in favour of EU interests (cf. Elgström 2000; Forwood 2001), we focus only on the negotiation process within the EU. The Cotonou Agreement could indeed be seen as the result of intra-European negotiations, rather than as an EU–ACP compromise. Our focus on the position of LDCs in the post-Lomé trade regime will confirm this point: despite ACP scepticism on the proposed duty-free access for all LDCs, article 37(9) of the Cotonou Agreement is almost a copy of the Council's negotiation mandate.

The intra-European negotiation process on Lomé reform can be summarized in three phases: the Green Paper of the Commission (November 1996), the Commission's negotiating directives (October 1997) and the Council's negotiation mandate (June 1998). Below we sketch this evolution, focusing more specifically on the place of LDCs in the new EU–ACP trade relationship.

After the 'incrementalist' changes of successive Yaoundé and Lomé agreements, the EU envisaged a more fundamental reform of the EU–ACP partnership and the Lomé trade regime in the 1990s (Holland 2002: 177–8). The Commission's Green Paper (EU 1996a) constituted the first concrete impulse to start this thought process. Four divergent scenarios are outlined, although the paper more or less indicates the Commission's preference for dividing the ACP group in smaller regions (Lister 1999: 153–4) and for establishing reciprocal trade liberalization (Forwood 2001: 427; Ravenhill 2004; McQueen 1998: 672).

On the position of LDCs, however, the Green Paper of 1996 is rather vague. The new principle of 'differentiation' is mostly applied to geographical categories

(ACP regions, p. iv) or to aid provision (targeted at the least developed countries, pp. 13, 41–2, 19–20). But it is unclear how the distinction between LDCs and other developing countries could be linked to the future EU–ACP trade regime, let alone that Ruggiero's tentative suggestion for duty-free market access for LDCs is mentioned. As a variation on the first scenario (*status quo*), there is a suggestion to conclude a separate agreement with the ACP LDCs, but it is unclear what this accord would look like and how it would relate to the general EU–ACP framework (pp. viii, 45, 65). The Green Paper also indicates that the scenario on extending the non-reciprocal GSP scheme to all developing countries, abolishing the ACP group's preferential treatment, implies a more generous treatment for the LDCs under the Enabling Clause (see above on paragraph 2d). Therefore the Commission links the application of this scenario with a multilateral commitment to lower tariffs on LDC imports (p. 66) – very much in the same vein as Europe's position towards the 1996 Singapore Conference.

Scenarios three and four on reciprocal trade relations do not refer to LDCs. The enumeration of plus and minus points of the different scenarios in the annex does not make mention of LDC trade provisions either.

This short overview shows that the Commission's Green Paper largely reflects the Union's low-profile attitude in 1996. Although this document again illustrates that the situation of LDCs is becoming a topic on the international trade and aid agenda (see above, and Chapter 1 of this volume), the EU is obviously not intending to take a leading role in opening its market for the LDCs.

After consulting EU member states and other actors, the Commission published its guidelines for the negotiation of a new EU–ACP agreement in October 1997. Whereas the Green Paper only gave limited, vaguely formulated and scattered references to the position of LDCs in the post-Lomé trade regime, these *negotiation guidelines* are much more explicit on this topic. The introduction already makes clear that a separate 'arrangement' (not an 'agreement') for market access (not aid) for all LDCs (not just ACP) is envisaged (EU 1997: 4). The guidelines further clarify that this arrangement would take the form of a GSP regulation, thus limited to market access, and outside the EU–ACP framework (pp. 26, 33). With hindsight two predictions are interesting to note: difficulties that may arise when non-reciprocal preferences are granted to LDCs who participate in a free trade area (p. 23), and LDC beneficiaries may no longer benefit from the commodity agreements for bananas, sugar and beef (p. 26).

Hence the above-mentioned acceleration of the LDC issue on Europe's international trade agenda is mirrored in the internal thought process on the reform of Lomé. At times (pp. 25, 33) the negotiating guidelines explicitly refer to the European LDC strategy of 2 June 1997.

These guidelines served as a basis for the elaboration of the Commission's negotiating mandate by the Council of Ministers in the first half of 1998. The trade chapter of this mandate was the main topic of contention within the EU, including the provisions on LDCs. All member states agreed that the medium-term option of the 1997 LDC strategy should be incorporated into the Cotonou Agreement. The debate within the Council (again along the North–South cleavage, as explained by Carbone in Chapter 3 of this volume) related to the timetable of implementation (*Agence Europe* 1998b; Holland 2002: 187) – not to the principle of granting DFQF market access to LDCs. The same holds true for the Agricultural Commissioner: although a permanent suspension of sensitive products would have been relatively easy to achieve, the Commissioner only wanted extended deadlines (see Van den Hoven in Chapter 4 of this volume).

Europe's negotiating mandate eventually contained the following stipulation: 'The Council and the Commission will start by the year 2000 a process which by 2005 will allow duty-free access for essentially all products from all LDCs building-ing on the level of existing trade provisions of the Lome Convention . . .'.[8] This provision – indeed the EBA *avant la lettre* decision of June 1997 – almost literally appeared in Article 37(9) of the EU–ACP Partnership Agreement, which was signed in Cotonou three years later (June 2000). Gibb called it a 'super-GSP' (Gibb 2000), only three months afterwards DG Trade entitled it 'Everything but Arms'. Table 2.3 recapitulates these parallels between the development of EBA on the one hand and the reform of Lomé on the other. Figure 2.1 visualizes the same story.

Table 2.3 The development of EBA and the reform of Lomé

EU-EBA and WTO trade agenda	*EU–ACP and post-Lomé reform*
Low profile	
WTO Singapore 12/1996	Green Paper Commission 11/1996
• Cf. international consensus • No autonomous EU initiatives	• Differentiation LDC: unclear how • EU-LDC agreement? vague • Maybe through GSP: only if multilateral agreement
Acceleration	
General Affairs Council 6/1997 (Table 2.1)	Negotiation directives Commission 10/1997
• LDC equivalent access as ACP from 1998 • *EBA avant la lettre* • 'Leading by example'	• Different trade regime for all LDCs (ACP and non-ACP) • Market access through GSP (not EU–ACP framework)
Consolidation	
'Everything but Arms'	Negotiation mandate Council 6/1998
• Weakened regulation (2001) after radicalization Commission proposal (2000) • Debate mainly on timetable	• 0 tariff for essentially all products in 2005, cf. Cotonou art.37(9) • Debate mainly on timetable

| EU low profile | EU acceleration | Radicalization | Consolidation |

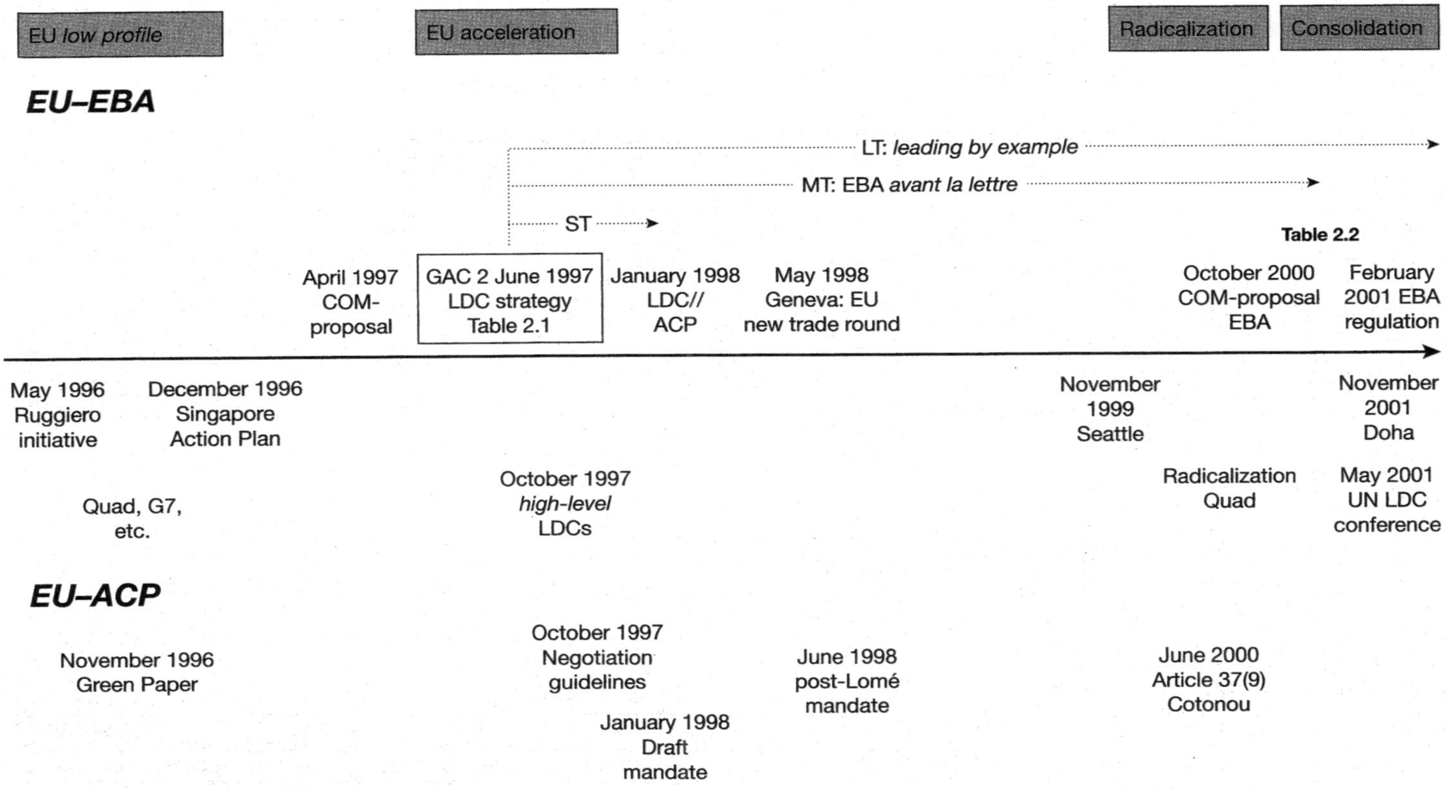

EU–EBA

| April 1997 COM-proposal | GAC 2 June 1997 LDC strategy Table 2.1 | January 1998 LDC// ACP | May 1998 Geneva: EU new trade round | October 2000 COM-proposal EBA | February 2001 EBA regulation |

ST →

--- MT: EBA avant la lettre ---

--- LT: leading by example ---

Table 2.2

| May 1996 Ruggiero initiative | December 1996 Singapore Action Plan | | | November 1999 Seattle | November 2001 Doha |

Quad, G7, etc.

October 1997 high-level LDCs

Radicalization Quad

May 2001 UN LDC conference

EU–ACP

| November 1996 Green Paper | October 1997 Negotiation guidelines | | | June 2000 Article 37(9) Cotonou |

January 1998 Draft mandate

June 1998 post-Lomé mandate

Figure 2.1 EU–EBA and EU–ACP agendas: timetable

The question now arises: *how* exactly are both dossiers interrelated? Below we hypothesize that the European LDC strategy plays a catalysing role in the broader reform process of the EU–ACP trade relationship. More specifically, it is argued that EBA plays an important role in the break-up of the ACP group and in the abolishment of more interventionist Lomé remnants.

Breaking up the ACP group

Holland (2004: 291) argues that:

> EBA has breached the long-established policy of offering the ACP preferential advantages over all other developing countries. To extend non-reciprocity to non-ACP LDCs implied, if not endorsed, a view that the ACP as a group was no longer the dominant organizing principle for EU Third World relations. . . . This would appear to have vindicated critics who saw the Lomé renegotiation process as the forerunner of the fragmentation of the ACP group.

Europe's preferential treatment of former colonies, to the detriment of some of the poorest non-ACP countries, has always been criticized (cf. Grilli 1993). There are many reasons why the EU insisted on 'differentiating' within the group of ACP countries. Among them is the increasingly widespread feeling in Europe that 'the ACP group is in reality neither a political group nor an economic entity. It grew up for essentially historic reasons and exists only in the framework of relations with the European Union' (EU 1996a: viii). It should be added that the political and economic importance of these countries has diminished throughout the 1990s, with the end of the Cold War (strategic importance of African countries), the increasing economic interdependence (emerging of trade partners in Asia and Latin America), Europe's focus on the near abroad (enlargement process and neighbourhood policy) and internal Commission reforms (cf. Babarinde and Faber 2004). This 'globalist' trend in EU trade and development policy is inextricably related to a decreased interest in the ACP group.

The question here is not so much what determined this globalist trend, but rather, how is Europe's LDC strategy related to this evolution? Europe's trade policy vis-à-vis LDCs clearly *reflects* this trend. The 1998 regulation to align LDC preferences with those of the ACP group already indicated the widening scope of EU trade and development policy, and this evolution was more radically enforced with EBA. Focusing on a 'cross-cutting' category such as the LDC – neither geographical nor historical-political, but defined by objective UN criteria – by definition implies a global approach. In principle any country could become a member of (cf. Senegal in 2001) or graduate from (cf. Botswana in 1994) the LDC category. EBA is also firmly embedded in the GATT/WTO rules: as an amendment on Europe's GSP regime it is legitimized by the 1979 Enabling Clause. WTO approval for such an arrangement is much easier to obtain than a waiver for trade schemes *à la* Lomé.

But the point here is that 'EBA' also plays a *catalysing* role. To explain this process, we have to go back to the short-term decision of June 1997 to grant all LDCs equivalent market access as the Lomé beneficiaries from 1998. This ostensibly limited decision – it concerns a relatively small tariff reduction for only nine of the poorest countries, since the other LDCs are already members of the ACP – has effectively narrowed down the range of future options to reform the EU–ACP trade relationship. It set off a 'path-dependent' process that almost inevitably led to a further differentiation between Europe's trade relations with *all* LDCs (including ACP-LDCs) on the one hand and the other ACP countries on the other. To continue the historical-institutionalist jargon (Pierson 1996), the 1998 decision to put LDCs' market access on the same footing as the ACP countries created a 'lock-in' situation, where the existence of 'sunk costs' renders it more difficult to choose a different 'path'.[9]

How exactly did this dynamic arise? First, it has to be remembered that, during the 1990s, the EU was aiming at the (gradual) establishment of reciprocal free trade with the ACP countries. The traditional system of unilateral preferences would be replaced with reciprocal liberalization. From the decision to grant non-ACP LDCs equivalent market access as the ACP group from January 1998 on the one hand, *and* the European option for free trade in the post-Lomé regime on the other, it follows that *all* ACP countries (both non-LDC ACP *and* ACP LDCs) would be discriminated against in favour of non-ACP LDCs. Non-ACP LDCs would preserve their ACP equivalent market access, but contrary to the latter group they would not have to negotiate tariff concessions of their own in exchange. In other words, this would entail discrimination between ACP LDCs (entering into free trade agreements with the EU) and non-ACP LDCs (with equivalent market access but without reciprocal concessions). As both belong to the group of least developed countries and the former traditionally appeared on the apex of the Union's preferential pyramid, such a situation was politically unfeasible. The 2 June decision indicates the wide support for an *extension* of ACP preferences to non-ACP LDCs, but a discrimination of these non-ACP LDCs *at the cost of* ACP LDCs would encounter resistance from a strong coalition of both 'traditionalist' countries (still preferring exclusive EU–ACP relations, e.g. France) and typical advocates of the LDC issue in trade and development (e.g. Scandinavian countries).

Therefore only two options remain. One is that the non-ACP LDCs also take part in the EU–ACP free trade agreements. It is however doubtful that they would opt for an agreement that necessitates reciprocal concessions for equivalent market access and without substantial additional benefits. This explains why the obvious option is to enforce the differentiation between LDCs and non-LDCs *within* the post-Lomé trade regime. Preserving unilateral trade preferences for ACP LDCs, in accordance with their non-ACP counterparts, essentially means the extension of the Lomé *status quo* for these countries, but it equally leads to the effective break-up of the ACP group as a political entity.

Concluding, what initially seemed to be a limited extension of ACP preferences to nine non-ACP countries turned out to entail greater differentiation within the ACP group. In the course of 1997 the LDC issue – initially raised by Ruggiero

– became functional in the thought process on the reform of the EU–ACP trade relationship. The concrete realization of the short-term decision to grant non-ACP LDCs equivalent market access was being prepared at the same time when the Commission published its negotiating guidelines (October 1997). This explains why the latter document is much more explicit on the role of LDCs in the post-Lomé trade regime than the 1996 Green Paper: the implementation of the June 1997 strategy had effectively limited the range of options. Given Europe's new commitments towards the LDCs, the possibility to continue an exclusive EU–ACP trade relationship had become even more difficult than before. Sooner or later an initiative such as EBA would have to materialize.

In turn, this EBA Regulation could imply a further differentiation within the ACP. Much depends on the strategy of ACP LDCs during the ongoing negotiations on Economic Partnership Agreements, a question that is addressed by Pilegaard in Chapter 8 and by Bilal in Chapter 11 of this volume.

Restructuring the Lomé trade regime

Several authors have pointed to the 'paradigmatic departure' (Holland 2003: 162) of Cotonou. Whereas the Lomé trade regime still contained some interventionist elements, inspired by the pleas for a 'New International Economic Order' (NIEO) in the 1970s – some called it a 'mini-NIEO' (Hveem 1980: 88–9) – the Cotonou Agreement establishes a much more neo-liberally inspired trade framework. Three points are worth mentioning: (1) the shift from non-reciprocity to reciprocal free trade agreements (albeit gradually), (2) the abolition of the export stabilization schemes STABEX and SYSMIN (although replaced by the more limited Flex mechanism) and (3) the pressure on commodity agreements with some ACP countries (although strictly speaking not part of the post-Lomé trade talks).

Without elaborating on explanations for this ideological shift in EU trade politics vis-à-vis developing countries (see Gibb 2000; Brown 2000; Ravenhill 2004; Hurt 2004; Arts and Dickson 2004), the role of the following factors is obvious: the general ideological climate since the 1980s, the establishment of the WTO, the failure of Lomé recipes for development of ACP countries, the decline of the latter's commodity power and Europe's changing economic interests.

Here too the question presents itself: what role (if any) does the EBA initiative play in this evolution? First of all, somewhat paradoxically, EBA indicates that most developing countries should engage in multilateral trade liberalization within the WTO and/or in bilateral Free Trade Agreements (FTAs) with the EU. Although EBA constitutes the most outspoken example of non-reciprocal preferences – an important aspect of the NIEO demands in the 1970s – it became the exception which proves the rule. Since EBA is limited to LDC beneficiaries, other developing countries that want an equivalent level of access to the European market will have to negotiate reciprocal FTAs. Developing countries that do not conclude such agreements fall back on Europe's 'normal' GSP system, with a less generous preferential margin than EBA. In the past decade FTAs between the EU and developing countries have indeed proliferated, for example with Mexico (1997),

South Africa (1999), Chile (2002) and the southern Mediterranean countries (since 1999). In the near future FTAs with MERCOSUR (negotiations since 2000) and the Gulf Cooperation Council (since 2001) may be concluded, and, in 2006, Trade Commissioner Peter Mandelson suggested negotiating an FTA with ASEAN, India, South Korea, and with Russia. Although EBA has not directly stimulated the proliferation of reciprocal free trade agreements, implicitly it defines which countries continue to benefit substantially from Europe's GSP regime. Countries not belonging to the LDC group better take the bilateral course of FTAs.[10]

Besides, the extension of Europe's GSP regime through EBA can hardly be seen as a late application of the NIEO demands. For one thing, Europe's unilateral market access is not complemented with a comprehensive 'trade and aid' package including more interventionist mechanisms that provide relatively high and stable prices. Although EBA allows the LDCs to export their sugar to the European market at a higher price than world market prices, it also renders the maintenance of existing commodity schemes between the EU and developing countries more difficult.

This brings us to the second and more important point. Granting completely free access to the European market – at least after a transition period – EBA hinders the functioning of interventionist commodity schemes *à la* NIEO. As soon as LDCs manage to export a substantial amount of a certain product to the European market, it becomes virtually impossible to sustain trade regimes providing guaranteed prices and quotas.[11] Therefore the establishment of LDC schemes such as EBA – although limited in terms of trade flows – facilitates the advancement of neoliberal trade schemes. This consideration on the ideological 'lock-in effects' of EBA seems rather theoretical – proposals for commodity schemes have disappeared from the international trade agenda (but see UNCTAD 2003b) – with the exception of sugar. More specifically, there are indications that EBA jeopardizes the continuation of Europe's Sugar Protocol with 17 ACP countries and India.

Between 1973 and 1975 the debates on the Sugar Protocol were 'one of the most hotly debated and, in the end, cliff-hanging components of the entire negotiations leading to Lomé' (Gruhn 1976: 256). The first article of Protocol 3 on ACP Sugar (Annex of the EU–ACP Cotonou Agreement) states that 'the Community undertakes for an indefinite period to purchase and import, at guaranteed prices, specific quantities of cane sugar, raw or white, which originate in the ACP states and which these States undertake to deliver to it'. ACP countries vainly hoped to extend this 'model' arrangement to other commodities during subsequent Lomé reforms (Ravenhill 1985: 211). This Sugar Protocol could, in a nutshell, be seen as a continuation of Europe's internal Common Market Organization for sugar. Developing-country protocol members benefit from similar price support mechanisms as EU producers – a guaranteed price of about three times the world market price – whereas other sugar exporters are virtually excluded from the European market. EU export subsidies are used to maintain this costly system, which leads to the dumping of surplus sugar on the world market.

In recent years various actors (e.g. Brazil in the WTO case against the EU, other sugar producers in the Doha negotiations, NGO campaigns, consumer lobbies, some EU member states) have fiercely criticized this European sugar regime. The current pressure for reform also results from the increased budgetary costs due to larger imports from non-ACP exporters, following enlargement and EU tariff concessions to Israel, Turkey and the western Balkan countries.

Does EBA add to this pressure? EBA gradually increases the tariff quotas for LDCs between 2001 and 2009 and at the same time the tariffs will be reduced to zero between 2006 and 2009. Several studies find that, after the end of the transition period, the effects of EBA on LDC's export growth will manifest themselves most outspokenly in the sugar sector. Cernat *et al.* (2003: 18) even suggest that 'Everything but Arms' could be better labelled 'Nothing but sugar'. When LDC sugar suppliers such as Sudan and Mozambique manage to increase their production and export capacity, at the expense of traditional ACP Sugar Protocol members (such as Mauritius, Fiji and Guyana), Europe's sugar regime may become unmanageable. But the main question is to what extent LDC producers will be able to export sugar to the EU. Disagreements between DG Trade and DG Agriculture on the EBA proposal of 2000 actually converged around conflicting estimates of the LDC's sugar export capacity.

But it is safe to say that the alleged effects of EBA have been used by policy makers advocating the liberalization of Europe's sugar regime. Although the agricultural community in Europe may have used EBA as a means to build a coalition with ACP countries within the WTO (see Van den Hoven in Chapter 4), it is clear that the trade community saw EBA as a stimulus for reforming Europe's sugar regime. This corresponds with Michael Brüntrup's thesis (see Chapter 10) about EBA as a 'Trojan horse' for sugar reform (see also Jennar 2004: 169). Indeed, during the EBA decision-making process, EU policy makers clarified that the ACP Sugar Protocol beneficiaries would have to 'adapt to a changing international regime' (Page and Hewitt 2002: 95; see also McQueen 2002: 106). At the same time, the British agriculture minister stated that EBA 'does add to the pressure for a reform of the sugar regime, including a reform of the price-fixing mechanisms' (House of Commons 2000). In 2003 a DG Trade official described the consequences of EBA in a rather straightforward way (House of Commons 2003):

> You have a closed system with, suddenly, additional imports coming in – your system explodes. We all know that the system will not survive in the way in which it is. We have a little time. The EBA effect for sugar will become really important from 2006 onwards. . . . We expect larger quantities of least developed country sugar to come into the Community and by then, therefore, we have to have a different sugar regime. Our present regime cannot survive with additional quantities coming in.

This is to the expense of some developing countries, but

> basically, we are coming round to understand that we have to send signals to these countries that they may still have another five, possibly ten, years, but they either become competitive or they move into other production lines.

It is a hard message but basically you cannot continue to produce against the markets.

Or in a nutshell, citing Agricultural Commissioner Fischler: "'Everything but Arms" is the best guarantee that the present sugar regime in Europe cannot survive' (House of Commons 2003).

These statements were made in the context of the Commission's preparatory work on a sugar market reform proposal. In one working paper EBA is again depicted as one of the major factors that make the present sugar regime untenable. There is some irony in this assertion, since the very same document states that ACP *and* LDC countries take more advantages from the existing system than from the proposed alternatives (EU 2003: 10). LDCs have indeed argued for an adaptation of 'Everything but Arms', deferring the tariff reduction (to 2016–19) *and* capping the sugar quotas after this transition period (LDC 2004). The Sudanese trade minister put it more simply: 'only by allowing us to sell sugar at a certain guaranteed price can EBA become meaningful to our economies' (*EUObserver* 3 March 2004). Nevertheless, according to the Commission (EU 2003), such an amendment of EBA would 'exact a high political price and harm the Community's credibility'. This may be another instance of lock-in effects ensuing from Europe's LDC strategy: it would be difficult for the EU to reconsider such a highly politicized and symbolic initiative as EBA, even if the supposed beneficiaries ask for an amendment.

Similarly, ACP and LDC countries criticized the 2004 Commission proposals on sugar reform. To date the future of the Sugar Protocol remains uncertain. The WTO panel on sugar stated that the EU must 'fully respect' its 'commitments to developing countries' (WTO 2004: 200). But the outlook of the protocol will also be influenced by the outcome of the WTO talks, by the agricultural reforms within the EU and Europe's bilateral free trade negotiations with developing countries – especially the Economic Partnership Agreements with the ACP regions. According to the Commission, the Sugar Protocol 'should be integrated into the EPAs in such a way that does not prejudice the EU's ['Everything but Arms'] commitment to LDCs for full market access for sugar from 2009 and that ensures full compatibility with WTO rules' (EU 2004).

Concluding, no matter what the empirical effects of EBA on the EU sugar market may be (see Chapters 9 and 10 of this volume), this initiative occupies an important place in European policy makers' discourse on the reform of the sugar market. EBA seems to play a catalyzing role in the shift from a more interventionist to a more neo-liberally inspired trade regime vis-à-vis the ACP. Although such a reform may be desirable in some respects, both ACP and LDC countries seem to prefer the current situation.

Conclusion

This chapter examined the political dynamics behind the Union's EBA initiative. Starting from a process-tracing analysis of the development of EBA, going back to

Europe's position on the Ruggiero initiative of 1996, two hypotheses were advanced. Each of them relates to a major theme in Europe's recent trade politics: the WTO agenda and the reform of Lomé. It was argued that the 'Doha hypothesis' sheds light on the timing of EBA and on the radicalization of the Commission (DG Trade) in 2000. However, the linkage between Europe's LDC policy and its objective to launch a new WTO trade round cannot account for the acceleration of the LDC issue in Europe's trade policy in 1997. The Council's LDC strategy of June 1997 – including EBA *avant la lettre* – coincided with the thought process on the reform of the EU–ACP Lomé trade regime. With hindsight Europe's LDC policy proved to be functional in the realization of two EU objectives in this reform process: greater differentiation within the ACP group and discouraging more interventionist trade arrangements.

From this perspective, both hypotheses are complementary rather than competing. Together they give a more comprehensive picture of the politics behind EBA than an exclusive focus on the role of EBA within Europe's WTO policy.

A historical-institutionalist perspective was used to shed light upon this rather empirical description of the consequences of Europe's LDC policy for EU–ACP trade relations. This analysis showed that Europe's LDC strategy created a path-dependent logic, favouring more globalist and neo-liberal options in the EU–ACP trade reform process. In other words, it gave rise to lock-in effects that made it more difficult for future policy decisions to sustain exclusive EU–ACP trade relations and interventionist trade arrangements.

This institutionalization is not merely a technical conclusion. Although this chapter did not elaborate on the underlying strategies of European actors, it should be stressed that policy and norm entrepreneurs did play a role in tracing out such processes. Strong European advocates for EBA (DG Trade within the Commission and the northern member states within the Council[12]) are traditionally critical of Europe's exclusive focus on the ACP group and of Lomé's interventionist ingredients. But this is not to say that there is a Grand Master Plan behind the design of EBA. The point is rather that the 'development of EBA' is affected by a broader normative evolution in favour of globalist and neo-liberal trade relations with the developing world.

The normative implications of these empirical observations also fall outside the scope of this chapter. However, in conclusion, some considerations should be touched upon. Concerning the break-up of the ACP group – once described as the 'trade union of the poor' by former President of Tanzania Julius Nyerere (Whiteman 1998: 32) – Stevens (1999: 11) correctly noted that:

> despite the difficulties of reaching agreement among 70 disparate states in three geographical regions, many crosscutting relationships have been developed during the period of Lomés I–IV and these should be nurtured. It would be a great shame if the EU were deliberately to jettison one of its most remarkable creations.

From this perspective the fading of the ACP group as a unitary political actor may be deplored.

With regard to the second evolution, namely the abandonment of Lomé's more interventionist trade arrangements, Arts and Dickson made a similarly critical evaluation: 'EU development cooperation policy has shifted away from making substantive and innovative attempts to contribute to the North–South dialogue ... to follow global trends much more than before ...' (Arts and Dickson 2004: 2–3). The question whether and how the increasingly neo-liberal outlook of Europe's trade policy contributes to economic development of the South indeed continues to be highly relevant. In this respect the ongoing EU–ACP negotiations on Economic Partnership Agreements will be an important test case.

Notes

I am grateful to all the participants of the Ghent symposium (5–6 December 2005) and of the ECPR Joint Sessions of Workshops in Uppsala (April 2004), and to Federica Bicchi, Annika Björkdahl, Ole Elgström, Knud Erik Jörgensen, Bart Kerremans, Dries Lesage, Steven Sterkx, Hendrik Vos, for their comments on earlier versions.

1 For example, an enumeration of Europe's priorities for Singapore by 'sources close to the Commission' (*Agence Europe* 1996) contains no single reference to the link between trade and development – not to mention the LDC issue.
2 See Sub-committee on LDCs, note of the meeting, WT/COMTD/LLDC/4, 23 September 1996.
3 However, Burma (Myanmar) was excluded from GSP preferences since 1997, because of practices of forced labour (see also Appendix 1.1 in Chapter 1 of this volume).
4 Lamy talked about a 'guillotine clause' that allows the Commission to take safeguard measures 'without consulting 36 expert committees' (*Agence Europe* 2001).
5 The subsequent chapters by Carbone and Van den Hoven focus on the divergent positions of EU actors in the EBA debate.
6 See the statements at http://www.wto.org/english/thewto_e/minist_e/min01_e/min01_statements_e.htm (accessed 17 May 2006).
7 Chapters 5, 6 and 7 of this volume elaborate on comparisons between EU and US trade policy vis-à-vis LDCs.
8 The mandate is not published, but this passage of the negotiation mandate is cited in another document by the European Commission (EU 1999: 8, 25). See also Gibb (2000: 9) and *Agence Europe* (1998a).
9 Matambalya and Wolf (2001: 141) made a similar suggestion on the impact of the 1997–98 decision: 'the unilateral extension by the EU of preferences usually reserved for ACP economies to non-ACP LDCs has changed the scenario, providing another reason for updated strategic considerations by the ACP States'.
10 Even LDCs may consider joining the Union's free-trade agreements (Economic Partnership Agreements) with the ACP regions more attractive than exporting under EBA (Babarinde and Faber 2004).
11 As mentioned above, the incompatibility between Europe's LDC initiatives and commodity agreements was already suggested in the Commission's negotiation guidelines of October 1997.
12 See the chapters by Carbone and Van den Hoven.

References

Agence Europe (1996), No. 6869, 7 December.
Agence Europe (1997), No. 6986, 2–3 June.

Agence Europe (1998a), No. 7236, 6 June.

Agence Europe (1998b), No. 7251, 27 June.

Agence Europe (2001), No. 7883, 18 January.

Arts, K. and Dickson, A.K. (eds) (2004) *EU Development Cooperation: from Model to Symbol?*, Manchester: Manchester University Press.

Babarinde, O. and Faber, G. (2004) 'From Lomé to Cotonou: business as usual?', *European Foreign Affairs Review*, 9: 27–47.

Brenton, P. (2003) 'Integrating the Least Developed Countries into the World Trading System: The Current Impact of EU Preferences under Everything but Arms', Policy Research Working Paper No. 3018, Washington DC: World Bank.

Brown, W. (2000) 'Restructuring North–South relations: ACP–EU development co-operation in a liberal international order', *Review of African Political Economy*, 27: 367–83.

Cernat, L., Laird, S., Monge-Roffarello, L. and Turrini, A. (2003) 'The EU's Everything but Arms Initiative and the Least-developed Countries', Discussion Paper No. 2003/47, Wider, United Nations University. Available at http://www.wider.unu.edu/publications/dps/dps2003/dp2003-047.pdf (accessed 8 May 2006).

Chaban, N., Elgström, O., and Holland, M. (2006) 'The European Union as others see it', *European Foreign Affairs Review*, 11 (2): 245–62.

DG Agriculture (2000) 'Everything but Arms (EBA) Proposal. First remarks on the possible impacts on the agriculture sector', Brussels: European Commission.

Elgström, O. (2000) 'Lomé and post-Lomé: asymmetric negotiations and the impact of norms', *European Foreign Affairs Review*, 5: 175–95.

EU (1996a) 'Green Paper on relations between the European Union and the ACP countries on the eve of the 21st century. Challenges and options for a new partnership', 20 November, Brussels: European Commission.

EU (1996b) '"A" Item Note to COREPER: Position of the European Union on the involvement of the Least Developed Countries in the WTO system', 12398/96, 3 December, Brussels: Article 133 Committee.

EU (1997) 'Communication from the Commission to the Council and the European Parliament. Guidelines for the negotiation of new cooperation agreements with the African, Caribbean and Pacific (ACP) countries', 29 October, Brussels: European Commission.

EU (1999) 'Joint analysis by EU and ACP experts for Negotiating Group 3, Economic and Trade Cooperation. Consequences for the ACP countries of applying the Generalised System of Preferences', CE/TFN/GCEC3/29-EN, ACP/00/177/99, 20 April, Brussels: European Commission.

EU (2000) 'Proposal for a Council Regulation amending Council Regulation (EC) No. 2820/98 applying a multiannual scheme of generalised tariff preferences for the period 1 July 1999 to 31 December 2001 so as to extend duty-free access without any quantitative restrictions to products originating in the least developed countries', 5 October, Brussels: European Commission.

EU (2003) 'Reforming the European Union's sugar policy: summary of impact assessment work', Commission Staff Working Paper, Brussels: European Commission.

EU (2004) 'Accomplishing a sustainable agricultural model for Europe through the reformed CAP – sugar sector reform', 14 July, Brussels: European Commission.

Forwood, G. (2001) 'The road to Cotonou: negotiating a successor to Lomé', *Journal of Common Market Studies*, 39: 423–42.

Gibb, R. (2000) 'Post-Lomé: the European Union and the South', *Third World Quarterly*, 21: 457–81.

Grilli, E. (1993) *The European Community and the developing countries*, Cambridge: Cambridge University Press.

Gruhn, I.V. (1976) 'The Lomé Convention: inching towards interdependence', *International Organization*, 30: 241–62.

Holland, M. (2002) *The European Union and the Third World*, Basingstoke: Palgrave.

Holland, M. (2003) '20/20 vision? The EU's Cotonou Partnership Agreement', *Brown Journal of World Affairs*, 9: 161–75.

Holland, M. (2004) 'Development policy: paradigm shifts and the "normalization" of a privileged partnership', in M. Green Cowles and D. Dinan (eds) *Developments in the European Union 2*, Basingstoke: Palgrave Macmillan, 275–95.

House of Commons (2000) 'European Scrutiny, Minutes of Evidence (para. 82)', 20 December.

House of Commons (2003) 'Minutes of Evidence (paras 170 and 207)', 20 March.

Hurt, S.R. (2003) 'Co-operation and coercion? The Cotonou Agreement between the European Union and ACP states and the end of the Lomé Convention', *Third World Quarterly*, 24: 161–76.

Hurt, S.R. (2004) 'The European Union's external relations with Africa after the Cold War: aspects of continuity and change', in I. Taylor and P. Williams (eds) *Africa in International Politics. External Involvement on the Continent*, London: Routledge.

Hveem, H. (1980) 'Scandinavia, the like-minded countries, and the NIEO', in E. Laszlo and J. Kurtzman (eds) *Western Europe and the New International Economic Order: Representative Samples of European Perspectives*, New York: Pergamon Press.

Jennar, R. (2004) *Europe, la trahison des élites*, Paris: Fayard.

Kerremans, B. (2004) 'What went wrong in Cancun? A principal–agent view on the EU's rationale towards the Doha Development Round', *European Foreign Affairs Review*, 9: 363–93.

Lamy, P. (2000a) 'What are the options after Seattle?', 25 January, Brussels: European Parliament.

Lamy, P. (2000b) 'Post-Seattle outlook for the developing countries', Brussels: European Parliament Development Committee, 21 February.

Lamy, P. (2001) 'Press Release', IP/01/261, 26 February.

Lamy, P. (2002) *L'Europe en première ligne*, Paris: Éditions du Seuil.

LDC (2004) 'Proposal of the least developed countries of the world to the European Union regarding the adaptation of the EBA in relation to sugar and the role of the LDCs in the future orientation of the EU sugar regime', LDC Brussels Sugar Group, 3 March.

Lister, M. (1999) 'The European Union's relations with the African, Caribbean and Pacific countries', in M. Lister (ed.) *New Perspectives on European Union Development Cooperation*, Boulder CO: Westview Press.

Matambalya, F. and Wolf, S. (2001) 'The Cotonou Agreement and the challenges of making the new EU–ACP trade regime WTO compatible', *Journal of World Trade*, 35: 123–44.

McQueen, M. (1998) 'ACP–EU trade cooperation after 2000: an assessment of reciprocal trade preferences', *Journal of Modern African Studies*, 36, 4: 669–92.

McQueen, M. (2002) 'EU preferential market access conditions for the least developed countries', *Intereconomics*, March–April, 101–9.

Moon, B.E. (2004) 'The trade agenda in the new millennium', in B. Hocking and S. McGuire (eds) *Trade Politics*, London: Routledge.

Orbie, J. (2003) 'EU development policy integration and the Monterrey process: a leading and benevolent identity?', *European Foreign Affairs Review*, 8: 395–415.

Page, S. and Hewitt, A. (2002) 'The new European trade preferences: does the "Everything but Arms" help the poor?', *Development Policy Review*, 20: 91–102.

Pierson, P. (1996) 'The path to European Integration: a historical institutionalist analysis', *Comparative Political Studies*, 29: 123–63.

Ravenhill, J. (1985) *Collective Clientelism: The Lomé Conventions and North–South Relations*, New York: Columbia University Press.

Ravenhill, J. (1986) 'Aid through trade: reforming the international trade regime in the interests of the least developed countries', *Third World Quarterly*, 8: 449–85.

Ravenhill, J. (2004) 'Back to the nest? Europe's relations with the African, Caribbean and Pacific group of countries', in V.K. Aggarwal and E. Fogarty (eds) *EU Trade Strategies: Between Regionalism and Globalism*, Basingstoke: Palgrave Macmillan.

Ruggiero, R. (1996) 'The road ahead: international trade policy in the era of the WTO', address to the fourth Sylvia Ostry Lecture in Ottawa, Canada, 28 May.

Smith, M. (1999) 'The European Union', in B. Hocking and S. McGuire (eds) *Trade Politics: International, Domestic and Regional Perspectives*, London: Routledge.

Stevens, C. (1999) 'The present state of the Lomé negotiations: the position of the EU and of the ACP states', in K. Schilder (ed.) *Farewell to Lomé? The Impact of Neo-liberal EU Policies on the ACP Countries*, Bonn: Terre des hommes/Kosa/Weed.

Stevens, C. and Kennan, J. (2001) *The Impact of the EU's 'Everything but Arms' Proposal: a Report to Oxfam*, Brighton: Institute of Development Studies.

UNCTAD and Commonwealth Secretariat (2001) *Duty and Quota-free Market Access for LDCs: an Analysis of Quad Initiatives*, London: Commonwealth Secretariat and Geneva: UNCTAD.

UNCTAD (2003a) *Trade Preferences for LDCs: an Early Assessment of Benefits and Possible Improvements*, New York and Geneva: UN.

UNCTAD (2003b) *Economic Development in Africa: Trade Performance and Commodity Dependence*, New York and Geneva: UN.

Van den Hoven, A. (2004) 'Assuming leadership in multilateral economic institutions: the EU's "Development Round" discourse and strategy', *West European Politics*, 27: 256–83.

Whiteman, K. (1998) 'Africa, the ACP and Europe: the lessons of twenty-five years', *Development Policy Review*, 16: 29–37.

WTO (1996) 'Comprehensive and integrated WTO plan of action for the least developed countries', 13 December, WT/MIN(96)/14, Geneva: WTO.

WTO (2004) 'European Communities export subsidies on sugar complaint by Brazil. Report of the Panel', WT/DS266/R, 15 October, Geneva: WTO.

3 EBA, EU trade policy and the ACP

A tale of two North–South divides

Maurizio Carbone

When the 'Everything but Arms' (EBA) regulation was adopted in February 2001, Pascal Lamy, the then Commissioner for Trade, enthusiastically stated: 'This is a global first. It is the first time that the European Union's trade policy has been substantially modified by the necessity of contributing to development policy' (*Washington Post* 28 February 2001). Linking trade and development has increasingly become a key priority for the European Union (EU). However, the proposal put forward by Lamy in September 2000 to liberalize all goods except arms and ammunitions coming from the least developed countries (LDCs) was resisted inside the European Commission, by EU member states, and by some developing countries. While other analyses concentrate on 'turf wars' between DG Trade and DG Agriculture (see Van den Hoven, Chapter 4 in this volume), this chapter, by focusing on different clashes, identifies two types of North–South divide in the process that led to the final adoption of the EBA regulation. The first north–south cleavage is in EU trade policy and occurs among member states. In particular, it is shown how member states' preferences fell into two broad categories: the liberal group, which supported the extension of preferential treatment to the LDCs for all products; the protectionist group, which cautioned against the potential negative impact of the EBA initiative on the Common Agricultural Policy (CAP) and on the EU budget. The final outcome, with the deferred liberalization of three 'sensitive' goods (i.e. rice, sugar, bananas) and the inclusion of some trade protection instruments, also reflects these disputes. The second part of the chapter looks at the North–South dynamics in EU development policy, focusing on the reactions from the ACP group to the proposal. In particular, this section demonstrates how the lack of consultation of the ACP group can be seen as part of a consistent strategy inside the EU that has gradually undermined the traditional partnership approach of the Lomé Convention. Moreover, though in line with the Cotonou Agreement, the EBA proposal, by extending preferential treatment to Asian LDCs, may have made a terminal contribution to the ACP unity and its privileged relationship with the EU.

North–South dynamics in EU trade policy

Trade policy in the EU is about reconciling internal factors – i.e. bureaucratic, sectoral, and national interests – and external aims – promoting multilateralism while maintaining tight relationships with (some) developing countries. The EU has progressively moved from a trade policy concerned with building the single market towards a more outward-oriented one. EU trade policy has therefore significant implications for the international trading system and for countries that look on the EU as an actor capable of promoting a development-friendly agenda in multilateral trade rounds (Woolcock 2005a, b). The EBA proposal is an example of how difficult it is to combine internal and external aims. The initial proposal by Lamy in September 2000 met with significant resistance from the Agriculture Directorate General and its Commissioner Franz Fischler (cf. Chapter 4 of this volume). But at the same time, a strong campaign was initiated by a group of member states and a number of associations of agricultural producers, which questioned the impact of the EBA initiative on the EU's agriculture sector and on the budget. Lamy (2002: 72; translation from French) describes this in his book:

> As soon as the proposal was distributed to the European Parliament and to the Council, and thus made public, reticences from the national capitals or economic sectors emerged. And I must say that their virulence surprised me. There is a big gap between rich countries' discourse about their responsibility towards the Third World, and concrete, even modest, measures that may translate this responsibility into practice.

This section argues that the resistance of a group of southern European countries contributed to watering down Lamy's initial ambitious proposal. It first analyzes how different 'trade cultures' along the liberal–protectionist dichotomy shape EU trade policy. Then, it applies this north–south cleavage to the policy making process of the EBA regulation.

The liberal–protectionist pendulum

Even though trade policy is amongst the most important common policies in the EU, the role of member states should not be underestimated. The Treaty of Rome transfers trade authority to a supranational entity. Seen through the lens of principal–agent theory, member states (principal) delegate trade authority to the European Community (agent). A second level of delegation, however, occurs from the Council of Ministers (principal) to the European Commission (agent), which negotiates trade agreements on behalf of the member states (Meunier and Nicolaïdis 1999; Nicolaïdis and Meunier 2005).[1] But the Treaty of Rome's provisions mainly concerned trade in goods. Throughout the 1980s and 1990s the emergence of new trade issues, considered by member states too sensitive to be left almost entirely to the discretion of the Commission, gave rise to a controversy between the European Commission and the member states about the issue of competence. Following a European Court of Justice ruling, the Treaty of Amsterdam (1997) established that exclusive EU competence in new trade issues can be created on a proposal by the Commission and decided by unanimity in the Council. The Treaty of Nice (2001) extended the role of the Commission but still left a number of sensitive sectors to member states' competence (Young 2004a; Smith 2004). In a nutshell, the main institutional actors in EU trade policy making are the European Commission, which initiates proposals, and the Council, which takes decisions by qualified majority voting. DG Trade plays a pivotal role, often advancing the cause of further liberalization and multilateralism. Other DGs (e.g. DG Agriculture, which is more protectionist; DG Development, which is concerned with the trade–development link; DG Environment, which wants to balance economic development and long-term sustainability) are often involved in the trade policy process, thus coordination may become a problem. Within the Council, the General Affairs and External Relations Council (GAERC), which has replaced the General Affairs Council (GAC) since 2002, coordinates trade policy issues. Before being discussed in the GAERC, the '133 Committee' (named after the relevant article in the EU Treaty) negotiates on the issues. In the case of more sensitive issues, negotiations take place in the COREPER. The European Parliament plays a mainly consultative role, which has raised issues of democracy and transparency. The European Court of Justice is also important, because through a series of judgements it has extended the scope of the common commercial policy (Smith 2001; Nicolaïdis and Meunier 2005).

This short overview shows how member states still exercise significant influence on EU trade policy. In addition to the institutional framework, different 'trade cultures', along the protectionist–liberal continuum, have important implications for final outcomes (Smith 2004). The pendulum between these two sides has swung over the years. Among the signatories of the Treaty of Rome, France and Italy are protectionists, whereas Germany and the Netherlands are liberals. With the first enlargement in the 1970s (i.e. United Kingdom, Ireland, Denmark) the liberalist side was reinforced. The southern enlargement in the 1980s (i.e. Greece, Spain, Portugal) brought in a new protectionist wave. With the Nordic enlargement in the 1990s (i.e. Austria, Sweden, Finland) the pendulum shifted again towards more liberalism. Finally, the eastern enlargement in 2004 has not substantially changed the balance between the two forces: in general, Poland and Slovakia may be associated with the protectionist side, whereas Estonia, the Czech Republic, Slovenia and Hungary can be seen as part of the liberal side (Woolcock 2005a; Nicolaïdis and Meunier 2005; Young 2004a). In short, when EU trade policy becomes politicized, France forms a protectionist alliance of mainly southern member states that opposes trade liberalization 'almost instinctively'. France is thus joined by Italy, Spain, Portugal and Greece, and often by Austria and Belgium. Germany and the United Kingdom generally lead the northern coalition of 'free traders', and are generally supported by the Netherlands, Sweden, Denmark, and Finland (Peterson and Bomberg 1999).[2] However, some degree of caution is necessary, as positions may vary depending on the topic and on domestic political factors. For example, France is protectionist in agriculture but somewhat liberal in services, with the notable except of audiovisuals. Germany has been reticent to start or openly support proposals to liberalize trade in agriculture. Ireland is liberal on trade, manufacturing, investment, and services, but protectionist on agriculture (Woolcock 2005a).

The question thus becomes how member states determine whether the EU as a whole is a 'fortress' or a force for liberalization. As a result of various multilateral trade rounds, tariffs have been substantially reduced (Hanson 1998). Yet the EU's 'nominal liberalism' may still be affected by various national factors. First, a few member states have resisted substantial reforms of CAP, aimed at cutting the system of price supports enjoyed by producers and at reducing the levies imposed on goods coming from abroad. Second, the EU has increasingly used a number of defence instruments to cater for particular member states that want to protect some sensitive sectors from 'unfair' external competition (see next section). Third, high tariffs are still maintained on some manufactured goods (i.e. footwear, leather, textiles and clothing), which again reflect the need of individual member states to protect a particular sector of their economy. Fourth, regulatory barriers to trade have become more prominent, which is largely a consequence of the different regulatory system in member states; this means that when the EU adopts common rules, approximation occurs at the most stringent level (Young, 2004a, b).[3] The next section examines how both trade cultures and various protectionist arrangements have affected the adoption of the EBA regulation.

EBA and member state pressures

In September 2000 Pascal Lamy launched a proposal for a regulation, formalized by the *Collège* on 5 October 2000, to grant duty-free and quota-free (DFQF) access to the EU market for the world's least developed countries, covering all goods except arms and ammunitions. For three products – i.e. sugar, rice, bananas – implementation was supposed to take effect within three years (European Commission 2000). This proposal was presented by Lamy in the GAC of 10 October 2000. In that venue member states did not openly oppose it, but when the discussion started in the 133 Committee, a major division between member states became evident. On the one hand, the protectionist member states expressed their fears about the impact of the EBA proposal on their agricultural sector. Concerned about the potential influx of products from LDCs, they argued that supporting LDCs should not jeopardize the future of workers in Europe. These countries are major producers of beet sugar (i.e. Belgium, Spain), rice (i.e. Italy, Greece, Spain), or bananas (France, Spain and Portugal's islands in the Caribbean and Atlantic) (AP 22 February 2001; *Agra Europe* 23 February 2001). Another key concern regarded the consequences for the EU budget as a result of the attraction into the EU of products at higher prices than world prices (*Agra Europe* 9 March 2001). France, in particular, argued that the EBA proposal would put the EU's commitment to the ACP countries at risk. On the other hand, the liberal member states argued that although their agricultural producers would be affected by the EBA regulation, the overall aim of the proposal (i.e. supporting the economic development of poor countries) justified a sacrifice of their national interest. The British government, in particular, had to resist the strong pressure by the sugar lobby and by various Conservative Party leaders, who accused the Labour Party of jeopardizing the entire agriculture sector in the United Kingdom and of sacrificing the livelihoods of many workers for an EU cause. More radically, Denmark, Sweden, and the Netherlands lamented the lack of ambition of the EBA proposal and called for an extension either to all products or to other developing countries. To clarify the consequences of the EBA regulation on the agriculture sector and on the budget, the group of protectionist member states asked the European Commission to carry out a series of impact studies. These requests were considered as delaying tactics by the Nordic countries, and for several weeks no significant progress was made in the negotiations (*European Voice* 7 December 2000).[4] France, which was holding the rotating presidency of the Union, did everything it could to postpone the issue, or at least not to have it adopted under its presidency (Pilegaard, Chapter 8 this volume).

The EBA discussion, however, was complicated by the parallel discussion on the reform of the rice, sugar, and banana sectors that was taking place in the Agriculture Council (Matthews and Gallezot, Chapter 9 this volume). In October 2000 the Agriculture Council postponed the restructuring of the rice sector as significant disagreements occurred between member states. In December 2000, the Agriculture Council agreed on a plan to extend the sugar regime for five additional marketing years (2001–06); at the same time it suggested that the Commission's proposal for a three-year phase-in for sugar under the EBA proposal be extended to five years. It also agreed to maintain the current system for bananas, while new quotas would be offered in the future. For ACP bananas, trade access would not be substantially improved, while a 'tariff only' system would enter into force no later than 2006. Peterson and Bomberg (1999) cogently argue that fragmentation is rarely a force for liberalization. Yet, some argue that the Commission may have used the EBA discussions to liberalize the sugar sector (see Brüntrup, Chapter 10 in this volume).

As a result of all these pressures, Lamy slightly modified his initial proposal. The *Collège* thus adopted a new proposal in January 2001, which further deferred liberalization for the three products, i.e. bananas from 1 January 2006; sugar from 1 July 2009; rice from 1 September 2009. For sugar and rice, duties will be reduced in three stages (20 per cent, 50 per cent and 80 per cent reduction respectively in 2006, 2007, 2008); for bananas, duties will be reduced by 20 per cent annually. To compensate for these delays, temporary measures to provide market access during the interim period were introduced: duty-free quotas for rice and sugar would be based initially on best figures for LDC exports during the 1990s, increased each year by a cumulative growth rate of 15 per cent; imports of sugar from ACP countries were to be excluded from this and, in accordance with the Cotonou Agreement, reviewed in 2008. Considering the potential problems that could be raised by member states in Council negotiations, the *Collège* gave Lamy some room for manoeuvre 'to discuss fine-tuning of the proposal' (Vahl 2001; IPS 17 January 2001).

Meanwhile, Sweden had taken on the rotating presidency of the Union. From the beginning Sweden expressed its intention of pushing for a free-trade line against the more protectionist countries, and its 'implacable opposition' to quotas, safeguard clauses, or exclusion of sensitive commodities from the final agreement (*Agra Europe* 12 January 2001). Lamy's modified proposal constituted the starting point for the discussion in the 133 Committee and in the COREPER. The deferred liberalization for the three products was welcomed by the protectionist group, whereas the liberal group preferred the initial Commission proposal. The discussions centred around certain protective instruments:

- *Rendez-vous clause.* France, supported by Spain, Portugal and Greece, wanted to re-evaluate the proposal in 2005 on the basis of an impact study of duty-free quotas and tariff reductions in the interim period before proceeding to full liberalization of the sensitive products. Belgium wanted only a technical re-examination, which would not question the principle of liberalization.
- *Safeguard measures.* Spain, Portugal, Belgium, and Greece asked that the EU would restrict imports of a product temporarily if their domestic industries were seriously injured or threatened by a surge in imports.
- *Rules of origin.* All the southern member states asked for further reassurance about the risks of 'triangular trade', and therefore called on the Commission to exercise tight control on the respect of rules of origin (*European Report* 24 February 2001; *Agra Europe* 23 February 2001).

At the end of the discussion in the COREPER on 21 February 2001, the Council was still polarized: nine member states were willing to accept the new Commission proposal, the remaining six member states were still reluctant. The week that preceded the GAC Council was decisive. Kofi Annan sent a *lettre magistrale* (Lamy 2002: 79) to the Swedish Prime Minister Goran Persson urging the EU to adopt the EBA proposal, which would be 'a clear signal that the world's richest countries are genuinely prepared to put into practice their oft-stated intention to accord priority attention to the plight of the world's poorest'. NGOs became more vocal, although some were disappointed that the initial proposal had been watered down (AP 22 February 2001). The Presidency and the Commission worked closely to find a solution. The Director General for Trade announced in the COREPER that new ideas for anti-fraud provisions concerning triangular trade would be set up. Lamy contacted all the trade ministers of the member states to gain further support for his proposal. The objective was to achieve a qualified majority, as explained by Lamy (2002: 77) himself: 'dans la bonne tradition des affaires communautaires, trouvons les voies d'un compromis possible. Un compromis qui réunisse la majorité qualifiée dont j'avais besoin. Mas pas au prix de concessions qui auraient vidé l'initiative de son sens.'

In the GAC of 26 February 2001 Lamy presented a statement, which was attached to the official minutes of the meeting, aiming at reassuring some of the hesitant member states. He conceded that whenever imports into the EU from LDCs for rice, sugar and bananas exceed imports in the previous marketing year by more than 25 per cent, the Commission would apply safeguard measures, including the suspension of trade preferences; he also stated that it would monitor existing rules of origin to avoid fraudulent behaviour. Most of the hesitant member states now felt reassured. France once again requested the insertion of a *rendez-vous* clause, which would oblige the Council to take a subsequent decision in 2005. Lamy agreed that the Commission would report in 2005, but made it clear that the review 'could change the proposal, but without calling into question the principle of liberalization and the timetable for liberalization' (*Agra Europe* 2 March 2001).[5] At the end of very intense discussions, the Presidency maintained that a qualified majority had been achieved. France remained the only member state to formally oppose EBA, while Spain seems to have remained silent as a sign of protest (*Financial Times* 27 February 2001; *European Report* 24 and 28 February 2001; Table 2.2 in this volume).

A final note concerns the role of the European Parliament. The treaty does not require consultation, but in November 2000 the Parliament requested voluntary consultation. The Council did not reply until late February 2001, refusing this request. The report adopted by the Parliament, with opinions of both the Committee on Development Cooperation and that on Agricultural and Rural Development, is symptomatic (European Parliament 2001: 14):

> Only formal consultation of the Parliament could have made the process of deliberation on the EBA proposal public, transparent and democratically acceptable. This did not happen. What instead happened was that massive influence was exerted behind the scenes, within the Commission, between member states and the Commission as well as between interest groups and the Commission in order to postpone duty-free access particularly for the three sensitive products, viz. bananas, rice and sugar.

Despite member states' scepticism, the Commission tried to involve the Parliament in the discussions. Lamy himself explained his proposal before various committees. In terms of substance, the Parliament in general welcomed the EBA initiative. Yet it criticized the Commission for not having taken adequately into consideration the needs of the ACP group (see next section) and regretted that 'under pressure from a number of member states, the Council has lengthened the period for opening up the European market to sugar, banana and rice imports from LDCs as compared with the original Commission proposal' (European Parliament 2001: 9). While this seems to be a fair criticism, the benefits of the EBA regulation, as enthusiastically pointed out by Lamy and various officials in DG Trade, should not be overshadowed by the exception related to the three sensitive products, which will eventually be opened to the LDCs; furthermore, to compensate for this delay LDCs were given duty-free import quotas rising each year from 2002.

North–South dynamics in EU development policy

While in the previous section the North–South cleavage in EU trade policy was discussed, this section is devoted to the North–South cleavage in EU development policy, focusing in particular on the (lack of) involvement of the ACP group in the EBA policy making process. This is particularly relevant as 40 of the 50 LDCs belong to the ACP group (cf. Appendix 1.1 in Chapter 1). Three interlinked claims are thus made: first, the adoption of the EBA proposal without a formal consultation of the ACP group is in line with the evolution of EU–ACP relations, in particular with the erosion of the partnership aspect; second, the EBA proposal, which is consistent with the idea of differentiation introduced by the Cotonou Agreement, reinforced the trend towards the undermining of the ACP group solidarity; third, the EBA proposal, in line with changes in EU development policy, for the first time granted a higher level of privileges to non-ACP countries than to some ACP countries.

The EU–ACP relationship: from protection to liberalization

Over the past 40 years, two broad tendencies have dominated the approach of the EU to the developing world: regionalism versus globalism. The regional approach – supported by France, Italy, Belgium, Spain and Portugal – recognizes the strategic links between the EU and its former colonies. The global approach – supported by Germany, the Netherlands, the United Kingdom, the Nordic countries – places more emphasis on poverty eradication (Grilli 1993). The EU's approach to developing countries that consists of a mix of foreign aid and trade preferences created a pyramid of privileges. While initially Africa and later the whole group of ACP countries were at the top of this pyramid, over the past years new countries have received similar privileges. In terms of external assistance, the EU has gradually broadened its activities to Latin America and Asia, and, more significantly, to the Mediterranean and then to Central and Eastern Europe. While this may imply that new partners have been offered virtually the same level of preferences and a considerable amount of foreign aid, a definite ending to the regional approach in EU development policy has not yet been set. In this sense Karen Smith (2004: 60–1) cogently argues that '[t]he globalists have won the argument in that there is a wider EU role in the world, although the regionalist legacy remains in the EU's preference to deal with third countries collectively'. The EBA regulation, however, may be interpreted as another attempt to depart from this.

The regional approach in EU development policy dates back to the Treaty of Rome (1957), when countries in Africa were 'associated' with the EU. Following the decolonization period, the Yaoundé Convention (1963–75) maintained the same system: a fixed amount of aid for five years, channelled through the European Development Fund, and trade preferential treatment based on reciprocal preferences. The Lomé Convention (1975–2000) was considered the most comprehensive, innovative and ambitious agreement for North–South cooperation.

Following the demands for a New International Economic Order, the EU made important concessions to the newly born group of ACP countries (Brown 2002). Three elements made the EU–ACP model very progressive. First, it was conceived as a partnership: decisions were not imposed by the EU, but taken together with ACP countries. Second, it was based on a 'contractual right to aid': resources were committed to the ACP countries for a five-year period. Third, it reversed previous trade preferences from reciprocal to non-reciprocal. Almost all ACP goods were allowed to enter the EU free of any tariff or quota restrictions (Raffer and Singer 2001).[6]

The development record of the Lomé Convention, however, was disappointing. Only a limited number of ACP countries managed to improve their level of development, while the majority underwent a process of steady deterioration. The expiration of Lomé IV in 2000 provided an opportunity for a profound rethinking of the EU–ACP development model. The new Partnership Agreement, signed in Cotonou on 23 June 2000, builds on the Lomé *acquis*, but for various aspects it represents a fundamental departure from it (Holland 2002; Hurt 2003; Babarinde and Faber 2005). First, although the idea of partnership is still present in print, the reality is very different. Rather than discussing with the ACP group, the EU follows trends set by international organizations, namely the World Bank and the World Trade Organization (WTO) (Arts and Dickson 2004). Second, aid allocations are now based on an assessment of each country's needs and performance, with the possibility to adjust the financial resources allocated through a system of rolling programming. Third, the trade regime is subjected to a profound transformation. While the trade pillar of the Lomé model was based on the principles of non-reciprocity and non-discrimination, the Cotonou Agreement on the contrary is based on reciprocity for non-LDCs and differentiation between ACP states. For non-LDCs, after a transitional period (2000–2007), new free trade agreements, the Economic Partnership Agreements, should be negotiated on a regional basis before January 2008. In contrast, LDCs will be able to maintain their existing preferential trade regime, that is, non-reciprocal trade preferences. In light of the 'serious economic and social difficulties hindering their development', the EU also committed itself in the Cotonou Agreement to ensure free access for 'essentially all' products from all LDCs by 2005 (Hurt 2003; Carbone 2005; Elgström 2000).[7]

These new developments should be evaluated against two different elements: the role that the EU plays or wants to play in the international arena; and the evolution of trade preferences in the EU. Whether a 'rival' or an 'alternative', the US has always been a point of reference in EU trade policy. In the 1960s and 1970s the EU was concerned with building a single market and with protecting its agricultural sector, while the US favoured multilateral trade liberalization, aiming at bringing the CAP under multilateral discipline. Since the mid-1980s the US has progressively shifted towards greater reliance on unilateral and regional/bilateral trade measures, whereas the EU not only wanted to become the champion of a stronger multilateral/liberal approach in international trade, but at the same time tried to place itself as 'the friend of the developing countries'. Following the failure of the WTO trade round in Seattle (1999), it reinvigorated the process for a development round and played a leading role in the launch of the Doha Development Agenda in 2001 (Van den Hoven 2004; Young 2004a; Nicolaïdis and Meunier 2005; Woolcock 2005a). The EBA proposal could thus be seen as an attempt of the EU to gain the support of the LDCs in the Doha context (see Orbie in Chapter 2). The second element to consider is that over the years trade privileges have been extended to a number of developing countries. Besides some form of privileges granted to southern Mediterranean countries, the EU has implemented a Generalized System of Preferences (GSP) scheme since 1971. The GSP is a non-contractual preferential trade arrangement in which benefits are autonomous and non-binding. While originally the main features of the scheme were quotas and ceilings, since 1995 the EU has provided trade preferences that vary according to the sensitivity of the products on the EU market (Stevens 2000). Before the adoption of the EBA, LDCs enjoyed special arrangements under the GSP, enjoying duty-free access for a large part of their industrial and mineral goods (Yu and Jensen 2005). Progressive extension and enhancement of the GSP meant that at the end of the 1990s the tariff difference between the Lomé trade regime and the LDCs became only 2 per cent (Dickson 2004). EBA further closed this gap and, in some cases, granted a higher level of privileges to a group of Asian countries than to some ACP countries.

EBA, ACP and the end of a privileged relationship

The adoption of the EBA regulation in February 2001 seemed for some a generous gesture from the EU to the developing world. For others, considering the limited amount of trade between the EU and the LDCs, it did not cost much to the EU, but it simply increased competition among the poor: in this sense, 'the EU robbed the poor to give to the poorest' (IPS 1 March 2001). As mentioned earlier, when the Cotonou Agreement was signed in June 2000, it was established that *in lieu* of the non-reciprocal preferential treatment, different regions within the ACP group would negotiate free trade areas with the EU and that free access for 'essentially all' products would be granted to the LDCs by 2005. Only three months later, the European Commission proposed to grant free access to 'all' goods but arms. Page and Hewitt (2002: 91) questioned the coherence of this approach: 'EBA contradicts and impedes the EU's policies of reciprocity and promotions of regions: it not only creates an alternative trade regime, but seems unilaterally to break existing agreements.' Françoise Moreau (2001: 16), who took part in the post-Lomé negotiations on behalf of DG Development, on the contrary argues:

> One particularity of the Cotonou Agreement is to combine special treatment for LDCs and the regional approach . . . The Community is committed to ensuring duty-free access for essentially all products from all LDCs by 2005 (Article 37.9). Nevertheless, believing that more rapid and radical action was necessary, the Community has adopted the necessary measures to liberalize all imports from LDCs.

Along a similar line, Holland (2004) maintains that the EBA regulation is consistent with the thrust of the Cotonou Agreement, which had already introduced the concept of differentiation among regions according to their development status. Nevertheless, the EBA initiative eliminated the need to belong to the ACP group for about half of the ACP countries. An important element of the Lomé Convention was its 'group-to-group' nature. The Cotonou Agreement, by introducing the idea of differentiation, had already undermined the unity of the ACP group. The EBA regulation may have contributed to damaging it for good. Furthermore, 'To extend non-reciprocity to non-ACP LDCs suggested – if not endorsed – a view that the ACP as a group was no longer the dominant organising principle for EU–Third World relations' (Holland 2002: 225). This for some has been a consistent trend since the late 1980s. As John Ravenhill (2004: 121–2) points out, over the years:

> the EU insisted that its obligations towards the ACP did not tie its hands in its external commercial policies in any way. Accordingly, throughout the life of the Conventions, the EU unilaterally took various actions that reduced the value of the trade preferences enjoyed by the ACP . . . The ACP, meanwhile, were placed in the somewhat awkward position of trying to encourage the EU to maintain trade restrictions on third parties in an attempt to preserve the major sources of advantages that the Conventions conferred on them.

In line with this, on 2 June 1997 the Council had adopted conclusions to grant LDCs that were not part of the Lomé Convention preferences equivalent to those enjoyed by the ACP countries, concessions that were eventually granted in January 1998. In sum, if combined with the increasing level of foreign aid going to other regions, EBA confirmed the trend that the ACP as a group has lost its privileged position in EU external relations.

This tendency is also confirmed by the fact that the ACP group was not involved in the debates before the official launching of the EBA proposal. The Cotonou Agreement obliges the EU to consult the ACP group when it intends to make changes that may impact on its members. Furthermore, Declaration XXIII established that the EU must 'examine all necessary measures to maintain the competitive position of ACP States on the Community market'. Nevertheless, the first time the ACP group officially heard about the EBA proposal was when Lamy presented it to the ACP–EU Joint Parliamentary Assembly on 10 October 2000. Lamy also met trade ministers from African countries in December 2000, reassuring them that the EU would be willing to pay special attention to developing countries' concerns in the framework of a new round of multilateral trade negotiations. African trade ministers 'welcomed and supported' the EBA initiative, but at the same time 'expected the EU to honour existing agreements' and 'further urge[d] that the EBA initiative takes into account the vulnerability of small, landlocked and island ACP states' (*Agra Europe* 15 December 2000). A similar conclusion was reached by the ACP–EU Joint Parliamentary Assembly held in Libreville, Gabon, on 19–22 March 2001, which, whilst welcoming the EBA proposal, deplored the lack of consultation of the ACP group and of the European Parliament and asked the European Commission to ensure that ACP exports would not be adversely affected and that their competitive position in the market would be maintained (McQueen 2002).[8] This lack of consultation is in line with the erosion of the partnership aspect in EU–ACP relations, as also shown by the asymmetrical negotiation process that led to the Cotonou Agreement (Elgström 2000).

It is not surprising that this lack of consultation and the loss of commitment by the EU to the ACP were used by a group of non-LDC ACP countries, mainly in the Caribbean region, aiming at maintaining their long-standing trade preferences. A statement by the Guyana Ministry of Foreign Affairs reads as follows: 'The unilateral action by the EU breached the Cotonou Agreement by not allowing Caribbean countries the opportunity to negotiate adequate transition provisions on their major exports to the preferential markets in Europe' (IPS 1 March 2001). Free access to the EU market was supposed to provide a significant advantage to LDCs over other developing countries.[9] Yet, although ACP countries have enjoyed non-reciprocal trade preferences since the mid-1970s, their exports have not performed well. In the post-Lomé debate and during the EBA negotiations, trade preferences seemed to be irrelevant for the poorest countries, with financial assistance being at the core of their demands (Bretherton and Vogler 2006). The Caribbean states, on the contrary, were very concerned about their exports. The future of bananas was already under tension because of a trade quarrel between the EU and the US. The region's rice exports were considered at risk under the pressure of Asian producers with lower production costs (*Financial Times* 21 March 2001). Similarly, the Sugar Association of the Caribbean argued that after the adoption of the Cotonou Agreement some of its members had made plans to build new estates and factories to take advantage of the growing demand. This investment would be jeopardized by cheaper producers in the Asian LDCs (IPS 6 December 2000). Similarly, Matai Toga, then Fiji's ambassador in Brussels and representing the ACP countries exporting sugar to the EU, manifested his concerns: 'The EU signed an agreement saying that current market access of commodity producers would either be maintained or improved but not reduced' (*European Voice* 1 March 2001). For all these reasons, the ACP even asked for an extension of the EBA regime to the entire group, but this request was rejected because of lack of compatibility with WTO rules (Pilegaard, Chapter 8 in this volume; interviews by the author).[10]

In the debates over the EBA proposal another key actor in EU development policy was not involved. While earlier analyses concentrate on the battles between DG Trade and DG Agriculture, in which DG Trade supported multilateralism and DG Agriculture protectionism, the role of DG Development is often ignored. From its creation, DG Development had 'bureaucratic interests' in expanding the scope of the ACP–EU relationship; therefore, 'in the early days of Lomé [it] was a promoter of the interests of the ACP, often fighting bitter bureaucratic battles with the Directorate for External Relations and the Directorate for Agriculture to attempt to secure an improvement in the terms of the commercial relationship' (Ravenhill 2004: 140). In the EBA case, although this initiative had significant impact on the ACP group, DG Development was left on the margin of negotiations. It should be noted though that, as a result of the reorganization of the Commission in 1999, the unit dealing with trade in the ACP group was transferred from DG Development to DG Trade: for Ravenhill this was 'a clear signal of the Commission's intentions that trade with the ACP would be subordinate to the overall principles of EU external trade relations' (Ravenhill 2004: 131). Similarly, for Page and Hewitt (2002: 94), this 'may have reduced appreciation of the development implications of trade measures'. While these explanations may be convincing, they do not take into account a significant difference inside DG Development: Commissioner Poul Nielson and his cabinet supported the EBA initiative, whereas senior officials in DG Development wanted to keep a privileged relationship with the ACP countries. DG Trade won an easy battle with DG Development, if it was ever fought, and paradoxically the transition period that was agreed for bananas, sugar and rice was achieved thanks to the intervention of DG Agriculture (and the southern EU member states).

Conclusion

The negotiation process over the EBA initiative has been very complicated. While the disagreements inside the Commission did play a key role in shaping the final outcome, this chapter has argued that strong divisions between member states should not be disregarded. Two North–South divides both in the field of external trade and international development have been identified. As for trade, on the one hand, a group of northern member states (i.e. Germany, the Netherlands, United Kingdom, the Nordics), which promotes a liberal agenda in international trade and a global approach in EU development policy, supported the EBA proposal in the name of further trade liberalization. On the other hand, a group of southern member states (i.e. France, Greece, Portugal, Spain, Italy), which supports a protectionist agenda in international trade and a regional approach in EU development policy, resisted the Commission proposal in the name of its potential impact on the CAP and on the EU budget.

This contribution has also discussed a second North–South cleavage in EU development policy. In the beginning, the relation between the EU and the developing world, and in particular the Lomé Convention, was considered a model for the future of North–South cooperation because of its innovative elements such as the principle of partnership, the contractual approach to aid and the non-reciprocal trade preferences extended by the EU to the ACP countries. Over the years the partnership has been eroded and replaced by a strong push for trade liberalization. The lack of involvement of the ACP countries in the discussion over EBA, though in breach of the Cotonou Agreement, confirms this trend. The marginal role played by DG Development, usually the defender of the ACP group, should be seen not only in the context of the loss of the trade expertise of DG Development to DG Trade, but also in the context of the new balance of power within the Commission, where the regional approach advanced by DG Development belongs to the past, to the pre-WTO world, and the globalist/multilateral approach proposed by DG Trade belongs to the present and even to the future. While this last point remains controversial, what is clear is that the traditional pyramid of privileges, with the ACP at the apex, is no longer recognizable. As Stevens (2000) cogently argued, a 'new' trade hierarchy may be created in 'new areas' of trade policy, such as agreements in services and intellectual property, but that time has not come yet.

Notes

1   It should be noted that when the EU concludes agreements with third countries in international negotiations, the Commission represents the member states, but it acts on the basis of negotiating directives adopted by the Council of Ministers. This mandate limits the Commission's margin for negotiations. The member states, through the Article 133 Committee, other committees, and by sending their own delegation to international negotiations, maintain constant control over the European Commission. In the context of WTO negotiations the delegations of the member states are regularly consulted, which leads third parties to accuse the Commission of inflexibility because of the constant need for consultation before a decision can be taken. The Council must then ratify all agreements. With the Maastricht Treaty the Parliament must give its assent to some international agreements (Smith 2001; Meunier and Nicolaïdis 2005).

2   A typical example of this dynamic could be the anti-dumping measures. In 1997 the European Commission, under strong pressure from France and its cotton producers, imposed anti-dumping measures on imports of unbleached cotton. These measures were not confirmed by the Council of Ministers, where the most liberal states prevailed. In late 1997 and 1998 the Commission, again facing pressure from France, reimposed provisional duties (Smith 2001).

3   Non-state actors also influence trade policy, although increasingly they lobby member states rather than the European Commission directly. For a long time, mainly the interests of producers were represented in Brussels. Since the early 1990s trade unions, consumer lobbies, and a wide range of non-governmental organizations have become more vocal (Smith 2004). The European Commission has also established consultations on trade policy with civil society. Such consultations are held regularly, but they 'have no real input into policy' (Woolcock 2005b: 244).

4   A study released by the Commissioner of Agriculture, Franz Fischler, in December 2000 showed that the impact on the farming sector in the EU would be greater than originally thought and that some industries might face significant costs. In particular, it was estimated that the impact on the sugar industry could be more than €1 billion. A similar study produced by DG Trade argued that the costs for the CAP would be less pronounced, if not marginal. Oxfam, a leading British NGO, published a very influential study which claimed that the costs for the EU of implementing the EBA proposal were considered 'very small, in comparison to the positive benefits it will bring for the least developed countries' (Stevens and Kennan 2001).

5   Denmark, in a unilateral declaration attached to the official minutes, stated that it would have preferred a more progressive proposal, yet it accepted the compromise.

6   Two instruments for stabilization of agricultural exports (STABEX) and mineral products (SYSMIN) were also adopted. STABEX, introduced by Lomé I, was meant to compensate ACP countries for the shortfall in export earnings due to fluctuations of prices or crop failures of several commodities (i.e. cocoa, coffee, tea, groundnuts). SYSMIN, introduced by Lomé II, was meant to compensate countries heavily dependent on mineral exports for their export losses. These two instruments have not been included in the Cotonou Agreement. A few agricultural products covered by the CAP were excluded from the Lomé trade regime, but were regulated through separate

trading protocols. The banana and rum protocol has represented a key resource for many small island Caribbean states, the sugar protocol for various countries such as Mauritius, Fiji, Guyana and Barbados, the beef and veal protocol for Southern African exporters.

7 See Orbie (Chapter 2) and Bilal (Chapter 11) in this volume, who further elaborate on the role of EBA and the LDCs in the EU–ACP relationship. DFQF entry into the EU for LDCs was introduced in 2001, long before 2005.

8 However, some disagreements occurred over this resolution. Some Members of Parliament (especially members of the Green parliamentary group) wanted to have a more critical resolution, criticizing the 'false labelling' of the EBA initiative, as there was no risk of LDCs exporting arms to the EU. On the other hand, a majority argued that a resolution of this kind 'on no account' could be passed (Southscan 1 April 2001).

9 It should be noted that some non-ACP LDCs also expressed their initial reservations about EBA. For instance, Abdukl Mannan of Bangladesh conceded that the EBA meant opening the EU market to products from developing countries, but still 'express my fear that it will all remain without effect'. The complaint was that it was not the EU's right to supervise the origin of products, the strict sanitary and phytosanitary standards, the safeguard measures to protect the CAP (IPS 27 February 2001). Although these issues are a constraint on LDCs' exports, Pilegaard in this volume claims that LDCs eventually welcomed the EBA proposal and actually 'ask for more of the same'. Finally, a group of non-ACP and non-LDCs (i.e. India, Brazil, Egypt) strongly criticized the EBA initiative (Page and Hewitt 2002).

10 The concerns of some ACP countries became part of the debate during the negotiations in the GAC and, according to Claire Short, the then British Secretary of State for Development, were used by EU member states and the big sugar companies as a sort of 'smokescreen' to keep their inflated European sugar prices and to resist the EBA proposal during Council negotiations. However, it is important to note that in the Agricultural Council of October 2000 the UK tried hard to enhance the preferential treatment for Caribbean bananas.

References

ACP–EU Joint Parliament Assembly (2001) Resolution on 'Everything but Arms', Libreville (Gabon), ACP–EU 3171/O1/fin.

Arts, K. and Dickson, A.K. (eds) (2004) *EU Development Cooperation: from Model to Symbol?*, Manchester: Manchester University Press.

Babarinde, O. and Faber, G. (eds) (2005) *The European Union and the Developing Countries: The Cotonou Agreement*, Leiden: Martinus Nijhoff Publishers.

Bretherton, C. and Vogler, J. (2006) *The European Union as a Global Actor*, London and New York: Routledge.

Brown, W. (2002) *The European Union and Africa: The Restructuring of North–South Relations*, London and New York: I.B. Tauris.

Carbone, M. (2005) 'Development policy', in M. Peter van der Hoek (ed.) *Handbook of Public Administration and Policy in the European Union*, Boca Raton FL: Taylor & Francis.

Dickson, A.K. (2004) 'The unimportance of trade preferences', in K. Arts and A.K. Dickson (eds) *EU Development Cooperation: from Model to Symbol*, Manchester: Manchester University Press.

Elgström, O. (2000) 'Lomé and Post-Lomé: asymmetric negotiations and the impact of norms', *European Foreign Affairs Review*, 5, 2: 175–95.

European Commission (2000) *Proposal for a Council Regulation amending Council Regulation (EC) No. 2820/98*, COM(2000)561.

European Parliament (2001) *Report on the Proposal for a Council Regulation amending Council Regulation (EC) No. 2820/98*, A5-0128/2001.

Gibb, R. (2000) 'Post-Lomé: The European Union and the South', *Third World Quarterly*, 21, 3: 457–81.

Grilli, E. (1993) *The European Community and the Developing Countries*, Cambridge: Cambridge University Press.

Hanson, B.T. (1998) 'What happened to Fortress Europe? External trade policy liberalization in the European Union', *International Organization*, 52, 1: 55–85.

Holland, M. (2002) *The European Union and the Third World*, New York: Palgrave.

Holland, M. (2004) 'Development policy: paradigm shifts and the "normalization" of a privileged partnership?', in M.G. Cowles and D. Dinan (eds) *Developments in the European Union 2*, London: Palgrave Macmillan.

Hurt, S. (2003) 'Co-operation and coercion? The Cotonou Agreement between the European Union and ACP states and the end of the Lomé Convention', *Third World Quarterly*, 24, 1: 161–76.

Lamy, P. (2002) *L'Europe en première ligne*, Paris: Éditions du Seuil.

McQueen, M. (2002) 'EU preferential market access conditions for the least developed countries', *Intereconomics*, March–April, 101–9.

Meunier, S. and Nicolaïdis, K. (1999) 'Who speaks for Europe? The delegation of trade authority in the EU', *Journal of Common Market Studies*, 37, 3: 477–501.

Moreau, F. (2000) 'The least developed countries in the Cotonou Agreement', in *The Courier ACP–EU*, May–June, p. 16.

Nicolaïdis, K. and Meunier, S. (2005) 'The European Union as a trade power', in C. Hill and M. Smith (eds) *International Relations and the European Union*, Oxford: Oxford University Press.

Page, S. and Hewitt, A. (2002) 'The new European trade preferences: does "Everything but Arms" (EBA) help the poor?', *Development Policy Review*, 20, 1: 91–102.

Peterson, J. and Bomberg, E. (1999) *Decision-making in the European Union*, New York: St Martin's Press.

Raffer, K. and Singer, H.W. (2001) *The Economic North–South Divide: Six Decades of Unequal Development*, Cheltenham and Northampton MA: Edward Elgar.

Ravenhill, J. (2004) 'Back to the nest? Europe's relations with the African, Caribbean and Pacific group of countries', in V.K. Aggarwal and E. Fogarty (eds) *EU Trade Strategies: Between Regionalism and Globalism*, Basingstoke: Palgrave Macmillan.

Smith, K.E. (2004) 'The ACP in the European Union's network of regional relationship: still unique or just one in the crowd?', in K. Arts and A.K. Dickson (eds) *EU Development Cooperation: from Model to Symbol*, Manchester: Manchester University Press.

Smith, M. (2001) 'The European Union's commercial policy: between coherence and fragmentation', *Journal of European Public Policy*, 8, 5: 787–802.

Smith, M. (2004) 'The European Union as a trade policy actor', in B. Hocking and S. McGuire (eds) *Trade Politics*, London: Routledge.

Stevens, C. (2000) 'Trade with developing countries: banana skins and turf wars', in H. Wallace and W. Wallace (eds) *Policy-making in the European Union*, Oxford: Oxford University Press.

Stevens, C. and Kennan, J. (2001) *The Impact of the EU's 'Everything but Arms' Proposal: a Report to Oxfam*, Brighton: Institute of Development Studies.

Vahl, R. (2001) '"Everything but Arms": free access for imports from least developed countries', *The Courier ACP–EU*, May–June, 30–1.

Van den Hoven, A. (2004) 'Assuming leadership in multilateral economic institutions: the EU's "Development Round" discourse and strategy', *West European Politics*, 27: 256–83.

Woolcock, S. (2005a) 'Trade Policy', in H. Wallace, W. Wallace and M.A. Pollack (eds) *Policy-making in the European Union*, Oxford: Oxford University Press.

Woolcock, S. (2005b) 'European Union trade policy: domestic institutions and systemic factors', in D. Kelly and W. Grant (eds) *The Politics of International Trade in the Twenty-first Century: Actors, Issues, and Regional Dynamics*, New York: Palgrave Macmillan.

Young, A. (2004a) 'The EU and world trade: Doha and beyond', in M.Green Cowles and D. Dinan (eds) *Developments in the European Union 2*, New York: Palgrave Macmillan.

Young, A.R. (2004b) 'The incidental fortress: the single European market and world trade', *Journal of Common Market Studies*, 42, 2: 393–414.

Yu, W. and Jensen, T.V. (2005) 'Trade preferences, WTO negotiations and the LDCs: the case of the 'Everything but Arms' initiative', *World Economy*, 28, 3: 375–405.

4 Bureaucratic competition in EU trade policy

EBA as a case of competing two-level games?

Adrian van den Hoven

Competing two-level games in EU trade policy

Trade policy making in the European Union (EU) sometimes resembles a dark art – shrouded in mystery and complex technical details. In many ways, 'Everything but Arms' (EBA) was an example of the dark art of EU trade policy. On the one hand, it serves as a beacon for the development-friendliness of EU trade policy by setting the benchmark for market access for the least developed countries (LDCs). On the other hand, the initial proposal covering all imports but arms was quickly transformed into everything but 'farms' when phase-in periods were introduced for rice, bananas and sugar. Given the contradictory results of EBA, one may question whether there is logic to EU trade policy. This chapter argues that bureaucratic divisions largely drive EU trade policy.

Studies of EU trade policy focus on intergovernmental bargaining between the 25 EU member states or on conflict between supranational and intergovernmental institutions (Meunier and Nicolaïdis 1999; Young *et al.* 2000). On the other hand, bureaucratic coordination problems in trade policy making have not received much attention by scholars.

The problem with the intergovernmental approach is that it caricatures the complex positions of the member states in trade policy making. The oft repeated definition of negotiations in the Council of Ministers is one of conflict between protectionist southern countries (led by France) and liberal northern countries (led by Germany or the United Kingdom).[1] This contribution adopts a bureaucratic competition approach that captures the nuances of member state positions to explain EU trade policy making.

By focusing on bureaucratic coordination problems, it is also possible to adapt Putnam's (1988) two-level game model to EU trade policy making. Indeed, his model assumes that linking domestic reform with international negotiations (external constraints) facilitates international cooperation and the adoption of domestic reforms. By combining Putnam's two-level game model with the bureaucratic politics model developed by Allison and Zelikow (1962/1999), this chapter will show that there are serious bureaucratic coordination problems in the EU trade policy.

Putnam's two-level game

In Putnam's two-level game, international negotiators are described as playing games at two levels. At the international level (level I) 'national governments seek to maximize their own ability to satisfy domestic pressures, while minimizing the adverse consequences of foreign developments' (Putnam 1988: 434). At the domestic level (level II) 'domestic groups pursue their interests by pressuring the government to adopt favourable policies, and politicians are seeking power by constructing coalitions among those groups' (Putnam 1988: 430). The key to a successful international negotiation is for the international negotiator to create 'synergistic linkages' between levels I and II that strengthen her/his position in both games.

Lee Ann Patterson (1997) has adapted Putnam's theory to the EU by examining agricultural policy reform as a three-level game that includes the international level (level I), the European level (level II) and the national level (level III). Although this approach is analytically useful, it is difficult to understand who is directing the process because there is no single actor (or chief of government – CoG) participating at all three levels. Thus, reforms just occur without anyone driving them. This makes it difficult to understand how the CoG uses external constraints ('synergistic linkages') at level I to facilitate the adoption of reforms at levels II and III.

The main problem with this approach is that it adds the national level (III) as a second ratification level even though trade policy and agricultural reform are ratified by the Council of Ministers at the EU rather than the national level. This contribution will use a more simple two-level game with the World Trade Organization (WTO) level as level I and the EU level as level II and the Commission as the CoG (see Figure 4.1).

One of the problems with the application of the two-level model to EU trade policy is that studies have focused on reform of Europe's Common Agricultural Policy (CAP) during the Uruguay Round rather than on the role of agriculture in cross-sector trade negotiations at the General Agreement on Tariffs and Trade, or GATT; the WTO since 1995). These studies tend to assume that the 1991–92 MacSharry reform of the CAP, named after the Commissioner for Agriculture at the time, was adopted mainly to allow the EU to resume GATT negotiations. In other words, the Commission used the external constraint of trade negotiations to produce a policy shift in agriculture.

Paarlberg (1997) questions the validity of the two-level game approach in his comparative study of agricultural policy reform in the EU and the US in the 1990s. For him, the real impetus for agricultural policy reform can be found only at the domestic level (or at the EU level in our case) where budgetary constraints force governments to reduce farm spending. Paarlberg also shows that synergistic linkages with GATT trade negotiations weakened the momentum for agricultural policy reform in the EU and the US by enabling rent-seeking farm unions to block domestic reforms because of competition with foreign farmers. Therefore, Paarlberg warns that internationalization of domestic policy reforms can also be used as a 'negative' synergistic linkage (Paarlberg 1997: 416).

Figure 4.1 Simple adaptation of Putnam's two-level game to the EU

This analysis will look at the EU trade policy as comprising a significant agricultural component and will focus on coordination problems between the EU diplomats responsible for trade and agricultural trade negotiations.

The competing two-level game model

Applying Putnam's model to the EU is difficult because the CoG (the Commission) is functionally and institutionally divided, unlike most national governments in international negotiations. Although the College of Commissioners is collectively responsible before the European Parliament, it functions as a divided institution. Indeed, individual Commissioners are responsible for specific functional issues such as competition, trade, environmental or agricultural policy before functionally divided Councils of Ministers representing foreign affairs, economics and finance, environment or agricultural ministers (Lewis 2000).

This functional division is dominant in trade policy for two reasons. First, the College of Commissioners makes limited contributions due to the extremely technocratic nature of trade policy and because trade negotiations take place in an international context. Second, the EU treaties restrict the participation of the European Parliament in trade policy making to a consultative role, which means that the Commission is primarily responsible before the Council of Ministers for this issue. However, there are two councils that take part in trade negotiations: the General Affairs Council (GAC) and the Agricultural Council (see Table 4.1).

By focusing on the divisive aspects of trade policy, it is possible to introduce Allison's model of bureaucratic politics in foreign policy making (Allison and

Table 4.1 The trade policy community

Actors with decision-making powers	*Actors with consultative powers*
• The Trade Commissioner and the General Affairs Council • The Agricultural Commissioner and the Agricultural Council	• The other Commissioners and the other Councils • The European Parliament

Zelikow 1962/1999). He demonstrated that bureaucratic agencies try to increase their power through participation in foreign policy making. When applied to EU trade policy, bureaucratic politics may be more problematic than in other, more centralized, political systems.

Bureaucratic coordination: a serious problem in the EU?

Weak bureaucratic coordination has been highlighted by many scholars of EU trade policy during the Uruguay Round. Ray MacSharry, the Commissioner for Agriculture during much of the Uruguay Round, once explained why he often disagreed with his colleague in charge of External Economic Relations, Frans Andriessen:

> There may be a difference of emphasis between myself and Mr Andriessen. He is the Commissioner responsible for external trade and is always, quite rightly, talking about the possibilities of compromise between one sector and another. I have a job to do in defending the EC's position on agriculture and I offer no apologies if I have to be tough or stubborn in doing it.
>
> (Vahl 1997: 128)

Frans Andriessen also hinted at the problematic coordination with his colleague responsible for agriculture by asking for more power over agricultural trade negotiations:

> It is practice in the Community that agricultural matters are very largely dealt with by the Agriculture Commissioner . . . We have to work out a formula which will make it possible that the overall responsibility [for the round] is not affected in a negative way by sectoral negotiations.
>
> (Vahl 1997: 128)

Bureaucratic divisions are also dominant in national policy making for EU affairs (Lequesne 1993: 47). During the Uruguay Round, German and British farm ministers regularly supported the Commissioner for Agriculture's [and France's] tough stance in GATT negotiations in spite of the official 'liberal' position of the German and British governments throughout most of the negotiations. German economics and agriculture ministers often expressed opposite views on the Uruguay Round negotiations, with the former calling for a flexible EU negotiating position and the latter demanding that Agricultural Commissioner MacSharry should not make any concessions to Europe's trading partners (Vahl 1997: 115).

The EU political system strengthens Allison's bureaucratic politics model because of a lack of coordination between councils in trade policy. During much of the Uruguay Round the GAC:

> failed to function effectively as the forum for coordinating EC policy and settling disputes that [arose] in technical Councils, and the technical Councils

... displayed considerable independence vis-à-vis each other as well as the Foreign Ministers. The Agriculture Council, for instance ... guarded its autonomy carefully, and in case of deadlock issues [were] referred to the European Council.

(Vahl 1997: 15)

Thus, there is ample evidence that both 'the Commission and Council face serious issues of internal fragmentation' (Christiansen 2001: 758).

Competing two-level games and 'Everything but Arms'

This chapter argues that trade policy is largely determined by conflicts between the Agricultural Commissioner and the Trade Commissioner, who are pursuing different strategies during the same set of international negotiations and reporting back to conflicting Councils of Ministers. Therefore the Trade Commissioner and the Agricultural Commissioner may even have opposing 'win-sets' (Putnam 1988) during trade negotiations.

To put it in Putnam's terms, the EU has two distinct CoGs for trade policy: the Trade Commissioner and the Agricultural Commissioner. They can both engage in multilateral trade negotiations (level I) with a view to gaining ratification in different institutional settings at the European level (level II). The Trade Commissioner needs the support of the GAC, while the Commissioner for Agriculture must be supported by the Council of Agricultural Ministers. Given that their credibility (their ability to deliver ratification) differs considerably, it would be highly unlikely if the Trade and Agricultural Commissioners were playing the same two-level game (see Figure 4.2). This chapter will examine the EBA initiative to assess the usefulness of a competing two-level games model to explain EU trade policy outcomes.

EBA: An initiative for internal consumption

Some background to the EBA initiative is essential to understand the trade policy making process in the EU. Announced with great fanfare in 2000, the EBA regulation was adopted in 2001 to provide duty-free and quota-free (DFQF) access to the EU market for almost all imports from the LDCs. Although it was ostensibly launched for the sake of development, it should really be considered an initiative appealing to an internal EU constituency.

EBA can be considered from two angles. First, the impact of the EBA on development is rather limited although it does serve as a model at the international level. Second, it was designed and implemented primarily to appeal to a domestic (EU) audience.

The economic impact of EBA on LDC exports to the EU has been examined by a number of scholars who generally conclude that the benefits, while positive, are quite small[2] (Cernat *et al.* 2003; Brenton 2003; also Babarinde and Faber and Brenton and Özden in Chapters 6 and 7 of this volume). With respect to the EU

L E V E L I	TRADE GAME		AGRICULTURAL GAME
	WORLD TRADE ORGANIZATION		
	TRADE NEGOTIATIONS (Trade Commissioner)	← informal coordination →	AGRICULTURE NEGOTIATIONS (Agricultural Commissioner)
	↑ *Commissioners defend EU mandate at WTO* ↑		
	TRADE COMMISSIONER	← majority vote in COLLEGE →	AGRICULTURAL COMMISSIONER
	CABINET	← informal coordination →	CABINET
	DG TRADE	← Inter-service consultations →	DG AGRICULTURE
	↓ *The Commission sends proposal for EU mandate for ratification by Council* ↓		
L E V E L II	↑ *The Council delegates authority (mandate) to negotiate on behalf of the EU* ↑ *to the Trade and Agricultural Commissioners*		
	GENERAL AFFAIRS COUNCIL	← Coordination by the rotating EU PRESIDENCY or by the EUROPEAN COUNCIL →	AGRICULTURAL COUNCIL
	(Trade or Foreign Affairs Ministers)	← limited coordination by Council Secretariat or by COREPER →	(Agricultural Ministers)
	133 COMMITTEE		SPECIAL COMMITTEE FOR AGRICULTURE
	(Ministry of Trade officials)	← various levels of coordination under the authority of the Prime Minister or the Foreign Minister →	(Ministry of Agriculture officials)

Figure 4.2 The coordination of trade policy in the EU

market (and EU producers), the impact is also considered to be negligible even in sensitive sub-sectors such as sugar because LDCs lack production capacity. Yet, despite its limited economic impact, the EBA proposal provoked considerable conflict between the Trade and Agricultural Commissioners. To explain this, EBA will now be examined as competing two-level games.

The Trade Commissioner's two-level game

This contribution hypothesizes that one game was directed by the then Trade Commissioner Pascal Lamy, who radicalized a concept that had been germinating within the EU trade policy community for several years: to improve access to the EU market for the LDCs. At level I (the international level), the objectives of the Trade Commissioner were:

- To send a signal to the WTO membership, composed largely of developing countries, that the EU was committed to a pro-development trade policy.
- To demonstrate that the EU was a leader in world trade by setting the standard of market access for LDCs that the other developed countries (notably the Quad – the US, Canada, Japan and the EU) should follow.
- To create a rift in the African, Caribbean and Pacific (ACP) group of countries that have historically benefited from a (WTO-incompatible) preferential trading regime with the EU.

At level II (the domestic or internal level), the objectives of the Trade Commissioner were:

- To respond to requests from the GAC to pursue a more development-friendly trade policy.
- To gain the support of development NGOs (non-governmental organizations) and the broader development community for the EU trade policy.

The Agricultural Commissioner's two-level game

Although EBA grew out of debates among the EU trade policy community, the agricultural policy community also played a key role in modifying the original proposal. This analysis hypothesizes that the role of the Agricultural Commissioner was not purely protectionist – to simply block the initiative. Instead, the Commissioner for Agriculture supported EBA but with some changes to serve his own objectives. At level I (international level), the Agricultural Commissioner's objectives were:

- To show that the EU was open to providing market access to developing countries and to counter one of the criticisms levelled at the CAP, namely that it prevents developing countries from exporting to the EU market.
- To prepare the phasing out of the special protocols between the EU and the ACP countries governing bananas and sugar (and to a lesser extent rice) that have been challenged in multilateral trade negotiations.

At level II (internal level), the objectives were:

- At first, to safeguard the interests of certain EU agricultural sectors – notably the sugar sector – threatened by the possible future development of sugar (and other agricultural products) exports from the LDCs to the European market.
- As the issue evolved, the Agricultural Commissioner shaped the regulation in such a way as to guarantee that the CAP reform would be carried through

for sensitive products – such as sugar or bananas – according to a specific calendar.

The genesis of EBA: born out of the trade policy community

EBA is often considered in the light of the WTO Ministerial Conference in Seattle in 1999 where the WTO failed to reach an agreement to launch a new round of trade negotiations. The link with Seattle was corroborated by the then Trade Commissioner, Pascal Lamy, who announced: 'The decision to proceed with the "Everything but Arms" initiative proves that the EU had heard the message developing countries had delivered in Seattle' (EU 2001).

However, as Jan Orbie points out in Chapter 2 of this volume, the idea of providing increased market access for the LDCs generated from discussions among the international trade community from 1996 to 2000. At the 1996 Singapore Ministerial Conference, the WTO Director General Renato Ruggiero encouraged the developed WTO members to provide greater market access to the LDCs as a gesture of good faith. As of 1997, the GAC outlined a pro-LDC trade policy that would provide LDCs equivalent market access as the ACP over the short term, duty-free access for substantially all products over the medium term and the establishment of a consolidated WTO preferential scheme over the long term. The GAC initiative was clearly a reaction to a 1996 proposal by the then Director General of the WTO Renato Ruggiero to eliminate duties and quotas affecting LDC exports. There was, therefore, a consensus in the GAC to develop a preferential arrangement for LDCs as of 1997.

Pascal Lamy's proposal of September 2000 was more radical than the GAC consensus, however, as the EBA proposal covered all goods with the exception of arms but including highly sensitive agricultural products. This radicalization of the LDC package provoked a reaction by some member states with important agricultural interests but it is questionable whether Commissioner Lamy had gone too far in the context of negotiations with the GAC.

By proposing EBA, the Trade Commissioner was playing an almost perfect two-level game. In reaction to the Seattle breakdown, where several poor African countries walked out of the negotiations, Commissioner Lamy was making a radical proposal at level I (international level) to facilitate market access for the LDCs. Internally (level II), the proposal appealed to development NGOs – such as Oxfam – that had been critical of EU trade policy – and to the GAC that expected the EU to play a leadership role on the international trade scene to get a new WTO round launched by 2001 and had been calling for a pro-LDC EU trade policy for many years. Although Lamy's proposal was subsequently weakened by introducing a phase-in for bananas, rice and sugar, this did not come about as a result of pressure in the GAC from the 'protectionist' southern member states.

The commonly held argument that EBA resulted from a conflict between 'liberal' northern member states and 'protectionist' southern member states – as elaborated by Maurizio Carbone in Chapter 3 of this volume – does not withstand the test of evidence. Indeed, opposition to EBA was also considerable in 'liberal' states like the UK – where opposition from the National Farmers' Union and Caribbean sugar exporters was very active (Bond 2005). Instead the pressure came from the Agricultural Commissioner and the EU Agricultural Council of Ministers.

The breaking point in the debate was, in fact, the release by Franz Fischler, then Agricultural Commissioner, of an internal study in December 2000 showing that the EU sugar industry could face costs of more than €1 billion because of EBA (ICTSD 2001a, b). Although an Oxfam study later concluded that the effect of EBA on sugar imports would be far less significant than the DG Agriculture study had demonstrated (Stevens and Kennan 2001), the impact of the latter study was determinant in the amendments made to the original EBA proposal.

On 17 January, the Commission modified its proposal by introducing phase-in periods for bananas (fully liberalized as of 2006), rice and sugar (as of 2009). During the transition period, the Commission proposed specific import quotas for the LDCs for these three products. Ironically, the import quotas introduced by EBA for these products for LDCs were not expected to have a substantial impact on EU producers because they were taken from existing quotas normally granted to ACP countries.

To what extent can we consider the amendments proposed by the Agricultural Commissioner a competing two-level game with Commissioner Lamy's two-level game? First, the 1996–2000 EU discussions on a package of LDC measures took place in isolation within the GAC and these discussions were ignored by the Agricultural Commissioner and Council. Clearly, the latter were taken by surprise by the strong opposition from farmers to Lamy's proposal for an EBA initiative. Although the proposal had been approved by the College of Commissioners, the Commissioner for Agriculture did not fully consider the potential impact of this initiative on sensitive products such as sugar. However, once alerted by the sugar industry (and others) of the potential risks associated with this initiative, the Agricultural Commissioner sprang into action.

To reassure his constituency (the EU farm lobby and Agricultural Council), the Commissioner leaked the results of a study demonstrating the potentially harmful impact of EBA on the EU sugar industry. In this way, he reassured his policy community that their interests would not be ignored. Yet the Agricultural Commissioner did not go so far as to request a permanent suspension of sensitive products from EBA – which would have been relatively easy to achieve. Indeed, the EU Generalized System of Preferences and the EU–ACP agreements both include a number of exceptions to protect sensitive products. Instead, the Commissioner for Agriculture proposed the phase-in of liberalization for the three sensitive products based on a very specific calendar.

To a large extent, this phase-in calendar could in itself be considered a two-level game linked to CAP reform. The EU has been engaged in a process of CAP reform for the past five years. The basic premise of the reform is to decouple subsidies from production to income support and to bring EU intervention prices into line with world market prices as a means to reduce budgetary expenditures. In other words, CAP reform is essentially about introducing stronger market forces in the agricultural sector while still supporting farmers through income support.

However, in order to carry out this complex and controversial reform, the EU engaged in a two-step reform process. In the first phase, beginning in 2001, most agricultural products, except the most sensitive, were subject to the reform process of decoupling. In the second phase beginning in 2005, the most sensitive sectors, such as sugar, were introduced into the reform process. The logic behind this two-step reform was a simple one: divide the agricultural lobby by providing the most sensitive sectors with more time in the reform process.

EBA thus served as international leverage to break the resistance to further reform in the sugar, banana and rice sectors. As Brüntrup argues in Chapter 10 of this volume, the EBA initiative became a veritable 'Trojan horse' for EU sugar market reform. Indeed, the DG Agriculture study on the impact of EBA on the EU sugar market may have been contested by Oxfam (Stevens and Kennan 2001) but was supported by the EU Agricultural lobby and national agricultural ministries (the Council of Agricultural Ministers). Therefore, the latter must agree that the CAP policies governing these products will need to be reformed as soon as the phase-in period for EBA begins. In fact, the farm lobby's opposition to EBA now ensnares it in the reform process because it cannot deny what the future impact will be (even though economists might argue that the impact of EBA will be small).

To make matters more difficult, EU sugar, rice and banana producers would need to request the amendment of EBA to block the reform process. Although the LDC countries themselves made this proposal to prevent reform of the EU sugar market (LDCs 2004), the EU rejected it in order to avoid affecting its international credibility. Indeed, EBA is a vital argument for the EU that the CAP is development-friendly. Therefore, the EBA initiative set the calendar for the second phase of CAP reform 'in stone'. As Franz Fischler remarked, 'Everything but Arms' is the best guarantee that the present sugar regime in Europe cannot survive' (cited in Orbie, Chapter 2 of this volume).

Competing 'reversed' two-level games

There is a second facet to the competing trade two-level game and agriculture two-level game because EBA has also served to undermine the EU–ACP preferential regime. From the DG Trade perspective, EBA can be seen as a reversed two-level game whereby the EU has used an internal regulation as a basis for a classification system of developing countries in the WTO. For several years now, the EU has been trying to reclassify the WTO membership because there is no clear definition of developing countries and because EU industries refuse to accept that emerging countries with competitive export industries – such as China or India – benefit from developing country exceptions to WTO liberalization commitments.

Since adopting the regulation, the EU has pressured the WTO to embed EBA in WTO rules by requiring the other developed and advanced developing countries to adopt similar preferential trade regimes. In addition to increasing market access for the LDCs, this would establish the differentiation principle among developing countries in the WTO. Indeed, by recognizing that LDCs represent the countries most in need in the WTO, the EU sets the ground rules for future differentiation based on economic need. By pressuring the emerging countries to provide preferential trading arrangements to LDCs, the EU also seeks to reclassify them as countries that do not require special treatment under WTO rules because a country that grants trade preferences is clearly not in a position to benefit from special treatment under WTO rules.

EU proposals to provide a 'G-90 round for free' and to provide exemptions for 'weak and vulnerable' countries also reflect its policy towards differentiation. Thus, from an EU perspective, three categories of developing countries exist in the WTO – each benefiting from a different level of special treatment:

- *LDCs* benefit from privileged market access to big markets and have very limited obligations under WTO rules.
- *'Weak and vulnerable' countries* benefit from limited privileged market access and have fewer obligations under WTO rules than other developing countries.
- *'Emerging' countries* have more obligations under WTO rules than 'weak and vulnerable' or LDCs (including a requirement to grant preferences to LDCs) but fewer obligations than developed countries.

The EU differentiation policy culminated in Hong Kong with an agreement that 'developed members, and developing country members in a position to do so' should grant DFQF access to LDC exports, and with the creation of a new category of developing countries referred to as 'small and vulnerable economies' (WTO 2005, annex F and paras 21 and 41).

Interestingly, the EU approach to developing country classification completely disregards the ACP group of countries as a classification *per se*. Indeed, 40 ACP countries are also LDCs but ten LDCs are not members of the ACP group and some 39 ACP countries are not LDCs. Thus, in addition to strengthening EU demands for differentiation between developing countries, EBA could provoke 'the effective break-up of the ACP group as a political entity' (see Orbie in Chapter 2).

From a DG Agriculture perspective, the EBA initiative serves an altogether different purpose by inciting the ACP group against further agricultural tariff liberalization. The ACP group benefit from substantial preferential access to the EU market for a number of key products such as sugar and bananas. However, this privileged access is being eroded – primarily by CAP reform whose objective is to reduce EU agricultural intervention prices. The phase-in of sugar, bananas and rice into the EBA initiative will erode the privileged position of the ACP countries on the EU market as competition from non-ACP LDCs increases. As explained by Carbone in Chapter 3 of this volume, non-LDC ACP countries feared that EBA would 'rob the poor to give to the poorest'. Yet, because CAP reform and EBA both arise from internal EU decisions, the ACP countries have no means to block this 'erosion' of their preferences.

On the other hand, the ACP countries do have a say in the WTO Doha Development Agenda (DDA) negotiations where decisions are made by consensus.

Given that they will lose out due to EBA, the ACP countries have expressed strong opposition to tariff reductions on their export products to the EU market – namely sugar, bananas and rice. Their objective is to preserve their market share even though they will face lower prices on the EU market due to greater competition from the LDCs.

Not surprisingly, this ACP opposition to tariff liberalization strengthens the negotiating hand of the Commissioner for Agriculture in the DDA negotiations by providing her/him with developing-country allies opposed to multilateral tariff liberalization. The EU would like to maintain relatively high tariffs on agricultural products to reduce the level of income support for EU farmers. In a more protected market, EU farmers will be able to sell their produce at higher prices.

Hence, internal EU policies at level II have provided EU negotiators with added political leverage at level I (in the WTO) in a kind of reversed two-level game. However, this policy will directly undermine the objectives of the Trade Commissioner because without a credible liberalization offer in agriculture (regardless of ACP concerns), she/he will be unable to negotiate an ambitious deal in the industrial and service sectors. It is not surprising, therefore, to see that the Agricultural Commissioner demonstrates a lot of understanding for the ACP countries in the WTO context but much less so when adopting internal EU CAP reforms.

Trade game		Agricultural game
International level (Level I)		
Differentiation between developing countries		ACP countries oppose tariff liberalization in WTO
Pressure on other big traders to give preferences		Strengthens negotiating position of EU
EU level (Level II)		
Satisfies 'differentiation' request of EU business		Sugar, banana, rice reforms 'locked in'
EU regulation defines 'differentiation'		Less WTO pressure on EU market (tariffs) at WTO level

Figure 4.3 Reversed two-level games

Conclusion

Despite the apparently contradictory nature of the EBA initiative of the EU, a breakdown of the policy process into separate, but competing, two-level games demonstrates a surprisingly clear logic. On the one hand, the Trade Commissioner launched a far-reaching public relations exercise to demonstrate the EU commitment to a development-friendly trade policy. At level I, this gave the Trade Commissioner more credibility to launch a new trade round at the WTO, while at level II it satisfied the requests of development NGOs and the GAC for a more development-friendly trade policy. At the same time, EBA has become the basis for an EU strategy at level I to introduce differentiation among developing countries in the WTO, which is a strong demand of the EU business community.

On the other hand, the Commissioner for Agriculture intervened late in the day at level II to protect his constituency (farmers) from the potential negative impact of EBA on the agricultural market by phasing in DFQF market access for rice, bananas and sugar. Yet EBA also served as a level I (international) constraint on further reform of the CAP at level II by locking in reform of EU rice, banana and sugar markets within a clearly defined calendar. At the same time, EBA has provoked strong reactions against agricultural tariff reductions from the ACP preference beneficiary countries at level I because EBA erodes their preferences. As a result, WTO pressure for tariff liberalization, which could threaten EU agricultural producers at level II, has been significantly weakened or at least counterbalanced by the ACP pressure.

We can see, therefore, that EU trade policy appears to be driven by, at times, very contradictory strategies – one directed by the Trade Commissioner and the other directed by the Agricultural Commissioner. The end result is a policy that lacks coherence or clear strategic direction.

Notes

This chapter reflects the personal opinions of the author only and does not, in any way, represent the views, opinions or position of his employer.

1   The preceding chapter of this volume by Carbone is partly along this line.
2   However, the adoption of EBA by a larger group of WTO members – along the lines of the commitment at the Hong Kong WTO summit in 2005 (see Chapter 12 in this volume) – could have a more significant economic impact than those studies demonstrate.

References

Allison, G. and Zelikow, P. (1962/1999) *Essence of Decision: Explaining the Cuban Missile Crisis*, New York: Longman.
Bond (2005) 'Everything but arms: a gesture of EU good faith?', BOND Networking for International Development. HTTP://www.bond.org.uk/eu/pre2002/arms.html.
Brenton, P. (2003) 'Integrating the Least Developed Countries into the World Trading System: The Current Impact of EU Preferences under Everything but Arms', Policy Research Working Paper No. 3018, Washington DC: World Bank.

Cernat, L., Laird, S., Monge-Roffarello, L. and Turrini, A. (2003) 'The EU's Everything but Arms Initiative and the Least-developed Countries', Discussion Paper No. 2003/47, Wider, United Nations University. HTTP: <//www.wider.unu.edu/publications/dps/dps2003/dp2003-047.pdf> (accessed 8 May 2006).

Christiansen, T. (2001) 'Intra-institutional politics and inter-institutional relations in the EU: towards coherent governance?', *Journal of European Public Policy*, 8: 747–69.

EU (2001) 'EU approves "Everything but Arms" trade access for least developed countries'. Press release, Brussels, 26 February.

ICTSD (2001a) 'Everything but Arms initiative under fire from EU farm lobby', *ICTSD Bridges Weekly*, 5, 1.

ICTSD (2001b) 'EU modifies "Everything but Arms" proposal under pressure from AG Sector', *ICTSD Bridges Weekly*, 5, 3.

LDCs (2004) 'Proposal of the Least Developed Countries of the World to the European Union regarding the Adaptation of the EBA Initiative in relation to Sugar and the Role of the LDCs in the Future Orientation of the EU Sugar Regime'. Proposal submitted on 3 March 2004 in response to the EU reform of the GSP regulation.

Lequesne, C. (1993) *Paris–Bruxelles: comment se fait la politique européenne de la France?*, Paris: Presses de la Fondation nationale de science politique.

Lewis, J. (2000) 'The methods of community in EU decision making and administrative rivalry in the Council's infrastructure', *Journal of European Public Policy*, 7: 261–89.

Meunier, S. and Nicolaïdis, K. (1999) 'Who speaks for Europe? The delegation of trade authority in the EU', *Journal of Common Market Studies*, 37: 477–501.

Paarlberg, R. (1997) 'Agricultural policy reform and the Uruguay Round: synergistic linkage in a two-level game?', *International Organization*, 51: 413–44.

Patterson, L.A. (1997) 'Agricultural policy reform in the European Community: a three-level game analysis', *International Organization*, 51: 135–65.

Putnam, R.D. (1988) 'Diplomacy and domestic politics: the logic of two-level games', *International Organization*, 42: 427–60.

Stevens, C. and Kennan, J. (2001) *The Impact of the EU's 'Everything but Arms' Proposal: a Report to Oxfam*, Brighton: Institute of Development Studies, University of Sussex.

Vahl, R. (1997) *Leadership in Disguise: The Role of the European Commission in EC Decision Making on Agriculture in the Uruguay Round*, Aldershot: Ashgate Publishing.

Young, A., Holmes, P. and Rollo, J. (2000) 'The European Trade Agenda after Seattle', Sussex European Institute Working Papers Series 37. Brighton: Institute of Development Studies.

5   The political dynamics behind US and EU trade initiatives towards the least developed countries

Dries Lesage and Bart Kerremans

In this chapter, the political dynamics behind US and European trade initiatives towards least developed countries (LDCs) will be investigated and compared on the basis of their main similarities and differences. The main purpose of this chapter is to explain these similarities and differences from a political point of view. The study will focus on the two initiatives that mark to a large extent the trade relations between the United States (US), the European Union (EU) and the LDCs, notably the US 'African Growth and Opportunity Act' (AGOA) and the European 'Everything but Arms' regulation (EBA). The decision of the World Trade Organization (WTO) at the Ministerial Conference in Hong Kong (December 2005) is also taken into account. As explained in Chapter 12 of this volume, members of the WTO promised to create a global system of largely duty-free and quota-free (DFQF) trade for the LDCs for at least 97 per cent of LDC products by 2008. After 2008, or after the actual implementation date, steps will be taken to liberalize the remaining 3 per cent. Of course, the implementation of this decision depends upon a successful conclusion of the entire Doha Round.

Comparing EBA with AGOA is not self-evident. Though both are unilateral pieces of legislation, their design, geographical scope and policy context are very different. Unlike EBA, AGOA is not explicitly directed at LDCs. Important non-LDCs such as South Africa or Kenya are AGOA beneficiaries, while all Caribbean and Asian LDCs are by definition excluded. As a result, a comparison between EU and US trade policies towards LDCs will always be somewhat artificial. Babarinde and Faber draw the same conclusion in Chapter 6.

AGOA is a unilateral programme to boost reform, economic growth and development in sub-Saharan Africa (SSA). The most important element of the Act is the granting of DFQF access to the US market for most products from eligible SSA countries. It was passed in Congress in the period 1999–2000 and signed into law by President Clinton on 18 May 2000. AGOA formed part of the broader 2000 Trade and Development Act. In August 2002, President Bush signed into law amendments to AGOA, also referred to as AGOA II, expanding the trade benefits. The July 2004 AGOA Acceleration Act (AGOA III) extends the programme for most products from 2008 to 30 September 2015, and further expands trade benefits. AGOA is a special scheme within the US Generalized System of Preferences (GSP) for developing countries. Under AGOA about 6,485 items can enter the US duty-free, while the standard GSP regime holds for 4,650 products.[1] Among the specific AGOA products, textiles and clothing are prominent, as these products are not covered by the US GSP (cf. Mattoo *et al.* 2003). Although a number of non-LDCs such as South Africa are actual or potential beneficiaries, AGOA is the most important US special initiative towards LDCs. At this moment 25 of the 37 AGOA eligible countries are LDCs.[2] Only one non-African LDC, Haiti, is a beneficiary of another far-reaching programme that includes extensive duty-free access: the 2000 US–Caribbean Basin Trade Partnership Act, legislation that benefits 24 Caribbean countries. The Asian, Pacific and African non-AGOA eligible LDCs can benefit from the standard GSP that is much less generous than AGOA.

In 2001 the EU adopted its 'Everything but Arms' regulation EC No. 416/2001, granting to all LDCs of the world immediate DFQF imports for all products, except arms and ammunition. Just like AGOA, EBA fits legally within the GSP framework; it is authorized by the WTO as an expanded GSP programme. Besides GSP, LDCs of the African, Caribbean and Pacific group (ACP) already enjoy preferential treatment under the 2000 Cotonou Agreement, the successor of the Lomé regime. Under the trade section of Cotonou, ACP members enjoy market access to the EU at lower tariffs than other developing countries do. The EU–ACP relationship also includes protocols on bananas, sugar and beef that specifically benefit imports from ACP countries (including quotas, and for sugar also price support), but they are under reform and drastically scaled back.

Similarities and differences, which can be drawn from the respective legal texts, are listed in Table 5.1. AGOA and EBA have in common that they were launched and adopted in about the same period (launched in 1996–97; adopted in 2000–01), but also that they, as pieces of unilateral legislation, seem to be situated within broader policy frameworks that envisage a move towards reciprocity between the US/EU and the LDCs in the form of bilateral Free Trade Agreements (FTAs), as they are called in the US, or Economic Partnership Agreements (EPAs) in the EU. Importantly, EPAs would apply only to ACP countries that are parties to the existing EU–ACP Cotonou agreement. Five differences catch the eye. First, AGOA is directed to one particular region, while EBA has a universal character, as it applies to all LDCs. Second, in order to be eligible under AGOA, SSA countries have to meet a substantial list of criteria concerning democratic governance, economic reform and consistency with US foreign policy. The EU imposes hardly any conditionality, as each country recognized by the UN as an LDC can benefit from EBA. However, the EU envisages a reciprocal legal framework (the EPAs) with the ACP countries that is likely to entail economic reform. Third, the US is not really pressing reciprocal FTAs with AGOA countries despite AGOA provisions in that sense, let alone with AGOA LDCs, while the EU nearly imposes its EPA initiative. Fourth, in addition to country eligibility, AGOA is based upon product eligibility, and special regulations for agriculture and apparel. EBA covers all products except arms and ammunition, with a transition period for bananas until 2006, and for sugar and rice until 2009. Fifth, EBA is only about trade, while an important characteristic of AGOA is that it also possesses a second pillar about

Table 5.1 AGOA and EBA: similarities and differences

US (AGOA)	EU (EBA)
Similarities	
• Special action for LDCs by providing more opportunities to trade around the same time • Move towards reciprocity in economic relations with LDCs	
Differences	
• Regionalism	• Universalism
• Strong conditionality	• Locking in reform by reciprocal agreement
• Soft FTA-ization	• Active pursuit of reciprocity
• Number of products excluded; special regulation for agricultural exports and apparel	• All products, with transition period for bananas, sugar and rice.
• Comprehensive programme for Africa	• Trade programme for LDCs

development-related issues, such as debt relief, technical assistance to promote economic reform, and support to infrastructure projects, as well as explicit support to US businesses; AGOA legislation calls on US agencies such as the Export–Import Bank and the Overseas Private Investment Corporation to step up their efforts to directly support concrete projects of US firms and investors. In this sense, AGOA resembles more the Lomé/Cotonou trade and development regime. This difference between AGOA and EBA is not that crucial, however, since EU development policy and export and investment promotion are provided through other EU instruments than EBA, as well as national policies. Therefore no special paragraph will be dedicated to this topic. Yet, it is interesting to note that the combination of trade and development provisions in AGOA, besides export and investment promotion for US business, was meant to remedy the perceived lack of cohesion and comprehensiveness in US policy vis-à-vis SSA.

Political explanations for main similarities

Timing

AGOA was signed into law on 18 May 2000. About nine months later (on 28 February 2001), EBA was adopted by the EU Council of Ministers. Is there any connection between the remarkably simultaneous timing of the EU and US initiatives? One possible explanation was the growing international political mood for this kind of initiatives as a result of the call by WTO Director General Renato Ruggiero to the developed world in the months before the WTO ministerial meeting in Singapore of December 1996. G-7 and Quad countries responded with some vague commitments. In Singapore, WTO members agreed in very general terms on a Plan of Action for the LDCs. It is difficult to ascertain whether the Ruggiero initiative was the deciding impetus to AGOA and EBA.

As far as the US is concerned, it is doubtful whether this is the case. In the decision-making process up to AGOA and its antecedents, no clear indications can be found of decisive WTO influence. The interest of American policy makers in African trade opportunities stemmed from different, endogenous sources. At the beginning of 1994 congressional interest in the economic dimension of US Africa policy increased as a result of growing concern among some Congressmen about the impact of the Uruguay Trade Round on Africa. They managed to insert into the 1994 Uruguay Agreement statutory language calling on the President to 'develop and implement a comprehensive trade and development policy for the countries of Africa'. In February 1996 the President submitted to Congress his first report on the subject. The report did not trigger much enthusiasm in Congress. It was claimed that it was neither very innovative, nor sufficiently ambitious. Unimpressed by the President's report, several members of Congress – including some people who had added the 'African' amendment to the Uruguay Agreement Bill (including Representative Jim McDermott (D), known as 'the father of AGOA') – formed the bipartisan congressional 'African Trade and Investment Caucus'. This happened in March 1996. A few months later, in September 1996, several members of the newly formed caucus introduced the 'African Growth and Opportunity End of Dependency Act'. This proposal was never adopted, but the idea of a comprehensive piece of legislation to promote development in Africa and stronger US–African economic relations was definitively put on the political agenda (Dagne 1998). On 24 April 1997, several members of the caucus introduced in the House of Representatives a second proposal, entitled the 'African Growth and Opportunity Act' (AGOA).[3] A comparable Bill was submitted in the Senate.[4] In June 1997, President Clinton launched his 'Partnership for Economic Growth and Opportunity', a plan of action that bore great resemblance to the proposed Bill. On that occasion he was also prepared to lobby Congress to approve the proposed AGOA (which happened in 1999–2000) and to invest political capital for that purpose. Clinton's trip to Africa – the first Africa tour by an American president – was part of his effort to add an African development component to his political legacy. In other words, AGOA stems to a large extent from political entrepreneurship by a very committed bipartisan group of Congressmen and the executive, this in a context of relatively muted opposition.

This does not mean that there was not any opposition to AGOA. There was. It came from lawmakers elected in districts with large textile and clothing interests, and from a substantial part of the congressional Black Caucus, divided as it was between principal support for African developmental initiatives, on the one hand, and concern about the lack of strong labour provisions in AGOA and its heavy reliance on the private sector on the other hand. The former explains AGOA's specific and complicated rules of origin for certain textile and apparel products. The latter explains why a substantial part of the House Democrats opposed AGOA even after the inclusion of a compromise on the rules of origin for certain textiles and apparel products. Seventy-eight of them voted against.[5]

As far as the EU initiative is concerned, Orbie shows in the second chapter of this volume that despite Ruggiero's call the LDC issue was not a high priority for the EU on the road to Singapore. A visible acceleration in the EU sensitivity toward the LDC issue can be noticed from June 1997 onwards, when the General Affairs Council started to formulate ambitious plans to improve the market access of LDCs. In a first phase, the Council envisaged equivalent market access for the nine non-ACP LDCs as for the ACP LDCs. A second phase would consist of duty-free access for essentially all LDC products and an appropriate mechanism to defend sensitive sectors. In October 2000, the European Commission (Pascal Lamy) laid down its proposal for EBA, a more radical plan than the just mentioned 1997 Council plan. An amended version of that proposal (with a transition period for sugar, bananas and rice, and stricter provisions on safeguards and rules of origin) was adopted by the Council in February 2001. EBA can be closely related to a parallel debate that took off around 1996: the reform of the Lomé regime, a derogation to the most favoured nation (MFN) principle of the WTO. Its WTO waiver would expire in 2000, and observers were not sure about its extension under the existing form. This happened first because the EU's insistence on the respect for the WTO provisions on preferential trade agreements suffered from the incompatibility of the (non-reciprocal) Lomé regime with these rules. For the EU such insistence became more important as a consequence of the rising number of preferential trade agreements concluded by other WTO members. Second, the Banana Protocol of Lomé had already caused serious trade conflicts with the US and with banana-producing countries in Central and South America. This underlined the problematic political sustainability of a non-reciprocal preferential trading regime in the WTO. From then onwards, within circles of the Council and the Commission, views advocating a 'globalist' and 'neo-liberal' relationship with the LDCs instead of the 'traditionalist' ACP relationship and its 'interventionist' components (cf. export quotas and price support for sugar) gradually gained ground. The member states that joined the EU in 1995 together with some incumbent ones showed less affinity to the special trade relationship with the former colonies, while some neo-liberally inspired member states rather preferred free market access without any other intervention, and an evolution to more reciprocity. In this respect EBA can be seen as a device to break up the traditional ACP regime. This explanation should be added to the role Ruggiero's 1996 call might have played, as well as the true willingness of actors like EU trade commissioner Pascal Lamy (1999–2004) to foster economic development in the LDCs.

In sum, idiosyncratic developments gave way to the materialization of both AGOA and EBA at about the same time. In the US, discomfort of activist Congressmen created momentum to launch a comprehensive programme to boost African development. The inevitability of a profound debate within the enlarged EU on the Lomé reform brought about EBA. Although no direct connection between the two initiatives can be noticed – entrepreneurship by the WTO leadership can hardly be considered as the decisive factor – maybe a common enabling political climate could be perceived. From the middle of the 1990s (1) the US proved willing to make a special effort for Africa, while the EU started to prepare a spectacular gesture towards all LDCs (instead of reducing commitment), and (2) both initiatives seemed to pin much faith on the benefits of free market access (instead of drastically enhancing aid, or establishing interventionist schemes like commodity agreements, etc.). It is difficult to explain this double parallelism over the Atlantic. A hypothesis about the mounting interest for LDCs at that time may be that the international idealism unleashed by the end of the Cold War was, notwithstanding the disappointments in Somalia, Rwanda and a lot of other places, not dead yet – to the contrary. Several political actors in both the US and the EU concerned with the Third World or Africa in particular remained willing to grasp the opportunity given by the end of bipolar rivalry. But because of disappoint-ment about traditional development aid, state-interventionist approaches and failed peacekeeping operations, they embraced a strongly market-based strategy, which was completely in line with the neo-liberal ideological consensus that reached its zenith in the 1990s. Moreover, this implied a creative recalibration of the old 'Trade, not Aid' maxim of the 1970s movement for a New International Economic Order (NIEO). In the 1990s, many commentators presented the remaining protectionism of the developed countries as one of the main causes of underdevelopment and poverty in the South. This vision was shared by both a number of NGO activists and neo-liberal politicians and economists. So, in the dominant discourse of the 1990s, the interventionist component of the NIEO had been dropped (see Orbie's chapter in this volume). An obvious positive side effect of this development strategy is its relatively low budgetary cost. In addition, the radicalization in respect of the LDC issue by Pascal Lamy after the highly contested and failed WTO summit in Seattle (December 1999), as well as the successful amendments to the initial AGOA proposal adding labour rights to the eligibility criteria,[6] could be seen as answers to the emerging and noisy anti- and alter-globalist movements on both sides of the Atlantic. In sum, EBA and AGOA responded to the willingness to help the most vulnerable countries in the world, but in a way that was consistent with the dominant ideological convictions, and compatible with politicized domestic interests.

Move towards reciprocity

Notwithstanding the unilateral character of AGOA and EBA, both Washington and Brussels are thinking about reshaping their policies vis-à-vis the LDCs towards reciprocal frameworks, wherein LDCs and developing countries in general open their markets more to American and European goods, services and direct invest-ment. This idea was present at the very start of AGOA and EBA policy making. A move to reciprocity, at least for the 41 ACP LDCs, is part of the transformation of the EU–ACP relationship as elaborated in the 2000 Cotonou Agreement. Thus far, non-ACP LDCs are excluded from this evolution. By 2008, the unilateral Lomé/Cotonou trade preferences should be replaced by reciprocal Economic Partnership Agreements (EPAs) between the EU and six ACP regions. Negotiations with regions are already under way. The EU wants EPAs to contain provisions not only on reciprocal free trade in goods, but also on trade in services, investment, competition policy, intellectual property rights, labour norms, and the like. An explicit objective of EPAs is the promotion and strengthening of regional integration within groups of ACP countries (EU 2002). Although entering into EPAs is not mandatory to ACP countries and even less to EBA eligible countries among them, it is very clear that the EU would consider refusal by ACP LDCs to join the EPAs as a setback for the EU–ACP reform effort.

In the US, the move to reciprocity is also present, but much less pronounced for the time being. The African Trade and Investment Caucus originally envisaged a US–SSA FTA by the year 2020 (McDermott 1996: 11). AGOA legislation itself contains a 'declaration of policy' stating that 'free trade agreements should be negotiated, where feasible, with interested countries in sub-Saharan Africa, in order to serve as the catalyst for increasing trade between the United States and sub-Saharan Africa and increasing private sector investment in sub-Saharan Africa'. The President is required to develop a plan in that sense. In his 2001 AGOA report to Congress the President stated that no AGOA country had expressed an interest in an FTA with the US, and that the administration prefers a phased approach. Most countries report that they need more time to reform and strengthen their economies before entering into an FTA. The US sees its Trade and Investment Framework Agreements (TIFAs) as a possible way to do this even if this does not mean that the conclusion of a TIFA automatically leads to FTA negotiations. The Bush Jr administration clearly sees them, however, as possible forerunners to FTAs (Office of the USTR 2001: 109–13). The TIFAs provide frameworks through which the US establishes closer economic cooperation with other countries. They contain very broad intentions to foster trade and investment between the parties, and establish a Council on Trade and Investment as a forum for bilateral consultation and dialogue and even for the settlement of bilateral trade and investment disputes. They focus on the economic policy reform commitments that the US considers to be necessary before FTA talks can be started. Prominent among these are reforms in the area of customs valuation, investment policy and intellectual property rights protection. As far as SSA is concerned, TIFAs have been concluded with South Africa, Nigeria, Ghana, the Common Market for Eastern and Southern Africa (COMESA) and the West African Economic and Monetary Union (WAEMU). FTA negotiations are currently limited to the Southern African Customs Union (SACU – Botswana, Lesotho, Namibia, South Africa and Swaziland).

How can these movements in the direction of reciprocity be explained? A legal explanation is that Lomé/Cotonou and AGOA, as unilateral schemes for countries of a particular geographical area (ACP and SSA respectively), are not compatible with WTO principles on MFN treatment and need a waiver – i.e. an exception to WTO legislation. They are also not covered by the 'Enabling Clause'. Under this clause, unilateral discrimination to the advantage of 'objective' categories such as the 'developing countries' or the 'least developed countries' (cf. EBA) is permitted, not unilateral discrimination that targets specific geographical areas only. The Lomé waiver expired in 2000. The waiver for unilateral preferences under Cotonou will expire in 2008. The EU chose to start a process towards reciprocal EPAs under the EU–ACP Cotonou Agreement, which are WTO-compatible under GATT Article XXIV if their content in terms of liberalization is sufficiently extensive and far-reaching. The US only recently requested a waiver for AGOA,[7] this under increasing pressure from countries like China, Pakistan and India. The US needs this waiver, as it runs its AGOA (and CBI) as a discriminatory modification of its GSP regime. Theoretically speaking, the EU, knowing which AGOA legislation was being prepared, could also have tried to transform its ACP regime into a modification of its GSP. For that purpose, together the EU and the US could have negotiated in the WTO a reform of the Enabling Clause to make unilateral trade preferences for particular regions WTO-compatible (e.g. new groupings such as the sub-Saharan region or the ACP). However, such a measure requires a consensus among the WTO membership. Given developing-country suspicion about developed-country strategies to divide them in order to weaken them, and the criticism from large developing countries, such a scenario has always been improbable (cf. Bilal and Rampa 2006: 30–1). It is also questionable to what extent the US would be prepared to invest political capital in such a negotiation. To the extent, however, that AGOA – and for that matter CBI – starts to substantially divert trade from non-AGOA developing countries to those covered by AGOA, one may expect the pressure to permanently legalize AGOA under the WTO rules to grow. This will probably push the US into increasing the number of African countries with which it concludes free trade agreements.

It is plausible that more factors, which are interrelated, are at play to explain the move to reciprocal agreements. For the EU and the US reciprocity is advantageous in terms of their export interests. Several manufacturing and service sectors are interested in improved market access, and profitable and predictable investment climates, in developing countries. At the same time, it has become clear that substantial progress on investment, competition policy and government procurement (three of the so-called 'Singapore issues') will be impossible during the current Doha Round in the WTO. The same holds even more for labour norms, an issue that some in the US and in the EU would like to add to the WTO agenda. Over the last decade international power relations within the WTO have shifted to the advantage of a group of emerging developing countries, of which the G-20 that was formed in 2003 is the most salient emanation. Bilateral negotiations between the US/EU and limited groups of developing countries transfer the discussion to another political arena where much more asymmetrical power relations than at the multilateral WTO level apply. Consequently, the US and the EU can more easily push through their 'WTO-plus' agenda in such talks than in the WTO. The result is a quite comprehensive bilateral treaty which is for both partners difficult to roll back; in other words, it binds future governments and generations, adding much to stability and predictability (Kerremans and Switky 2000: 150–1; Feinberg 2002: 131). There is more to this than power politics based on material self-interest, however. The US and the EU, as well as some partners in the developing world, assume the ideological posture that implementing the WTO-plus agenda fosters economic reform, competitiveness, and attractiveness of the country as an investment location.

Political explanations for main differences

Regionalism versus universalism

AGOA: special programme for sub-Saharan Africa

EBA is a scheme that focuses on a group of countries, based on a universally applied criterion: the recognition as a least developed country. AGOA starts from another philosophy: it is focused on SSA as a particular geographical area. As such, it fits better into the geographical approach that characterizes the US policy on unilateral trade preferences for the developing world. Even if the US has its own GSP regime, it is supplemented by additional preferences targeted at specific geographical areas, most prominently in the western hemisphere.[8] This approach allowed the US to gear its unilateral preference policies to other substantive policy interests or requirements. Drug eradication is an obvious example, but other security-related or wider foreign policy-related interests have been important too, especially, but not only during the Cold War. The US sees its trade policies as instruments for the achievement of wider foreign and security policy objectives. This is not only the case for its unilateral preferences, but even more so in its approach on FTAs, especially since 9/11. The politicization of Latin American immigration in the US, for instance, played an important role in US interest for Mexico's proposal on NAFTA and its zeal on concluding the Central American Free Trade Agreement (CAFTA). Oil and terrorism-related concerns are prominent in the enthusiasm of the US for FTAs in the Middle East. Business interests matter too, but these can work both ways. They can help explain why the US government invests political capital in certain preferences or trade agreements. They cannot explain however why in some cases – like CAFTA or the free trade agreements with countries like Morocco, Bahrain, Oman and Qatar – the US government needed to convince US business to show some interest in the preferences or agreements it wanted to grant or conclude, and to manifest themselves accordingly.

The regional approach in the US policy on unilateral trade preferences results in discrimination among developing countries in terms of the conditions of their access to the US market. This is even so among the LDCs, where 15 Asian and Pacific LDCs lack the kind of preferential treatment to the US market that the LDCs covered by AGOA and CBI enjoy. It concerns the following countries: Afghanistan, Bangladesh, Bhutan, Cambodia, Kiribati, Laos, Maldives, Myanmar, Nepal, Samoa, Solomon Islands, Timor-Leste, Tuvalu, Vanuatu and Yemen. This is in contrast with Europe's trade policy, where Asian LDCs have arguably been the largest beneficiaries since the 'EBA *avant la lettre*' decision to grant LDCs equivalent market access as their ACP counterparts since 1998.

This US policy creates a risk of trade diversion among the LDCs themselves. And it all reflects the fact that the group of LDCs has never been that relevant as a separate category in the external trade policy of the US, or at least that such categorization has always been secondary to geo-strategic and business-driven imperatives. The latter results in preferential schemes that are geared to the specific interests of the US in a particular region, and that are largely affected by the extent of domestic opposition and support for increased competition from that region. AGOA is a clear example of this.

Indeed, as indicated above, AGOA was largely triggered by the activism of a sub-group of congressional members – the African Trade and Investment Caucus – and that used a mixture of arguments, some of which might be applicable to all LDCs, and some of which were typical for the US–African relationship. Moreover the category 'SSA' was the relevant one, not the distinction between LDCs and other countries. As already mentioned, the congressional African Trade and Investment Caucus, supported by business groups such as the Corporate Council on Africa and NGOs, felt about the middle of the 1990s that there was a need for a better Africa policy. US involvement in Africa during the Cold War was problematic. Governments were supported according to their geopolitical affiliation, not according to their good governance or human rights record. For the rest policy focused on conflict and human disasters. After the Cold War, SSA did not receive much attention from Washington. There was no 'grand strategy'. The Somalia and Rwanda traumas added to the already existing 'Afro-pessimism'. Trade and investment in relation to economic development have never been important topics in US policy on Africa; administrations were said to be stuck to traditional and unproductive forms of official aid. President Clinton's 1996 report to Congress (cf. *supra*) did not remove frustration about this. Representative Jim McDermott (D) put it as follows:

> Unfortunately, the President's response fell short of our minimum expectations. There has been no debate or serious discussion within the administration, no re-evaluation, no creative thinking about a new, more productive engagement as buyers and sellers as opposed to donor and recipient. Unfortunately, masquerading as a trade and development policy are an assortment of programs and initiatives that do not work well together, have no central focus, policy or direction. It is a compilation of the programs and initiatives that are trapped in the cold war mentality and is almost a paternalistic approach to sub-Saharan Africa.
>
> (McDermott 1996: 9)

The essence of the alternative agenda of the African Trade and Investment Caucus could be resumed as follows: (1) the case for a comprehensive framework for US–Africa relations, (2) a strong focus on trade, investment and the development of the private sector as a vital and neglected motor to economic development and 'self-reliance', and as a possible substitute for a drastic enhancement of aid, (3) the recognition that public sector action is still crucial with respect of health, education, and other services, (4) a view on SSA as a vast market of buyers and sellers, instead of a charity case, (5) the conviction that these countries should be granted considerably more generous market access to the US, (6) the idea that US trade benefits and aid should be targeted at well performing states as regards economic reform, good governance, etc., and (7) the case for creating and financing direct export and investment opportunities for US business (Dagne 1996, 1998; McDermott 1996). This agenda was ultimately endorsed by President Clinton in his Partnership for Economic Growth and Opportunity initiative, an initiative that largely overlapped with the proposed AGOA. A factor that certainly played a role here was the prospect of large investments in infrastructure and the concomitant potential benefits for US companies if the local governments would develop some goodwill vis-à-vis the US, and the wave of privatizations that opened opportunities for American investments in the region. Some even claim that this 'Africa-as-a-last-frontier-for-US-business approach'[9] needs to be seen as part of a US strategy to counter the preponderance of Western European capital and investment in this part of the world.

What about the regional focus of US trade policy towards developing countries after the Hong Kong decision on DFQF market access for LDCs by 2008? This decision points at a policy shift in the US, although the coverage of 97 per cent of LDC products allows the US to exclude a broad range of sensitive products among which most probably textiles and clothing. In the Hong Kong ministerial declaration, the commitment to liberalize the remaining 3 per cent is formulated rather vaguely, as there is no commitment to a timetable to complete the DFQF treatment. How can this shift towards recognition of LDCs as a relevant category be explained? Probably, an institutional element is at play here. The executive branch has in general a more positive attitude towards trade liberalization than broad segments of Congress. It is the executive, more specifically the US Trade Representative (USTR), who negotiates in the WTO, within the confines of the Trade Promotion Authority granted by Congress. Unlike unilateral pieces of legislation, such as AGOA, or bilateral FTAs, in the WTO setting the US executive possesses a lot of room of manoeuvre to negotiate comprehensive and quite far-reaching multilateral deals, while at the same time Congress, politically speaking, faces a higher threshold to vote down the entire draft multilateral agreement. For the USTR, coming back from a WTO gathering with a multilateral commitment to the LDCs is easier in terms of circumventing domestic resistance than introducing a similar proposal in Congress aimed at a unilateral Bill. As in this decision only LDCs are concerned, it is hardly conceivable that this issue will be a decisive element for Congress to reject the final Doha agreement, a scenario that is unlikely anyway. But as regards the contents of this decision, it is still difficult to explain the US move. A special initiative for the LDCs has been on the official WTO and G-7 agendas for a long time, but before Hong Kong the US was not in a hurry to make strong commitments. Anyhow, the Bush Jr administration wants to promote development through free trade (and 'Aid for Trade'), rather than massive increases of official development assistance. It is also interested in strengthening its soft power in the South – in an international political context in which the US has lost a lot of valuable soft power throughout the Third World (due to Iraq and other issues) – knowing that the EU already runs a scheme that goes further than this WTO commitment. EBA may have functioned as an impetus. More research is necessary on the US position in Hong Kong, but these are plausible factors. The

US commitment could be considered as an idealistic and strategic move, knowing that the 3 per cent margin gives some flexibility to appease the most tenacious protectionists.

EBA: universal UN list of LDCs

EBA's embeddedness in the EU's approach to development policy is different from that to AGOA in the US. Although the EU had developed a special GSP regime directed at a number of Latin American countries in the 1990s, and although it gradually developed preferential trade regimes with its near neighbourhood (Central and Eastern Europe and the Mediterranean), a special far-reaching project for one single continent does not fit in Europe's trade policy since 1975. Since its first enlargement in 1973, the EC has generally adopted a more universal approach in its trade politics towards developing countries. The traditional relationship with ACP was already more universal than the Eurafrican-inspired Yaoundé Agreements. When some aspects of the Lomé Convention became controversial in the 1990s, and while the strong willingness to support vulnerable countries by means of trade preferences remained intact, turning to the LDCs as an objective intercontinental category was a more logical step than starting to advantage one single continent. The objective LDC criterion was also a legitimate one on the basis of which the ACP could gradually be broken up, establishing discrimination between LDC ACP and non-LDC ACP countries. Moreover, in Europe the LDC category has always been a highly relevant one in development policy and NGO circles.[10] More recently, extra arguments to embark upon a landmark initiative for LDCs were that the EU could give a substantial follow-up to the WTO call to radically improve trade opportunities for LDCs, that this would create goodwill among LDCs for further WTO negotiations, and that this would make its comprehensive but rather vague 'harnessing globalization' discourse more concrete.

Strong conditionality versus locking in reform by reciprocal agreement

AGOA: fostering economic reform, political stabilization and democratic consolidation

In strong contrast with EBA, AGOA is characterized by strong conditionality in function of country eligibility. First of all, AGOA countries have to meet the general GSP criteria of the US.[11] Second, AGOA contains an additional list of important criteria, although they are formulated in rather vague terms: a market-based economy (which implies, among other things, minimization of government involvement in the economy through measures such as price controls and government ownership of economic assets); the rule of law and political pluralism; the elimination of barriers to US trade and investment, including measures to create an environment conducive to domestic and foreign investment, as well as protection of intellectual property; poverty reduction policies, investment in health care and education, investment in physical infrastructure, and promotion of private enterprise; anti-corruption policies; worker rights, including the right to organization and collective bargaining, minimum age, prohibition of forced labour, minimum wages, maximum working hours and occupational safety and health. (This is broader than the so-called 'core labour standards' of the ILO.) It is the President who designates countries as eligible (sec. 104). An important nuance to this apparently burdensome conditionality is that the Act states that in order to be eligible a country 'has established, or is making continual progress toward establishing' the above-mentioned eligibility requirements. Another requirement is that countries do not engage in activities that undermine US national security or foreign policy interests, do not commit gross violations of human rights, do not support or sponsor terrorism, and do cooperate in efforts to combat the latter. In sum, the text leaves the President much room for interpretation, which can work in both directions. At this moment 37 of the 48 SSA countries enjoy AGOA preferences, of which 25 are LDCs. Of the 11 excluded SSA countries, 9 are LDCs (see Appendix 1.1 in Chapter 1).

It is difficult to assess the intrusiveness of AGOA conditionality, but there are some indications that it should not be exaggerated. Comoros, Somalia and Sudan did not show any interest in AGOA from the start. A number of countries were not designated from the very beginning (Angola, Burkina Faso, Burundi, Democratic Republic of Congo, Gambia, Sierra Leone, Swaziland, Côte d'Ivoire), because of reasons concerning the political criteria and economic reforms, but acquired AGOA status by 2006. Until now Equatorial Guinea, Liberia and Togo have never got AGOA status, because of a combination of serious problems as regards political pluralism, rule of law and human rights, the undermining of US foreign policy interests (Liberian support to rebels in Sierra Leone) and insufficient economic reform. The Central African Republic, Côte d'Ivoire, Mauritania, Eritrea and Zimbabwe lost their AGOA status, partly or entirely on the basis of very compromising violations of the elementary political criteria (*coup d'état*, massive human rights abuses, government-sponsored violence against a UN-monitored cease-fire). In sum, no country has ever been denied AGOA status on purely economic grounds, not even on 'minor' infringements of the political criteria, which frequently occur in several of the AGOA eligible states (think of the two Congos, Rwanda, Nigeria, Uganda). All this points at a pragmatic implementation of the requirement list (Office of USTR 2001, 2005) even if assessing US motives in this regard is not easy. The text of the decisions in which the termination of the eligibility of countries is announced tends to be cursory.[12] One cannot overlook, however, that even pragmatic implementation has led to the exclusion of eight applicant countries, and probably the discouragement of three others to show any interest.

Yet some nuances could be added to this overall conclusion. First, we have to take into account the broader context. Several AGOA countries are subject to the quite intrusive conditionality of the IMF and World Bank[13] – policies that receive the full support of the US, even if it is a matter of debate to what extent they are steered by it (cf. Bird and Rowlands 2003: 1261–4) – and national official development assistance programmes. Second, AGOA was not the main incentive to reform in most beneficiary countries, but can be an extra stimulus to continue reform. Third, AGOA is about substantial trade preferences and not that much about financial aid; given the importance of trade opportunities for particular local economic and political elites, AGOA may for some countries be a deciding factor to maintain or intensify reform. Fourth, the explicit political requirements as well as the emphasis on labour rights as forms of conditionality for African countries are typical features of AGOA. (The IMF and World Bank are legally not allowed to apply such an explicitly political conditionality.)

But how can the decision to include country eligibility criteria in AGOA be explained? First, the US Congress is traditionally very reluctant to approve unconditional aid that generates considerable costs to the US (in terms of budget or unilateral trade preferences). Even increasing the reserves of the IMF in the aftermath of the financial crises of 1997–98, in order to be more capable to maintain global financial stability, was extremely difficult for Congress (cf. Mosley 2001: 605). Concessions had to be made to overcome staunch isolationist resistance. Lawmakers must be reassured that they are not carrying coals to Newcastle; there are limits to their idealism. Therefore, AGOA had to target countries that are visibly on the way to structural political and economic reform; it is also these countries that in the long run, as stable and growing economies, will create more business opportunities for US firms, and advance US national security interests. In this respect, it is even remarkable that AGOA conditionality is not more detailed and stricter. Moreover, AGOA exclusion may be an incentive for some countries to start reform. Excluding 11 poor countries might look somewhat harsh, but in the long run, it will help these countries better than just granting them AGOA status, their institutional and economic structures being so deficient that they will never be able to grasp a big deal of the potential economic opportunities that AGOA offers. In fact, AGOA conditionality should not be considered as a sheer compensation for US generosity, it also forms an integral part of the renewed US development policy. This idealistic reading of conditionality directed at promoting domestic reform and private market forces was for instance obvious in the discourse of the African Trade and Development Caucus.

Second, influencing the domestic policies of other countries has always been an important part of US foreign policy, both for realistic and idealistic reasons (see, e.g., Hentz 2004). US foreign investments are spread all over world. They require political stability and a profitable investment climate. In addition, it is strongly believed in the US that good governance, a market-based economy and democracy are mutually reinforcing, and that these factors render countries more peaceful, prosperous and better equipped to combat phenomena such as terrorism and international crime. So a policy of stimulating these factors, or reform to achieve them, by means of conditionality is considered to advance US national security. This strategy has become even more relevant since the end of the Cold War, something that brought about worldwide democratization and rendered the second-best strategy of supporting dictatorial US-minded regimes both less legitimate and less 'necessary'. Locking-in pro-market reform in function of US economic and strategic interests is also an important motivation for the growing number of reciprocal FTAs that the US has already concluded or is negotiating (cf. Feinberg 2002: 131). Examples are the FTAs with a number of Andean countries (where US investors are worrying about the rise of left-wing radicalism), as well as the FTAs with Chile, Morocco, Jordan, Oman and Bahrain, the negotiations with the United Arab Emirates and Panama, and the bold plan of a US–Middle East Free Trade Agreement by the year 2013. Besides shaping the international environment, or pursuing a set of 'milieu goals' conducive to US interests (Wolfers 1962), the internationalist current in US politics traditionally sees it as its mission to actively promote political and economic freedom wherever in the world.

Third, AGOA conditionality may be seen as a kind of compensation for what we called the 'soft FTA-ization' (cf. *infra*). It makes possible to insert elements of the 'WTO-plus' agenda into the US–SSA relationship. A final remark should be made about the domestic institutional dimension of conditionality. In US policy making, notwithstanding the existing divergence between departments in the administration, the integration of trade policy and foreign policy occurs more easily than in Europe.

Again, the 2005 Hong Kong deal on LDCs thwarts this policy. In the WTO language no hint at conditionality is mentioned. It is likely that the executive has made use of its institutional freedom of movement at the WTO forum to neglect congressional sensitivities, supposing that Congress will not torpedo the Doha Round because of the LDC issue. But for the market access to the 3 per cent non-eligible LDC products, it is not excluded that for AGOA LDCs (and possibly the other LDCs) conditionality will be maintained.

EBA: locking-in reform postponed until EPAs?

Countries recognized by the UN as LDCs are automatically eligible for EBA. They do not need to fulfil any other criteria. However, under the EU GSP (currently Council Regulation No. 980/2005) countries may lose their EBA status on the basis of the temporary withdrawal provisions of the European GSP regulation. These provisions are about serious violation of core labour rights, unacceptable trade practices and violation of international agreements as regards fisheries. The EU has not legally bound itself to exclude countries that visibly violate these provisions. The Commission and the Council are allowed to choose not to take action. In 1997, GSP Council Regulation No. 552/97 excluded Myanmar from GSP benefits because of its forced labour practices. Consequently, it has never been granted EBA status. All other 49 LDCs benefit from EBA. How can this purported generosity be explained? A possible explanation is that within the particular polity of the EU reaching a consensus about a detailed list of substantial criteria, and about the synergy between trade policy and foreign policy, is very difficult. Divergence with the US is not as great as it looks at first glance, however. As aforementioned, the intrusiveness of AGOA conditionality should not be exaggerated. Moreover, a number of EU governments apply conditionality through other channels, such as their official development assistance and their leverage over IMF and World Bank.

There is more. Forty-one of the world's 50 LDCs are party to the Cotonou Agreement. Cotonou envisages reciprocal EPAs between the EU and six ACP regions; as mentioned above, EPA negotiations are now under way. Cotonou already includes political requirements: democracy, good governance, human rights, anti-corruption policies, and so on, but formulated in rather broad terms. These principles are to reappear in the EPAs. In addition, the EU wants the EPAs to contain a large number of 'WTO-plus' provisions (on services, investment, competition policy, intellectual property, labour rights, etc). Within EPAs, LDCs will be granted differential treatment (in the form of longer transition periods to open up their markets). Only nine non-ACP LDCs will be excluded from the EPAs and continue to benefit from unilateral trade benefits. The evaluation of the generosity of the EU will depend on the extent to which unwilling ACP LDCs are able to refuse EPAs, or at least the 'WTO-plus' provisions, while keeping their DFQF access to the European market. Anyhow, in the Cotonou Agreement both the EU and ACP commit themselves to enter into EPA negotiations. The initiative has obviously come from Brussels. Notwithstanding the asymmetrical power relationship between the EU and the ACP, the outcome of the negotiations remains unclear. It is possible that some ACP countries will not enter into an EPA in the end, or just sign an EPA that is much less ambitious than the European Commission would like, because they do not feel ready, or because they disagree with Europe's terms. In the Cotonou agreement it is provided that in the event a non-LDC ACP country does not sign the EPA, the EU will examine all possibilities to offer the country a WTO-compatible trading arrangement which is equivalent to the former (Article 37(6)). This can be called a leap into the unknown, and a not very attractive one. The situation of ACP LDCs is different. Most probably, LDCs not joining an EPA will keep their EBA status, since discrimination among LDCs is not WTO-compatible. Of course, the EU can make use of other instruments – such as official development assistance – to persuade LDCs. Moreover, not entering EPAs may leave some LDCs in a rather isolated position within the context of the strengthening of regional trade arrangements that the EPA process is underscoring. (See the discussion in Chapter 8 on Zambia, and Chapter 11 in this volume.)

Restrictive product eligibility versus total free trade

AGOA: import-sensitive products more strictly regulated or excluded

About 6,485 items (eight-digit level in the US Harmonized Tariff Schedule) can enter into the US duty-free under AGOA, while the standard GSP for developing countries provides preferential treatment to approximately 4,650 items.[14] In order to be eligible, products have to be determined as 'not import-sensitive' by the President (that is, by the USTR) taking into account the advice from the US International Trade Commission (USITC). Among the excluded items are some textile articles, certain steel products, canned peaches and apricots, broken rice and dehydrated garlic (Office of USTR 2005: 10). Agricultural products subject to a tariff-rate quota remain subject to such a quota, however, which means that the quantity of an imported agricultural product that exceeds the in-quota quantity cannot be eligible for duty-free treatment.[15] As has been described above, apparel, another important product category for several SSA countries, is subject to a number of restrictive rules of origin. Some – among which the World Bank – have claimed that without the restriction on apparel imports made from fabric produced in third countries,[16] the export opportunities of these countries to the US market would be substantially higher (cf. Brenton and Ikezuki 2004). The 3 per cent margin in the December 2005 Hong Kong deal gives a lot of possibilities to deny DFQF market access to sensitive products that are important to LDCs.

EBA: unlimited duty-free and quota-free access, but strict rules of origin

In terms of market access, EBA seems more generous than AGOA at first glance. Notwithstanding the transition periods for rice, sugar and bananas, EBA grants unlimited DFQF access for all products, except arms and ammunition. This seeming generosity is overshadowed, however, by the quite burdensome rules of origin of the European GSP to which EBA is subject, as is shown by Brenton and Özden in Chapter 7 of this volume. The modification to the GSP rules in EBA, namely the possibility of regional sourcing of intermediary products ('regional cumulation') among LDCs, is not very helpful in mitigating the effects of these restrictive rules (Inama 2002; UNCTAD 2003). This is the political price proponents of the actual EBA regime had to pay to protectionist elements in the EU who are concerned about the possible trade diversion and import effects of much more liberal rules of origin. EBA is indeed very open to LDC exports that respect the rules of origin.

'Soft FTA-ization' versus 'active pursuit of reciprocity'

Although the US and the EU have in common that they are interested in the 'FTA-ization' of their trade relations with developing counties, as far as SSA and ACP are concerned the EU applies a much more ambitious strategy than the US. At this point, only one LDC – Lesotho – is involved in an FTA negotiation with the US, this as part of the ongoing – but slowly progressing – negotiations between the US and SACU. In comparison, 40 ACP LDCs are a party in current EPA negotiations with the EU. Therefore, the American posture can be labelled 'soft FTA-ization', the European 'active pursuit of reciprocity'.

Soft FTA-ization

There are different reasons for the hesitancy on the part of the US, certainly compared with the EU. An important one among them concerns the political economy of FTAs in the US. Such agreements tie the US commitments on market access for an indeterminate period of time. Permanently excluding sensitive sectors or products from such access is possible but difficult. There are in the first place the relevant WTO rules. But, more important, through the conclusion of FTAs the US is building and expanding an FTA legacy. And that legacy affects the kinds of demands future FTA partners raise vis-à-vis the US. If the US asks for product exclusions in an FTA today, it increases the probability that it will be exposed to similar demands by other countries with which it will negotiate an FTA in the future. And that is problematic. As the US Congress needs to approve the FTAs that the US administration concludes, a sufficiently large coalition in favour of such an FTA needs to be constructed. Given the lack of political party discipline in Congress – certainly in comparison with the situation in most EU member states – the construction of such a coalition needs to happen on the basis of the merits of each case. As a starter, given the bounded nature of the commitments required and the difficulty to avoid complete liberalization in the longer run – eventually after a long transition period – more domestic opposition may be expected than in the case of unilateral tailor-made preferences for sensitive products. Consequently, a larger counter-coalition that supports free trade will need to be constructed. That is only possible in case sufficient access to the market of the trading partner can be offered. And 'sufficient' means that, first, access for US exporters needs to be DFQF, and second, that the market of the trading partner needs to be sufficiently large so that the expected export opportunities are substantial. Under these conditions, business associations with export interests will be prepared to mobilize in favour of an FTA and to promote it to the public, and derivatively to Congress, accordingly.

The problem with many AGOA countries is that they are small and poor. They represent only relatively small purchasing power, even if some of them may present attractive investment opportunities. The incentives for business mobilization in favour of an FTA with these countries are small. The opposition from American import-competing interests is in many cases strong because of the sensitive nature of the products the AGOA countries export most. In addition, to the extent that it concerns textile and clothing, and a range of agricultural products (or their processed derivatives), the geographical concentration of the former in the US, and the overrepresentation of the latter in the US Senate, leads to an opposition coalition that is often much stronger than its possible supportive counterpart. In some cases, security or strategic interests may compensate for that and may tilt the balance in favour of support for an FTA. This explains the rapidly rising US interest for the Middle East since 9/11 and since the war in Iraq. The 13 criteria for the choice of FTA partners – as defined by the Bush administration in May 2003 – clearly indicate this (US GAO 2004: 7–9). But for many AGOA LDCs it is difficult to point to such interests, at least for now. Consequently, US FTA-ization will occur, but only softly.

From the point of view of African countries, since Congress has to renew the Act, the future of unilateral AGOA preferences is unclear after 2015 (and even earlier – namely 2007 – for apparel produced with third-country fabric by AGOA-eligible LDCs). This uncertainty may be an argument for African countries to consider an FTA rather sooner than later.

Active pursuit of reciprocity

As already mentioned, the EU felt quite uncomfortable with the WTO incompatibility of its Lomé/Cotonou regime, while because of path dependence it remained committed to maintaining it one way or another, instead of dropping it and just going on with a WTO-compatible GSP or LDC regime. In terms of political feasibility in a new context of growing power and assertiveness of non-ACP developing countries such as China, India and Brazil, 'saving' the special EU–ACP relationship was believed to be possible only by transforming it into 'regional trade agreements' under GATT Article XXIV. Continuing the regime without a waiver – an illegal situation – has never been a serious policy option for a multilateralist EU in a WTO capable of enforcing its rules. Note that getting the waiver for the 2000 Cotonou Agreement had already been accompanied by suspicion and contestation from non-participating developing countries. What is more, the EPA project is motivated not only by legal concerns but also by political and economic considerations, more specifically the logic that a reciprocal open trade and investment regime fosters economic growth, political stability and business opportunities.

The institutional setting helps to explain the transatlantic divergence on this matter. In the EU, the Council of Ministers delivers a mandate to the Commission to negotiate, and approves the agreement in the end; final ratification in the national parliaments appears to be a mere formality. In the US, Congressmen are the principal decision makers, and they are not that much bound by party discipline. Because of the size of their constituencies, US Congressmen are inclined to be more sensitive to highly localized special interests than EU ministers, who pursue a more 'common interest', in which local interests are to some extent transcended. This explains why EU officials meet less internal opposition to reciprocal agreements.

Conclusion

In this chapter we examined the political dynamics behind US and EU trade preferences towards LDCs, and elaborated explanations for the main similarities and differences. We can conclude that there is divergence between the US and the European approaches, but it is smaller than it looks like at first glance. As far as LDCs are concerned, at this moment the US actually grants extensive trade benefits to one Caribbean and 25 African LDCs through CBI and AGOA, while the European EBA initiative covers 49 LDCs. This difference is due to the idiosyncratic trade and development policy making processes on both sides of the Atlantic. However, at the December 2005 WTO ministerial summit in Hong Kong, the US agreed to a plan to grant DFQF market access to all LDCs by the year 2008. This decision points at a US move to a more universal approach, and thus growing policy convergence over the Atlantic, although the provision that by 2008 only 97 per cent of LDC products should be covered gives room to the US and other WTO members to exclude tens of important product categories, including items of textiles and apparel.

A second difference is about conditionality. Political and economic conditionality appears to be one of the cornerstones of AGOA legislation. However, the Hong Kong deal on LDCs may eliminate conditionality to the AGOA LDCs within a few years, at least for 97 per cent of their products. In EBA, hardly any conditionality is applied. Again, the EU seems to be more generous. Yet, in the same text as where the idea of EBA was announced – the 2000 EU–ACP Cotonou Agreement – it was foreseen that by 2008 49 LDCs would enter into the reciprocal EPAs between the EU and six ACP country groupings. Brussels hopes that every EPA will include a comprehensive 'reform' package in the form of political provisions, as well as provisions directed at the liberalization of services, open and stable investment regimes, protection of intellectual property rights, labour and environmental norms, etc. In other words, the plan is to lock in reform through bilateral treaties. The outcome of the negotiations remains unclear, but it is obvious that both LDC and non-LDC ACP countries find themselves in an asymmetrical power relation with the EU. In this respect, as both the US and the EU are convinced that good governance and an open market economy are necessary conditions to development, policy divergence between the two is not that large, though in AGOA and Cotonou different instruments are used.

This leads us to the third great difference. For 49 ACP LDCs, EBA is intended to be a temporary regime, awaiting the EPAs. The US rather opts for 'soft FTA-ization'. Anyway, the European EPA formula for the ACP will be more WTO-compatible than the current US AGOA legislation for SSA. If the US does not get a WTO waiver to continue AGOA, chances are real that it will promote bilateral free trade agreements with AGOA countries or regions more strongly as well. Fourth, AGOA denies and restricts free market access for a lot of products, while EBA gives DFQF access to all products, except arms and ammunition, another indication of greater European generosity. But at the same time EBA is subject to very restrictive rules of origin, which is an important reason for the disappointingly low utilization rate of EBA among LDC exporters.

In sum, the EU approach towards LDCs is more generous, but there are several 'checks and balances' attached to it. The basic reasons are that in the (enlarged) EU the commitment to the LDCs as a policy-relevant category is much stronger than in the US, and that in the EU polity protectionist pressures have more difficulties to exert decisive influence than in the US, where institutional – especially congressional – characteristics more rapidly lead to the politicization of trade policy. There is a huge possibility, however, that once the US has implemented the 2005 Hong Kong decision, the transatlantic difference will be strongly reduced.

Notes

1 Sec official AGOA website at http://www.agoa.gov (accessed 9 February 2006).
2 Based on the list of the UN Office of the High Representative for the LDCs, see http://www.un.org/special-rep/ohrlls/ldc/list.htm (accessed 9 February 2006), as far as the LDCs are concerned, and on the list of eligible countries in the *Federal Register* (Vol. 70, 2005, No. 177), as far as the AGOA countries are concerned.
3 House of Representatives 1432 (105th Congress). The Bill was introduced by Rep. Phil

Crane (R-IL) and co-sponsored by 53 other members. The Bill that ultimately passed – the Trade and Development Act of 2000 (Public Law 106-200) – was House of Representatives 434 (106th Congress). For the Trade and Development Act, see Public Law (P.L.) 106–200, in 114 Stat. 251–306.

4 Section 778 (105th Congress). It was introduced by Sen. Richard Lugar (R-IN).

5 Roll Call 145, 106th Congress.

6 Crucial in this regard was the adoption of the Gejdenson Amendment by the House International Relations Committee, see House Report 106–19 Part 1, p. 13. This amendment added point (F) to Section 104 (a)(1) of the Bill.

7 WTO documents G/C/W/508, G/C/W/509, and G/C/W/510.

8 Namely the Caribbean Basin Initiative (CBI), which is provided for by the Caribbean Basin Economic and Recovery Act, and the preferences for the Andean countries as provided by the Andean Trade Preference Act (ATPA) as amended and renewed by the Andean Trade Promotion and Drug Eradication Act (ATPDEA).

9 The last-frontier-for-American-business refers to a statement made by President Clinton when he presented his 1996 report on a comprehensive trade and development policy for the countries of Africa. Many have interpreted this reference as inspired by a concern for the disproportionate influence of European investors in SSA.

10 See Arts 17, 19, 41, 48 of the first Lomé Convention (1975).

11 They include *inter alia* political (not for communist countries that are not members of the WTO and that are dominated or controlled by international communism), economic (not for members of disruptive commodity export cartels, and countries that conduct expropriation policies and their equivalents without compensation), security-related (countries that provide a safe haven to terrorists), and labour-related (countries that decline to take steps to grant internationally recognized worker rights to workers, or that have failed to eliminate the worst forms of child labour) conditions. See 19 USC 2462.

12 See for instance such announcements for Mauritania (*Federal Register*, Vol. 70, 2005, No. 247), and Eritrea and the Central African Republic (*Federal Register*, Vol. 69, 2004, No. 1), and Appendix 6.2 of this volume.

13 Angola, Botswana, Namibia, South Africa, and Swaziland being the exceptions.

14 Likewise, the import limitation rule applicable in the US GSP system does not apply to the eligible products from the AGOA countries (see 19 USC 2463(c)(D)).

15 This quota limit is provided by the US GSP system (19 USC 2463 (b)(3)) and has not been changed by AGOA. Note, however, that the SSA economies depend to a large extent on agriculture. This sector currently covers 35 per cent of their GNP, 40 per cent of their exports, and 70 per cent of their employment (Bread for the World 2003).

16 Note that a special import monitoring and safeguard system is applied to these products, and to apparel produced from regionally produced fabric (sec. 112 (b)(3)(C) of P.L. 106-200).

References

Bilal, S. and Rampa, F. (2006) *Alternative (to) EPAs: Possible Scenarios for the Future ACP Trade Relations with the EU*, Maastricht: ECDPM.

Bird, G. and Rowlands, D. (2003) 'Political economy influences within the life-cycle of IMF programmes', *The World Economy*, 26: 1255–78.

Booker, S., Minter, W. and Colgan A.-L. (2003) 'America and Africa', *Current History*, 101: 195–9.

Bread for the World (2003) *AGOA 2003 and African Agriculture*, Washington DC: Bread for the World.

Brenton, P. and Ikezuki, T. (2004) 'The Initial and Potential Impact of Preferential Access to the US Market under the African Growth and Opportunity Act', World Bank Policy Research Paper, No. 3262, April. Washington DC: IBRD.

Dagne, T. (1996) 'Africa Trade and Development: Clinton Administration Policy and Issues for US–sub-Saharan Africa Trade Relations', Congressional Research Service, Report for Congress No. 96-639, 16 July, Washington DC: Congressional Research Center.

Dagne, T. (1998) 'Africa: Trade and Development Initiatives by the Clinton Administration and Congress', Congressional Research Service, Report for Congress No. 98–92, 2 March, Washington DC: Congressional Research Center.

Dagne, T. and Sek, L. (2000) 'African trade and investment: proposals in the 106th Congress', Congressional Research Service, Issue Brief for Congress No. IB98015, 29 August, Washington DC: Congressional Research Center.

EU (2002) 'Commission Draft Mandate 9 April 2002: Explanatory memorandum', Brussels: European Commission.

Feinberg, R.E. (2002) 'Regionalism and domestic politics: US–Latin American trade Policy in the Bush era', *Latin American Politics and Society*, 44: 127–51.

Feinberg, R.E. (2003) 'The political economy of United States' free trade agreements', *The World Economy*, 26: 1019–40.

Hentz, J.J. (2004) 'US involvement in sub-Saharan Africa', in I. Taylor and P. Williams (eds) *Africa in International Politics*, London and New York: Routledge.

Inama, S. (2002) 'Market access for LDCs: issues to be addressed', *Journal of World Trade*, 36: 85–116.

Kerremans, B. and Switky, B. (eds) (2000) *The Political Importance of Regional Trading Blocs*, Aldershot: Ashgate Publishing.

Mattoo, A., Roy, D. and Subramanian, A. (2003) 'The Africa Growth and Opportunity Act and its rules of origin: generosity undermined?', *The World Economy*, 26: 829–51.

McDermott, J. (1996) 'Statement. Hearing "US Trade with sub-Saharan Africa" before the Subcommittee on Trade of the Committee on Ways and Means', House of Representatives, Serial 104–90, 1 August.

Mosley, P. (2001) 'The IMF after the Asian crisis: merits and limitations of the "long-term development partner" role', *The World Economy*, 24: 597–629.

Office of the USTR (1997) 'A comprehensive trade and development policy for the countries of Africa', Second Report, Washington DC: Office of the USTR.

Office of the USTR (2001) 'Comprehensive Report of the President of the United States of America on US Trade and Investment Policy toward sub-Saharan Africa and Implementation of the African Growth and Opportunity Act', The First of Eight Annual Reports, Washington DC: Office of the USTR.

Office of the USTR (2005) 'Comprehensive Report of the President of the United States of America on US Trade and Investment Policy toward sub-Saharan Africa and Implementation of the African Growth and Opportunity Act', The Fifth of Eight Annual Reports, Washington DC: Office of the USTR.

UNCTAD (2003) *Trade Preferences for LDCs: an early Assessment of Benefits and possible Improvements*, Geneva: UNCTAD.

US General Accounting Office (2004) 'International Trade: Intensifying Free Trade Negotiating Agenda Calls for Better Allocation of Staff and Resources', Report 04-233, Washington DC: General Accounting Office.

Wolfers, A. (1962) *Discord and Collaboration: Essays on International Politics*, Baltimore MD: Johns Hopkins University Press.

6 Exports by least developed countries in sub-Saharan Africa

The role of preferential systems, geography and institutions

Olufemi Babarinde and Gerrit Faber

Countries in sub-Saharan Africa (SSA) have enjoyed trade preferences for a very long time. The reciprocal preferences that were part of the Treaties of Yaoundé and Arusha, concluded in the 1960s between some SSA countries and the European Union (EU), were succeeded by non-reciprocal preferences under the Lomé Conventions (1975) that will continue until 2008 under the Cotonou Agreement (2000). The United States (US) and other industrialized countries introduced Generalized Systems of Preferences (GSPs) in the 1970s, offering preferential market access on a non-reciprocal basis for all developing countries. Despite the seemingly generous preferential market access, exports by SSA economies have been marginalized in terms of global market share – from an abysmal 3.74 per cent in 1980 to a paltry 1.49 per cent in 2003 (UNCTAD 2004).

After the conclusion of the Uruguay Round (1986–94), the future value of non-reciprocal preferences seemed dwindling as Most Favoured Nations (MFN) rates fell substantially. A few years later, it appeared that preferential margins had remained significant for a number of products that were important for developing countries, due to selective and limited MFN liberalization. New initiatives were launched to improve preferential market access for least developed countries (LDCs). Thus, the 1996 WTO Ministerial meeting in Singapore launched the idea of offering special preferences to these countries. In 2001, the EU introduced its 'Everything but Arms' (EBA) regime that offers the LDCs duty-free and quota-free (DFQF) access to its market on a non-reciprocal basis. At the same time, the Lomé preferences are being transformed into reciprocal free trade areas. For its part, the US introduced a special preferential system for African countries in 2001 – the African Growth and Opportunity Act (AGOA) – that offers more generous preferences than the GSP but demands reciprocity on political and economic issues.

The effectiveness of these preferential systems in stimulating exports has been the subject of several intellectual enquiries. Much of the scholarly attention has been directed to the rapidly increasing exports of clothing/apparel by Lesotho and Madagascar under AGOA and the somewhat more general increase of SSA exports to the US under that system (UNIDO 2004: 13). This chapter will discuss the relative efficacy of EBA and AGOA in promoting exports by SSA economies.

In recent debates on the causes of economic growth and development, integration in the world economy through trade and capital flows is considered an important element. On both theoretical and empirical grounds it has been emphasized that trade performance is also dependent on economic growth. Institutions and geography have been proposed as other important factors in the growth equation. Thus, a complex relationship exists in which trade is important, but other factors are as well. For example, Rodrik *et al.* (2002) find that in this web of relationships institutions are crucial for economic growth. Following this approach, trade performance is positively related to institutional quality (and vice versa). In order to exclusively measure the effectiveness of AGOA and EBA, we will control for institutional quality.

One of the salient differences between AGOA and EBA is the benchmark for being accepted as a beneficiary country. The US has a number of criteria concerning domestic and foreign policies, while the EU only has the benchmark of being on the UN list of LDCs. One might argue that the US only offers preferences to economies where a minimum of institutional quality is present, which is a basic condition for developing export capacity. This will directly increase the success of AGOA compared with EBA. Indirectly, the eligibility criteria may encourage countries to improve their institutional quality. This brings us to hypothesize that *AGOA is more effective in promoting exports than EBA, as it makes eligibility for preferences dependent on institutional quality.*

Among the factors that determine the export performance of SSA countries, the quality of domestic infrastructure is likely to be important. For the median landlocked country, Limão and Venables (2001) find 50 per cent higher transport costs compared with the median coastal economy. In addition, they are able to explain most of Africa's weak trade performance by poor infrastructure. Thus, we will control for transport costs when analysing the effectiveness of preferential systems.

In the remainder of this chapter, the next section will discuss the state of the SSA condition, in order to justify the need for generous and special concessions for these countries. The third section is a brief review of the vast and growing literature on the interconnectedness of trade and development. In section four, the discussion will contrast the similarities and differences between the EBA and AGOA regimes, which will be followed by a section that discusses the empirical analysis. The chapter concludes with a summary, and identifies potential future research.

The sub-Saharan African condition: justifying EBA and AGOA

The African condition at the dawn of this century, in relative and absolute terms, is in an appalling state. Consider the following. In 2002, the total gross national product (GNP) of SSA was US$311 billion in nominal terms, thus representing roughly 1 per cent of the world's total GNP.[1] Contextually, it means that almost 700 million population of SSA produced a combined GNP that was approximately 3 per cent the national output generated by an estimated 288 million people of the

United States. There were other countries with much smaller populations whose individual GNPs exceeded the aggregate performance of SSA in 2002. Among them were Australia (US$384 billion in GNP and 20 million population), Brazil (US$495 billion and 174 million population), Canada (US$702 billion and 31 million population), South Korea (US$473 billion and 48 million population), the Netherlands (US$378 billion and 16 million population), and Spain (US$597 billion and 41 million population). This is quite consistent with the pattern of the past two decades or so, whereby the aggregate output of SSA has been roughly equal to, or exceeded by, what many German or US states have individually produced. To further underscore the relative collective weakness of SSA countries, consider the well established fact that many in the world league of Fortune 500 multinational companies (MNCs) boast annual turnover that exceeds the national output of most countries in Africa. For example, in 2004, five of the top 15 MNCs worldwide recorded at least US$100 billion sales receipts each, a feat that was only matched in GNP by South Africa at US$113 billion.[2] Moreover, Nigeria was the only SSA to have a relatively respectable GNP at roughly US$40 billion in 2002, which nine of the top 15 MNCs enjoyed or surpassed in annual sales receipts.

Furthermore, whereas many SSA economies expanded between 2001 and 2002 by as much as 15.3 per cent (Angola), 9.4 per cent (Rwanda), 7.7 per cent (Mozambique) and 6.7 per cent (Uganda), to mention a few, many also contracted by as much as 12.7 per cent (Madagascar), 7.2 per cent (Guinea-Bissau) and 5.6 per cent (Zimbabwe) over the same period. The average *per capita* income for the sub-region was roughly US$450 in 2002, hardly enough spending money for an American or a European university student during a semester. It is thus not surprising that in the World Bank's 2004 classification of countries by *per capita* income, 39 (or 81 per cent of) SSA countries fell in the unenviable category of 'low-income' countries, which represented 61 per cent of all such countries worldwide.[3] That means the average African survives on less than US$2 per day, far less than the typical primary school pupil collects in daily allowances in much of Europe and North America. In fact, according to the World Bank and the United Nations, almost one in every two Africans lives below the poverty line.

The SSA condition has been exacerbated by the continent's population explosion at an average annual growth rate of 2.7 per cent between 1980 and 2001, compared with the average annual economic growth rate of 2.6 per cent during the 1990–2001 period. Moreover, agricultural output growth was 2.8 per cent, while the growth of industry and manufacturing output was 1.7 per cent and 1.6 per cent respectively, and the services sector output growth was 2.8 per cent between 1990 and 2001.[4] Furthermore, the trade of SSA was approximately US$230 billion in 2002, representing an abysmal 1 per cent of total world trade. What is even more, the share of intra-African trade in the continent's total trade volume has hovered at 10 per cent (IMF 2004). What this means is that for a variety of reasons, explicable and otherwise, the typical African country is more likely to procure a product from Europe and/or from North America than from a neighbouring African country. This has translated into a mountain of debt for the continent. For instance, the debt burden for the subcontinent soared from US$177 billion in 1990 to US$230 billion in 2001 (World Bank 2004).

Compared with other parts of the world, especially in the southern hemisphere, the SSA condition is equally troubling. Indeed, in just about every category of social, economic and even political measurements, SSA countries prop up global rankings. Even when the rate of return on investment is higher in SSA than in any other region for MNCs, the sub-region still lags in capital inflow. For example, the *per capita* foreign direct investment (FDI) flow into SSA was roughly US$18 in 2001, a stark contrast with Latin America's roughly US$132, East Asia and Pacific's US$26 (excluding Japan), the euro zone's US$893, the US's US$454 for the same period.[5] Additionally, Africa's share of global FDI in 1998 was a paltry 1.7 per cent in 1998, compared with Latin America's 9.2 per cent, East Asia and Pacific's approximately 7 per cent, the euro zone's 36.5 per cent and the US's 17.5 per cent. Even five of the 15 most corrupt countries in 2004 were in SSA, according to Transparency International's corruption perception index.[6] Furthermore, measured in terms of human poverty index, human development index, physical quality of life index, and *per capita* HIV/AIDS infection, SSA countries and their people occupy the unenviable position of being (among) the poorest and most vulnerable in the world. In a global context, therefore, African economies are profoundly susceptible and peripheral.

According to several studies by the United Nations Economic Commission for Africa (UNECA) and the World Bank, it is estimated that in order for abject poverty to even be halved on the African continent by 2015, its countries would have to grow their economies by at least 7 per cent per annum. This is quite a daunting task, given the continent's precarious history since the 1960s, and given the limited efficacy of myriad economic strategies that have been attempted in the past to kindle its development. In this era of globalization and economic liberalization, it seems African countries would need to reconsider their approach to trade and investment, the twin engines of economic growth.

Trade, openness and economic development

The diverging economic development of nations over time has been the subject of research for economists since the very start of their science. And the last word has not been said, although many insights have been gained during two and a half centuries of the debate. Excellent reviews of that literature already exist; hence, that effort will not be needlessly repeated here.[7] For the purposes of this chapter it is useful to point to the theories of international trade that promise individual economies that implement free trade that they will achieve the maximum level of welfare attainable, given their resources. The more countries participate in free trade, the better the results (Bhagwati 2002). Although trade theories are logically convincing and have relevant messages for practical policy making, empirical research has not brought complete certainty. There are still many methodological problems. For instance, in a cross-country empirical analysis, the World Bank concluded that 'trade goes hand-in-hand with faster growth' (World

Bank 2002: 5). However, the World Bank notes that causality is more difficult to prove. Rodrik *et al.* (2002) review much of the recent empirical literature on the determinants of economic growth. They advance three lines of thought. First, they posit theories that hypothesize that geography is the main explaining variable for economic growth. The second school of thought puts international trade or the integration of a country into the world economy at the centre of the explanation, while in the third strand of thought, institutions are regarded as the critical factor for economic growth.

Much energy has been devoted to finding instruments for the explaining variables – trade/integration and institutions – in order to exclude reverse causality, that is, from growth to trade and institutions.[8] After putting these in a combined estimation procedure, Rodrik *et al.* find that 'the quality of institutions trumps everything else' (2002: 4). Furthermore, they find many links among the explaining variables. One of them, and highly relevant for our research, is that institutional quality has a positive and significant effect on integration in the world economy. Islam and Montenegro (2002) have also investigated and confirmed this relationship, be it in a reversed direction of cause and effect. They argue that there are at least four reasons why more open economies have better institutions.

First, economic agents compete better with better institutions, and thus countries will try to improve their institutions, in order to attract economic agents and ultimately increase overall economic welfare. Second, openness brings more competition among agents, which will make rent seeking and corruption more difficult. Third, better institutions are demanded to manage the risks that are associated with trading with unknown partners. Finally, there is a learning process based on the institutional conditions under which foreign agents work. Consequent to their empirical research, Islam and Montenegro find that 'openness in trade is significantly and consistently *correlated* with measures of institutional quality that focus on economic features such as the rule of law, corruption and government effectiveness measures' (2002: 14). It seems plausible to posit that there is a dual causality between trade openness and institutions. Rodrik *et al.* find that the impact of a change in institutional quality on trade openness is three times larger than the effect of a change in openness on institutional quality (Rodrik *et al.* 2002: 8). Following this, we hypothesize that *AGOA is more effective than EBA in stimulating exports, as it makes preferences dependent on institutional quality*.[9] The two preference donors select beneficiaries on widely different benchmarks. The US has a number of criteria concerning domestic and foreign policies, while the EU only has the benchmark of being on the UN list of LDCs. One might argue that the US only offers preferences to economies where a minimum of institutional quality is present, which is a basic factor for the promotion of economic development and export development.

In order to analyze this proposition, it is necessary to make some remarks on institutional quality. There are several definitions of institutions. One definition is that institutions establish the 'rules of the game' for a society. This is not far from North's definition that defines institutions as the formal and informal constraints on political, economic and social interactions. Institutions that establish an incentive structure that reduces uncertainty and promotes efficiency are considered to be 'good' institutions. At a more concrete level, institutions may be defined as particular organizational entities, procedural devices and regulatory frameworks (IMF 2003). Such institutions may have a positive effect on economic performance by promoting better policies. Examples of institutions that promote positive economic performance via better policies include trade agreements that bind tariffs between signatory countries (to the extent that tariffs are set and predictable), and statutory provisions that establish the independence of a central bank (which removes the manipulation of interest rates for political expediency). One may thus try to measure institutional quality in absolute/relative terms based on some established global metrics, or according to how economic agents perceive them. For particular purposes, perceptions matter most, especially for investors. Furthermore, in the medium/long term, perceived institutional quality will not remain higher than real institutional quality.

An overview of EBA and AGOA

Everything but Arms

The EU has a long tradition of granting preferential market access. In fact, the establishment of the EEC in 1957 included preferential access for overseas countries and territories. These preferences evolved eventually into the Lomé Convention preferences, and continued under the Cotonou Agreement until 2008. Many beneficiary countries are now negotiating reciprocal free trade arrangements (Economic Partnership Agreements or EPAs) with the EU. Among them are many LDCs. At present, it is not clear whether these countries will opt for EPAs or EBA.[10] In 2002, the beneficiary countries in SSA overwhelmingly continued to export under the ACP preferences (UNCTAD 2003: 48).

EBA evolved out of the EU GSP, which the supranational entity first applied in 1971. The EU felt that it had to harmonize the preferential systems for both ACP and non-ACP LDCs after the 1996 WTO Ministerial meeting in Singapore. This was accomplished in 1998 by granting the latter group of LDCs the same preferential treatment as the ACP group. EBA goes a step further: by abolishing tariffs as well as quantitative restrictions it will offer even more favourable market access than the Lomé preferences, always considered as the top of the 'pyramid of preferences'. EBA was introduced in March 2001 for an undefined period. In contrast to the Cotonou Agreement and the EPAs that will result from it, EBA is a unilateral gesture by the EU, not bound by international law. For example, the EU may unilaterally invoke the safeguard measures of EBA, thus temporarily withdrawing preferential treatment.

Eligibility

EBA has been created in favour of, in principle, all LDCs. The main yardstick for eligibility is being on the UN list of LDCs. This list contains 50 countries, of which only Myanmar has been excluded from the EBA regime. A majority of 34 LDCs is in SSA (see Appendix 1.1 in Chapter 1). In principle, all may use EBA to get preferential access to the EU.

Product coverage

There are a few exceptions on free access, beyond what the title of the system implies. Some very important products will be brought under the system in a gradual way. The tariff on bananas has been reduced step by step, to zero on 1 January 2006. Free entry for rice and sugar will be phased in between 2006 and 2009 by expansion of the duty-free tariff quotas, to be replaced by quota-free entry in 2009. The Commission monitors the preferential imports of these sensitive imports very closely. As far as the gradual phasing in of free access gives rise to serious problems to EU producers, including 'serious disturbance to EU markets and their regulatory mechanisms', the EU will apply safeguard measures.

Preferential margins

The LDCs in SSA have been exporting to the EU under the Lomé preferences since 1975. These preferences cover almost 100 per cent of ACP exports. Thus, ACP LDCs' exports to the EU already enjoy free entry. The main exceptions are in agriculture, where there are specific duties and entry prices for particular products, both processed and unprocessed. A recent UNCTAD study mentions specific MFN rates on cane molasses, fresh tomatoes (plus entry prices), sweet corn, garlic and sorghum (UNCTAD 2003: 50). EBA will abolish these barriers. The tariff quotas for rice and sugar appear to provide ample room for expanding trade by the beneficiary countries.

Although the coverage of EBA is very complete, the effective preferential margins are often low or zero. In 2002, the EU imported US$8.5 billion worth of goods from the ACP LDCs. Of this, only US$2 billion was dutiable, the rest entered at zero MFN rates from any source (UNCTAD 2003: 38 and 48). The conclusion is that the added export stimulus that can be expected from the EBA regime for the SSA LDCs is in the area of agricultural products.

Rules of origin

As an extension of the GSP, the rules of origin of that system also apply for the EBA scheme. The most important difference with the Cotonou preferences is the larger room for accumulation of origin under the latter system. The rules of origin under EBA are that a change of heading under the Harmonized System must have taken place in the originating country. Accumulation of origin is allowed for members of the Association of South East Asian Nations (ASEAN), the South Asian Association for Regional Cooperation (SAARC), the ANDEAN and the Central American Common Market (CACM). For a number of products more rules apply. This is the case for fish and fish preparations and for clothing and textile products.

For the latter products, there is the requirement of double-stage transformation. In a somewhat bitter tone, a study by UNCTAD draws the conclusion that:

> much of the evidence of the link between origin requirements and low utilization derive from the discussion papers and debates arising from the UNCTAD Working Group on Rules of Origin and later Sessional Committee on Rules of Origin. These intergovernmental bodies met regularly at UNCTAD from early 1970 until the mid-1990s. Since little has changed in the GSP rules of origin since their inception, many of the findings of the studies and reports presented at these meetings remain fully valid.
>
> (UNCTAD 2003: 71)

Brenton and Özden (Chapter 7 of this volume) show that less restrictive rules of origin may induce substantial export flows in particular exports by LDCs.

African Growth and Opportunity Act[11]

On 18 May 2000, US President Bill Clinton signed the AGOA into law as Title 1 of the US Trade and Development Act of 2000. It was the culmination of a protracted and chequered history that dates back to the second term of the Clinton presidency, when the on-again, off-again Africa Growth and Opportunity Bill was first mooted. Lesage and Kerremans (Chapter 5 of this volume) present more details on the parliamentary history of AGOA. The Bill, which was presented to members of the US Congress as a measure that would not only help spread US values, primarily (economic) freedom in Africa, but also concomitantly create economic opportunities for US businesses via trade, foreign direct investment, and technology transfer, was intended to liberalize the African market in order to benefit from globalization. The Bill, which the President touted as a win–win undertaking for both the US and the African continent, either 'died' or was 'dead on arrival' many times on Capitol Hill due to opposition from various constituencies, but for different reasons. For instance, powerful interest groups in the US, most notably the textile industry/lobby, opposed the Bill, arguing that many of its provisions would seriously threaten US jobs. Similarly, African governments opposed the Bill, because they deemed its litany of eligibility requirements too onerous, unpalatable, and a threat to their economies.

The original AGOA bill has since been re-enacted as part of the 2002 Trade Act, which President George W. Bush signed into law in August 2002. Otherwise known as the AGOA II legislation, it improved upon and clarified aspects of the original AGOA Bill. Among the changes in AGOA II were the addition of Botswana and Namibia, neither of which qualified for this concession under AGOA I, to the category of 'lesser developed beneficiary countries' to utilize fabric manufactured from anywhere in the world. The special concession was granted to the two SSA countries, because their *per capita* income was less than US$1,500 (according to the World Bank's 1998 classifications, which were employed for determining eligibility). Mauritius also got the permit to use these rules of origin.

Additionally, AGOA II allows hybrid cutting, that is, fabric cutting that occurs both in the US and in AGOA countries, unlike under AGOA I, when fabric cutting that occurred in both the US and an AGOA country was deemed ineligible.

Objectives

One of the objectives of AGOA and its trade concessions is to encourage SSA countries to promote free market institutions and structure, increase trade and investment activities between the US and SSA, stimulate economic growth in SSA, and facilitate the integration of SSA into the global economy. The underpinning of the AGOA strategy is to use trade and investment, the twin engines of economic growth, to alleviate poverty, bridge the economic welfare divide, and foster the development of SSA. Through AGOA, SSA countries would have access to much-needed US credit and technical know-how. Concomitantly, AGOA would nurture capacity building in SSA, which, in turn, would create additional market opportunities and stronger economic partners for the US business community.

Eligibility

The AGOA list of eligibility criteria at country level is quite long. As AGOA is a derivation of the GSP, there is a list of eligibility criteria that applies to all countries that want to benefit under the GSP. The criteria are rather diverse. A country will not qualify for AGOA if it is a communist country (unless it is member of the Bretton Woods institutions), a member of a commodity cartel, supports another country that has significant adverse effects on US trade, does not comply with international law, supports terrorism, does not meet certain minimum labour standards (or make progress towards them). In deciding on the GSP status of a country the US President will take into account the level of economic development, whether other developed countries give preferential treatment to that country, the trade policy and protection of intellectual property rights of the country and whether the country has taken action to reduce trade-distorting investment practices and barriers to trade in services. Under AGOA a number of specific eligibility requirements have been enacted. The SSA country that wants to receive AGOA benefits should have or be making progress toward establishing:

- A market-based economy that protects private property rights and minimizes government interference.
- The rule of law and political pluralism.
- Rules of the international trading order (national treatment, protection of intellectual property rights, etc.).
- Policies to reduce poverty, including providing basic public services and access to them, and promoting the development of private enterprise.
- Programmes to combat corruption and bribery.
- The protection of minimum labour standards.

Furthermore, a country is not eligible if it undermines US national security or foreign policy interests, or engages in gross violations of internationally recognized human rights or supports acts of international terrorism. Accordingly, and based on the recommendation of the United States Representative (USTR), 34 SSA countries were initially determined to have fulfilled the aforementioned criteria, according to a 2 October 2000 proclamation by President Bill Clinton. Subsequently, the US government added Swaziland (2001), Côte d'Ivoire (2002), Gambia and the Democratic Republic of Congo (2003) and Angola and Burkina Faso (2004) to the list of eligible countries. In contrast, and relying on the eligibility criteria, the US government revoked the eligibility of Central African Republic and Eritrea (2004) and Côte d'Ivoire (2005). Appendix 6.2 gives a summary of the reasons for not accepting countries as AGOA beneficiaries. All told, President Bush signed a proclamation on 30 December 2003 that declared 37 SSA countries eligible for AGOA benefits in 2004.

Product coverage

Virtually all products of AGOA SSA countries may be exported to the US free of duty, in accordance with the provisions of the Act or its GSP provisions. Indeed, more than 95 per cent of US imports from AGOA beneficiary countries in 2003 qualified for duty-free concession treatment. This was possible because of at least three important AGOA provisions. First, all products that relevant agencies of the US government determine to be not import-sensitive, when imported from SSA, are to be accorded duty-free protection by the President. Thus, in December 2000, the President granted duty-free treatment to over 1,800 tariff products (including footwear, luggage, handbags and watches). Similarly, the President granted duty-free treatment to almost 5,000 products that are available to non-AGOA GSP beneficiary countries through 30 September 2015. Second, the AGOA scheme also provides duty-free and quota-free concessions to apparel made: of US yarns and fabrics; of SSA yarns and fabrics (subject to a cap); in designated LDCs (the 'lesser developed countries' as discussed above) of third-country yarns and fabrics (subject to a cap); and of yarns and fabrics not produced in commercial quantities in the US. Third, other eligible apparel includes certain cashmere and merino wool sweaters, and hand-loomed, hand-made, and ethnic fabrics. All told, very few exports of AGOA beneficiary SSA countries do not qualify for duty-free concessions.

Rules of origin

The GSP rules of origin – in principle, a 35 per cent increase in value added in the beneficiary country – apply to AGOA exports as well. Special rules apply for textiles and clothing, as discussed under the heading of product coverage.

Empirical analysis

This section is devoted to a discussion of the empirical enquiry, that is, the data and the method of analysis. From the foregoing, it is apparent that the criteria for the EBA and the AGOA schemes differ considerably, although there are somewhat comparable welfare criteria in the EU and US initiatives. For example, the US has domestic policy/institutional/foreign policy criteria for eligibility that the EU does not have, at least not in such an operational form. In other words, whereas it is possible for any given SSA country's eligibility for benefits to change from one year to another under the AGOA regime, the continuity of eligibility for SSA countries under the EBA scheme is more certain. Under the EBA scheme, eligibility for benefits does not vary from year to year, but instead depends on whether the beneficiary country is a LDC. In any event, the number of eligible SSA countries for this enquiry, depending on the period covered, will likely differ for the two preferential regimes.

Relative institutional quality

To find out whether AGOA really discriminates between SSA countries on their institutional quality, we will test the hypothesis that *the institutional quality of AGOA-eligible countries is higher than in SSA countries in general and EBA countries in particular.*

The data for institutional quality were obtained for SSA countries from the World Bank Governance and Anti-corruption Data set.[12] Table 6.1 shows the average scores of the variables, on a scale that runs from −2.5 to +2.5. The lowest score, −2.5, is for the worst institutional quality, while +2.5, or the highest score, represents the best institutional quality. In general, the table shows low scores for all SSA countries on all indicators. There is a general pattern in the table – the average scores for AGOA countries are somewhat higher than for all SSA, while the average scores for EBA are somewhat lower than for the SSA category. This applies for all variables. It confirms our hypothesis that AGOA-eligible countries have better institutional quality than EBA countries by virtue of the more stringent vetting criteria of the US preferential scheme.

In general, the scores per country show that the degree of correlation between the scores at the country level is high. Although the score for the AGOA beneficiary countries is better on average, a few of them have relatively low scores. If we take the scores for the Rule of Law indicator, for example, it is striking that a few of them have scores that are less than −1 on the −2.5/+2.5 scale. This holds true for Republic of Congo, Cameroon, Côte d'Ivoire (removed in 2005), Kenya, Nigeria and Rwanda. The higher score for AGOA countries is mainly due to a few countries that have relatively high scores, viz. Botswana, Cape Verde, Mauritius, Namibia and South Africa. Of these, only Cape Verde is also eligible under the EBA scheme. Our conclusion, therefore, is that on average, AGOA selects countries that have a higher institutional quality than SSA in general, although a few have relatively weak performance on some governance indicators.

Table 6.1 Quality of governance in SSA countries and subgroups, 2002

Average	Voice and accountability	Political stability	Government effectiveness	Regulatory quality	Rule of law	Control of corruption
SSA	−0.63 (0.72)	−0.54 (1.01)	−0.71 (0.58)	−0.65 (0.59)	−0.67 (0.64)	−0.60 (0.58)
AGOA	−0.44 (0.68)	−0.30 (0.90)	−0.52 (0.51)	−0.45 (0.48)	−0.43 (0.55)	−0.42 (0.56)
EBA	−0.75 (0.65)	−0.60 (0.99)	−0.87 (0.47)	−0.79 (0.49)	−0.77 (0.50)	−0.69 (0.48)

Source: the data were obtained/calculated from the World Bank, 'Governance Research Indicators Dataset'.
Standard deviations in parentheses.

Geography

Transport costs as such hamper trade just as tariffs and non-tariff barriers to trade. For many poor countries transport costs outweigh trade barriers. 'For the majority of sub-Saharan African countries, the tariff incidence amounts to less than 2 percent, while the transportation cost incidence often exceeds 10 per cent' (World Bank 2001). Pure distance and natural obstacles such as seas and mountains increase transport costs. Although improvements in transport technology have reduced transport costs substantially, distance between trading partners remains a significant factor in the explanation of trade flows. Gravity models are rather successful in explaining bilateral trade flows by using distance as the variable that encompasses transaction cost in international trade. In many trade relations, distance is an adequate proxy for the cost of transport, insurance and of crossing borders. However, in trade among very unequal partners, transaction cost may not be proportional to distance. Low road quality, inadequate port facilities, high cost of crossing borders and inefficient service suppliers on the part of the poorer partner may increase transaction cost substantially. This applies even more for landlocked countries. Limão and Venables (2001) find that land distance adds a much higher amount to transport cost than does sea distance. Being land-locked adds costs that cannot be fully explained by land distance. Apparently, transit has its own cost in the form of delays, uncertainty, special charges by the transit country, and transport coordination problems. As a result, 'the representative landlocked [SSA] economy has transport costs 50 per cent higher and trade volumes 60 percent lower than the representative coastal economy', according to Limão and Venables (2001).[13]

Thus, the distance between an exporting SSA economy and the economy of destination is not sufficient to control for transaction cost. We will include two variables in our estimations. First, we propose the land distance in Africa, that represents the generally higher cost of land transport in general and the low quality of transport infrastructure in SSA countries in particular. For this variable we take the distance between the geographical centre of the exporting SSA country and the seaport through which the country ships its exports. Second, we control for being landlocked by including a dummy variable that represents the cost of transit.

Stimulus on exports

We employ a gravity model to analyse the effectiveness of the two preferential systems. This approach is frequently used to model bilateral trade flows in order to test the effects of common borders, common language and culture, the change of trade policy regimes and other phenomena in international trade relations. The model is based on Newton's law that states that the gravity between two objects is positively related to their masses and negatively related to the distance between them. Tinbergen (1962) conducted one of the pioneering studies in this field in the early 1960s. Linnemann (1966), Leamer and Stern (1970) and Anderson (1979), among others, provided the theoretical underpinning of the gravity model. The general form of the gravity equation that we used for this enquiry is:

$$\ln X_{ij} = \beta_0 + \beta_1 \ln GDP_i + \beta_2 \ln GDP_j + \beta_3 \ln Distance_{ij} + \mu \tag{1}$$

where:

- X_{ij} represents export from country i to country j. In our analysis, the exporting countries are all 48 SSA countries (see Appendix 1.1 in Chapter 1) that are eligible under AGOA, EBA and/or 'Lomé-style preferences', depicted as i. The countries j are the destinations for countries i's exports in 2002, as reported in the *2004 IMF Direction of Trade Statistics.*
- β_0 is a constant.
- GDP_i is the 2002 gross domestic product of the exporting country as given in the UNDP *Human Development Report 2004.*
- GDP_j is the 2002 gross domestic product of the importing country, also obtained from the *Human Development Report 2004.*
- $Distance_{ij}$ is the distance between the geographical centres of the exporting and importing countries. Distances were calculated from the coordinates given in the *CIA Factbook,* 2005.
- μ is an error term.

In order to control for variables that are not included in the general gravity equation, we include variables for the internal distance in the exporting SSA economies and transit countries and a dummy for the status of being landlocked. Finally we control for institutional quality. The dummies for AGOA and EBA are used to find out whether these preferential systems have an impact on the exports of the countries that export under these systems. This expands the general form of the gravity equation into:

$$\ln X_{ij} = \beta_0 + \beta_1 \ln GDP_i + \beta_2 \ln GDP_j + \beta_3 \ln Distance_{ij} + \beta_4 \ln DtoSeaport$$
$$+ \beta_5 DummyLLD + \beta_7 POLSTAB + \beta_8 RULEOFLAW + \beta_9 DummyAGOA$$
$$+ \beta_{10} DummyEBA + \mu \tag{2}$$

where:

- DtoSeaport is the distance from the geographical centre in the exporting SSA economy to the nearest seaport in order to take land distance in SSA into account. Seaports were taken from Export 911 at www.export911.com.
- Dummy LLD is 1 for landlocked SSA economies and 0 for coastal economies.
- POLSTAB and RULEOFLAW are variables for political stability and the rule of law in the exporting countries in 2002. These were taken from the World Bank *Governance Research Indicators.*
- Dummies for AGOA and EBA are 0 if there is no preferential treatment and 1 if the particular destination applies one of the two preferential systems.

Discussion of the results

The estimation results are presented in Table 6.2. The first equation is the most simple gravity equation. Compared with the other, 'augmented' equations, this simple form explains relatively much of the variations in exports by SSA economies. All explaining variables are highly significant and have the expected sign. The second equation shows that being landlocked significantly reduces exports compared with coastal economies, as we expected. The larger distance to the nearest seaport is largely responsible for this barrier on exports, as the coefficient of the dummy for being landlocked falls by 80 per cent and becomes insignificant after the inclusion of the variable for the distance to the nearest seaport (equation 3). The latter variable is more general: both coastal and landlocked economies that have a large distance from their geographical centre to the nearest seaport are significantly hampered in their exports. In equation 4, two governance variables are included. Political stability is not significant and does not have the expected sign. One might speculate that this is caused by the 'resource curse', to which many SSA countries are susceptible. Thus, resources (oil and other minerals in particular) may simultaneously promote exports and undermine political stability (Sachs and Warner 2001). The variable for the rule of law has the right sign and is significant. This confirms the expectation that economies that have higher institutional quality will have a better export performance. The effectiveness of AGOA and EBA is captured in equation 5. Both preferential systems have a positive sign but only AGOA has a significant effect on SSA exports. The earlier finding that AGOA selects beneficiaries that have better institutions, combined with the result of equation 4 that a better rule of law promotes exports, probably explains the effectiveness of AGOA. The ineffectiveness of EBA may be caused by the low-quality institutional environment in which SSA LDC exporters operate, and/or by the circumstance that these exporters have an alternative to EBA. The latter might be relevant, as it is a well established fact that many exporters continue to use the 'Lomé-style' preferences instead of EBA. Thus, we substituted the EBA dummy for a Lomé dummy (equation 6). This results in a significant coefficient of the right sign, indicating that such preferences are effective. Finally, we left out the net oil-exporting SSA countries in 2002 (Angola, Cameroon, Democratic Republic of the Congo, Chad, Côte d'Ivoire, Democratic Republic of the Congo, Equatorial Guinea, Gabon, Nigeria, Republic of the Congo, Sudan). Oil exports have a large impact on the pattern of destination of exports, and preferences have no effect on these exports, as MFN tariffs are zero. The result is reported under equation 7. It is striking that the governance indicators have become insignificant, just as the distance to the nearest seaport. In contrast, the landlocked dummy now has a much higher coefficient than before, while the dummies for AGOA and Lomé preferences are significant as well. The change compared with equation 6 is that the coefficients of the two preference systems are now of comparable value, while the significance of the coefficient of the Lomé dummy is higher than the one for the AGOA dummy. This still leaves the question open of the effectiveness of the EU and US preferences for the LDCs only. Equation 8 is the same as the

Table 8.2 Estimation of gravity equations for 2004 exports in 2005

Dep. var LOG(EXPORTS) 2,443 observations	Equation							
	1	2	3	4	5	6	7 1,841 obs.	8 1,347 obs.
C	7.639712	7.844034	9.324245	8.311230	8.338763	7.983183	7.930154	9.668524
LOG(GDP origin)	1.006751	0.978702	1.059299	1.012403	1.018214	1.020793	1.024848	0.589156
LOG(GDP dest)	0.774771	0.775437	0.783769	0.788078	0.767486	0.714689	0.693855	0.649867
LOG(DISTANCE)	-1.441416	-1.448038	-1.482493	-1.500559	-1.488464	-1.442570	-1.392600	-1.302599
DUMMY LLD		-0.387895	-0.084073*	-0.233484	-0.226110*	-0.237319	-0.451697	0.236151*
LOG(DtoSEAPORT)			-0.235051	-0.113428	-0.124600	-0.114863	-0.071009*	-0.473798
POLSTAB				-0.019137*	-0.019175*	-0.025444*	-0.023454*	0.067333*
RULEofLAW				0.304714	0.289927	0.295204	0.077844*	0.029045*
DUMMY AGOA					0.957591	1.306953	0.861281	0.799281*
DUMMY EBA					0.179996*			
DUMMY LOME						0.713293	0.757801	0.738608
R squared	0.387978	0.391431	0.396686	0.398589	0.400608	0.406576	0.433550	0.305544
Adj. R squared	0.387225	0.390432	0.395448	0.396858	0.398389	0.404381	0.430765	0.300869

Note:
* Not significant at a 95 per cent confidence interval.

previous one, but was estimated for the LDCs only. We find that AGOA has an insignificant effect on the exports of these countries, while the 'Lomé-style' preferences have a significant effect. Distance to the nearest seaport is a significant hampering factor for these countries.

Returning to the research hypothesis (AGAO is more effective in promoting exports than EBA, as it makes eligibility for preferences dependent on institutional quality), we can conclude that for 2002:

- EBA does not have an observable effect on the exports of the beneficiary countries in SSA.
- SSA LDCs use the 'Lomé-style' preferences, and these are effective in stimulating the exports by these countries and for the SSA group at large.
- AGOA is effective for the beneficiary countries. However, as an instrument to promote exports by SSA LDCs, AGOA does not have a significant impact.
- Geographical factors have an important impact on SSA exports. The distance between exporting and importing country is significantly hampering exports. There is a separate local factor in the shape of being landlocked and/or being far from a seaport. The latter factor is particularly strong for the LDCs (equation 8).
- Variables of institutional quality have a rather low explanatory power. Political stability is an insignificant variable, while the rule of law is often significant albeit with a relatively low coefficient. Probably this is a result of the fact that institutional quality is low in almost all SSA countries and thus cannot explain much of the variations among these countries' exports.

A few remarks concerning these conclusions should be made. First, the equations were estimated for 2002. In that year, EBA was new. This may partly explain the low utilization of the opportunities offered by EBA. Thus, in later years economic operators may be better informed and may make better use of EBA. The phasing in of DFQF access for bananas (2006) and rice and sugar (2009) will also promote the utilization of EBA.

Second, our empirical research shows the incomparability of AGOA and EBA. The two systems are often mentioned together as measures in favour of the LDCs. We have shown that AGOA does not have a significant effect on SSA LDCs exports, although it is effective for a large number of *other African countries than LDCs*. EBA is only accessible for LDCs – and not effective either, but 'Lomé-style' preferences under Cotonou are effective *for these least developed countries*. Thus, a better comparison would be between AGOA and 'Lomé-style' preferences. Equation 6 addresses this and shows that the two are effective, while AGOA has a higher coefficient (1.31 against 0.71), indicating a bigger impact on exports. This difference is due to the selectiveness of AGOA and the different rules of origin, as argued by Brenton and Özden (see next chapter of this volume).

Should the EU apply a set of criteria comparable to what the US has for AGOA? It might be argued that Cotonou is a step in this direction. In 2008, the 'Lomé-style' preferences will come to an end, and will be replaced by either EPAs or non-reciprocal preferences (GSP or EBA). It is to be expected that most SSA LDCs will opt for EPAs (Babarinde and Faber 2004). If that happens, the LDCs concerned will have to fulfil the obligations of EPAs in terms of trade liberalization, policy reforms and regulatory coordination. Whether this will effectively promote the institutional quality of the SSA LDCs depends on the function of EPAs as a commitment mechanism for both the ACP countries and the EU (Faber 2005; Bilal in Chapter 11 of this volume). For this to happen, all parties should share the conviction that EPAs are beneficial, and positive and negative sanctions should be available to help overcome developing partners to overcome external shocks that undermine their capacity to meet their obligations and to sanction EPA members that do not live up to their obligations.

Appendix 6.1

Exports by sub-Saharan African countries, 1980 to 2003, in value (US$million) and average annual change

Value

1980	1990	1995	2000	2001	2002	2003
76,009	69,544	76,537	92,035	87,824	90,704	111,097

Change

1980–90	1990–00	2000–01	2001–02	2002–03
–0.5	3.2	–4.6	3.3	22.5

Source: UNCTAD *Handbook of Statistics 2004* (New York and Geneva, 2004).

Appendix 6.2

Arguments given to reject countries for AGOA, or with delay of trade preferences, as of 2003

Angola 'Not AGOA eligible, largely because of concerns related to economic management and human rights'.[a]

Burkina Faso 'Not AGOA eligible, largely because of concerns related to its foreign policy and activities related to the outbreak of the crisis in the Côte d'Ivoire.'

Burundi 'Not AGOA eligible, largely because of concerns related to economic reform, rule of law, and labour and human rights.'

Democratic Republic of the Congo 'AGOA eligible, with delayed implementation of AGOA trade benefits. Democratic Republic of the Congo (DROC) will become eligible for AGOA trade benefits upon formation of a transitional government.'[a]

Equatorial Guinea 'Not AGOA eligible, largely because of concerns related to economic reform, rule of law, political pluralism, labour and human rights.'

continued

Liberia 'Not AGOA eligible, largely because of concerns related to economic reform, rule of law, corruption, human rights, and the government's destabilizing policies in the region, particularly its participation in the conflict in Sierra Leone.'

Sierra Leone 'AGOA eligible. Sierra Leone became eligible for AGOA trade benefits in October 2002. Implementation of Sierra Leone's trade benefits under AGOA had previously been delayed pending progress in stabilizing its political and security situation.'

Togo 'Not AGOA eligible, largely because of concerns related to economic reform, political pluralism and rule of law, corruption, poverty reduction and human rights.'

Zimbabwe 'Not AGOA eligible, largely because of concerns related to its poor performance on economic management, rule of law, political pluralism, corruption, and human rights.'

Source: USTR (2003).

Notes:

Three countries (Comoros, Somalia and Sudan) did not apply for AGOA. The review was made by the inter-agency Trade Policy Staff Committee.

a Declared eligible in 2004.

Notes

An earlier version of this chapter was presented at the biannual conference of the European Union Studies Association (EUSA) in Austin TX, 31 March–2 April 2005 and in the conference 'Everything but Arms': All about Nothing?', Ghent, 5–6 December 2005. The authors thank the participants in these conferences and Harry Garretsen, Piet Keizer, Marc Schramm and Joppe van de Ree of the Utrecht School of Economics for their stimulating comments. The authors are responsible for all remaining errors.

1 The data for these and related comparisons in this section of the chapter were obtained from World Bank (2004).
2 This and the subsequent comparisons were based on data in the '*Financial Times* Survey: FT 500,' *Financial Times*, 27 May 2004, pp. 10–15, and World Bank (2004).
3 This and the subsequent comparisons were based on data from World Bank (2004).
4 Ibid.
5 Ibid.
6 http://www.icgg.org/corruption.cpi_2004_data.html (accessed 11 July 2006).
7 See, among others, Easterly (2001) and Winters (2004).
8 Geography is the only realistic independent explanatory variable.
9 Pursuing this line of thought, one might posit that trade preferences as such have a relatively small effect on economic growth, as trade openness does comparatively little to improve institutional quality, the main cause of economic growth.
10 We have argued elsewhere that the two schemes are mutually exclusive and that it is likely that most of them will opt for an EPA (Babarinde and Faber 2004).
11 This section relies on, *inter alia*, the fourth annual report on AGOA (USTR 2004) and http://www.agoa.gov/ (accessed 11 July 2006).
12 Available at http://info.worldbank.org/governance/kkz2002 (accessed 11 July 2006).
13 Pilegaard discusses transport costs as a barrier to Zambian exports in Chapter 8.

References

Anderson, J. (1979) 'A theoretical foundation for the gravity equation', *American Economic Review*, 69 no 1: 106–16.

Babarinde, O. and Faber, G. (2004) 'From Lomé to Cotonou: business as usual?', *European Foreign Affairs Review*, 9, no 1: 27–49.

Bhagwati, J. (2002) *Free Trade Today*, Princeton NJ: Princeton University Press.

CIA (2005) *The World Factbook*, available at http://www.cia.gov/cia/publications/factbook/fields/2011.html (accessed 11 July 2006).

Easterly, W. (2001) *The Elusive Quest for Growth: Economists' Adventures and Misadventures in the Tropics*, Cambridge MA: MIT Press.

Faber, G. (2005) 'Economic Partnership Agreements and regional integration among ACP Countries', in O. Babarinde and G. Faber (eds) *The European Union and the Developing Countries*, Leiden and Boston MA: Martinus Nijhoff Publishers.

IMF (2003) *World Economic Outlook 2003*, Washington DC: International Monetary Fund.

IMF (2004) *Direction of Trade Statistics Yearbook 2004*, Washington DC: International Monetary Fund.

Islam, R. and Montenegro, C.E. (2002) 'What determines the Quality of Institutions?', Background Paper for the World Development Report 2002, Washington DC: World Bank.

Leamer, E.E. and Stern, R.M. (1970) *Quantitative International Economics*, Boston MA: Allyn and Bacon.

Limão, N. and Venables, A.J. (2001) 'Infrastructure, geographical disadvantage and transport costs', *World Bank Economic Review*, 15, 3: 451–79.

Linnemann, H. (1966) *An Econometric Study of International Trade Flows*, Amsterdam: North-Holland.

Rodrik, D., Subramanian, A. and Trebbi, F. (2002) 'Institutions Rule: The Primacy of Institutions over Geography and Integration in Economic Development', CEPR Discussion Paper Series No. 3643, London: Centre for Economic Policy Research.

Sachs, J. and Warner, A. (2001) 'Natural resources and economic development: the curse of natural resources', *European Economic Review*, 45: 827–38.

Tinbergen, J. (1962) *Shaping the World Economy: Suggestions for an International Economic Policy*, New York: Twentieth Century Fund.

UNCTAD (2003) *Trade Preferences for LDCs: An Early Assessment of Benefits and Possible Improvements*, New York and Geneva: UNCTAD.

UNCTAD (2004) *Handbook of Statistics 2004*, New York and Geneva: UNCTAD.

UNIDO (2004) *Industrial Development Report 2004: Industrialization, Environment and the Millennium Development Goals in sub-Saharan Africa*, Vienna: United Nations Industrial Development Organization.

UNDP (2005) *Human Development Report 2004*, New York: UNDP.

United States Trade Representative (USTR) (2003) '2003 Comprehensive Report on US Trade and Investment Policy toward sub-Saharan Africa and Implementation of the African Growth and Opportunity Act'. The Third of Eight Annual Reports (Washington DC: 2003) Available at: http://www.ustr.gov/Trade_Development/Preference_Programs/AGOA/Section_Index.html (accessed 11 July 2006).

United States Trade Representative (USTR) (2004) '2004 Comprehensive Report on US Trade and Investment Policy toward sub-Saharan Africa and Implementation of the African Growth and Opportunity Act'. Available at: http://www.ustr.gov/Trade_Development/Preference_Programs/AGOA/Section_Index.html (accessed 11 July 2006).

Winters, L.A. (2004) 'Trade liberalisation and economic performance: an overview', *Economic Journal*, 114: F4–F21.

World Bank (2001) *Global Economic Prospects and the Developing Countries: Making Trade work for the Poor, 2002*, Washington DC: World Bank.

World Bank (2002) *Globalization, Growth and Poverty*, New York: Oxford University Press.

World Bank (2004) *2004 World Development Indicators*, Washington DC: World Bank.

7 The effectiveness of EU and US unilateral trade preferences for LDCs

Rules of origin in the clothing sector

Paul Brenton and Çaglar Özden

The 2001 Doha Ministerial Declaration reaffirmed the commitment of the World Trade Organization (WTO) to the least developed countries (LDCs) through trade preferences and trade-related technical assistance. The declaration lays down the objective of 'duty-free, quota-free market access for products originating from LDCs' and pledges to 'consider additional measures for progressive improvements in market access for LDCs' (paragraph 42). This chapter discusses how the design and implementation of policies to achieve the first objective are crucial in determining how much market access preferences actually provide. Trade preferences should be designed to help developing countries access global markets in industries in which they have a comparative advantage. Trade preferences can also play a crucial role in assisting the process of export diversification away from dependence on traditional commodity exports that leads to vulnerability to commodity price fluctuations. Labour-intensive products should form the basis for global competitiveness and for a more diversified export base for the LDCs, given their level of development and their relative endowments of factors of production. These products are typically subject to relatively high levels of duty in developed countries so that preferences can be an important stimulant to the establishment of supply capacities in the LDCs. However, the rules of origin that define trade preferences also often limit the extent to which these preferences in labour-intensive products can be exploited.

This chapter focuses on the 'Everything but Arms' (EBA) initiative of the European Union (EU) and compares and contrasts it with the preferences of the US towards African and Caribbean LDCs under the African Growth and Opportunity Act (AGOA) and the Caribbean Basin Initiative (CBI). The preferences of the EU and US cover different countries, in particular, Asian LDCs that are not eligible for the extended preferences that have been offered to African and Caribbean countries by the US (see also Appendix 1.1 in the introductory chapter of this volume). There is also different commodity coverage, as the US schemes do not provide for duty-free and quota-free (DFQF) access for all products. For example, textiles and a range of agricultural products are effectively excluded. The different schemes also have different rules of origin and the chapter discusses how these might explain the different supply responses that have been observed. Even though

EBA offers DFQF access to LDCs, it appears to have had little impact on the exports of LDCs to the EU in aggregate. The majority of preference-receiving countries obtain very little benefit from the EBA, reflecting the fact that their exports are still dominated by commodities (such as cocoa, coffee, minerals) which are not subject to duties in developed countries.

Whereas Chapters 5 and 6 of this volume compare EBA and AGOA with regard to the underlying political dynamics and the role of market size, geography and institutions respectively, this contribution mainly concentrates on the role of the rules of origin in the clothing sector. The clothing sector is a key sector for many developing countries since they can exploit their comparative advantage in low labour cost operations. In addition, production technology is relatively simple, start-up costs are comparatively small and scale economies are not important. These all favour production in low labour cost locations. At the same time, many clothing products remain subject to relatively high tariff barriers in the preference-granting developed countries. The chapter shows that for a number of LDCs preferences appear to have contributed to a substantial increase in exports, but only when the rules of origin have been accommodating. In the case of the EBA, restrictive rules of origin for clothing products severely constrain LDCs in their ability to diversify and expand exports to the EU.

The trade impact of EBA

EBA was launched by the then Commissioner Lamy as evidence that the EU was serious about 'getting the most disadvantaged to share in the fruits of trade liberalization' (EU 2001). However, the introduction of EBA has not led to any apparent increase in the share of LDCs in EU imports and has not prevented a continuation of the long-term decline in the share of ACP (Africa, Caribbean and Pacific countries) LDCs of the EU market (Figure 7.1). This reflects that the vast majority of EU imports from the LDCs (99.5 per cent in 2001) were already entering DFQF prior to EBA due to existing preferences and that many countries' exports are dominated by products that are subject to zero Most Favoured Nation duties.

Exports from LDCs to the US show a slightly different pattern (Figure 7.2). The share of ACP LDCs in US (non-oil) imports has been mildly increasing since 2000, the year in which AGOA was signed into law. In contrast the import share of the non-ACP LDCs has been declining. It is worth bearing in mind that at present the EU market is much more important for LDCs than the US market. In 2004, EU (non-oil) imports from LDCs amounted to around US$15 billion whilst US imports from LDCs were just over US$6 billion.

These broad trends in LDC exports to the EU and the US do not reveal the contribution of trade preferences granted to the exports of the LDCs. Figure 7.3 seeks to capture this for a single year by presenting the value of preferences, which is the margin of preference [equal to the duty that would have been paid without preferences] multiplied by the value of exports for each product summed across all products divided by the total value of exports for each of the (non-oil exporting)

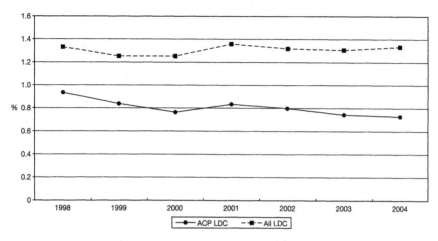

Figure 7.1 LDC share of EU imports (non-oil): no apparent impact of EBA

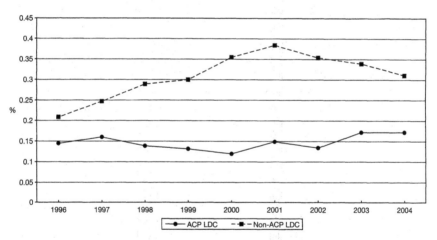

Figure 7.2 LDC share of US imports (non-oil): recent increases for ACP but decline for Asian LDCs

countries that receive preferences under both the EBA and AGOA. The calcu-lations take into account that many of the ACP countries are also eligible for preferential access to the EU market under the Cotonou Agreement. Finally, the value of preferences is based on preferences actually requested and captures that preferences may not be fully utilized. The main culprit for such under-utilization is the rules of origin that will be discussed in more detail below.

Figure 7.3 shows that for the majority of countries preferences do not amount to substantial amounts of the value of exports to the EU and the US. Only for one country, Malawi, does the value of preferences exceed 10 per cent of the value of exports for both the EU and the US. Malawi's preferences in the EU are driven

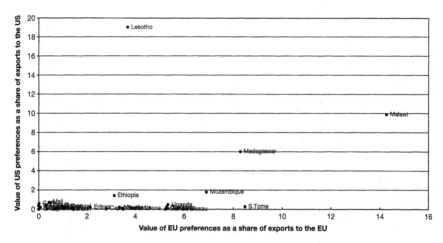

Figure 7.3 Value of preferences in the EU and the US for African LDCs in 2002

primarily by sugar, whilst preferences in the US are derived from tobacco. Lesotho has significant preferences in the US amounting to almost 20 per cent of the value of exports. However, for the majority of the 27 countries depicted in the figure the value of preferences to the EU and US amount to a small fraction of exports to these markets. In 2004–06 a small number of African LDCs, including Uganda, Tanzania and Cape Verde, have been able to increase exports of clothing to the US under AGOA. The high tariffs on these products entail that the value of US preferences for these countries are now likely to be more substantial than is depicted in the figure.[1]

EU and US preferences for clothing

The clothing sector has been a major example where developing countries have been able to significantly increase and diversify exports with positive effects on incomes, employment and poverty.[2] Trade preferences that assist countries in achieving international competitiveness in clothing are likely to have a significant impact on the beneficiaries. Figures 7.4 and 7.5 show EU and US imports of clothing from ACP LDCs (mainly Africa), distinguishing between knitted clothing (HS61) and non-knitted clothing (HS62). The reason for making this distinction is that the rules of origin requirements have different implications for the two types of products, as we will discuss in more detail below. Figures 7.6 and 7.7 show similar figures for the non-ACP LDCs, mainly countries in Asia.

Figures 7.4 and 7.5 both show strongly growing exports of clothing from the ACP LDCs to the US while at the same time exports to the EU have stagnated. While the dollar value of ACP LDC exports of clothing (both categories combined) to the US exceeded those to the EU by 40 per cent in 1996 they were almost six times greater in 2004. However, the growth of exports of clothing to the US has not been broadly based across countries. Three countries (Haiti, Lesotho, and

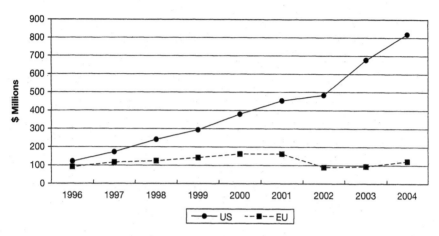

Figure 7.4 EU and US imports of knitted clothing from ACP LDCs

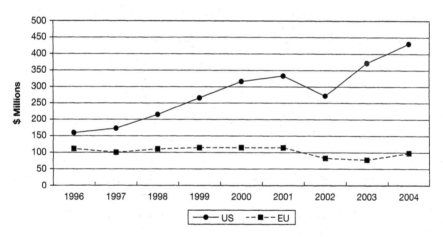

Figure 7.5 EU and US imports of non-knitted clothing from ACP LDCs

Madagascar) accounted for 94 per cent of US imports of knitted clothing from ACP LDCs and 80 per cent of imports of non-knitted clothing. Nevertheless, other countries appear to be emerging as exporters of clothing to the US, with six countries (Cape Verde, Ethiopia, Malawi, Mozambique, Tanzania and Uganda) exporting more than US$1 million of clothing in the first nine months of 2005.

The situation regarding the non-ACP LDCs is rather different. These countries do not receive preferences for their clothing exports to the US but are eligible for duty-free access to the EU (subject to the rules of origin). Figures 7.6 and 7.7 show that non-ACP LDC exports to the EU are increasing and most of the growth is taking place in knitted clothing products. Since 2000, growth in exports to the EU has substantially exceeded that to the US.

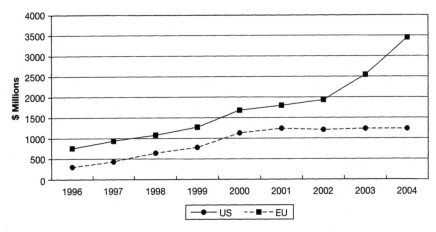

Figure 7.6 EU and US imports of knitted clothing from non-ACP LDCs

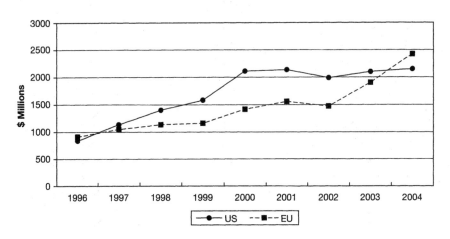

Figure 7.7 EU and US imports of non-knitted clothing from non-ACP LDCs

So, trade preferences appear to have played a crucial role in the expansion of a small number of ACP countries' exports of clothing to the US. At the same time EU preferences appear to have done little to support the development of supply capacities in clothing in these LDCs. We now discuss how the different rules of origin under the EU and US preferential schemes are likely to explain this differential performance.

When the US grants preferences for clothing products, such as under the CBI, the products requesting preferential access must satisfy the following conditions in the rules of origin. They must be

• Assembled from domestic or US-made and cut fabric, manufactured from domestic or US yarn.

- Cut and assembled from domestic or US fabric made with domestic or US yarn, sewn in Caribbean countries with US-formed thread.
- Knitted to shape (other than certain socks) from domestic or US yarns, and knitted apparel cut and wholly assembled from fabric formed in one or more beneficiary countries or in the US, from US yarn.

In short, the rules of origin for apparel require that articles need to be made from domestic or US fabric that in turn has to be produced from domestic or US yarn.

AGOA has substantially less restrictive rules of origin. The basic rule is that qualifying clothing articles must be made from US *or* sub-Saharan (regional) fabric or yarn. However, compared with all other preference programmes, AGOA grants special rules for countries that are designated as 'lesser developed'. These countries may use third-country fabric and yarn (for example, from China) and still qualify for AGOA preferences. As of today 24 countries are qualified for apparel preferences and all have been designated as 'lesser developed countries', with the exception of South Africa.[3] The special rule expires on 30 September 2007, but can be renewed by Congress, as has happened in the past. Also, AGOA limits imports of apparel made with regional or third country fabric to a fixed percentage of the aggregate apparel imported into the US. The cap is around 2.5 per cent for 2006. But is not a constraint on current export flows. It is the third-country fabric rule that has allowed countries such as Lesotho, and more recently Uganda and Tanzania, to take advantage of US preferences and expand production capacities and employment in the sector.

EU rules of origin for clothing require production from yarn. This entails that a double transformation process must take place in the beneficiary, with the yarn being woven into fabric and then the fabric cut and made up into clothing. Countries cannot import fabrics and make them up into clothing and receive preferential access, which constrains the value of the scheme for countries that do not have an efficient textile industry. The basic EU rule is slightly more flexible than the basic US rule, since clothing producers can globally source the yarn, whilst to be eligible for US preferences producers must use US yarn. However, the EU rules do not allow producers in African LDCs the flexibility they have under AGOA to source fabrics globally.

Finally, the restrictive rules requiring production from yarn have a different impact on the two broad types of clothing products, knitted and non-knitted. The rules of origin requirements are more costly for non-knitted items, since they prevent firms from sourcing fabrics (the key input) from the most appropriate and least-cost locations. For knitted items, since there is typically no fabric involved, this rule is less costly to satisfy. This can help to explain the trends for the LDCs in the graphs above. The liberal rules of origin that allow global sourcing of fabrics has allowed African LDCs to expand exports of both knitted and non-knitted items. The structure of clothing exports to the US and the EU for the non-ACP countries shows that in the US market, where there are no preferences, exports of non-knitted products are more important than exports of knitted products. In contrast, knitted products are more important in exports to the EU. There are preferences for both types of clothing products but the rules of origin for knitted products are easier to satisfy. For example, in 2004 Bangladesh exported US$1.25 billion of non-knitted products to the US and US$0.5 billion of knitted clothing. In the same year Bangladesh exported around US$2.7 billion of knitted clothing to the EU and US$1.9 billion of non-knitted clothing.[4]

Thus, the rules of origin governing clothing products are a crucial element explaining the differential supply responses to the available preferences for LDCs in the EU and the US. We return to this issue in more detail below but first discuss the prospects for the future development of the clothing sector in LDCs in the face of the recent removal of quotas on China and India that some commentators suggest will devastate suppliers in small developing countries.

The future of LDC exports of clothing

On 1 January 2005, the 30-year-old quota system regulating imports of textiles and clothing products into rich countries was finally dismantled. This occurred despite a last-gasp attempt by certain importing countries, in alliance with a number of developing countries that had benefited from the restrictions on China and other Asian countries, to delay the reform of the most protected manufacturing sectors. Much has been written about the likely impact of these reforms and the fear that markets will become swamped by Chinese products, with adverse implications for other developing-country producers that export to the developed countries. In the face of fierce competition from China is it feasible for small LDCs to develop capacities to export clothing products?

Clearly, it is too early after the removal of quotas to draw firm conclusions about the subsequent impact. Here we look at information on imports of textiles and clothing products in to the EU and the US in the first six months of 2005 and show that the impact of the removal of quotas is likely to be more nuanced than many commentators have suggested and that there are opportunities for many developing countries to continue to export mainly clothing products, given a favourable domestic climate.

While US imports from China have increased strongly since the ending of the quotas, imports from a number of other developing countries have also increased significantly (Figure 7.8). US imports from Bangladesh, a country that many thought would be hit hard, increased by more than 20 per cent in the first half of 2005. In fact US imports from a range of countries across Africa, Asia and South America increased. On the other hand, imports from a range of developing countries in Africa, Asia and South America as well as imports from developed countries declined. In absolute terms the largest declines in imports are from Hong Kong, Korea, Mexico, Taiwan and Macau, respectively.[5]

Figure 7.9 shows a similar situation in the EU market. Imports from China have increased strongly but so have imports from a number of other developing countries, including Egypt, Cambodia, Bangladesh, Madagascar and Vietnam. Large declines in imports have also been recorded for Macau and Hong Kong. There

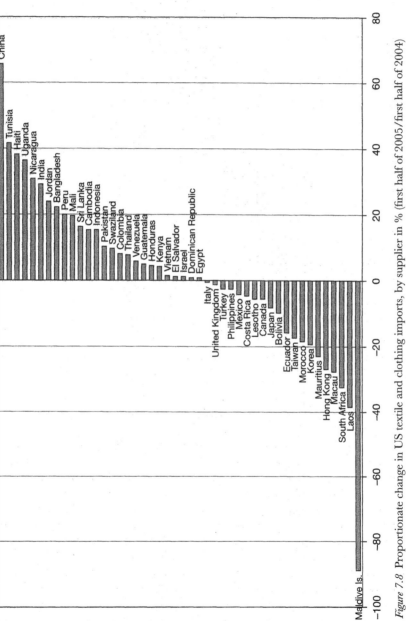

Figure 7.8 Proportionate change in US textile and clothing imports, by supplier in % (first half of 2005/first half of 2004)

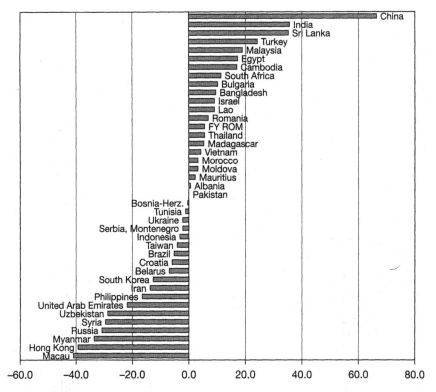

Figure 7.9 Proportionate change in EU textile and clothing imports, by supplier in % (first half of 2005/first half of 2004)

have also been significant reductions in imports from a range of countries in Eastern Europe, the Middle East and Asia.

The changes for countries such as Sri Lanka and Bangladesh are in sharp contrast to some of the predictions of the impact of the end of textile and clothing quotas that suggested that 1 million jobs would be lost in Bangladesh and that one-half of factories in the industry in Sri Lanka would close down (as reported in Oxfam 2004). It is too early to conclude with confidence that there will not be a major negative impact on these countries. Buyers in developed countries may be postponing decisions to change sources to China while there is uncertainty concerning protection in the EU and US against Chinese products. Nevertheless, the fact that a number of countries that were expected to be hit hard by the removal of quotas against China managed to increase the value of their exports to the EU and the US, even in product categories in which Chinese exports have grown the fastest, suggests that opportunities for a range of developing countries to export, especially in the clothing sector, will remain.

While global buyers will review their sourcing strategies, many have indicated that they will not risk placing all their orders with China and will seek to maintain a more diversified sourcing structure. In addition, China cannot fill each and every niche. Textiles and clothing have a large number of niches, which vary by country due to vastly differing tastes. Even a small share of a small niche of the US or a large European country market can have a substantial economic impact on a small developing country.

It is worth stressing the differences between the EU and US markets. Large buyers in the US, such as Walmart, look to suppliers who can satisfy economy-wide demand for standard products. The EU market remains considerably fragmented along national lines. Footwear is a sector in which the EU and the US imposed quantitative restrictions against China and other East Asian suppliers in the late 1980s, but which were subsequently removed in the 1990s. China now accounts for around 70 per cent of US imports of footwear. China's share of EU imports of footwear is less than 15 per cent. Finally, China and India are experiencing high growth rates. Rising domestic demand will reduce some of the excess supply that can be exported. Rising wages will reduce competitive margins.

What are the elements that are likely to comprise a successful strategy to support the clothing sector in developing countries?

Review domestic trade policies to remove constraints on clothing exports

For clothing producers the ability to effectively source fabrics and other inputs from the global market is a crucial factor in the ability to compete. Many developing countries apply high import duties to products used as inputs in the textiles and clothing industries. This is a major constraint to competitiveness and capacity to export final products. Thus, local producers in these and other developing countries are paying considerably higher than world prices for their inputs. In many cases there are drawback schemes to reimburse exporters for these duties. However, poor implementation often leads to delays in payment and exporters have to incur other costs, in terms of paperwork and time.[6] Thus, many developing countries continue to shackle their clothing sector with restrictive duties on the inputs they use.

Given the imperative of being able to satisfy short delivery times, the time and the costs of satisfying customs procedures on both imported inputs and the exported product as well the availability, cost and speed of transport services are important determinants of competitiveness in the clothing sector. In many developing countries, and especially in Africa and South Asia, long customs clearance times and poor transport infrastructure act to push producers further away from key global markets.[7] For example, in Bangladesh onerous documentary requirements and complicated customs procedures entail that it takes an average of 57 days to satisfy all import requirements and 35 days to satisfy export procedures, much longer times for import (24 days) and export (20 days) than in China. Similarly in Ethiopia the average import requires 57 days and the average export 46 days to satisfy the necessary procedures.[8] Thus, initiatives, such as customs reform, improvement of port and transport infrastructure and the stimulation of competition among transport service providers, that reduce customs clearance and transport times are important measures to support the competitiveness of the clothing sector.

Improve the business environment

Many countries have lower labour costs than China in the production of clothing – the relevant metric is the price per one standard minute. Moldova, for example, has per-minute costs that are only two-thirds of those in China. Labour costs are also lower in Bangladesh than in China. Many countries in Africa also have lower labour costs than China. However, in many of these countries the advantage of low labour costs is undermined by high indirect costs resulting from a hostile business environment. For example, the World Bank estimates that the cost of doing business in Africa is as much as 40 per cent above that of other developing regions. Countries that implement policies to provide a favourable business climate will support firms in being able to compete in both domestic and overseas markets.

Exploit non-labour cost advantages

Labour cost is only one element that influences the sourcing decisions of global buyers. Proximity and speed of turnaround can be equally important. This puts added emphasis on customs procedures and capabilities and transport capacities. Many buyers, particularly in Europe, are turning to products with very limited shelf lives and hence short production runs so that flexibility can give firms a critical competitive edge. In addition, labour and environmental standards are increasingly becoming a key issue for many buyers that may affect their sourcing decisions. Reports in the press conjecture that the continued success of the clothing industry in Cambodia – exports to both the EU and US increased substantially in 2005 – reflects a strategy of enhancing labour standards that has led to increased quality and has captured the attention of international buyers. In addition, it has been suggested that the constraints on cutting labour costs have led factory owners to push the government to tackle corruption and unnecessary bureaucratic rules.[9] This issue is ripe for more detailed analysis and assessment.

Increasing the effectiveness of preferences: reform the rules of origin

Whilst developed countries can assist the LDCs in addressing the key issues above through technical assistance and development support they can also help the LDCs adjust to the more competitive environment for the export of clothing products by increasing the effectiveness of preferences granted to these countries. Preferences can be enhanced, and the commitment to improve market access opportunities for LDCs made in the Doha Declaration fulfilled, through a fundamental reform of the rules of origin to allow LDCs permanent access to the global inputs they need to be able to develop long-run competitiveness.

The role of the rules of origin

Rules of origin are necessary to ensure that only products from beneficiary countries are granted trade preferences and avoid products from other countries being transhipped through the beneficiary to avoid the payment of tariffs in the final market. Avoiding trade deflection is in the interest of the country that grants the preference as well as the one that receives it. However, rules of origin for trade preferences are set by the preference-granting country and are often manipulated to achieve other objectives, such as protecting domestic producers. When domestic interests are allowed to influence the scope and terms of rules of origin, the outcome tends to be far more restrictive than is necessary to prevent trade deflection. Too often, the result is that market access for the beneficiaries is limited, and the objective of promoting developing country exports is undermined.[10] In practice, products that are important for many developing countries – such as textiles, clothing, and processed agricultural products – are often excluded from preference schemes (pointing to the need for duty-free access for *all* products). When preferences are made available for sensitive products, they are usually accompanied by particularly restrictive rules of origin.

When a product is produced in a single stage or is wholly obtained in the beneficiary country, then its origin is relatively easy to establish. In all other cases rules of origin must specify the methods to be used in ascertaining that the product has undergone 'sufficient working' or processing or been subject to a 'substantial transformation' in the beneficiary country. Such tests are designed to determine that products have not been transhipped from a non-qualifying country or been subject to only minimal processing. The higher the level of working that is required by the rules of origin, the more difficult they are to satisfy and the more they constrain market access (relative to what would be required simply to prevent trade deflection).

For many products, and for almost all sensitive products, including clothing, the current EU rules of origin link the implied definition of 'substantial transformation' to the sourcing of raw materials.[11] Thus, a clothing producer in Africa who imports fabrics from Asia may not receive preferences. A cannery may not use fish originating from outside the preferred jurisdiction. A producer of bakery products may not use imported flour. In effect, the rules of origin deny producers in developing countries freedom to choose the source of their inputs, which can mean that production capacities that could have had a substantial economic and development impact are denied preferential access to the EU. In some cases it may mean that investment in such capacities may not take place.

It is sometimes asserted, and often by those in developed rather than developing countries, that strict rules of origin are needed so as to stimulate the emergence of integrated production structures in developing countries to maximize the impact on employment and to ensure that it is not just low value-added activities that are undertaken in the developing countries. However, strict rules discriminate against small developing countries where the possibilities for local sourcing are limited. Second, there is no evidence that strict rules of origin over the past 30 years have done anything to stimulate the development of integrated production structures in developing countries. In today's globalized world strict rules of origin constrain firms in developing countries in integrating into global and regional production networks and in effect act to dampen the location of any value-added activities.

If needed inputs are competitively produced by local firms, exporters will always source locally to avoid transport and other trade-related costs. However, if the right inputs are not available locally at a competitive price, then producers must look to overseas suppliers. When rules of origin prohibit the use of imported inputs they may force exporters to use materials of higher cost, thus undermining their ability to compete in global markets. The aim of trade preferences, of course, is to stimulate exports and export diversification in beneficiary countries and so to provide a boost toward achieving global competitiveness and sustainable economic activity. That objective can be completely undermined by rules of origin that dictate the use of high-cost inputs.

The opportunity for reform in the EU

The reform of rules of origin of the Generalized System of Preferences (GSP) that govern EBA preferences, currently being considered by the EU, is a critical opportunity to support exporters in the LDCs.[12] EU trade preferences would be considerably enhanced if producers in small developing countries were allowed to choose freely the source of the inputs they require, a freedom denied by the current rules. The opportunity to give meaning to existing preferences will be lost, however, if protectionist interests succeed in maintaining or even increasing the restrictiveness of the rules of origin.

The current EU rules of origin are product-specific, sometimes complex, and often restrictive. Their restrictiveness is reflected (1) in low utilization rates of preferences and (2) in the significant expansion of exports under other preference schemes that have more liberal rules. They are particularly restrictive with respect to products of comparative advantage for Africa and low-income countries, namely, processed agricultural products and clothing. For the non-ACP LDCs that are eligible for the EBA but for no other EU preference scheme, less than 50 per cent of the available EBA preferences are being utilized. The principal export of Bangladesh to the EU is clothing, yet exporters request preferences for only half of their clothing exports. Why? Because they must use the cheapest and most appropriate fabrics in order to be competitive. The best source of such fabrics may be China, but EU rules of origin disqualify from preferences clothing made from Chinese fabrics.

Utilization rates understate the restrictive impact of rules of origin. The EU's restrictive rules of origin for key products such as clothing can be prohibitive for small firms in low-income countries, keeping them out of the market altogether. Utilization rates show the share of *actual exports* that are eligible for preferences but do not request them. They do not capture the potential export capacities stifled by restrictive rules of origin. The differential supply responses in Africa to US and EU preferences for clothing illustrate this principle. Liberal rules of origin have strongly stimulated US imports of clothing from African LDCs, while EU imports have stagnated because of strict rules of origin. This suggests, and is supported by anecdotal evidence from companies themselves, that there is a substantial export potential to the EU that is being constrained by restrictive rules of origin and which is not captured in data on utilization rates.

If the full market-opening opportunities of EBA are to be realized, a significant relaxation of EU rules of origin will be required. Recognizing that rules of origin have constrained the developmental impact of the GSP, the European Commission has proposed a value-added rule to define origin for all products. A preferable alternative would be to give developing countries, especially LDCs, the flexibility of satisfying *either* a value-added rule *or* a change-of-tariff-heading requirement. At what level should the value-added requirement be set and what degree of cumulation should be allowed? The Blair Commission (Commission for Africa 2005) proposed a value-added requirement on all products of no more than 10 per cent, which would allow African exporters the flexibility to source inputs and to exploit their comparative advantage in labour-intensive products.

The issue of cumulation

Cumulation is an instrument that allows producers to import materials from a specific country or regional group of countries without undermining the origin of the final product. In so doing, it offsets the restrictiveness of a particular set of rules of origin. However, as long as the most efficient producer of the required inputs is excluded from the area of cumulation then the offset will be partial and may well be worthless. We have no strong empirical evidence of the importance of cumulation provisions, but the information we do have does not suggest a strong impact.[13]

If the value-added requirement is low enough, there is no need for cumulation. If it is high, then the rules must allow LDCs to source inputs globally if they are to be able to exploit their comparative advantage. Current EU proposals for limited regional cumulation are likely to do little to mitigate the restrictiveness of high value-added requirements. Global cumulation, by contrast, would allow sourcing of inputs from regional partners and help promoting regional integration; by not limiting cumulation to the region, it also would avoid excluding the lowest-cost source of inputs. However, a low value-added requirement (10 per cent) common across all products would be more transparent, simpler for firms to satisfy, and easier to administer by customs and other agencies. Setting a high value-added requirement (such as 35–40 per cent) and allowing limited regional cumulation is most unlikely to provide for a substantial easing of the rules of origin. It could even make them *more* restrictive.

Fears that a low value-added requirement or global cumulation would benefit mainly China are overstated. In fact, the benefits to China probably would be very small. Many producers in developing countries already choose to use Chinese inputs, because the cost penalty of not using the least expensive inputs is often greater than the tariff preference. Restrictive rules of origin and limited cumulation will not induce these producers to use other sources of inputs. By contrast, a low value-added requirement (or global cumulation) will allow developing-country producers that have chosen for competitive reasons to use Chinese inputs to receive preferences and, in principle, realize higher returns for their exports. If competitive inputs are available locally they will always be used. Global cumulation will benefit China only in cases where producers previously sourced inputs domestically or from a country in an area of cumulation solely for the purpose of receiving preferences.[14]

Conclusion

Reform of the rules of origin governing EBA preferences for the LDCs offers the EU a crucial opportunity to improve market access for LDCs and other developing countries and to enhance the value of their trade preferences. Current EU rules of origin severely limit the ability of producers in small developing countries to source inputs on a global basis and still receive preferences. Trade preferences should be designed to help countries reach global competitiveness in industries in which they have a comparative advantage. In the globalized economy such competitiveness must be based on the freedom to source inputs from the most suitable and least expensive location. The global market exacts a high penalty on producers that use inappropriate or high-cost inputs. The US experience with AGOA shows that a bold approach to rules of origin can provoke substantial supply responses from developing countries and help them build a more diversified export base. It is important that the US now entrenches the flexibility it allows exporters in sourcing inputs to clothing products by making the third-country fabric provision permanent, by moving to reduce the current 35 per cent value added requirement for other products and by offering DFQF access to all LDCs for all products.

By reforming the rules of origin to provide a value-added requirement of no more than 10 per cent across all products in EBA (with the alternative of satisfying either the value-added rule or a change-of-tariff-heading requirement) the EU would widen access to its market in a manner consistent with the Doha process and with the ongoing adjustment to the expiration of quotas on textile and clothing products.[15] The impact of liberalizing the rules of origin on EU firms will be at most minimal. Products from LDCs are unlikely to be competing with products produced in the EU. Even a doubling of EU imports from LDCs would increase the share of LDCs in (non-oil) EU imports to less than 3 per cent and hence a much smaller share of EU consumption. In the US, where the textiles and clothing industry has proved to be very effective in trade policy lobbying, African LDCs are able to export with non-restrictive rules of origin. Hence, the key factor determining whether the EU reforms its rules of origin in a way that enhances the EBA and supports exporters in the poorest countries is political will.

Notes

The views expressed here are those of the authors and should not be attributed to the World Bank. We are grateful to Gerrit Faber and Jan Orbie for comments and suggestions.

1 The data come from Brenton and Ikezuki (2005). Unfortunately, data after 2002 have not been made available to us by the European Commission.

2 Kabeer and Mahmud (2004) suggest that the production of garments for export in Bangladesh has generated 1.6 million 'new' jobs most of which were captured by women. Many of these workers tend to be migrants from poorer areas. These authors also find that wage levels for garment workers were double that of other workers involved in non-tradable activities. There is, however, some evidence to suggest that workers in this sector are vulnerable to changing employment contracts and the increasing casualization of work (see Nadvi 2004).

3 Mauritius has joined the group of countries eligible for this third-country fabric rule after an amendment to the AGOA Acceleration Act of 2004 and following intense efforts by its government. The amendment limits Mauritius to a cap of about 27 million m^2 equivalents.

4 This is also reflected in the structure of ACP countries' exports to the EU. For example, the value of exports of knitted items from Mauritius to the EU was almost four times the value of exports of non-knitted products.

5 The declines for Hong Kong, Taiwan and Macau may reflect that under quotas a portion of mainland China's exports were handled by middlemen in these countries and recorded as their exports. Hence some of the recorded increase in China's exports reflects this reorganization of trade and part of the falling prices of imports from China is the result of the avoidance of the handling charges of these middlemen (see Mayer 2005).

6 In Bangladesh, for example, it has been reported that reimbursement takes 58 days on average and requires 6 per cent of additional expenditure to obtain the refund cheque (WTO 2005).

7 Transport cost as a barrier to trade is also discussed in Chapters 6 and 8 of this volume.

8 Source: World Bank Doing Business Database, www.doingbusiness.org.

9 See, for example, 'Labor standards help Cambodia keep customers', *International Herald Tribune*, 11 May 2005.

10 In seeking to persuade the Council to accept the EBA proposal, the Commission declared that 'granting of the regime is subject to strict compliance by the beneficiary countries with all the provisions applicable in this context, notably as regards the rules of origin' (General Affairs Council, 6602/1, 26 February 2001).

11 Block and Grynberg (2005) draw this out very clearly for processed fish.

12 See the EU rules of origin webpage at http://ec.europa.eu/taxation_customs/common/publications/info_docs/customs/index_en.htm (accessed 16 May 2006).

13 See, for example, UNCTAD and Commonwealth Secretariat (2001).

14 There is also the notion that more restrictive rules of origin are necessary to prevent fraud. This is misplaced. Prevention of fraud requires effective control whatever the nature of the rules of origin. With weak control mechanisms there can be fraud whether the rules of origin are restrictive or not.

15 If a beneficiary country feels that this is not commensurate with its development objectives it should be allowed to petition for a permanent derogation of more restrictive rules on its exports to the EU.

References

Block, L. and Grynberg, R. (2005) 'EU Rules of Origin for ACP Tuna Products (HS Chapter 16.04)', mimeo, London: Commonwealth Secretariat.

Brenton, P. and Ikezuki, T. (2005) 'The value of trade preferences for Africa', in R. Newfarmer (ed.) *Trade, Doha and Development*, Washington DC: World Bank.

Commission for Africa (2005) 'Our Common Interest: Report of the Commission for Africa'. Available online at http://www.commissionforafrica.org/english/report/introduction.html (accessed 15 May 2006).

EU (2001) 'EU approves "Everything but Arms" trade access for least developed countries'. Press release, Brussels, 26 February.

Kabeer, N. and Mahmud, S. (2004) 'Globalisation, gender and poverty: Bangladeshi women workers in export and local markets', *Journal of International Development*, 16: 93–109.

Mayer, J. (2005) 'Not totally naked: textiles and clothing trade in a quota-free environment', *Journal of World Trade*, 39: 393–426.

Nadvi, K. (2004) 'Globalisation and poverty: how can global value chain research inform the policy debate?', *IDS Bulletin*, 35: 20–8.

Oxfam (2004) 'Stitched up. How Rich-country Protectionism in Textiles and Clothing Trade prevents Poverty Alleviation', Oxfam Briefing Paper, April.

UNCTAD and Commonwealth Secretariat (2001) 'Duty and Quota Free Market Access for LDCs: An Analysis of Quad Initiatives', London and Geneva: UNCTAD and Commonwealth Secretariat.

WTO (2005) 'Options for Least Developed Countries to improve their Competitiveness in the Textiles and Clothing Business', Subcommittee on Least Developed Countries, WT/COMTD/LDC/W/37, Geneva: World Trade Organization.

8 Symbolic *and* effective?

An LDC perspective on duty-free and quota-free market access

Jess Pilegaard

As the most comprehensive market access initiative for least developed countries (LDCs) ever offered by the European Union (EU) or any other developed country, the 'Everything but Arms' (EBA) initiative would appear to be a decisive break with established trade and development policies (Smith 2000). As argued by then Trade Commissioner Pascal Lamy (Lamy 2002: 72, author's translation):

> no one had ever accepted to go beyond giving market access for essentially all products originating in the LDCs. This simple diplomatic euphemism basically signified that each and everyone reserved the right to limit imports of sensitive products, such as agricultural products or textiles.

EBA, on the other hand, would go beyond anything ever put on offer to the LDCs: the prospect of complete duty-free and quota-free (DFQF) access to the European market.

However, appearances can be deceiving. Critics were quick to point out a number of major flaws, the most important being the decision to defer market access on three of the more important product groups, namely sugar, rice and bananas. The exclusion of these products from the EBA initiative substantially reduced the immediate real value of the concession (Brenton 2003; Gibb 2006). To the cynics, it merely confirmed the hypocrisy of EU trade and development policy: EBA was basically a dose of hot air wrapped in symbolism (Jennar 2004). However, judging from the reactions of the LDCs, and the continued insistence of LDC trade negotiators on the importance of DFQF market access, the EBA initiative apparently hit the spot: the LDCs liked it and are currently asking for more of the same.[1] The LDCs would prefer a multilateralization of the initiative, giving it a legal standing in the WTO, whereby future conflicts would be subject to the Dispute Settlement Mechanism, but they are not questioning the utility of increased market access.

Ironically, experience suggests that increased market access may in fact be of limited immediate value to a good number of the LDCs. Structural constraints that limit their ability to effectively supply any major increases in demand would seem to significantly dilute the real value of initiatives like EBA.[2] However, in spite of the limited results achieved post-EBA, the LDCs have chosen to maintain DFQF access as the central objective in their multilateral trade policy. The present chapter attempts to explain this paradox.

The following section provides a bit of historical background on the LDC as an official classification device and the preferential trade regime that the LDC status confers upon a developing country. Focusing on the experience of Zambia, the chapter then proceeds with a cursory analysis of some of the constraints that limit the export capacity of LDCs and hence the utility of market access initiatives such as EBA. This analysis is based on an investigation of the Zambian sugar industry, followed by a more general discussion of the major internal barriers to trade, as identified by Zambia's Diagnostic Trade Integration Survey (DTIS). Against this background, the last section of the chapter attempts to explain the persistence of the DFQF agenda. Drawing on theoretical insights from the literature on international negotiations, it is argued that the popularity of the DFQF market access agenda has more to do with the politics of LDC negotiations than with immediate economic utility.

Background: UNCTAD and the least developed countries

In the early 1960s, the developing countries were seen as a rather homogeneous group of states, faced with broadly similar challenges, and eventually destined to follow a similar development path, cf. Rostow's highly stylized *Stages of Economic Growth* (1960). By the time of the first United Nations Conference on Trade and Development (UNCTAD) in 1964, there was growing acknowledgement of the need for a more differentiated classification, and the first session of UNCTAD thus drew special attention to the 'less developed' of the developing countries.

From the time of the second UNCTAD in 1968, the notion of 'least developed country' was gradually established as an official designation, although there was no agreed list of LDCs. Based on the work of UNCTAD in identification and classification of developing countries, the United Nations (UN) Committee on Development Planning recommended a list of countries and a set of criteria to the General Assembly in 1971. The list was gradually expanded from the 1970s to the 1990s, Botswana being the only country to actually graduate from the list in 1994.

An important part of the UNCTAD/LDC agenda was centred on trade preferences. The idea of extending trade preferences to boost the economic development of the developing countries goes back to the period of decolonization and political debates spurred by the declining terms of trade for agricultural commodities. The newly independent countries in Africa and Asia were facing declining world market prices for their main export commodities, and were consequently finding it extremely difficult to raise the foreign currency needed to finance their social and economic development policies. The newly independent countries needed foreign currency to purchase the technology that would eventually permit them to reach the 'take-off' stage, but their only real source of income was extremely uncertain due to downward fluctuations in the world market prices for primary products. Classical trade theory would have developing countries exporting agricultural produce while importing high-technology manufactures from the developed world: the developing countries exploiting their abundance of land and labour while the developed countries concentrate their efforts on more capital-intensive production. However, falling prices for agricultural produce made it increasingly difficult for developing countries to finance the desired import of technology from the developed countries. The worsening terms of trade basically made the development strategies advocated by classical economics increasingly unrealistic: selling bananas by the metric tonne was no fast track for technology modernization and economic prosperity. An increasingly prominent perception was that only the development of manufacturing sectors in the economies of the developing countries could provide stability in terms of job creation and export earnings.

The theoretical works of Raoul Prebisch and Hans Singer popularized the argument that the developing countries had to develop their manufacturing base in order to kick-start economic development. The economic theses developed by Prebsich and Singer made the case in favour of creating non-reciprocal tariff preferences to spur the export of manufactures from the developing countries. By giving developing countries privileged access to sell manufactured goods in the developed world, these countries would be given an opportunity to diversify their production structure and thus lessen their dependence on export earnings from primary products. In short: developing countries should develop their own industries to substitute expensive imports from the developed world, and start exporting manufactured goods that would fetch a higher and more stable price.

The 1947 General Agreement on Tariffs and Trade (GATT) had no provision to assist developing countries through preferential trade arrangements. Indeed, in 1947 the notion of 'developing country' did not really exist.[3] The first UNCTAD meeting in 1964, held under the chairmanship of Raoul Prebisch, then chairman of the UN's Economic Commission for Latin America, had initiated an analysis of how targeted trade preferences could be extended to developing countries. In 1968, the idea of a Generalized System of Preferences (GSP) whereby the industrialized countries could grant trade preferences to all developing countries was tabled at UNCTAD II. The introduction of this system necessitated a general waiver from the GATT agreement, which prohibited discriminatory trade practices. This waiver was granted in 1971 in the form of an 'Enabling Clause', which created the legal framework for the GSP. The clause was first adopted for a period of ten years, but it was subsequently renewed in 1979, for an indefinite period of time.

Under the Enabling Clause, preferential treatment (discrimination) in favour of developing countries is allowed, but the party extending the preferential treatment may not discriminate *between* developing countries, *except* for the benefit of LDCs. The GSP is the most extensive example of an attempt to utilize trade preferences as a tool to foster economic development in the developing countries (Cernat *et al.* 2003).

Successive UNCTAD conferences adopted specific LDC resolutions up through the 1970s, emphasizing the need for special measures to be adopted in favour of the LDCs. The same period saw the majority of the LDCs lagging still further behind. Determined to address this increasing marginalization of the LDCs, the General Assembly decided to follow the lead of UNCTAD by convening a special UN Conference on the LDCs, which was held in Paris in September 1981. The conference approved a special Substantial New Programme of Action (SNPA), which, however, failed to halt the seminal decline of the LDCs. The second UN Conference on the Least Developed Countries was held in Paris in 1990. The outcome of the conference echoed the concern that had been voiced during the past decades, and suggested a new programme of action to address the mounting challenges facing the LDCs.

The first three decades of special action programmes placed great emphasis on the need for special trade preferences for the developing countries in general and the LDCs in particular. The EBA initiative is thus firmly lodged within this historical tradition: it is discriminatory in the sense that it privileges the exports of LDCs, making it easier for this group of developing countries to sell their goods on the European market. Still, during the first three decades, trade preferences in favour of the LDCs were a relatively minor addendum to the multilateral trade system and the core business of the GATT: the LDC's received preferential treatment, but they did not play an active role in the GATT (Woolcock 2002: 3).

The criteria for belonging to the group of LDCs have been revised on a number of occasions since 1971. At present, there are three criteria: a low-income criterion, a human resource weakness criterion and an economic vulnerability criterion. In addition, the population must not exceed 75 million. (See Chapter 1 for a more elaborate discussion of the criteria.)[4]

Any country satisfying these criteria is structurally disadvantaged and the LDCs are thus almost by definition unable to exploit market access on a larger scale (the main exemption being Bangladesh, which was included on the original list of LDCs, before the introduction of the population ceiling) (Page and Hewitt 2002: 99). There are currently 50 LDCs on the UN's official list (see Appendix 1.1 in Chapter 1), Zambia being one of them.

An LDC is by definition poor, but there are several other developing countries with large segments of the population living in extreme poverty, that do not classify as LDCs, and that are consequently prevented from exploiting the preferential trade arrangements (e.g. India and Pakistan, Kenya and Zimbabwe). There are a number of other, semi-official classifications, including the UN-backed 'Landlocked Developing Countries', and the category of 'Small Island States'. The more general 'Lesser Developed Countries' – often abbreviated LLDC – is also common. In the present context, however, focus is on the 50 LDCs covered by the EBA initiative.

In order to provide some perspective on the 'structural disadvantages' facing the LDCs, the following section provides a more detailed analysis of the international trade performance of Zambia.

Zambia: a competitive producer priced out of the market

With two-thirds of the population living on less than US$1 a day, Zambia's domestic market is too small to support the sustained high growth in production and employment that would be necessary to achieve a notable reduction in poverty levels. Private sector development and export diversification are consequently necessary for achieving broad-based economic growth in Zambia. Recent years have witnessed concerted efforts to spearhead this development. However, in spite of a remarkable increase in non-traditional exports (NTE),[5] Zambia remains heavily dependent upon export earnings generated by a limited range of raw materials such as copper and cobalt. This dependence makes the Zambian economy highly sensitive to changes in external demand: following years of steadily declining copper prices, Zambia's share in world exports thus declined from 0.038 per cent in 1990, to just 0.014 per cent in 2003.[6] During the same period, the direction of trade flows has changed considerably; exports to the EU and Japan have declined, while the regional market (especially South Africa) has grown in importance (see Table 8.1).[7] In general terms, Zambia remains a marginal player in the global economy. Instead of becoming more integrated in the global economy, Zambia has become more integrated in the regional economy.

Zambia is obviously not representative of the LDCs as a whole, but in terms of global trade, the country does face a number of challenges or constraints that are almost endemic to the group of LDCs. A number of these problems can be exemplified through an analysis of the Zambian sugar industry, and the manner in which this industry has responded to the EBA initiative.

The Zambian sugar industry[8]

Zambia Sugar, which is by far the largest sugar producer in Zambia, has since 2001 been controlled by the South African company Illovo Sugar. In addition to South Africa and Zambia, Illovo holds a dominant position in Malawi, Swaziland, Tanzania, and Mozambique. It is estimated that the Zambian sugar industry is one of the five most cost-efficient in the world. As mentioned in Chapter 10 of this volume, Zambia is one of the six net exporting LDCs in sugar. Zambia is capable of *producing* sugar at a price that is highly competitive. However, Zambia's

Table 8.1 Direction of Zambia's international trade, 1990–2002 (%)

Type of country	Destination of exports			Origin of imports		
	1990–92	*1995–97*	*2000–02*	*1990–92*	*1995–97*	*2000–02*
Low-income	33.5	48.7	66.7	40.3	62.1	82.7
High-income	66.5	51.3	33.3	59.7	37.9	17.3

Source: Adapted from DTIS (2005: 11).

competitiveness is severely weakened by high transport costs, i.e. an under-developed infrastructure and lack of direct access to a shipping port. The total costs of getting a pound of Zambian sugar on the shelf in a supermarket in London is consequently much higher than the actual production costs. This means that other sugar producers, who benefit from a more developed infrastructure and easier access to shipping facilities, are able to price Zambian exporters out of the market. Or so they would be *if* the market for sugar were a free market. It is not. On the contrary, the sugar market is one of the most convoluted markets in the world. And that is basically the main reason why Zambia still has a sugar industry.

In 2004, Zambia Sugar produced 230,000 tonnes of sugar, exporting approximately half of the production.[9] Of this export, 27,000 tonnes went to the European market. Seven thousand tonnes were exported under the Sugar Protocol of the Cotonou Agreement, which guarantees a minimum price that is roughly equivalent to the internal price of sugar in the EU. Another 12,000 tonnes of sugar were exported under the Special Preferential Sugar agreement at a price approximately 15–20 per cent below the internal EU sugar price. Finally, Zambia exported 8,000 tonnes of sugar under the EBA initiative at a price roughly equivalent to the price of Special Preferential Sugar.

Approximately 25 per cent of Zambia's sugar exports were thus destined for the EU market. However, the earnings from the EU market constituted more than 40 per cent of the total sugar export earnings in 2004. The earnings stemming from the EU market have been rising steadily since 2001 because of new quotas under the EBA arrangement and adjustments to the Sugar Protocol (see Gibb 2006: 13; Chapter 10 in this volume).

According to Illovo, export earnings from the European market have acted as a catalyst for foreign investments in the Zambian sugar industry. Since 1996 over US$37 million have been invested in the Zambian sugar industry. The first major wave of investment was initiated in 1995, when the British sugar company, Tate and Lyle, became the major shareholder in Zambia Sugar. Over the following five years, US$30 million were invested in the sugar industry. About 75 per cent of this investment went into factory plant and machinery, signalling that the aim has been value addition in future sugar production. Since Illovo took over Zambia Sugar a further US$4 million have been invested, and again about 75 per cent of this has gone to factory plant and machinery. Illovo aims at expanding both the production volume and the production types that are being exported to the European market.

The present investments in the Zambian sugar industry are, according to Illovo, specifically motivated by the prospect of the full implementation of the EBA initiative in 2009, when Zambia will be able to export all types of sugar without duties or quotas being applied. (At present, EBA quotas are for raw cane sugar only.) This means that after 2009, a much higher proportion of the value addition will take place in Zambia. This will have a positive effect on employment levels and stimulate additional transfer of technology. It is estimated that employment at the factory level will rise, although expectations vary somewhat. In addition to this, the expansion of sugar production post-2009 will improve the market of cane sugar producers in Zambia. It is estimated that formal employment will rise by approximately 500 persons. The increase in the informal sector will arguably be much more important, as benefits from expansion will be felt in the cane growing community more generally.

As explained by Michael Brüntrup in Chapter 10 of this volume, the fall 2005 reform of the EU sugar regime should see a fall in the internal EU price of sugar over a number of years. Even though the outlook for the Zambian sugar industry would have been better without a reform of the EU sugar policy, Illovo still estimates that the overall effect will be positive.[10] This is primarily due to the fact that the reform creates certainty over a longer period of time. Over 2005–15, Zambia expects to be able to profit from the preferential access to the EU market where sugar prices – while steadily decreasing – are still expected to be 20–25 per cent higher than world market prices. Illovo thus estimates that increasing export volumes and the broader range of product types that can be exported to the EU market will compensate for the price reductions.

The Zambian sugar industry will also profit from an expected fall in EU sugar exports over the coming years. Because of the high transport costs, Zambian sugar will not be able to access markets where EU sugar currently holds a dominant position. However, since Zambia exports a large part of its domestic production at world market prices, it will still benefit from the increase in world market prices that will follow from a fall in EU sugar exports.

The EU sugar reform was received with mixed feelings in Zambia. The Zambian sugar industry is not interested in a general liberalization of the EU sugar market. There are other, more efficient sugar producers, with a much better export infrastructure, who would be able to outcompete Zambian sugar. The Zambian sugar industry is – in other words – still dependent on preferential treatment. Sugar is but one example, but it serves to highlight both the opportunities and the challenges that are associated with an initiative like EBA. The value of the initiative lies in the fact that it is discriminatory: it provides for a preferential treatment that is necessary for Zambian sugar to be competitive. The EBA initiative may have spurred investment, but only because it is discriminatory and because some minimum price differential is expected to remain in force. Market access is only interesting in so far as other potential suppliers (Brazil, Thailand, South Africa) can be prevented from entering the market. Without this preferential treatment, a country like Zambia looses its competitive edge. Less competitive LDC sugar producers are obviously facing an even more difficult situation.

Barriers to trade: beyond market access

As argued above, the international sugar trade is highly regulated. While developments in the Zambian sugar industry may provide valuable insights, it is arguably necessary to broaden the scope of analysis in order to obtain a more comprehensive understanding of the challenges currently facing Zambia.

Zambia's DTIS, which has been undertaken under the guidance of the Integrated Framework, provides a broader overview of the constraints facing

Zambian exporters.[11] The following provides a summary discussion of the major challenges facing Zambian exporters. Simplifying the analysis somewhat, the discussion will be structured around just five headings: market access, trade policy and customs administration, transport, quality and safety standards, and the somewhat vague 'enabling business environment'.

Market access

As argued above, market access is not the main obstacle facing Zambian exporters (DTIS 2005: vii).[12] As an LDC, Zambia stands in the centre of a cobweb of preferential trade agreements that confer duty-free access to most of the exports Zambia currently has to offer.[13] On any given product, Zambian exporters have a range of different export promotion schemes to choose from, ranging from the universal Most Favoured Nation (MFN) standard rate to the preferential (discriminatory) levels utilized under, *inter alia*, the GSP, the Cotonou Partnership Agreement, the EBA initiative, and AGOA. In addition, for the most important products exported by Zambia (copper and raw materials) the MFN tariffs are in fact either zero or extremely low, making tariff preferences irrelevant.

Still, as argued above, the discriminatory levels have been and continue to be very important for exporters of Zambian sugar. The immediate impact of the EBA initiative may have been limited, but as the analysis of the Zambian sugar industry suggested, trade preferences continue to play an important role for developing country exporters. These exporters are consequently concerned by the overall tendency for the standard MFN rates to fall, as this movement represents a *de facto* erosion of their competitiveness (see, e.g., Dickson 2004). With a gradually diminishing competitive edge, most LDCs will have to start addressing the domestic factors that act as barriers to increased exports, e.g. the transaction costs of cross-border trade, policy harmonization, and infrastructure or supply-side constraints more generally (see below).

Trade policy and customs administration

Like the majority of the LDCs, Zambia needs to strengthen the institutions that are responsible for developing, negotiating, and implementing trade policies. While Zambia performed remarkably well as LDC coordinator in 2005, the fact is that the *Financial Times* has more full-time reporters writing about the Doha Round than Zambia has professional staff actually negotiating it. There is a dearth of technical expertise and the limited capacity of the Ministry of Commerce, Trade, and Industry has clearly been stretched to the limit over the past 12 months, which have seen not only the regular WTO negotiations, but also increased movement on the Economic Partnership Agreement (EPA) with the EU (see below).[14]

The operational institutions, such as the Zambian customs administration, need to be overhauled and thoroughly modernized. Efforts have been under way for some years, but the complaints from the private sector continue unabated: the multiple control procedures and cumbersome physical inspections make for very long clearing processes, adding costs to the exporter while creating incentives for corrupt practices. Anyone having crossed an international border in Central/ Southern Africa will know how exhausting an experience it can be. Bringing a truckload of taxable goods along does not simplify matters.[15]

Transport

Zambia is big. Travelling from one end of the country to the other will easily take up to three days, provided you stick to the main roads, drive a 4 × 4 vehicle with all essentials (including a full jerrycan), avoiding both potholes and pit stops. The greater part of Zambia's road network was built in the decade immediately following independence (1964). Failure to ensure proper maintenance has led to a steady deterioration of the network. Unsurprisingly, there is a strong correlation between the quality of road infrastructure and transport costs. During the rainy season, when roads are particularly difficult to pass, transport costs rise dramatically. Bad roads increase the costs of traders, who systematically overload their trucks in order to recoup some of the extra costs, thus further aggravating the situation.

Irrespective of the physical state of the road network, the numerous checkpoints on most African roads represent an additional hurdle. At one point, the main road from Lagos in Nigeria to Abidjan in Côte d'Ivoire apparently displayed a staggering 69 checkpoints scattered over less than 1,000 km. That is equivalent to approximately seven checkpoints per 100 km.[16] There are fewer checkpoints in Zambia, but enough to make life difficult for commercial truck drivers.

High transport costs make goods more expensive. In a study reported by the WTO's *World Trade Report*, it is suggested that for the majority of the sub-Saharan countries, the share of international shipping costs in the value of trade is five times higher than the trade weighted *ad valorem* duty actually paid (WTO 2004). High transport costs increase consumer prices for imported goods and undermine the competitiveness of exporters in foreign markets. African countries, which have the highest transport cost rates in the world, thus also have the lowest share of international trade.

The domestic transport costs can be prohibitive, and with bulk imports from South Africa, small producers in the rural areas are finding it hard to compete. In the shops of the capital, Lusaka, you will often find that imported goods are price-competitive, even with products where domestic producers (from a theoretical point of view) *should* have a massive competitive advantage. The domestic production that is available in the shops is basically from the area of greater Lusaka (within a radius of 100 km) (DTIS 2005: viii).

The obstacles that stem from the long distances and the weak infrastructure are even more pronounced when it comes to exports. Zambia being landlocked, would-be exporters need to move their products across international borders in order to access a shipping port.[17] The three major regional ports – Durban in South Africa, Dar-es-Salam in Tanzania, and Beira in the Republic of Mozambique – are at a real distance of more than 1,500 km. Because of the dismal state of the

Beira access road, this option is not utilized to the same extent as the other two corridors: Copperbelt–Lusaka–Johannesburg–Durban, and Lusaka–Copperbelt–Kapiri–Mposhi–Dar-es-Salam.[18]

Fresh vegetables and cut flowers are exported via air freight to international markets. Production is consequently limited to farms that are close to the international airport of Lusaka. Consignments sent to Europe (80 per cent of total production) are settled in euros. Air freight charges are high and still predominantly in US dollars. Minor fluctuations in the exchange rate will often have a disproportionate effect on the economic viability of the emerging business. Limão and Venables (2000) thus estimate that a 10 per cent increase in transport costs (which is not unreasonable, given exchange rate fluctuations) will lead to a reduction in trade by approximately 20 per cent. Few emerging businesses in Zambia are capable of handling fluctuations of this magnitude.

In summary: distance matters. As argued by Hirst and Thompson, 'the distance variable is the most consistent and significant of the variables explaining international trade' (Hirst and Thompson 2002: 258). With distances in excess of 2,000 km, some estimated 58 per cent of all trade disappears.[19] Add another 5,000 km, and 97 per cent of all trade disappears. These figures underline a simple, yet very important fact: a large proportion of Zambia's trade with the developed countries is basically artificial. If it were not for discriminatory trade preferences, Zambian products would not make it in the competition with other low-cost suppliers. As Zambia's preference margins are gradually eroded by the diminishing MFN rates, Zambian trade flows are increasingly focused on the neighbouring countries, cf. Table 8.1.

Quality and safety standards

Like most LDCs, Zambia lacks an adequate quantity of quality testing services. When the bulk of Zambian exports were made up of copper and cobalt, the lack of proper standards was a minor concern. However, with a burgeoning export of cut flowers, fresh vegetables, and other agricultural products, Zambia has to meet the food safety and agricultural health safety standards of the major export markets. Most of the necessary testing takes place in Lusaka, if not in Europe, and the lack of international certification means that the tests often have to be repeated all over again at the final destination. The Zambia Bureau of Standards does not have a mandate to effectively coordinate the different government bodies involved in testing and assessment, and the services offered to exporters leave a lot to be desired. Implementation of the Sanitary and Phytosanitary Standards (SPS) and Technical Barriers to Trade (TBT) Agreements remains a sizeable challenge for Zambia.

The weakness of the testing regime in Zambia represents a serious impediment to the growth of NTEs to high-income markets overseas. Without a credible and internationally recognized testing regime, a range of Zambian products that would benefit from DFQF access under the EBA initiative risk being rejected at the port of entry for non-compliance with the relevant SPS and TBT Agreements.

Similarly, there is also a growing demand on companies to adopt environmental management systems (ISO 14000 Series Standards), total quality management (ISO 9000 certification), and social codes of conduct.[20] On all counts, Zambian companies are far behind.

Enabling business environment

This rather broad heading is arguably a residual category for all the supply-side constraints and problems that do not fall under any other heading. Most important in this connection is the willingness of the private sector to actually exploit the opportunities that are being offered for Zambian exports. Two of the most often cited constraints in the Zambian business sector are the high cost of and limited access to finance, macroeconomic instability and lack of policy predictability.

The limited access to finance and the high costs involved are clearly the main challenge facing Zambian companies. The vast majority of private businesses rate the limited access to low-cost financing as the number one impediment hindering private sector growth. The costs of actually borrowing money vary with the size of the firm in question: the smaller the firm, the higher the costs and the more lenders will insist on collateral that far exceeds the amount in question. As the vast majority of Zambian capital is 'dead' – i.e. non-registered and consequently worthless as collateral – less than 20 per cent of the smaller firms in Zambia actually have loans in the financial institutions.[21] Fiscal austerity measures to prevent government borrowing from 'crowding out' the private sector and interventions to lower inflation rates may bring down interest rates, but private business is risky business in LDCs, and lenders are likely to insist on being amply compensated.

Macroeconomic instability has long been a major stumbling block for private investors, but the past two to three years have witnessed sustained improvements in the overall management of the economy, leading to a steady decrease of the inflation rate. Ironically, this period of macroeconomic stability has led to a significant appreciation of the kwacha, whose value against the US dollar rose by more than 20 per cent during the latter half of 2005. This massive appreciation was apparently fuelled in part by a steady increase in the demand for Zambian copper, in part by a decreasing government demand for US dollars following Zambia's attainment of the HIPC completion point (debt relief under the Heavily Indebted Poor Countries Initiative) in late 2005. Still, regardless of how the appreciation of the kwacha came about, the fact remains that exporters of non-traditional products such as flowers and vegetables are getting less and less kwacha for their merchandise.[22] In the long run this imbalance would supposedly even itself out as local prices adjust to the strength of the Kwacha. However, deeply ingrained inflationary expectations make for relatively sticky prices, and the majority of the smaller Zambian companies cannot afford to live in anything but the immediate situation.

Zambia in the EPA negotiations

Just like several other ACP LDCs, Zambia is facing another challenge in its external economic strategy formulation: the EU offer to negotiate EPAs with ACP regions. Zambia has been relatively active in the discussions surrounding the EPAs offered by the EU under the Cotonou Agreement. There were serious doubts as to whether the proposed EPA would be beneficial for Zambia, and the argument in favour of choosing the existing EBA option was often heard: why should Zambia open her markets for European exporters when she already enjoyed near-universal market access under the terms of the EBA initiative?[23] Zambia had much to lose and little to win. Still, Zambia eventually opted for the EPA solution. There are probably several different motives behind this decision, but a fundamental consideration was the fact that an EPA would strengthen the policy of regional economic integration, which Zambia would be pursuing regardless of the offer from the EU. As argued above, Zambian exports are increasingly focused on the regional markets (cf. Table 8.1), and the Zambian Ministry of Commerce, Trade, and Industry has consequently taken a rather active position in the different regional trade negotiations.

Complicating the picture somewhat is the fact that Zambia is part of two different regional economic trade agreements, under which member states are conducting EPA negotiations in parallel: the Southern African Development Community (SADC) and the Common Market for Eastern and Southern Africa (COMESA). Zambia has decided to join the 16 members of COMESA – the ESA (Eastern and Southern Africa) group – who have opened EPA negotiations with the EU.[24] Zambia is consequently grouped with the Democratic Republic of the Congo and Zimbabwe, but separated from Angola, Mozambique and Tanzania, which are negotiating within the SADC group (under the shadow of South Africa; see also Box 11.1 in Chapter 11). This regional overlap of institutions and memberships has raised a number of technical issues that have yet to be resolved. However, for Zambia the arguments in favour of the ESA grouping were substantial: Lusaka hosts the COMESA Secretariat, and the Zambian government was one of the pioneers in developing the Free Trade Area protocol in 2000, and is actively promoting the development of a COMESA customs union by 2008.

The ESA–EPA negotiations were launched in Mauritius in February 2000, with a road map comprising six overall negotiation clusters (development issues, market access, agriculture, fisheries, trade in services and trade-related areas) and the development of national and regional negotiation structures. Each ESA country would establish a National Development and Trade Policy Forum (NDTPF), mandated to follow and discuss the ongoing EPA negotiations. Zambia developed its National Impact Assessment Study under the guidance of the NDTPF in late 2004. The key concern was obviously linked with the prospect of increasing competition from European exporters, and emphasis was consequently put on the need for long transition periods and substantial financial assistance to overcome the supply-side constraints facing Zambia. As mentioned above, the costs and benefits of moving from EBA to EPA were the subject of some debate. In the end, the prospect of accessing larger amounts of trade-related financial assistance clearly played a significant role.

The EPA negotiations have to be concluded in 2006, so that the agreements may enter into force before the end of 2007. After a difficult start, the negotiations in the ESA–EPA are showing progress. The prospect of increased competition from EU exporters is still haunting ESA negotiators, who are consequently stressing the need for asymmetry and favourable terms in the form of special and differential treatment. For ESA governments, the potential losses in terms of forgone tariff revenues are daunting. Zambia is on the defensive, hoping for the best in the form of long asymmetric transition periods coupled with generous financial and technical assistance, but fearing the worst in the form of another tidal wave of deregulation and economic liberalization (as experienced under the harsh structural adjustment programme of the early 1990s).

Conclusions

Like most other developing countries, Zambia has a very large untapped potential for economic growth. Unlike many developing countries, however, Zambia is actually beginning to exploit these opportunities, which are typically concentrated in natural resource and labour-intensive activities such as agriculture, agro-processing, textiles and garments, and light manufacturing. According to most estimates, Zambia would have a comparative advantage in the production of a range of agricultural products, including cotton, tobacco, coffee, and paprika. However, this would-be comparative advantage in markets that are relatively saturated (with declining world market prices) may not be sufficiently solid to attract the financing that is needed to actually develop the potential. Zambia's production structure is not that much different from the production structure of other developing countries which – by fate of nature – are endowed with a geography that is more conducive to international trade, and who are consequently able to export at a lower price.

As an LDC, Zambia is almost by definition a marginal player in the international trade system. If it were to become a more important exporter, it would arguably not remain an LDC for long. Seen from behind the desk, the solution is straightforward: banking on the sectors that are currently experiencing strong economic growth, Zambia needs to invest time, energy, and resources in overcoming the constraints identified in the DTIS. Zambia's bilateral (US, UK, the Netherlands, Sweden) and multilateral (EU, World Bank, UNDP) development partners are stepping up efforts within this field (i.e. the 'Aid for Trade' agenda), with an ambitious programme providing financial and technical assistance for trade expansion and private sector development. However, moving from the obvious to the actual implementation of this remedy remains a daunting challenge.

In the short run, the options that are open to Zambia are few and unconvincing. The limited use of increased market access opportunities offered by EBA clearly underlines the difficult situation confronting Zambia. There has been no surge in exports to the EU market. If the EPA negotiations lead to the introduction of reciprocal free trade with the EU, Zambia's domestic producers may be hurt in the short run – although the EPA process could be beneficial in terms of regional integration in COMESA and development aid from the EU. There are no quick fixes to the challenges that are preventing Zambia from exploiting the possibilities offered by increased access to high-income markets. EBA was hardly perfect, but the modest impact of the initiative does underline the limited immediate value of increased DFQF market access.

Explaining the attractiveness of a strategy that does not work

Seeing the objective shortcomings of the EBA initiative, it should come as no surprise that its actual impact has been limited. The EBA beneficiaries already enjoyed privileged access to the EU market; the vast majority for several years through the Lomé Conventions, the minority since the decision to grant LDCs equivalent market access as the ACP countries from 1998 (see Chapter 2 in this volume). The EBA preferences provided broader product coverage, but given the preferences already extended to LDCs, the impact would necessarily be limited. Second, even if EBA were to stimulate an increasing demand for LDC products, few exporters would be able to significantly increase their supply. There are evidently vast differences between the LDCs, but as a whole, this group of exporters would not be expected to significantly increase export volumes (not in the short run, at any rate). Seen against this background, the EBA initiative may be described as a rather modest improvement in market access extended to a group of countries that are largely incapable of exploiting the (limited) possibilities on offer. Simple as this conclusion may seem, it certainly raises a pertinent question: if EBA is of limited immediate value, why have the LDCs embraced not only the EU initiative, but made DFQF access more generally the single most important issue in the Doha Round?

In order to address the question, this final section looks first at the more recent history of the DFQF position, and second at the internal dynamics of LDC trade negotiations.

The recent history of the DFQF issue

As explained above, the calls for preferential market access have been heard for many years in the international trade negotiations, but it was apparently the first WTO Director General, Renato Ruggiero (1996), who in connection with the Singapore Ministerial in 1996 introduced the concept of DFQF market access as a legitimate object of negotiation in the context of the WTO. The Singapore Ministerial Declaration and the Action Plan adopted by the Ministerial both made explicit reference to the situation of the developing countries and the LDCs (*Agence Europe* 1996). The official discussions in Singapore left the LDC issue open; the Singapore Plan of Action provided for 'positive measures', but it stopped short of imposing obligations on any one. The calls for improved market access thus resurfaced in connection with the aborted Ministerial in Seattle, and received new support by the EU EBA initiative and the UN Third LDC Conference, held in Brussels just months after the approval of EBA in early 2001.

During the 1990s, the LDCs developed a more independent standing in the international trade negotiations and gradually came to play a more important role in the GATT/WTO negotiations (Woolcock 2002; Young 2004). The LDCs introduced biannual meetings at ministerial level and a rotating chairmanship to help provide greater coherence and continuity to the LDC position. With support from the UN Office of the High Representative for the LDCs, UNCTAD, and even the WTO Secretariat, the LDCs gradually developed a more distinct international profile.

Meeting in Tanzania in July 2001, the LDC trade ministers thus resolved to adopt a common position prior to the Fourth WTO Ministerial to be held in Doha, Qatar, in November 2001. The Zanzibar Declaration calls on the Doha Ministerial to agree on a 'binding commitment' on DFQF market access 'for all products from LDCs on a secure, long-term and predictable basis'.[25] On the same occasion, the LDC trade ministers decided to make the LDC meeting a recurrent institution, timed to precede the biannual WTO Ministerial. The Dhaka Declaration, adopted by the LDC trade ministers meeting in Bangladesh in May 2003 (in the run-up to the Cancun Ministerial), reiterated the call for improved market access, stressing the determination of the LDCs to obtain a 'binding commitment from . . . trading partners guaranteeing a substantive and concrete increase in the market share of the LDCs in world trade'.[26] The Livingstone Declaration, adopted by the LDC trade ministers meeting in Livingstone, Zambia, in June 2005 in preparation for the Hong Kong Ministerial in December 2005, also had DFQF access as the most important demand. The first of the 39 demands put forward in the declaration thus calls on the WTO members to agree to a '[b]inding commitment on DFQF market access for all products from LDCs to be granted and imple-mented immediately, on a secure, long-term and predictable basis, with no restrictive measures introduced'.[27]

As can be seen from the LDC declarations presented above, the issue of DFQF market access has been at the top of the LDC group's negotiating agenda over the past decade, and certainly in the run-up to the Hong Kong Ministerial. And this issue has allegedly been 'crowding out' other, equally important themes on the WTO agenda (agriculture, NAMA, services, etc.). Instead of addressing specific LDC concerns across the range of negotiation topics, the 50 LDCs have been consistently hammering the demand for DFQF market access.[28]

In order to understand the LDC stance as it emerged during the 1990s the following section provides a brief theoretical discussion of the character of the LDC group as an international negotiator.

Analysing LDC negotiations

The first and arguably most critical point to note about the LDCs is that it is an artificial or 'imposed' interest group. This group of countries was defined by external, objective criteria and thus created by a purposive political act rather than as a result of specific economic incentives. This is in contrast, for example, with the Cairns group of agricultural exporters, who most obviously share a limited and specific common interest in liberalizing international trade in agriculture.[29] Membership of the LDC group confers a number of economic benefits, most notably access to preferential trade schemes, but these benefits were not the result of the LDCs' active lobbying. On the contrary: the benefits were bestowed upon the LDCs as part of the UN-led process of constituting the grouping. From a theoretical point of view, the LDC grouping is not a *natural* coalition, but rather a political creation.

In terms of negotiation theory, the LDC group can arguably be likened to an extremely weak and underdeveloped policy network. There are few formal structures and there is very little political and administrative continuity between the chairs that are supposed to rotate every six months. The group rarely meets in plenary and when it does, the delegations are generally quite narrow (comprising mostly government officials and few, if any, representatives of the private sector). At best, there will be one full ministerial every two years. The Office of the UN High Representative for LDCs and the UNCTAD and WTO secretariats provide some logistical support, but it is limited and not systematic. Within this rather loose network there are thematic groups that meet somewhat more frequently (primarily in Geneva), but that is the exception, not the rule.

Bargaining in a network like the LDC group is not naturally efficient. There are high transaction costs stemming from the global distribution of the LDCs and the ensuing high transport costs. The LDCs have only limited resources for this type of coordination activities, and most meetings are consequently financed by external funds. Further compounding the problems facing the LDC group is the relative scarcity of information. The LDCs lack information about each other, about their negotiating partners, and about the WTO. These two handicaps, the high transaction costs and the scarcity of information, are obviously linked, but addressing one will not necessarily solve the other.

Loose networks with few formalized structures generally have a large number of *de facto* veto powers. This introduces a bias in favour of the lowest common denominator and thus a bias in favour of continuity: it is easier to postpone policy decisions than to enact policy changes, and the founding policies of the LDC group are consequently rather 'sticky'. As a loose network, the LDC group is not a particularly effective negotiator. And to the extent that the group is actually capable of improving the trade terms of the LDCs, this will *ipso facto* benefit the entire group of LDCs, presenting the network with a relatively pronounced collective action problem (see Elster 1993: 125).

These theoretical considerations would provide a plausible explanation to the question raised at the beginning of the chapter: the LDCs basically maintain the DFQF market access strategy because the loose network structure of the group is conducive to continuity more than anything else. Irrespective of the dismal record of preferential trade schemes, the LDCs continue promoting the strategy because they are unable to agree on a new negotiation mandate (Elster 1993: 141). While being attractively simple, this explanation is hardly sufficient: the LDCs may lack technical capacity in international trade negotiations, but that does not imply that they are only passive 'victims' of the constraining negotiation structure.

The concept of reinforcement may shed additional light on the persistence of the DFQF position (Elster 1993: 82–8).[30] The strategy has a number of advantages that may help explain its continued popularity among the LDCs. The first advantage of the DFQF position is the simple fact that it is agreeable to all the LDCs. This may seem to be a relatively trivial observation, but, the LDC group being a political artefact rather than a natural coalition of interested parties, these countries only have a limited number of common interests in the multilateral trade talks. Some LDCs – Bangladesh being the prime example – are relatively well positioned to take advantage of globalization. Others – such as Zambia and Malawi – have become increasingly marginalized in the global economy. For a major oil-producing country like Angola, trade preferences are essentially redundant. (MFN tariffs on crude oil and diamonds are zero, and Angola does not really export anything else of value.) The small island states face a number of very different challenges and their trade interests are likely to differ accordingly. Similarly, in the actual WTO negotiations, there are important differences of opinion inside the LDC camp. The major sugar producers all have a stake in the continuation of the highly regulated sugar trade. Some are obviously more vulnerable than others (high-volume producers like Mozambique and Sudan are arguably less vulnerable than the small, inefficient producers in the Caribbean), but all have a positive interest in safeguarding the preferential trade agreements.[31] The major LDC cotton producers, on the other hand, are following a much more liberal position, arguing in favour of abolishing all subsidies and distorting tariffs. For the West African LDCs Benin, Burkina Faso, Mali, and Chad, cotton represents more than 60 per cent of all agricultural export revenues, and up to 30 per cent of total export revenues. Liberalization of the sugar trade would hurt LDCs, while liberalization of the cotton trade would yield significant benefits for LDC producers.

Few LDCs have a clear conception of their trade interests in the multilateral trade negotiations, and aggregating the positions of the different LDCs would not necessarily produce a much clearer picture. To the extent that the group is to follow a common negotiating position, the latter will have to be relatively broad and inclusive. Some of the LDCs obviously stand to benefit more than others from the DFQF agenda, but in principle it is a position that is agreeable to the entire group of countries. For a group as politically and economically diverse as the LDCs, a relatively straightforward negotiating mandate is of paramount importance.

Second, and partly related to the first point, the demand for DFQF access has the distinct advantage of being based on an analysis that is clear, consistent, intuitively correct, and emotionally effective. The clarity of the negotiating mandate yields a number of immediate benefits. Backed by economic 'textbook logic', the LDC demand for DFQF access bears the stamp of approval of the mainstream establishment: economists from the World Bank and the IMF have endorsed the idea, and irrespective of the practical difficulties involved (i.e. the fact that most LDCs may in fact be incapable of exploiting the opportunity) the case for DFQF market access is certainly justified theoretically (see, e.g., Bhagwati 2001). Moreover, the position is relatively easy to grasp even for the LDCs, who have a critical shortage of experienced and knowledgeable trade negotiators. All else being equal, it is a lot easier explaining the merits of DFQF market access than it is to justify the intrinsic value of the 'Swiss formula' approach to tariff reductions. Finally, the basic message is easily conveyed, which means the LDCs have important supporters in the broader Western community and in a number of important political parties in the developed countries. This links up with Adrian van den Hoven's analysis of EBA as an 'initiative for internal consumption', appealing to the European development community (see Chapter 4 in this volume). The support of the international community and their domestic constituencies obviously represents a massive reinforcement of the DFQF agenda (the bulk of the LDC negotiating infrastructure being directly or indirectly financed by the same community).

Reinforcement may shed additional light on the persistence of the DFQF position, but it still leaves the LDCs in a rather passive role. The recommendation included in Zambia's DTIS actually suggests an additional explanation that is centred on the purposive behaviour of the LDCs, as opposed to the objective circumstances under which they find themselves. Zambia's DTIS clearly states the limited importance of increased market access: 'Market access is not currently a binding constraint to export growth. Most of Zambia's existing exports face zero or low tariffs and qualify for preferential access to the major developed countries and regional markets.' Zambia's DTIS is adamant on this point, arguing that 'Zambia should focus on realizing improvements in non-tariff aspects . . . strengthening its trade and behind the border policies . . . and removing supply-side constraints . . . to increase its competitive strength' (DTIS 2005: vi).

In the context of the multilateral trade talks, the study does emphasize that 'Zambia needs to participate actively in the global and regional trade negotiations to ensure that its longer-term interests are adequately safeguarded in the outcome'. However, the study simultaneously notes that Zambia still needs to 'determine its long-term trade interests in order to develop a clear national strategy that will inform its participation in the ongoing WTO and EPA negotiations with the EU' (DTIS 2005: 3). In order words: Zambia does not at present have a clear conception of its strategic trade interests.

Given the structure of the multilateral trade system, a relatively insignificant country like Zambia can only hope to have an impact by working through broader coalitions; and the LDC group is arguably the most suitable platform for Zambian trade diplomacy. Zambia may attempt to influence the DFQF position at the margins (including special reference to special Zambian concerns in the Ministerial declarations), but Zambia cannot expect to change the core of the LDC negotiation mandate.

However, by actively supporting the DFQF position, Zambia can in fact promote other key trade interests. An important advantage of the DFQF position is the fact that other delegations – especially the OECD countries – are loath of moving down this path. This may seem strange, given the limited practical consequences, but governments are arguably risk-averse, and the safest hedge against the potential long-term dynamic effects of DFQF access for the LDCs is obviously to exclude the most vulnerable (and, typically, the best protected) sectors from the negotiations. This reluctance is exemplified by the extended deadlines for sugar, rice and bananas under the EBA Regulation, and by the absence of a clear timetable for liberalization of the remaining 3 per cent in the Hong Kong declaration. The demand for DFQF market access basically forces the developed countries on the defensive, where they have to offer some form of compensation to the LDCs in order to safeguard their sensitive sectors. The LDCs have very limited influence on the course of the multilateral trade negotiations, but the DFQF position certainly makes the most of this rather modest influence.[32]

In summary, theories of negotiation can shed some light on the persistence of the DFQF agenda. At the most basic level, the loose network structure of the LDC group makes for continuity of policy, as evidenced in the relatively consistent LDC line from the mid-1960s to the early twenty-first century. In addition, the DFQF strategy has a number of characteristics, which may inadvertently reinforce the political attractiveness of the position. Finally, at the level of strategic action, some LDCs may actually be able to benefit indirectly from the DFQF position by forcing the other negotiating parties on the defensive, and extracting some form of compensation, i.e. the promise of additional Aid for Trade.

Summary: symbolic *and* effective?

EBA was launched as a strategic initiative, but was arguably never expected to have a major impact on the ground. It was first and foremost a symbolic gesture. Ironically, the LDCs seem to have embraced it as such, and instead of critiquing the initiative, they are currently lobbying for more of the same. This chapter argued that the popularity of the initiative with the LDCs has little to do with economics, and everything to do with politics. The immediate real economic effects of increasing LDC market access are rather limited: few LDCs have the potential to exploit the new opportunities. The case of Zambia amply illustrates that many factors may be in the way of using the preferences on offer: customs administration, transport infrastructure, quality and safety standards and others.

Still, the LDCs have by and large embraced the EBA initiative, calling for more of the same. The position makes little sense from an economic point of view, but for the LDCs as a negotiating group, the call for DFQF access has the clear advantage of rallying all LDCs around a common theme while clearly demarcating the LDC group as an entity in the international trade negotiations, and forcing the developed countries to offer the LDCs a substitute for market access. This substitute is not necessarily satisfactory, but arguably much better than what they would otherwise have been offered.

Notes

This chapter is based on Jess Pilegaard's PhD research at the Danish Institute for International Studies/Institute of Political Science, University of Copenhagen. It reflects the personal opinions of the author only and does not, in any way, represent the views, opinions or position of his employer.

1 See e.g. the Zanzibar Declaration of the LDC trade ministers in 2001 (annex 1).
2 The same applies for the US-sponsored African Growth and Opportunities Act (AGOA). See e.g. *Times of Zambia*: 'Zambia has failed to take advantage of the AGOA', 16 January 2006.
3 Notwithstanding the lack of special provisions in favour of the less economically developed countries, roughly half of the original contracting parties could in principle be designated as 'developing countries': Brazil, Chile, the Czechoslovak Republic, China (pre-revolution), Cuba (pre-revolution), India, Lebanon, Myanmar (Burma), Pakistan, South Africa, Sri Lanka, Syria, and Rhodesia (Zimbabwe) (see Bown 2004: 59).
4 See the UN Office of the High Representative for the LDCs, Landlocked Developing Countries and Small Island Developing States. Available online at http://www.un. org/special-rep/ohrlls/ldc/ldc%20criteria.htm (accessed 10 May 2006). It is the UN Committee for Development Policy that makes the recommendations for inclusion and graduation, which are then endorsed by the UN Economic and Social Committee and submitted to the General Assembly, which has the authority to make a final decision.
5 NTEs include engineering products (e.g. copper rods, cables, wire), textiles, processed foods (e.g. sugar, molasses, honey and beeswax), building materials, primary agricultural commodities, animal products such as crocodile meat, poultry, fish and leather products, gemstones, floricultural products, and electricity. NTEs increased from 8 per cent of export earnings in 1990 to almost 38 per cent in 2003 (DTIS 2005: v).
6 Since 2004 copper prices have witnessed a steady increase (DTIS 2005: v).
7 The distribution reflected in Table 8.1 is based on official figures. Trade with neighbouring countries like the Democratic Republic of Congo (DRC), Zimbabwe, and Angola is likely to be much more important than suggested by the official figures.
8 The following section is based on material obtained from Illovo and interviews conducted in Zambia in late 2005.
9 Zambia Sugar is by far the dominant producer. The second largest producer, CFL in Kafue Flats, produces less than 10 per cent of the volume produced by Zambia Sugar (see DTIS 2005: xii).
10 See the press statement on Illovo's website at http://www.illovo.co.za (accessed 10 May 2006).
11 The Integrated Framework for trade-related technical assistance to the LDCs is a 'joint venture' between the World Bank, the International Monetary Fund (IMF), the International Trade Centre, United Nations Development Programme (UNDP), WTO and UNCTAD. Mandated by the 1996 WTO Singapore Ministerial, the overall objective of the Framework is to assist the LDCs in expanding their participation in the global economy, thus enhancing their economic growth and sustaining their poverty reduction strategies.
12 While market access is not an objective constraint for the majority of the LDCs, there are obviously differences between the countries in question. Major cotton, rice, and sugar producers would thus be likely to benefit from increased market access in these specific sectors.

13 However, the existing export structure, which reflects the distorted incentives facing Zambian exporters, may not be the most accurate measure of Zambia's actual export potential.

14 Under normal circumstances, the LDCs would elect a new coordinator every six months. However, in mid-2005 it was decided to extend Zambia's tenure first another six months (to include the Hong Kong Ministerial), and then another four months (up to the 31 April 2006 deadline). The UK provided financial and technical support to the Ministry during 2005 (interview done in Zambia in late 2005).

15 Delays of two to four days for trucks are not uncommon at the main transit border, Chirundu (bordering Zimbabwe). The Beit Bridge crossing between Zimbabwe and South Africa has average delays of up to six days (February 2003), which represents an estimated loss of earnings per vehicle of US$1,750. At the Lusaka International Airport, shipment clearance may take up to four days. Even so, Zambia is clearly not the worst performer: according to the ECA (2004) the average delays at the customs of sub-Saharan countries is no less than 12 days (compared with just five and a half in Central and East Asia).

16 2003 figure taken from the ECOWAS home page. See also Robert Guest, whose *Shackled Continent* (2005) includes an amusing but rather tragic description of a particularly testing journey from Douala to Bertona in Cameroon.

17 The *Economic Report on Africa* (ECA 2004) suggests that transport costs for landlocked countries are on average 35 per cent higher than for countries that have direct access to the sea.

18 Incidentally, there are discussions on the possibility of opening a fourth corridor, from the Copperbelt/North Western Province to Walvis Bay harbour in Namibia.

19 Again, the closest shipping port from Lusaka is more than 1,500 km away. And that is obviously only the starting point of an even longer journey to markets in the developed world.

20 See *Times of Zambia*, 'Exporting to the European Union', 16 February 2006.

21 Guest (2005) has an interesting discussion of the economic literature on this matter.

22 See *Development Zambia*, 23, February 2006.

23 See *The Post*, 'Zambia to lose $15m if it maintains pact with EU', 1 July 2005.

24 COMESA (like SADC) includes countries that are not part of the ACP group and thus not eligible for participating in an EPA. COMESA has 19 members, but only 16 will be conducting EPA negotiations (Angola, Egypt and Swaziland are not in the ESA group).

25 See the Zanzibar Declaration of the LDC trade ministers in 2001 (Article 4).

26 See the Dhaka Declaration of the LDC trade ministers in 2003 (Article 15 ii).

27 See the Livingstone Declaration of the LDC trade ministers in 2005 (Article 1).

28 Interview done in Zambia in late 2005.

29 The Cairns Group is a coalition of 17 competitive agricultural exporters, including both Organization for Economic Cooperation and Development countries like Australia and Canada and developing countries like Brazil and Colombia. The coalition seeks to promote international free trade in agriculture, and is one of the staunchest critics of the EU Common Agricultural Policy.

30 Elster uses the example of behaviour that '... has valuable or pleasurable consequences ...', where '... our perception or registration of that fact strengthens or reinforces our tendency to engage in it'.

31 On 3 March 2004, the LDC sugar producers submitted a letter to the EU Commission, appealing for an extension of the sugar preferences, i.e. safeguarding the price level offered to suppliers of EBA sugar.

32 See e.g. *Times of Zambia*, 'LDCs vow not to compromise', 13 December 2005.

156 *Jess Pilegaard*

References

Agence Europe (1996), No. 6876, 16 December.

Bhagwati, J. (2001) 'Targeting rich-country protectionism', *Finance and Development*, 38: 14–15.

Bown, C. (2004) 'Developing countries as plaintiffs and defendants in GATT/WTO trade disputes', *World Economy*, 27: 59–80.

Brenton, P. (2003) 'Integrating the Least Developed Countries into the world trading system: the current impact of EU preferences under 'Everything but Arms', *Journal of World Trade*, 37: 623–46.

Cernat, L., Laird, S., Monge-Roffarello, L. and Turrini, A. (2003) 'The EU's Everything but Arms Initiative and the Least-developed Countries', Discussion Paper No. 2003/47, Wider, United Nations University. Available online at http://www.wider.unu.edu/publications/dps/dps2003/dp2003-047.pdf (accessed 8 May 2006).

Dickson, A. (2004) 'The unimportance of trade preferences', in K. Arts and A. Dickson (eds) *EU Development Cooperation – from Model to Symbol*, Manchester: Manchester University Press.

DTIS (2005) *Zambia's Diagnotic Trade Integration Survey*, Integrated Framework. Available online at http://www.integratedframework.org (accessed 10 May 2006).

ECA (2004) *Economic Report on Africa: Unlocking Africa's Trade Potential*, Addis Ababa: Economic Commission for Africa.

Elster, J. (1993) *Nuts and Bolts for the Social Sciences*, New York: Cambridge University Press.

Gibb, R. (2006) 'The European Union's "Everything but Arms" development initiative and sugar: preferential access or continued protectionism?', *Applied Geography*, 26: 1–17.

Guest, R. (2005) *The Shackled Continent*, London: Macmillan.

Hirst, P. and Thompson, G. (2002) 'The future of globalization', *Cooperation and Conflict*, 37: 247–65.

Jennar, R. (2004) *Europe, la trahison des élites*, Paris: Fayard.

Lamy, P. (2002) *L'Europe en première ligne*, Paris: Éditions du Seuil.

Limão, N. and Venables A. (2000) 'Infrastructure, Geographical Disadvantage and Transport Costs', Mimeo, Washington DC: World Bank and New York: Columbia University Press.

Page, S. and Hewitt, A. (2002) 'The new European trade preferences: does the "Everything but Arms" help the Poor?', *Development Policy Review*, 20: 91–102.

Rostow, W.W. (1960/1971) *The Stages of Economic Growth*, Cambridge: Cambridge University Press.

Ruggiero, R. (1996), 'The Road Ahead: International Trade Policy in the Era of the WTO', address to the fourth Sylvia Ostry Lecture in Ottawa Canada, 28 May.

Smith, M. (2000) 'Trade: EU may end duty for nations', *Financial Times*, 21 September.

Woolcock, S. (2002) 'The Changing Nature of Trade Diplomacy'. Paper for the BISA Panel on *Economic Diplomacy in the Twenty-first Century*, London: London School of Economics and King's College.

WTO (2004) *World Trade Report 2004*, Geneva: WTO.

Young, A. (2004) 'The EU and world trade: Doha and beyond', in M. Cowles and D. Dinan (eds) *Developments in the European Union 2*, Basingstoke: Palgrave Macmillan.

9 The role of EBA in the political economy of CAP reform

Alan Matthews and Jacques Gallezot

The motivation for the 'Everything but Arms' (EBA) initiative was to enhance the role of trade preferences as a European Union (EU) development cooperation policy instrument from the point of view of the least developed countries (LDCs). The European Commission's view was that there was a real risk that these countries were becoming increasingly marginalized in the world economy. Apart from this altruistic motive, the initiative was intended to present the EU as a champion of development in the ongoing efforts at the time to launch a new multilateral trade round.

The EU's Generalized System of Preferences (GSP) had provided for more favourable tariff treatment for LDCs. At the Singapore Ministerial Conference of the World Trade Organization (WTO) in 1996, WTO members pledged to carry out an action plan to improve access to their markets for products originating in the LDCs. In 1997, the Council of Ministers called for the Singapore conclusions to be implemented by granting LDCs not party to the Lomé Convention preferences equivalent to those enjoyed by signatories and, in the medium term, duty-free access for essentially all their exports. Council Regulation (EC) No. 602/98 granted LDCs not party to the Lomé Convention preferences equivalent to those enjoyed by the African, Caribbean and Pacific (ACP) signatories to the Convention. The Cotonou Agreement (Article 37) stated that the Community would start a process which, by the end of the multilateral trade negotiations and at the latest in 2005, would allow duty-free access for essentially all products from all LDCs building on the level of the existing trade provisions of Lomé IV and which would simplify and review the rules of origin, including cumulation provisions, that apply to their exports.

In September 2000, the Commission issued a press statement proposing to go beyond previous Community commitments by granting unrestricted duty-free access to all products (except arms) from all LDCs. Page and Hewitt (2002) somewhat critically describe the context for this decision. In February 2001, the Council adopted the so-called 'EBA Regulation' (Regulation (EC) 416/2001). The provisions of this Regulation were subsequently incorporated into the GSP Regulation (EC) No. 2501/2001. The EBA Regulation foresees that the special arrangements for LDCs should be maintained for an unlimited period of time and not be subject to the periodic renewal of the Community's GSP. Therefore, the date of expiry of Council Regulation (EC) No. 2501/2001 does not apply to its EBA provisions.

The significance of the EBA Regulation was to extend deep trade preferences to LDCs on products excluded from the EU's other preferential schemes, such as Cotonou and the GSP. A total of 919 tariff lines (out of the 10,500 tariff lines in total) were affected, almost entirely agricultural products covered by the EU's Common Agricultural Policy (CAP). Only imports of fresh bananas, rice and sugar were not fully liberalized immediately. Duties on those products are being gradually reduced and duty-free access was granted for bananas in January 2006 and will be granted for sugar in July 2009 and for rice in September 2009. The extent to which this delayed liberalization for these three products was due to concern over the impact on EU producers and the CAP will be considered later in this chapter. However, the pressure to delay full liberalization for these products came at least as much from other developing countries whose preferential access to the EU market would be eroded by the EBA initiative. For example, the ACP countries welcomed the fact that 'the full liberalization of sugar, rice and bananas, which constitute very important export products for many of the LDCs, will not be implemented until 2009, thereby taking into account the legitimate concerns of ACP commodity-producing countries' (ACP–EU Joint Parliamentary Assembly 2001).

It was recognised from the outset that the greater access under EBA would have implications for future reform of the CAP. Indeed, those with a Machiavellian cast of mind might argue that it was a deliberate attempt by one arm of the Commission (DG Trade) to force change in another EU policy area (DG Agriculture), particularly with respect to the EU sugar regime. The EBA Regulation noted that:

> In the light of the fact that the arrangements for the common organization of the markets in sugar, rice and bananas are currently being revised or are due to be revised, the Regulations regarding these reforms will have to take account of duty-free access for the LDCs from the outset when they establish new general import arrangements.

The ACP–EU Joint Parliamentary Assembly statement expressed its concern that '[the EBA initiative] is aimed at eventually securing liberalization of trade in all agricultural products at low prices and that, if it is not improved, it could rob the trade protocols attached to the Cotonou Agreement of their substance' (ACP–EU Joint Parliamentary Assembly 2001).

The first objective of this chapter is to explore whether, in practice, EBA has influenced the trajectory and pace of CAP reform either in general or with respect to the specific commodity regimes identified as sensitive in the regulation. The chapter finds evidence that the EBA impact was indeed important in the reform of the EU sugar and rice regimes but that, apart from these two products, EBA was not otherwise a factor taken into account in the most recent 2003 CAP reform process. The chapter reviews *ex ante* projections of the likely impact of EBA access for agricultural markets, and compares these with *ex post* evidence on the actual increase in trade to date, recalling that barriers for bananas were only eliminated on 1 January 2006 and barriers remain on sugar and rice until 2009. While some *ex ante* forecasts warned of the need to take account of the EBA factor in considering CAP reform, there is little evidence from the *ex post* trade statistics of any export surge which might cause complications except, again, in the case of sugar.

While evidence that EBA has had a direct impact on CAP reform is limited, there may be indirect effects of the EBA initiative which may turn out to be important in the longer term. One such indirect effect is that EBA increased the number of WTO members which have preferential market access to the EU market and thus, by implication, a stake in the continuation of a high-price EU agricultural policy. In this way, the EU may have hoped to diminish the pressure from developing countries for more radical CAP reform. Also, by making the demand that other developed countries should also introduce EBA market access terms for LDCs, the EU puts pressure on its negotiating partners to liberalize their agricultural policies, to the extent that additional LDC exports to these countries might force faster reform of these policies than might otherwise have been the case. Neither argument appears to hold much water on closer examination.

A second indirect effect might be called the demonstration effect of EBA in the context of the negotiations of the EU with ACP countries on a successor to the trade provisions of the Cotonou Agreement. The EU has proposed forming reciprocal free trade areas called Economic Partnership Arrangements (EPAs) with a number of ACP regions. ACP countries are being asked to offer duty-free access to most EU products (albeit over a transition period) and will be seeking improved market access in return. Their obvious benchmark is EBA equivalent status, and this demand will be further encouraged by the fact that each of the six ACP negotiating regions has at least one LDC member. Extending EBA equivalent access to non-LDC ACPs would offer a group of countries with vastly greater (if still limited) supply capacity unrestricted access to CAP-protected markets. The consequences for the CAP would then be very different to those outlined below.

Ex ante EBA impact on CAP reform

The reform impact of EBA depends on the volume of additional imports expected from LDCs and the way these additional imports influence the EU market balance and interact with the market support instruments of the CAP. Two widely different assessments were offered in the negotiating phase of EBA in studies undertaken for Oxfam by Stevens and Kennan (2001) and by DG Agriculture (2000). Stevens and Kennan argued that EBA would affect LDC trade only for products on which they currently paid an import tax in the EU and where they had a supply capacity. Sifting through 1997 EU trade statistics, they identified 2,939 items imported from at least one LDC, but for only 502 of these was the export value from the whole LDC group more than US$500,000. Of these, only 11 at that time did not have duty-free and quota-free (DFQF) access, and these were the items for which EBA would make an immediate difference (Table 9.1).

Table 9.1 Import barriers on LDCs' exports to the EU that will be affected by EBA, 1997

CN 1997	Description	Current import restrictions (1999[a])	
		Non-ACP LDCs	ACP LDCs
02023090	Frozen bovine boned meat	9.8%+€332.6/100 kg	0%+€332.6/100 kg; Protocol K0%+€28.8/100 kg
04069021	Cheddar (excl. grated or powdered and for processing)	No preference	K€63.9/100 kg
07099060	Fresh or chilled sweetcorn	No preference	€10.1/100 kg
08030019	Bananas, fresh (excl. plantains)	No preference	€508/1,000 kg (K0)
10059000	Maize (excl. seed)	No preference	€75.19/T
10062017	Long-grain husked brown- rice, length/width ratio >=3, parboiled	Bangladesh K€109.82/ 1,000 kg; no preference	P€75.57/1,000 kg
10063098	Wholly milled long-grain rice, length/width ratio >= 3, (excl. parboiled)	Bangladesh K€232.09/ 1,000 kg; no preference	P€160.51/1,000 kg
17011110	Raw cane sugar, for refining (excl. added flavouring or colouring)	No preference	K0; Protocol 0
17011190	Raw cane sugar (excl. for refining and added flavouring or colouring)	No preference	K0; Protocol 0
17019910	White sugar, containing in dry state>= 99.5 % sucrose (excl. flavoured or coloured)	No preference	K0; Protocol 0 (for one item out of two)
17031000	Cane molasses resulting from the extraction or refining of sugar	No preference	K0

Sources: Stevens and Kennan (2001), based on Eurostat (1998); Taric (1999).

Note:
a 'K' denotes rate within quota; 'P' denotes ceiling.

Table 9.2 LDC global exports in relation to EU global imports, 1997

FAO product group	HS codes[a]	LDC global exports as a % of EU imports from Extra-EU, 1997
Beef and veal	020110/20, 020210/20*	15.7
Beef and veal, boneless	020130, 020230*	0.4
Cheese (whole cow milk)	0406*	0.02
Green corn (maize)[b]	070990*	no LL DC exports
Bananas	0803*	0.7
Maize	1005	5.9
Rice	100610/20/30/40	5.3
Sugar (centrifugal, raw)	170111/12*	7.4
Sugar refined	170191/99	44.0
Molasses	1703	2.9

Sources: Stevens and Kennan (2001), based on Eurostat (1998); FAO (1998).

Notes:
a The HS codes included in the FAO product group, according to FAO's concordance. An asterisk
   denotes that the HS codes shown (and used to obtain the EU import data on which the
   percentages in the next column are based) are broader in coverage than the FAO product group.
b The HS code listed in FAO's concordance indicates that this is sweetcorn.

They then asked what would happen to EU imports if the LDCs could divert to the EU their entire global exports. Table 9.2 shows, for each broad product group and using statistics from FAO and Eurostat, the value of LDC global exports in 1997 as a proportion of total EU imports from all sources of the products that might be affected by EBA. They argued that the picture painted for most products is of the LDCs as marginal suppliers. For four of the ten products (as both types of rice are included in the FAO 'rice' group), LDC global exports are less than 1 per cent of EU global imports, and for a further four they are less than 10 per cent (this includes raw sugar). They concluded that only in the cases of beef and veal and refined sugar (and the latter is not a heavily traded commodity) is it plausible to suppose that LDCs could have a significant absolute impact on EU markets.

An initial assessment from officials in DG Agriculture provided a very different assessment. The DG Agriculture paper began by recognizing that the LDCs together have very small net exports that they could export to the EU. Even when account is taken of greater export surpluses of individual LDCs, it admits these appeared to be quite limited and would probably not cause major problems as far as the most sensitive products are concerned. Its more apocalyptic tone was due to three factors. First, it argued that LDCs would be likely to import agricultural products to meet their domestic consumption needs and export part of their own domestic production to the EU. It acknowledged that this type of triangular trade (import/export swap) would be completely legal and pointed to existing evidence of it happening in the sugar sector. Second, it argued that the proposed EBA would apply current GSP rules of origin that allowed regional cumulation for origin purposes between LDCs and two regional groupings, ASEAN and SAARC,[1] as well as the EU. Regional cumulation would allow LDCs to export as their own goods products that had been imported from one of these regions and processed adding at least 100 per cent to the import value.[2] Third, it pointed to the possibilities of bilateral cumulation between the EU and LDCs with more limited value added if a processing company operated both in the EU and in an LDC. It could export from the EU using export subsidies and then re-export from the LDC to the EU at the domestic market price ('carousel' arrangement).

In its empirical estimates, the DG Agriculture paper focused on the likelihood of swap trade. It developed a 'ready reckoner' examining the impact of LDCs exporting 10 per cent of their total production to the EU over time. On this basis (and excluding the sensitive products of rice, sugar and bananas, which were discussed in greater detail and which arguments are reviewed later), it projected this could result in an additional 4.5 million tonnes of cereals (excluding rice), around 1.5 million tonnes of vegetables and slightly less than 1 million tonnes of fruit. In addition, it projected increased exports of 22,000 tonnes of skimmed milk powder, a similar amount of beef and more than 100,000 tonnes of sheep meat.

It went on to consider the probability of these trade flows emerging, pointing out the difficulties LDCs would have in the short term in meeting Sanitary and Phytosanitary Standards in fruits and vegetables and animal products. It also recognized that the price gap for wheat between EU and world market prices would make it unlikely that LDCs would find it worthwhile to engage in swap trade, although the incentive would be higher for maize. It was also possible that additional LDC exports would displace third country exports (trade diversion) rather than EU domestic production. However, even though it was unlikely there would be major problems in the short term, the paper warned that LDCs could progressively generate market problems for the EU. It hinted that these competition problems might have to be taken into account in discussions on reform of EU commodity regimes.

However, again apart from the three sensitive commodities which are considered in more detail below, there is no evidence that EBA concerns have driven subsequent CAP reform. In the 1990s, there were two major reforms of the CAP. The MacSharry reform in 1992 for the first time made a switch from market support to direct support for farmers' incomes, the latter linked to production limitations. In 1999, the Agenda 2000 agreement intensified the 1992 reforms. As a result, EU market price support, the most trade-distorting form of support, which accounted for 85 per cent of total support in the 1980s, fell to 50 per cent before the June 2003 reform (OECD 2005). Export subsidies fell from 25 per cent of the value of farm exports in 1992 to 5.2 per cent in 2001 and in absolute terms from US$10 billion to US$2.8 billion a year.

The changes in the form of support agreed as part of the Mid-term Review of Agenda 2000 in Luxembourg in June 2003 marked a further significant step in the reform process. The main innovation of the 2003 reform concerned the design of the EU direct payment schemes with a move from coupled to decoupled payments. As a result of those changes, and the subsequent reform of the tobacco, cotton, olive oil and hops regimes, it is estimated that up to 90 per cent of EU direct payments will be eligible for the minimally distorting or non-distorting Green Box category under WTO rules. It is noteworthy that only in connection with rice EBA is mentioned as a possible factor in reform in any of the Commission documentation setting out its justification and rationale (EU 2002, 2003; DG Agriculture 2003).

Ex post EBA impact on CAP reform

While we find no evidence that concerns about EBA competition played a role in the June 2003 CAP reform (again excepting the sensitive products), it is possible that the competition effect has been underestimated and that actual trade flows are larger than expected. The relative importance of EBA preferential imports in 2002 compared with other sources of EU agri-food imports is shown in Table 9.3. In total, they amount to 0.44 per cent of the EU total, although of course for individual commodities their importance could be greater.

Table 9.3 EU imports of agro-food products under various regimes, 2002

Regime	Country eligible	Value of imports (€ million)	Share in total imports (%)
Preferential imports from developing countries		13,316	20.01
Non reciprocal preferences			
Cotonou	Africa, Caribbean, Pacific	5,500	8.26
GSP (excluding Eastern Europe)	Almost all developing countries	4,257	6.40
GSP 'plus' (drugs)	Countries fighting drug trafficking	1,714	2.58
'Everything but Arms'	Least developed (except Myanmar)	294	0.44
Others	Overseas territories.	399	0.60
Reciprocal preferences			
Bilateral agreements with developing countries	Maghreb, Mashrek, etc.	1,153	1.73
Imports under a zero MFN duty from developing countries	All developing countries	15,567	23.39
Imports under a non-zero MFN duty from developing countries		11,724	17.61
Total imports from developing countries		40,737	61.20
Total EU imports of agro-food products from third countries		66,559	100.0

Sources: Data from Gallezot, based on Taxud and Taric-Eurostat. Figures for 2002, chapters 1 to 24 of the Harmonized System.

Table 9.4 LDC agricultural exports, 2000 and 2003

	2000			2003		
Exports to	EBA US$000	Total US$000	EBA/Total (%)	EBA US$000	Total US$000	EBA/Total (%)
EU	80,664	1,450,846	5.6	166,147	1,506,725	11.0
Other	494,420	2,562,593	19.3	688,200	5,038,847	13.7
Total	575,085	4,013,439	14.3	854,347	6,545,572	13.1

Sources: BACI (Cepii) and Taric (DG-Taxud).

Note: Agriculture as defined by the WTO.

While the absolute amount of EBA preferential imports is small, for these agricultural products benefiting from an additional preferential advantage due to EBA (referred to here as EBA products), there has been a doubling in the volume of exports to the EU during the implementation phase of the initiative (Table 9.4). The trend is more striking when compared with the exports of EBA products from other (non-LDC) ACP countries. Between 1996 and 2000, the exports of non-LDC ACP countries to the EU decreased at a rate relatively close to that of the fall in LDC exports (a fall of 19 per cent for exports of EBA products from non-LDC ACP countries, a fall of 16 per cent for LDC exports). On the other hand, after 2000 the growth of LDC exports to the EU contrasts with those of other ACP countries: exports of EBA products from African LDCs doubled and those of Asian LDCs tripled, while those of non-LDC ACP countries only increased by 25 per cent.

While this seems to underline the success of EBA in stimulating additional exports in the agri-food sector from LDCs, more detailed evaluation highlights that this growth has been concentrated on a narrow range of products and a limited number of countries. In 2003, there were only seven products that represented each more than 1 per cent of the total exports in EBA products to the EU. This selection covers 92.5 per cent of EBA exports to the EU (Table 9.5). By comparing 2003 with the pre-EBA initiative period, it can be noted that this selection criterion includes 86 per cent of EBA exports to the EU in 2000 and 90.1 per cent in 1996. It can be noted that certain products that represented a significant share of exports to the EU in 1996 and 2000 no longer appear in this selection in 2003. These are live poultry and bovine meat as well as bananas. On the other hand, exports of cane sugar multiplied threefold between 2000 and 2003. LDCs, which sent a third of their sugar exports to the EU in 1996, sent two-thirds of the total in 2003.

The LDCs that represent more than 1 per cent of the value of exports to the EU in products benefiting from an advantage with the EBA initiative are, compared with the previous periods, more numerous in 2003 (Table 9.6). There were, in 2003, 14 countries (out of 48) that cover 95.8 per cent of exports to the EU for these products. These are mainly African countries, at the head of which we find

Table 9.5 Exports of products benefiting from an EBA preferential advantage, from LDCs to the EU, 1996, 2000 and 2003

Product	HS6 code	1996 LDC exports to EU US $000	1996 % of value Share of exports to EU	1996 % of value of total exports to EU	2000 LDC exports to EU US $000	2000 % of value Share of exports to EU	2000 % of value of total exports to EU	2003 LDC exports to EU US $000	2003 % of value Share of exports to EU	2003 % of value of total exports to EU
Turkeys, ducks, geese, guinea fowls ...	10599	3,814	100.0	4.1	–	–	–	–	–	–
Meat of bovine animals, boneless, frozen ...	20230	4,891	69.9	5.2	–	–	–	–	–	–
Tomatoes, fresh or chilled	70200	1,714	71.2	1.8	2,790	77.5	3.5	4,208	59.7	2.5
Garlic, fresh or chilled	70320	–	–	–	–	–	–	1,797	66.1	1.1
Vegetables, nesoi, fresh or chilled	70990	9,098	77.9	9.7	10,794	63.0	13.4	24,507	80.3	14.8
Roots and tubers neso, fresh or dried ...	71490	–	–	–	2,797	90.3	3.5	–	–	–
Bananas and plantains, fresh or dried ...	80300	11,912	85.9	12.7	–	–	–	–	–	–
Corn (maize), other than seed corn	100590	2,385	8.1	2.5	–	–	–	–	–	–
Grain sorghum	100700	4,119	68.0	4.4	5,685	40.0	7.0	2,500	33.2	1.5
Cane sugar, raw, solid form, w/o added as ...	170111	32,043	45.0	34.1	35,268	33.7	43.7	105,642	66.4	63.6
Cane molasses from extraction ...	170310	12,454	56.3	13.3	10,244	74.6	12.7	11,648	74.3	7.0
Oilcake etc. from vegetables fats ...	230690	2,147	81.4	2.3	1,826	46.1	2.3	3,365	64.2	2.0
LDC exports to EU of products selection		84,576	14.5	90.1	69,406	12.1	86.0	153,667	22.3	92.5
All LDC exports to EU (EBA advantage)		93,840	16.1	100	80,664	14.0	100	166,147	24.1	100
LDC exports to all destinations (EBA advantage)		582,785	–	–	575,085	–	–	688,200	–	–

Source: BACI (CEPII).

Note: Only those products that represent more than 1% of the total value of exports to the EU are included.

Table 9.6 LDC exports to the EU for products benefiting from an EBA preferential advantage

	1996			2000			2003		
	LDC exports to EU US $000	% of value		LDC exports to EU US $000	% of value		LDC exports to EU US $000	% of value	
LDC		Share of exports to EU	of total exports to EU		Share of exports to EU	of total exports to EU		Share of exports to EU	of total exports to EU
Bangladesh	5,463	68.1	5.8	6,243	47.0	7.7	10,375	50.8	6.2
Burkina Faso	–	–	–	–	–	–	4,190	59.5	2.5
Congo	–	–	–	5,960	72.2	7.4	2,791	40.0	1.7
Ethiopia	–	–	–	–	–	–	9,664	23.1	5.8
Madagascar	15,062	86.9	16.1	1,369	33.8	1.7	1,971	70.8	1.2
Malawi	13,412	59.8	14.3	13,295	76.9	16.5	41,766	55.9	25.1
Mali	4,615	7.2	4.9	2,932	55.4	3.6	–	–	–
Mozambique	2,148	9.5	2.3	920	3.9	1.1	6,612	28.6	4.0
Myanmar	2,146	2.7	2.3	–	–	–	–	–	–
Nepal	–	–	–	1,141	2.4	1.4	5,525	15.6	3.3
Niger	–	–	–	–	–	–	–	–	–
Senegal	4,357	42.3	4.6	8,097	63.4	10.0	9,844	25.7	5.9
Somalia	11,458	13.4	12.2	–	–	–	–	–	–
Sudan	12,370	11.6	13.2	17,650	13.1	21.9	19,349	14.2	11.6
Tanzania	8,207	78.4	8.7	7,948	30.2	9.9	13,239	22.4	8.0
Togo	–	–	–	1,622	10.8	2.0	2,894	9.6	1.7
Uganda	1,419	5.4	1.5	2,494	25.1	3.1	3,515	25.2	2.1
Zambia	7,817	89.2	8.3	6,778	20.0	8.4	27,402	78.1	16.5
LDC exports to EU of countries select	88,475	15.2	94.3	76,449	13.3	94.8	159,137	23.1	95.8
All LDC exports to EU	93,840	16.1	100	80,664	14.0	100	166,147	24.1	100
All LDC exports for all destinations	582,785			575,085			688,200		

Source: BACI (CEPII).

Note: Only those countries that represent more than 1% of the total value of exports to the EU are included.

Malawi (25.1 per cent of the value of exports to the EU), Zambia (16.5 per cent) and Sudan (11.6 per cent). For these three countries, the value of exports to the EU has risen sharply since EBA was implemented (it tripled for Malawi and Zambia). These are the countries for which the additional sugar quota have been particularly important. We conclude from this detailed examination of actual trade flows by country and commodity that there is no *ex post* evidence to suggest that EBA imports have grown by amounts which are likely to cause CAP market imbalances.

A further feature of LDC trade in agri-food products with the EU is that only a small proportion of it is actually conducted under the terms of EBA, with exporting countries appearing to prefer apparently less advantageous preference schemes such as Cotonou, as was also argued by Babarinde and Faber in Chapter 6 of this volume. For non-agricultural products (mainly textiles and clothing), stricter rules of origin seem to be an important determinant of this preference (Brenton and Özden, this volume). For agri-food products, the situation in 2003 is set out in Table 9.7. Even for EBA products, i.e. products for which EBA actually provided some extra tariff advantages compared with the previous situation, around 23 per cent of agri-food products enter under the Most Favoured Nation (MFN) regime. A further 56 per cent enter under the Cotonou Agreement, even though EBA provides duty-free access (and not Cotonou). Possible explanations for this behaviour, based on interviews with importers, appear to be the small size of the Cotonou/EBA preference margin differential, which gives little incentive to use EBA as well as an entrenched use of ACP administrative forms (OECD 2005). As a result, the overall importance of EBA as a scheme for the import of agri-food products into the EU remains very small.

Table 9.7 The EBA utilization rate for agricultural products and for products where the initiative introduced a real preferential advantage, 2003

Import regime	EU imports 'EBA products' from LDCs		EU imports agricultural products from LDCs	
	€000	%	€000	(%)
MFN	35,259	23	250,862	15
Cotonou	86,669	56	1,156,923	71
EBA	34,143	22	225,794	14
Total	156,071	100	1,633,579	100

Sources: SAD (Eurostat); Taric (DG-Taxud).

CAP reform and EBA-sensitive products

Sugar

Three sensitive products where liberalization is being phased in over a transitional period were identified in the EBA Regulation: sugar, rice and bananas. The competitive threat was recognized, and for these products we are more likely to see evidence of a knock-on effect on CAP reform. The significance of sugar from the perspective of this paper is that not only is there clear evidence that concern about additional EBA imports played a role in shaping the Commission's reform proposal, but the EBA beneficiaries themselves have forcefully engaged in attempting to influence the trajectory of reform, to the extent that they proposed forgoing the main advantage of EBA – DFQF access – for a limited transitional period in return for a less drastic reform package (Brüntrup Chapter 10 of this volume). This has created an unusual alliance between sugar producers in the EU and a cohort of the world's poorest countries. Brüntrup argues that the Commission skilfully used the threat of open-ended LDC imports to push through its favoured reform strategy based on price reductions – what he calls the 'Trojan horse' strategy – rather than compromise on the quota reduction strategy favoured by EU and ACP producers.

The LDCs as a whole are net importers of sugar. Their consumption amounts to about 3.4 million tonnes and production to about 2.6 million tonnes of raw sugar, leaving them with a net deficit of about 0.7 million tonnes. Thus, production is insufficient to meet domestic demand (LMC 2004). Only a few countries are net exporters. Although there are 50 countries that fall under EBA, sugar exports are dominated by a handful of countries. However, EBA arrangements do not require beneficiary countries to be net exporters, only that sugar exported to the EU must be domestically produced to meet the rules of origin. EBA countries have a big incentive to export their domestic production at the high EU price and re-import their domestic needs from the world market. Thus, once quotas are removed in 2009, the pattern of exporting countries could change, depending on the sugar price prevailing in the EU market at that time.

The key issue with regard to EBA is that, prior to reform, the reference price for EU sugar was two to three times the world price. The likely effect of this on full implementation of EBA in 2009 was that the EU would act as a 'suction pump' for sugar production in EBA countries, fuelling growth in the industry which would further increase the volumes of sugar entering the EU through the agreement (EU 2003). Various estimates of the possible volumes involved have been made. Stevens and Kennan (2001) provided a lower-bound estimate based on the difference (in 1997) between global LDC exports and exports to the EU in that year of 100,000 tonnes. The initial Commission estimate suggested that 2.7 million tonnes could be imported, of which 1.3 million would arise from increases in LDC production (DG Agriculture 2000). This was subsequently revised down to 900,000 tonnes after account was taken of infrastructure costs and constraints to expansion faced by countries which are landlocked, politically unstable or face other such problems (DG Agriculture 2001). Other authors give estimates of 2.4 million tonnes (Mitchell 2004) and between 0.5 million and 3.9 million tonnes (LMC 2004). A more recent estimate that takes account of the post-reform prices and includes possible swap trade has suggested a maximum level of imports of 2.2 million tonnes (EU 2005). The wide variation in these estimates partly relates to different assumptions about the likely price on the EU market in the future as well as the proportion of domestic sugar production that might be exported to the EU.

The background to the EU sugar reform is explained by Brüntrup in Chapter 10 of this volume. Now that the reform is agreed, the question arises whether it is sufficient and sustainable in the light of EBA access. The July 2004 reform proposal by the Commission was projected to decrease EU-25 production from 19.7 million tonnes to 12.2 million tonnes by 2012/13. Total preferential imports were expected to amount to 3.9 million tonnes after full implementation of EBA (EU 2005). This included a projected figure of 2.2 million tonnes for EBA imports and 1.3 million tonnes for ACP/India. The Commission's projected fall in EU production of 7.5 million tonnes would be sufficient for the EU to comply with the WTO ruling, to eventually remove export subsidies and to absorb EBA imports with scope to absorb an additional 0.4 million tonnes above the projected level (EU 2005). The sugar reform agreement in November 2005 was less ambitious than the July 2004 proposal. Also, some analysts believe that the EU supply response to a fall in the sugar price will be much lower than what the EU Commission has projected. For example, Gohin and Bureau (2006) expect the reform to reduce EU production by only 2.7 million tonnes, enough to cope with the WTO panel report but not with the elimination of export subsidies or the growth in EBA imports.

On the other hand, there is considerable uncertainty about the likely volumes of EBA imports after 2009. These will depend on the EU price relative to the world price and the ability of the EU to monitor the origin of sugar imported under EBA. Some expert opinion suggests that the EBA export increases projected by the Commission are unlikely to materialize, given that the reform has reduced the profitability of supplying the EU market. Stevens (2006) quotes one industry view that suggests that, if non-LDC ACP countries continue to be constrained by the Sugar Protocol export quantities, the net additional impact of EBA, given the reform, is likely to be less than 100,000 tonnes. Even if non-LDC ACP countries were given EBA-like unlimited access to the EU market at the new reference price, the additional volume of imports from ACP countries under all preferential regimes would be just over 1 million tonnes, according to this source. If these lower figures turn out to be more realistic, then EBA is unlikely to be a factor threatening the sustainability of the reformed EU sugar regime. However, a particular problem could arise after 2009 when EBA quotas disappear and with them the ability of the EU to insist that the refiners pay a minimum price for EBA sugar. The EU would have an obligation to pay the EU reference price for ACP sugar purchased under the Protocol. But if the EU sugar refineries were no longer interested in buying ACP sugar because EBA sugar was available at less than the reference price, this could require the EU to directly purchase ACP sugar with consequent difficulties for its disposal.

Rice

Rice was one of the few products where specific Common Market Organization changes were introduced in the June 2003 Luxembourg Council decision. At that time, EU rice production benefited from an intervention price at €298.35 per tonne (paddy rice). In addition, producers received a direct payment of €52.65 per tonne multiplied by the reference yield and amount paid per hectare, within Maximum Guaranteed Areas (MGA). The intervention price equated with roughly twice the world market price for rice. As for sugar, the fear was that LDCs might export, in line with the rules of origin, the totality of their domestic rice production to the EU, while importing their domestic consumption requirements from the world market. Another fear was that the LDCs might import raw rice, process it and then export it back to the EU, adding sufficient value so as to meet the rules of origin requirements.

The Commission's original proposal in June 2002 was designed to address these fears by decreasing the rice intervention price to world market levels while compensating producers with increased direct aid. Its proposal noted that:

> In the rice sector, the market situation is characterized by considerable public intervention stocks of around a quarter of annual production. A further deterioration of the market imbalance can be expected from the implementation of the Everything but Arms Initiative. By 2009/10, total public rice stocks in the EU are expected to reach an unsustainable level.
>
> (EU 2002)

The Commission proposed a one-step reduction of the intervention price by 50 per cent to a basic price of €150 per tonne for 2004/05 in line with world prices. It also proposed a private storage scheme that would be triggered when the market price would fall below the basic price. Safety net intervention would be established at €120 per tonne. The global price reduction would be compensated at a rate of 88 per cent, equivalent to the total cereals compensation over the 1992 and Agenda 2000 reforms. This implied compensation of €177 per tonne, including the existing payment of €52 per tonne. Of this, €102 per tonne multiplied by the 1995 reform yield would become an income payment paid per farm. The remaining €75 per tonne multiplied by the 1995 reform yield would be paid as a crop-specific aid reflecting the role of rice production in traditional production areas. The MGAs would be reduced to the 1999–2001 average or the current MGA, whichever was lower.

The final Council compromise was close to the Commission proposal. It involved a 50 per cent cut in the intervention price to €150 per tonne, triggering intervention limited to a maximum quantity of 75,000 tonnes per annum. Compensation payments were set at a level of €177 per tonne of which €75 per tonne were granted as a crop-specific payment. The national MGAs were reduced to the lower of the 1999–2001 average or the current MGA. Finally, the Commission was mandated to negotiate tariff quotas for rice imports availing of the WTO procedures for this purpose.

The logic of the reform was spelled out in one of the impact studies undertaken by the Commission (EU 2003). Reducing the support price for rice by around 50 per cent was projected to translate into a very sharp fall in EU domestic prices towards world market levels, which would boost EU rice competitiveness while reducing the attractiveness of the EU market as an export market. The fall in prices is accompanied by the granting of direct payments, which partly maintain the production potential of the EU rice sector. In contrast, the fall in market prices would encourage rice consumption, which would increase strongly relative to *status quo* levels. Whereas total imports were projected to represent some 30 per cent of total EU consumption by 2008/09 before rising to 80 per cent under a *status quo* policy, the substantial drop in the internal market price would enable the EU market to lessen its dependence on imported rice. The EU market would be less attractive as an import market, since domestic prices would develop at world market levels. As for sugar, a clear link can also be made in the case of rice between the reform that took place and concern about the impact of additional EBA imports.

Bananas

Bananas constitute the third of the sensitive products, but LDC access has been totally liberalized since 1 January 2006. The EU's import regime for bananas has been significantly changed, first in response to the introduction of the EU single market in 1993 and more recently in 2006 in response to a series of challenges in the WTO.[3] Prior to 1993, in the absence of a common EU policy on the import of bananas, several member states had their own import controls. The 1993 regime, designed to replace these various national arrangements, was a very complex one, based on a system of quotas differentiated by source, category and by group of economic activity. One quota was reserved for traditional ACP suppliers who could export duty-free within this quota. A second quota was reserved for MFN suppliers (principally Latin American exporters) who paid a duty of €100 per tonne on bananas exported within their quota. Out-of-quota imports were subject to effectively prohibitive tariffs of €850 per tonne (€750 per tonne for ACP suppliers) falling to €680 per tonne at the end of the Uruguay Round implementation period. Following a second GATT challenge to this regime, the EU entered into a Banana Framework Agreement with most of the Latin American exporters that provided a higher tariff quota and a lower tariff under this quota. This regime was again challenged in 1996 and again the complaint against the EU was largely upheld. After years of prevarication within the WTO, the EU and US reached an agreement in 2001 to resolve the dispute. This agreement committed the EU to a series of phased implementation steps, ending with the introduction of a tariff-only regime for banana imports by 1 January 2006. This agreement was underpinned by two waivers granted at the November 2001 WTO Ministerial Conference at Doha in which it was stated that the tariff-only regime 'would result in at least maintaining total market access for MFN banana suppliers'.

In January 2005, the EU proposed a tariff of €230 per tonne, to be imposed on bananas imported from MFN countries under this tariff-only regime. Latin American exporters deemed this to be too high and called for arbitration. The arbitrators ruled that the regime did not satisfy the WTO waiver requirement. In September 2005 the EU submitted a revised proposal with a significantly lower tariff of €187 per tonne together with a duty-free quota for ACP exporters. This was also deemed unacceptable by the arbitrators. Subsequently, the EU decided unilaterally to adopt a tariff-only regime from 1 January 2006 which implements a €176 per tonne MFN tariff and a duty-free quota for ACP exporters. Honduras, Nicaragua and Panama have indicated that they will challenge the new tariff-only regime so the 'banana war' will continue (see Anania 2006 for details).

The EU's stubbornness in resisting these international pressures for reform of its banana import regime is rooted in its commitment to the Banana Protocol to the Lomé IV Convention that required it not to place any ACP state as regards access to its traditional markets in the EU in a less favourable situation than in the past or the present. When EBA was introduced, EU consumption was estimated at around 3.934 million tonnes of which 854,000 tonnes were EU production, 2.420 million tonnes were imported at €75 per tonne duty and 660,000 tonnes were ACP imports at zero duty (DG Agriculture 2000). The very substantial gap between the internal EU price and the world market price (€660 per tonne as compared with €360 per tonne in 1999–2000, according to the same source) created a potential incentive for LDCs to redirect banana production and increase exports to the EU market, disturbing the delicate balance created by the import regime. In practice, however, this potential threat to the regime from increased LDC imports was never considered a serious one. Although total banana production in LDCs amounted to around 5.7 million tonnes and thus exceeded EU consumption by almost 2 million tonnes, most LDCs do not produce exportable bananas. Total LDC exports at that time only amounted to 26,000 tonnes, all of which came from ACP LDCs within the ACP quota (Cape Verde, Madagascar and Somalia) which was not filled in any event.

A recent modelling exercise, one of the few that tries to take explicit account of EBA, confirms this view (Anania 2006). The model is calibrated to 2002, in which year net exports from EBA countries of 50,000 tonnes were assumed. With the implementation of EBA and the continuation of the pre-2006 regime, EBA exports to the EU (including from ACP LDCs) are projected to grow to 133,000 tonnes. (A figure for total exports is not given in the paper.) However, this figure is based on generic export supply elasticities as well as some *ad hoc* modification to the underlying trends in population and *per capita* income which otherwise would have led to decreased or no exports from EBA countries. Thus, it really should be seen as an indicative figure rather than a forecast. Despite the fact that the ending of the transition period for EBA bananas and the introduction of the tariff-only regime were timed to coincide on 1 January 2006, there seems little evidence of any other link between the two events. The EU authorities seem to have been satisfied that EBA bananas were not in principle different from ACP bananas and that any growth in these exports was not likely to add to supply on the EU market beyond what was factored in from ACP countries. Unlike in the case of sugar and rice, therefore, there is no evidence that concern about the impact of EBA imports was a factor in reform of the EU's banana regime.

The role of EBA in WTO negotiations

The CAP has been heavily criticized both by developing countries and by development NGOs within Europe for damaging the growth and trade prospects of poor countries and for being inconsistent with the EU's development policy objectives. In response to these criticisms, the Council of Agricultural Ministers has argued that the EU has developed its agricultural trade policy so as to provide preferential access to developing-country exporters under a variety of schemes (DG Agriculture 2002). Following an informal meeting in Killarney, Ireland, in May 2004, the Agricultural Council highlighted the ways in which the EU has tried to communicate its food safety regulations and provide technical assistance to help developing countries meet these standards as further evidence of its commitment to facilitating trade in food and agriculture (EU 2004).

In this context, EBA may have a significance beyond its immediate trade effects by improving the 'development credibility' of the CAP. As Van den Hoven suggested in Chapter 4 of this volume, the EU may have hoped to co-opt the support of the LDCs (32 of the 50 LDCs are WTO members, out of a total membership of 150 by the time of the Hong Kong Ministerial at the end of 2005) for its cautious approach to further agricultural trade liberalization. These countries now have a stake in the continuation of EU protection, particularly for agricultural products, as further liberalization leads to an erosion of the value of their preferences. Also, having committed to full access for LDCs, the EU could make the extension of DFQF access by all developed countries, and indeed some developing countries, an offensive demand in the negotiations. For some of its trading partners, opening their agricultural markets fully to LDC imports could require changes in their domestic agricultural policies similar to those required for sugar and rice in the EU, quite apart from any market access gains the EU might hope to make through the general tariff cutting negotiations. It is thus not surprising that the EU has been the main champion of this demand in the Doha Round negotiations.[4]

The Doha Declaration, in paragraph 42, commits WTO members:

> to the objective of duty-free, quota-free market access for products originating from LDCs. In this regard, we welcome the significant market access improvements by WTO Members in advance of the Third UN Conference on LDCs (LDC-III), in Brussels, May 2001. We further commit ourselves to consider additional measures for progressive improvements in market access for LDCs.

In fact, many other developed countries, and some developing countries, have already taken steps to implement this commitment. New Zealand and Australia offer DFQF access since 2001 and 2003 respectively. Japan announced its '99 per cent initiative on Industrial Tariffs' in 2001, while Canada's LDC Market Access Initiative announced in 2003 extends DFQF access to all products except supply-managed agricultural products (dairy, poultry, eggs). The US gives enhanced market access opportunities for 25 LDCs of the 37 sub-Saharan African beneficiaries under the African Growth and Opportunity Act (AGOA). Among the major developing countries, Singapore and Hong Kong already offer DFQF access on virtually all products, including products from the LDCs. In many, though not all, cases, however, agricultural products remain excluded from these arrangements.

Against this background, the agreement in the Hong Kong Ministerial Declaration that developed-country members, and developing-country members declaring themselves in a position to do so, would implement DFQF market access for products originating from LDCs by 2008, or earlier if the implementation period of a new agreement begins before then, must be welcomed. There were, of course, qualifications. In particular, the obligation is interpreted as DFQF access for at least 97 per cent of LDC products defined at the tariff line level. Depending on the number of tariff lines with LDC exports, this will normally allow an importing country to exempt its principal sensitive products from DFQF treatment. Although the text includes a 'best effort' provision to 'take steps to progressively achieve' full product coverage, there is no deadline as to when this should be achieved. Also, while developing countries called for a binding commitment, the agreement refers to providing DFQF access on a lasting basis. The possibility of excluding sensitive products from DFQF access means that other developed countries can exempt sensitive agricultural products such as rice in Japan, sugar in the US or poultry meat in Canada from their LDC offers. Given the limited supply capacity of LDCs, this suggests that this agreement will not create particular difficulties for the management of agricultural policy in other developed countries.

The EU's strong support for full DFQF treatment by all developed countries did not appear to earn it much reciprocal support in the agricultural negotiations at the Hong Kong Ministerial. The EU went into the Ministerial seeking a high level of ambition in the final outcome, meaning that it was prepared to offer significant cuts in its agricultural support provided some of the more advanced developing countries made significant offers on industrial protection and services. However, its offer of an average farm tariff cut of 46 per cent was criticized as too low by the US, the Cairns group of agricultural exporters and the G-20, which wanted developed countries to cut tariffs by 54 per cent while developing countries do so by 36 per cent (ICTSD 2005). Significantly, developing countries presented a collective show of strength during the meeting when all of the developing-country groupings – the G-20, the ACP group, the LDC group, the African Union, small and vulnerable economies, the G-33 and G-90 – held a joint press conference to underline their 'shared interest in the development dimension of the round and their expectations for a comprehensive development outcome'.[5] The joint statement by the group – referred to as the G-110 – underlined their objectives to seek the elimination of agricultural export subsidies by 2010; the need for substantial reductions in trade-distorting support; and the importance of substantial improvements in market access for products of export interest from developing countries in developed country markets.[6] Apart from Switzerland, the EU was alone in refusing to accept the 2010 date for the elimination of export subsidies, and the final declaration ultimately compromised on 2013, although with the proviso that a substantial part of the reduction is realised by the end of the first half of the implementation period. Although the EU argued that the offers on manufactures and services at Hong Kong were far too limited to provide the basis for a deal, it found itself blamed for the lack of a breakthrough in the talks by refusing to put a more generous agricultural offer on the table. Rather than being seen as a gesture of good faith and a sign of the development credentials of the EU in the negotiations, EBA appears to have been interpreted more as a fig leaf designed to disguise its reluctance to make an offer that was deemed adequate particularly by the major developing country players in the G-20.

The role of EBA in the EPA negotiations

There is a further channel whereby the introduction of EBA could lead to accelerated CAP reform. The EU is currently engaged in renegotiating its preferential access arrangements for ACP countries under the Cotonou Agreement. The Cotonou Agreement is a comprehensive aid and trade agreement concluded between 77 ACP countries and the EU, signed in June 2000 in Cotonou (Benin). The Cotonou Agreement builds on former ACP–EU cooperation (the Yaoundé and Lomé Conventions), and includes economic and trade cooperation as well as aid. Under the four successive Lomé Conventions (1975–2000), the EU granted a preferential trade regime to ACP countries through trade preferences, commodity protocols and other instruments of trade co-operation as well as financial and technical aid. Under Cotonou, the current non-reciprocal tariff preferences will be maintained until 31 December 2007 under the terms of a WTO waiver from its rules governing non-discriminatory treatment of third countries. Starting from 2008, a set of reciprocal Economic Partnership Agreements (EPAs) will replace them, following negotiations that began in September 2002.

The EU operates on the assumption that the EPA negotiations will be conducted on a regional basis, with regions that have functioning regional integration processes and mechanisms. The outcome should be WTO-compatible, meaning that the ACP countries must open their borders to 'substantially all' EU exports. Those countries that do not wish to open their markets to EU products after 2008 can choose to revert to the GSP regime. Because the ACP countries include both LDCs and non-LDCs, some of them can benefit from EBA status while others cannot.

There will be pressure on the EU to offer reciprocal concessions to offset the opening up of ACP economies to its exports. For the ACP countries, the obvious benchmark would be EBA status for all ACP countries. This would extend DFQF access to countries with substantially greater supply capacity than the LDCs have. On sugar, for example, if these countries were offered a similar deal to the LDCs, ACP exports to the EU could reach 3.5 million tonnes (EU 2003). Indeed, if their entire production was exported to the EU, this would represent 6 million tonnes. Negotiations with MERCOSUR could further increase this quantity (EU 2003), although it is noteworthy that sugar (and beef) were excluded entirely from the EU's liberalization offer under its Free Trade Agreement with South Africa.

If EBA were to become the benchmark for the ACP in the EPA negotiations, it might be argued that the main contribution of EBA to CAP reform has yet to come.

Conclusion

As a general conclusion, EBA has not played a significant role in the evolution of CAP reform apart from the two specific exceptions of sugar and rice. The overall volume of exports, or potential exports, from LDCs in CAP products is just too small to create market management difficulties for CAP-supported products. Sugar and rice are the two commodities where LDCs do have real supply capacity, and full unrestricted access for these products will be available only from 2009. The reform of the EU rice and sugar regimes in 2003 and 2005, respectively, was undoubtedly motivated in part by the desire to make the EU market a less attractive outlet for these countries and thus diminish the volume of additional imports. As Brüntrup argues in Chapter 10 of this volume, once the EBA decision was a reality, the Commission used the threat of open-ended LDC imports to push through its favoured reform strategy based on price reductions against the wishes of those who favoured a quota reduction strategy. In the case of sugar, it is even possible that the November 2005 reform will not have cut EU production sufficiently to accommodate the possible increase in EBA imports. In this situation, the reform makes provision for further unilateral quota cuts to ensure that the EU sugar market is balanced. But, apart from these products, EBA has not influenced CAP reform. Looking ahead, however, in the context of the EPA negotiations between the EU and the ACP countries under the Cotonou Agreement, EBA may yet play a role as a benchmark that ACP countries will use in seeking greater access to the EU market in return for liberalizing their own markets towards EU exports. While it is too early to guess at the shape of a final agreement, any move to extend more generous preferential access to ACP countries for CAP-supported products would have much greater implications for the CAP simply because of their greater supply capacity.

Nor did EBA prove of much assistance in the ongoing Doha Round negotiations. In part, this might have been because the EU's scheme of DFQF access for LDCs is no longer quite as unique as it was. Nearly all developed countries now offer significant duty-free access to LDCs. However, the EU's scheme does cover sensitive agricultural commodities such as rice and sugar, unlike those of the US and Japan. It is also the case that the EU remains the most important importer of agri-food products from the developing world. The 2003 CAP reform has decoupled the vast bulk of direct payments to farmers from production. But these indicators of openness to agri-food imports from developing countries were not enough to overcome their suspicion that the EU was intent on maintaining substantial support to its own farmers while seeking significant reductions in the protection developing countries provide to their industrial and service sectors. In the words of Kamal Nath, India's commerce minister, 'We have been seeing an amazing development in the discussions in Hong Kong whereby the developed countries talk in the plenary halls of a "Round for Free" for developing countries. Then they move to the green room and continue to ask for a "Round for Free", this time for themselves'.[7] This reaction suggests that offering EBA access has done little to improve the development credentials of the CAP in the eyes of developing countries.

Notes

The authors are grateful to Jean-Christophe Bureau, Christopher Stevens and the editors for comments on a draft. Alan Matthews thanks the Advisory Board for Development Cooperation Ireland for its support for the project 'Coherence between Ireland's Official Development Cooperation Activities and other Policy Areas in particular Agricultural Trade and Support Policies' on which this chapter draws.

1 ASEAN countries comprise Myanmar, Thailand, Vietnam, Indonesia, Malaysia, Brunei, Singapore, Philippines. SAARC countries comprise Pakistan, India, Bangladesh, Maldives, Sri Lanka, Nepal, Bhutan.
2 This appears to be based on a misunderstanding of GSP rules of origin. Regional cumulation within the meaning of Commission Regulation (EEC) No. 2454/93 applies where a product used in further manufacture in a country belonging to a regional group originates in another country of the group, which does not benefit from the arrangements applying to the final product, provided that both countries benefit from regional cumulation for that group.
3 The tortuous history of the GATT and WTO banana disputes is recounted in Weiss (2003) and Vranes (2003).
4 The Commission, in its Explanatory Memorandum when presenting the EBA proposal to the Council, noted: 'It will show developing countries in general, and the LDCs in particular, that after Seattle the Community is continuing to take the initiative on trade liberalisation, and will testify to its genuine efforts to take on board the needs and concerns expressed by these countries regarding a new round of multilateral trade negotiations' (p. 3).
5 For an explanation of the coalitions in the Doha Round negotiations (G-20, etc.), see Van Dijck and Faber (2006).
6 See the Joint Statement by the G-110, available online at http://www.g-20. mre.gov.br/conteudo/statement_16122005_02.htm (accessed 17 May 2006).
7 Quoted by Jenny Ricks, Assistant Coordinator of the Trade Justice Movement, in her report from the Hong Kong Ministerial. Available online at http://www.tjm.org.uk/wto/hongkong/day4.shtml (accessed 25 January 2006).

References

ACP-EU Joint Parliamentary Assembly (2001) 'Resolution on 'Everything but Arms'', ACP-EU 3171/01/fin, Libreville, Gabon.

Anania, G. (2006) 'The 2005 Episodes of the "Banana War" serial: An Empirical Assessment of the Introduction by the European Union of a Tariff-only Import Regime for Bananas', TradeAG Working Paper 06-02. Available online at http://tradeag. vitamib.com (accessed on 16 May 2006).

DG Agriculture (2000) 'Everything but Arms (EBA) Proposal. First remarks on the possible impacts on the agriculture sector', Brussels: European Commission.

DG Agriculture (2001) 'Everything but Arms (EBA) Proposal: possible impacts on the agriculture sector', Brussels: European Commission.

DG Agriculture (2002) 'Facts and figures on EU Trade in agricultural products: open to trade, open to developing countries', MEMO/02/296, Brussels: European Commission.

DG Agriculture (2003) 'Mid-term Review of the Common Agricultural Policy: July 2002 Proposals, Impact Analyses', Brussels: European Commission.

Dijck, P. van and Faber, G. (eds) (2006) *Developing Countries and the Doha Development Agenda of the WTO*, Abingdon and New York: Routledge.

EU (2002) 'Communication from the Commission to the Council and the European Parliament: Mid-term Review of the Common Agricultural Policy', COM(2002)394, Brussels: European Commission.

EU (2003) 'Reforming the European Union's Sugar Policy: Summary of Impact Assessment Work', Brussels: European Commission.

EU (2004) 'Facilitating Food and Agriculture Trade: EU biggest Global Food Importer', IP/04/627. Press release, 11 May, Brussels.

EU (2005) 'Reforming the European Union's Sugar Policy: Update of Impact Assessment', Commission Staff Working Document, SEC(2005)808, Brussels: European Commission.

Gohin, A. and Bureau, J.C. (2006) 'WTO Discipline and the CAP: The Constraints on the EU Sugar Sector', TradeAG Working Paper, forthcoming.

ICTSD (2005) 'Low Ambitions Met: Members Adopt Declaration', International Centre for Trade and Sustainable Development, Bridges Daily Update on the Sixth Ministerial Conference, Issue 7.

LMC (2004) 'EU sugar reform: the implications for the development of LDCs', Oxford: LMC International.

LMC (2005) 'EU Sugar Reform. The LDC Proposal: The Development Dimensions', Oxford: LMC International.

Mitchell, D. (2004) 'Sugar Policies: Opportunity for Change', World Bank Policy Research Working Paper No. 3222, Washington DC: World Bank.

OECD (2005) 'Preferential Trading Arrangements in Agricultural and Food Markets: The Case of the European Union and the United States', Paris: Organisation for Economic Cooperation and Development.

Page, S. and Hewitt, A. (2002) 'The new European trade preferences: does "Everything but Arms" (EBA) help the poor?', *Development Policy Review*, 20: 91–102.

Stevens, C. (2006) 'Why Unwinding Preferences is not the same as Liberalisation: the Case of Sugar', IIIS Discussion Paper 137, Dublin: Trinity College.

Stevens, C. and Kennan, J. (2001) 'The impact of the EU's "Everything but Arms" proposal: a report to Oxfam', Brighton: Institute of Development Studies.

Vranes, E. (2003) 'From Bananas I to the 2001 Bananas settlement: a factual and procedural analysis of the WTO proceedings', in F. Breuss, S. Griller and E. Vranes (eds), *The Banana Dispute: An Economic and Legal Analysis*, Vienna and New York: Springer.

Weiss, F. (2003) 'Manifestly illegal import restrictions and non-compliance with WTO dispute settlement rulings: lessons from the banana dispute', in E. Petersmann and M. Pollack (eds) *Transatlantic Economic Disputes: the EU, the US and the WTO*, Oxford: Oxford University Press.

10 EBA and the EU sugar market reform

Development gift or Trojan horse?

Michael Brüntrup

The 'Everything but Arms' (EBA) initiative of 2001 has made three notable exceptions to its commitment for duty-free and quota-free (DFQF) access of least developed countries (LDCs) to the EU market: longer transition periods have been imposed for sugar, bananas, and rice. Despite the delayed opening of the EU market for EBA sugar, it is precisely sugar that presently constitutes the highest preferential value for LDCs – at least in the short and medium term and given the present high EU sugar price under the current Common Market Organization (CMO) for sugar. This European price for sugar is more than €600 per tonne, which is more than three times the world market price. The EU itself projected that the EBA exports would attain 3.3 million tonnes per year in 2013 at a value of almost €2 billion.[1]

However, in June 2005 the EU proposed a reform of the EU sugar market including a substantial reduction of the sugar price of about 40 per cent. As a result, by 2013 exports of EBA beneficiaries might fall to 2.2 million tonnes and export revenues might decline by about €1 billion relative to the unchanged CMO. The final reform reduced the price drop to 36 per cent. Certainly, all actors who have benefited from the high sugar prices will loose. But whereas EU producers (and to a smaller extent traditional preferential exporters from Africa, the Caribbean and the Pacific, ACP) will receive high cash compensations for losses, EBA countries are not considered, since the very high losses of these LDCs are 'only' computational against the expected high future exports. They are nevertheless the most vulnerable and needy of all losers. Therefore, the most important impact of EBA on LDCs will partially be nullified by the sugar market reform.

From this perspective, there are strong arguments supporting the thesis (see also Chapters 2 and 4) that the high motivation for the inclusion (and the transitional period) of sugar in the EBA initiative was to destabilize the European sugar market system. Without EBA, a strengthened quota management system would have saved the system with its extremely high prices – although with major difficulties in balancing the interests of different countries and their sugar sub-sectors, and perpetuating the existence of uncompetitive EU sugar producers. Thus, the EBA sugar imports constituted a 'Trojan horse' to the EU CMO for sugar, which made a price cut almost inevitable. This is not to argue against the price reform, which was necessary in light of the highly distorted and costly EU sugar regime, but to hint to a highly unfortunate economic and political signal towards LDCs.

The remainder of this chapter is structured as follows: the next section shows that sugar is key to the EBA initiative from the European side, but also for many developing countries. Subsequently an assessment is made of the likely impact of EBA on (sugar producing and exporting) LDCs at the time of its introduction, e.g. without reform of the European CMO for sugar. The following section describes the setting that pressed for the reform of the sugar market, and the major options available. Then the reform, as it was finally decided, is briefly presented, as well as the role that EBA played in shaping this outcome. The chapter proceeds with a discussion of the impact of EBA relative to the unreformed CMO for sugar scenario.

In the conclusion, it is argued that the European Commission has used EBA to bring forward a reform in the sugar sector in the spirit of the Common Agricultural Policy (CAP) reforms – alignment with world market prices and decoupled direct payments – and that it has set the scene for further reforms by breaking up the big sugar alliance. For LDCs, the European sugar market is still attractive due to its high and stable prices and long-term perspective until 2015, but the export profits (the rents) and thereby the likely investments are clearly reduced. It is warned that if there are no 'compensations' for the imputed profit losses to EBA countries, this political deal would leave a 'bad taste' of EBA, tariff preferences and the development orientation of the EU in reforming its trade and agricultural policies. This could have negative repercussions for the overall worldwide liberalization process, making a precedent case that liberalization negatively affects the poorest countries in particular.

The EU sugar market order: a highly sensitive issue

When the EBA initiative was announced in 2000, a storm of protest went through parts of the agricultural sector in Europe. According to Oxfam (2000: 1), the protests were 'launched by the National Farmers' Union and parts of the multi-national sugar industry, labelling it a threat to UK sugar beet growers'. But also other groups joined the aforementioned protest against including sugar in the EBA initiative, particularly sugar-exporting ACP countries that had preferential access to the EU. These Sugar Protocol ACP countries tried to ensure that EBA sugar would not undermine their interests (ACP–EU 2001). Only three of these countries are LDCs, namely Tanzania, Madagascar and Malawi.

The opposition of these actors to EBA stems from their vested interests in the EU sugar regime. The essential features of the highly protected EU sugar market can be summarized as follows:

- An intervention price is used to determine the minimum price that triggers official sugar purchases. This intervention price in turn is used as a basis to set prices at various processing stages.
- Specific tariffs of, at present, over €400 per tonne of white sugar (roughly €320 for raw sugar), a figure amounting to 130–260 per cent of the world market price (which has in recent years ranged between US$160–US$300 per tonne),

and the permanent use of special agricultural safeguard measures total to a protection of more than €700 per tonne which have until now served to shield the market against any non-preferential imports.

- To contain overproduction, quantitative target output quotas are set and allocated to the member countries. A distinction is made between regular A-quota sugar and B-quota sugar, which is roughly 40 per cent cheaper.
- Surpluses (so-called C-sugar) are sold on the world market, i.e. exported in the form of sugar and sugar products manufactured by the sugar-processing industry. In addition, all preferential sugar imports are re-exported. Part of these transactions profit explicitly from official export subsidies (in particular the re-export of preferential imports from ACP countries at a cost of €0.8 billion to €2 billion per year in 1995 to 2005, depending on the EU world market price gap and excess sugar in the EU), another part benefits implicitly from high administrative prices, with mandatory charges levied on the sugar industry and ultimately paid by the consumer.

There are two systems that grant a number of ACP countries preferential access to the EU sugar market:

- Under the Sugar Protocol, a present total of 20 ACP countries enjoy irrevocable duty-free import quotas amounting to a total of roughly 1.3 million tonnes of white sugar equivalents per year. Mauritius alone accounts for 38 per cent of this quota, and Fiji, Guyana, Jamaica, and Swaziland together account for another 43 per cent. For India there is a similar arrangement in place for 10,000 tonnes.
- The Special Preferential Sugar arrangement is a non-binding EU commitment that allows further duty-free exports of raw sugar to cover the specific needs of certain sugar refineries. In recent years this has meant a volume of some 150,000–300,000 tonnes per year. The beneficiaries of this agreement are also mainly ACP countries and India.

Besides opposition against including sugar in EBA, other but less fervent concerns were raised against rice and banana liberalization. The protests led to three seemingly minor but in reality important exceptions from full liberalization in EBA for three sensitive products – bananas, rice and sugar. By introducing long transition schemes, the most interesting elements of EBA for the LDCs were delayed for many years.[2]

The then Trade Commissioner Pascal Lamy conceded in an interview in 2001 that the three sensitive products represented 40 per cent of the newly liberalized exports of LDCs into the EU, whereas the non-sensitive products represented 60 per cent (EU 2001). In an early computational experiment using a worldwide computable general equilibrium model, Cernat *et al.* (2003) found that without quantitative import restrictions, 'in value terms, looking at the aggregate exports of LDCs, the increase associated with EBA is very concentrated in sugar and sugarcane, which account by themselves for almost all the changes in values'. After some years of implementation, sugar is still clearly dominating the impact of the EBA initiative (cf. Matthews and Gallezot in Chapter 9 of this volume).

In the case of sugar, up to 1 July 2009, when market access to the EU will be entirely free, EBA countries are allocated sugar import quotas (for raw sugar only). Quotas started from existing imports of 74,000 tonnes in 2001–02, with the quota then rising by 15 per cent per year up to 197,335 tonnes in 2008. The quota allocation to different countries and producers is managed by the European Commission via a complicated (and non-transparent) system of quota application by and approval of the LDC sugar group (Garside *et al.* 2005). In parallel, starting in 2006, non-quota tariffs are set to be reduced to zero in three stages of 20 per cent, 50 per cent and 80 per cent.

Sugar in EBA: probably the main 'development gift' for LDCs

While sugar exports from LDCs are still being substantially hindered by quotas, future years could see a substantial raise. The size of the sugar export surge will determine the value of the entire EBA initiative to a large degree. The direct impact of EBA on LDC sugar sectors depends on their own sugar production and exports, and on the internal distribution of revenues within LDCs.

As Jess Pilegaard also pointed out in Chapter 8 of this volume, LDCs are not homogeneous with regard to sugar production and consumption. 'As a whole, the LDCs have a net deficit approaching one million tonnes per annum' (LMC 2004: 7). The production of sugar is concentrated on some 22 LDCs that have formed the LDC sugar group.[3] In several other countries sugar mills are no longer operational but a production potential probably exists (LMC 2004).

There are at present six net exporting LDCs (Ethiopia, Malawi, Myanmar, Sudan, Zambia and Angola) and two that are in a process of rehabilitation and close to becoming net exporters (Mozambique and Tanzania). Only Malawi and Tanzania export refined sugar, the others raw sugar only. As mentioned, three LDCs have already preferential though quota-restricted market access to the EU under the ACP Sugar Protocol – Malawi 21,000 tonnes, Madagascar 11,000 tonnes, Tanzania 10,000 tonnes.[4]

In recent years there has been considerable privatization and rehabilitation in several sugar-producing LDCs, most often under foreign investors (LMC 2004; Garside *et al.* 2005). These foreign direct investments are key to assessing the impact of EBA, since in LDCs very often neither liquidity nor know-how nor management capacities are sufficiently available. Foreign investors are attracted by preferential agreements offering export rents, but will also consider overall economic policies such as foreign exchange and money transfer and country risks. All this has consequences for supply capacity and supply response. Thus, foreign investment climate, production efficiency and export performance, comparative advantage and (preferential) trade regimes are inextricably linked.

The sugar price that LDC producers can expect when exporting to the EU under EBA depends on the CMO. When the EBA initiative was implemented in

February 2001, the CMO for sugar was in force as described above, with a very high reference price of €632 per tonne for white sugar, and derived prices for raw sugar and beets according to standard transformation, processing and handling margins. Comparably high prices were paid to ACP Sugar Protocol country exporters (there are minor adjustments for raw cane sugar), and these prices were also granted to LDCs under EBA. This discussion thus relates to the impact of EBA on LDCs under the CMO for sugar valid at the time of the EBA introduction.

EBA impact on LDC sugar exports to the EU

Several attempts have been made to assess the medium and long-term investment and supply response to the EBA initiative. Global trade studies including developing countries and sugar markets commonly use the GTAP (Global Trade Analysis Project) database and model. In principle this global approach is most appropriate because it reflects interdependences of markets for capital, production factors and output. But for the time being the GTAP is hardly capable of predicting the impact of EBA in combination with EU sugar policy reform, since it is based on oversimplified assumptions and weak data. For instance, it takes no individual consideration of most LDCs, which are mostly hidden within the cluster 'Rest of Sub-Sahara Africa', it assumes uniform hypothetical supply elasticities and transport costs across all countries and, until version six (released 2005), no account of preferences is taken (Achterbosch *et al.* 2004; Huan-Niemi and Kerkelä 2005). In addition, it seems that the restrictive sugar trade policies of the few African LDCs which are explicitly modelled in GTAP are not correctly taken into account (Keck and Piermartini 2005).

In studies trying to at least partially adapt global models to reflect the impact of the EU sugar reform under EBA on LDCs, the exports from LDCs to the EU vary from 0.2 million to 2.9 million tonnes according to various parameters: the degree of price depression, the substitutability of LDC and EU sugar, and the extent of swaps (Berkum *et al.* 2005). Under the assumptions that that the price drops by 33 per cent, that swaps are allowed, that LDC cane sugar is an almost perfect substitute for EU beet sugar if properly refined, and that capital fixed in beet refineries is written off in the medium term in favour of investment in cane refineries (either in the EU or in LDCs), a volume of about 2.7 million tonnes or US$1.6 billion seems to be the most realistic long-run projection.

Given the limitations of global trade studies to reflect the impact of detailed policy changes, many studies use more detailed partial models of agricultural markets, sometimes including sweeteners and some rudimentary interactions with other markets. For instance, Adenäuer *et al.* (2005) use a regional optimization model of the European farm sector coupled with a simplified world multi-market model and derive EBA sugar imports under unchanged prices of 3.1 million tonnes in 2009. However, due to the complex realities of sugar markets – such as conditions of monopsony, imperfect information, production risk and associated quota risks, economies of scale, sunk investment costs, limited tradability of quotas, rent seeking and political economy – modelling is difficult and limited by many assumptions. Data availability and reliability are major constraints even under European conditions, and much more so for developing countries where market imperfections and complex multi-goal rationalities of farm-household economic behaviour are more accentuated.

One of the most thorough attempts to look deeper into the supply response capacity of LDC sugar producers is LMC (2004) which attempts to individually model the supply response of 22 EBA beneficiaries under certain assumptions of sugar production costs and a minimum expected internal rate of return on investment costs which amount to at least 65 per cent of total production costs (in Europe). This industrial investment approach is probably justified for sugar, certainly more than for other agricultural products, since most of the production is carried out on joint plantations/refineries or under close contract farming schemes. Sugar processing for export is always a large-scale industry with its own support infrastructure (electricity, water, quality services, etc.). Even medical care and education are provided to secure high labour morale and standards. Therefore, sugar production and processing are rather insulated from the vagaries of fragile economic and social conditions in LDCs.

Since the investment conditions in LDCs are still more risky than in industrialized and even 'normal' developing countries, the basic required internal rate of return in LMC (2004) was set at 20 per cent. The LMC study then determines the most competitive producers on the EU market, assuming that the EU internally liberalizes the sugar market. Under this hypothesis, first expected production capacities of LDCs are calculated, which are then compounded to result in an aggregated supply response curve by combining them with fixed quota productions for EU and ACP countries as well as liberalized isoglucosis competition within the EU (Figure 10.1).

The resulting EU-25 equilibrium price without quotas (but shielded from the world market) is estimated to be about €400 per tonne in 2015, a number similar to other studies including one by the EU which finds €350–€450 per tonne (EU 2003). At that price, EBA countries would supply about 0.5 million tonnes raw value. LDCs that are competitive and supply to the EU include Sudan, Malawi and Mozambique, while others such as Ethiopia and Senegal would also be competitive but would prefer to sell to other (national and regional) markets with more attractive prices (see below). It is worth noting that most preferential ACP suppliers are not competitive, in particular Mauritius and the Caribbean countries are losers. These results are more or less in line with other studies (EU 2003; Oxfam 2005a).

With higher than free equilibrium price in the EU, the attractiveness of sugar production and export will be higher, and so will be investments in several LDCs, as well as Congo, Laos, Madagascar, Nepal and Zambia. With price cut scenarios of 20 per cent, investments are calculated to be US$1 billion, and production of LDCs will increase from the present 2.8 million tonnes to about 4.5 million tonnes, and export to the EU to 2.7 million tonnes. With a reduced minimum internal rate of return of 10 per cent the projections even amount to 4 million tonnes of EBA sugar supply.

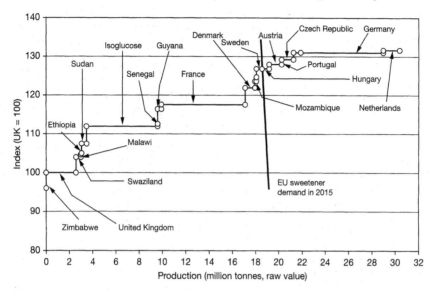

Figure 10.1 The hypothetical EU sweetener market under a liberalized EU sugar market: prices and quantities in 2015

Source: LMC (2004: 30)

These independent calculations confirm the EU's own assessments that predict a massive increase of LDC sugar under constant EU sugar prices (cf. Table 10.1, column 'no reform').[5] The EU counted with 3.5 million tonnes of EBA imports in 2012–13 at an unreformed price of €560 per tonne.[6] This means that, when keeping ACP imports constant and reducing exports to 0.6 million tonnes (which will have to be reduced to zero if export subsidies, as defined by the WTO case of Brazil against EU, also include all direct and indirect (cross) subsidies, see below), EU production would drop by more than 40 per cent to 12.2 million tonnes.

EBA impact on income generation and internal distribution

Up to here, the impact of EBA was only analysed at the aggregated national level and in terms of export and import volumes and gross values. Since in the political debate about EBA and sugar market reform distributional issues receive utmost attention, analyses on distributional impacts have been reviewed. These reviews confirm that 'studies assessing the impact of preference erosion have largely disregarded within-country impacts across different parties' (Garside *et al.* 2005; cf. Tangermann 2002). Information on net income and distributional effects is indeed difficult to obtain or generate, which is partially due to the characteristics and limitations of the different methodological approaches described above:

- Sectoral approaches can look into the details of factor use and production of the sugar sector and its different players as well as internal adaptation costs, but rarely do they consider economic opportunity costs. If sugar output and

Table 10.1 Projections of the impact of different sugar reform models in the EU

Model	Base year	2012/13 reform	2012/13 no reform
Prices			
Institutional price (€/t)	631.9	385.5	560.0
Cumulative reduction in institutional price[a] (%)		39	
Quantities (million tonnes)			
Consumption	15.9	16.0	16.0
Quota	17.4	[17.4]	[17.4]
Cumulative increase in isoglucose production	–	0.3	0.0
Estimated EU production under quota	16.7	12.2	11.4
C sugar production	3.0	–	–
Total EU-25 production	19.7	12.2	11.4
Total imports (million tonnes)	2.3	3.9	5.2
of which ACP/India	1.3	1.3	1.3
of which EBA/SPS	0.2	2.2	3.5
of which MFN	0.1	0.1	0.1
of which Balkans	0.3	0.3	0.3
Total exports (million tonnes)			
of which non-Annex 1	0.4	0.4	0.4
of which A and B with refunds	1.1	0.0	0.2
of which eq. ACP	1.6	0.0	0.0

Source: EU (2005).

Note:

a Technical reduction of 11% on Institutional prices in the no-reform scenario.

trade increase, e.g. due to policy reform, opportunity costs reduce gross revenue gains because production costs increase too, and alternative gains from the use of production factors such as land are not realized. On the contrary, if sugar production and export are reduced, the real loss to the exporter is lower than the gross revenue loss because of reduced costs and/or alternative uses of production factors.

- Microeconomic multi-sector approaches (farm-household, agricultural programming models, etc.) are able to look at some of these issues but most often do not incorporate interactions with non-farm sectors, or do so in a grossly simplified way, particularly concerning markets and their structures. In addition, such models hardly exist nor are they available for sugar producers in LDCs.

- Global general equilibrium models take into account alternative uses of production factors, markets and prices, and are thus able to distinguish between effects on the sugar sector and on the economy as a whole. However, they do this in a very superficial way, especially for poor developing countries (if at all, see above), which makes a sound evaluation of complex policy adjustments highly questionable. In particular, the ownership of production factors and the distribution of rents and value added and their changes have hardly been analysed. Very often, the central information provided by these studies beyond gross production and trade is national welfare, which is generally dominated by price effects on the consumer side.

Another specific problem is that sugar markets are not transparent, even in Europe (Adenäuer *et al.* 2005). In most developing-country cases, market price mechanisms are absent or profoundly skewed, and information on remuneration of cane producers, wages, administration, taxes, levies and profits is absent (Mitchell 2004; Larson and Borell 2005; Garside *et al.* 2005). One reason for this particular intransparency is that the sectors are not open markets, but vertically integrated to a very high degree: at least in the way of contract farming between a few sugar factories and outgrowers, and at the maximum by single integrated production/ processing enterprises. A second reason is that the markets are not structured as ideal polypolies but as national monopolies or oligopolies. The third reason is that local sugar markets are often among the most regulated and protected ones in these countries. This is explained, fourth, by their high politicisation from the side of very influential factory owners, from the side of well organised workers unions, and the international preference systems which imply political decisions on quota alloca- tions. In several LDCs, governments hold shares in sugar companies. All this leads finally to a high degree of rent seeking behaviour, corruption and intransparency of the distribution of gains. Despite these limitations, several case studies seem to allow the following rough indications of distribution, in particular poverty orientation, of sugar production in LDCs.

In many LDCs, sugar is produced entirely within large enterprises, from cane to refinery (estates/mills). In these cases, workers' salaries constitute the bulk of the value added that goes to poorer sections of the population. In some case studies it is found that wage work in estates of SSA is an important income source, better- paid than other wage employment and significantly increasing household income (Tschirley and Benfica 2000; Pletziger 2003; Oxfam 2004) compared with local smallholder farming. Tschirley and Benfica (2000) relate their findings to African multi-country research that finds 'strong evidence of a positive relationship between total household income and the level and income share of off-farm earnings'.[7] Many sugar companies in LDCs offer additional social services for their workers and even for the local communities. The following passage refers to Southern Africa (Todd 2001: 3):

> With the exception of Swaziland, governments in the region levy little or no tax on revenue from the sale of sugar under the EU and US preferential access arrangements. The sugar factories support large settlements, with the com- pany typically providing or contributing directly to schooling, healthcare, and housing. The sugar producers are major employers in these countries. Their ability to assist with social provision stems in part from the high prices derived

from the sale of sugar at preferential prices to the EU and, to a much lesser extent, the US.

There is no doubt that compared with Western social standards and probably with standards in formal urban sectors in LDCs, these jobs do not provide comparable benefits. NGOs in particular are very sceptical of the role of large estates and sugar factories in providing adequate social benefits to workers. They generally advocate smallholder sugar production (Forum Umwelt und Entwicklung 2004). However, the fact that the competition for jobs in sugar factories and estates is very high (Oxfam 2004) shows that it provides better conditions than local alternatives.

In some LDCs, a considerable proportion of cane for industrial sugar production is bought from farmers, for instance 70 per cent in Swaziland and 30 per cent in Madagascar (Buntzel-Cano 2005). This kind of smallholder production is overwhelmingly assessed as positive for poverty reduction. It is interesting to note that smallholder farms are also important providers of wage work, although the remuneration of workers is even lower than on estates (Tschirley and Benfica 2000; Forum Umwelt und Entwicklung 2004; Oxfam 2004).

Thus the effect of sugar production on rural poor household incomes, through wage or smallholder remuneration, is generally described as positive in LDCs, although the evidence is anecdotal. However, it should be recalled that this is only partly attributable to highly priced exports to Europe – the US has similar trade and preference agreements. The main reason is that local sugar prices are generally much higher than prices on the world market and sometimes even the EU market. In most countries, the share of exports is modest or very modest compared with local sales (only in Mozambique, Madagascar and Zambia does the share of exports exceed 40 per cent), and there are numerous indications that sugar prices in LDCs are very high compared with world market prices (LMC 2004).

In fact, in most countries government protective trade policy measures, such as tariffs, licensing, consumption quotas and direct government trading, are the main reasons for these high prices. These are more important factors than the remoteness of the markets – although the remoteness has a clear influence on some landlocked countries (e.g. Cooksey *et al.* 2003; Berkum *et al.* 2005; LMC 2004). For instance, the Southern African Development Community (SADC) has its own Sugar Protocol attached to its regional trade policy, regulating exchange between SADC members until at least 2012 (Lincoln 2005). By their relative size, the sugar industry exerts strong political influence on trade policies at national and regional level. This is at the expense of consumer interests who have to pay more for sugar. Taking into account that sugar provides on average 8 per cent of the caloric intake in developing countries (Chenoweth 2000), this is an important burden, and it is even a higher burden on low-income households who have a proportionally higher consumption of sugar (and other basic food) than high-income groups.

The interests and objectives of these government interventions are complex and not without contradictions. In several countries (e.g. Ethiopia, Sudan, Madagascar) governments or related organizations such as pension trust funds, have invested heavily in the sugar industries. The trade unions of sugar industries, often privatized state enterprises, are among the only organized workers in these largely informal economies. By making them participate in the rents they are converted into important allies in upholding protective policies. For some countries in Southern Africa, the threat of pending land reforms are an additional argument for estate and mill owners to distribute rents down to (potential) land holders, thereby increasing the number of beneficiaries of high sugar prices.

Overall, it seems that in many LDCs there is a positive impact of EBA exports on rural households directly involved into producing and transforming local sugar. Negative impacts on consumers are directly attributable not to EBA but to the general protectionism in the sugar sectors of LDCs, to which the EU sugar policy is indirectly contributing by providing arguments against more liberalized trade.

Reform of the EU sugar market

Reasons and options

As has been pointed out, sugar is particularly interesting in the context of EBA, since it is probably the only product which is both highly protected in the EU and for which a high (though still hypothetical) production capacity exists in LDCs. The large benefits are linked to the high EU sugar prices that are enshrined and assured in the CMO. This CMO was scheduled to expire at the end of June 2006. There were at least four reasons for the sugar market reform. First, it is no longer in line with the EU vision of agricultural markets. Since 1992, CAP reforms have had a thrust toward lower prices and a decoupling of subsidies from production. Apart from colliding with rules of the World Trade Organization (WTO, see below), the old price-supporting policies are expensive, opaque, producing over-supply and reducing competition. The costs of the CMO for consumers are estimated at up to €6 billion.[8] The lack of competition on the European sugar market is probably even more important than the lack of efficiency: none of the quotas, be it on the level of country, factory or producer, is freely tradable. The average national production costs within the EU vary from about €250 per tonne to more than €600 per tonne (EU 2004). Large efficiency differences between factories and farmers are also reported. As a matter of fact, the majority of transfers from the CMO for sugar benefit the most prosperous farmers in the EU who own the best soils and are generally larger than comparable non-sugar producers. Since the relation of profitability between already reformed crops and non-reformed sugar has been growing in recent years, this has become a politically untenable situation.

Second, sweeteners increasingly compete with sugar. A high sugar price makes such substitution more attractive. Halting such products would result in an ever-growing extension of the CMO for sugar such as has already been the case for isoglucosis.

Thirdly, export subsidies, claimed to be the most trade-distorting policies, have been attacked in the WTO for many years. For the time being, under the Uruguay

Agreement on Agriculture (AoA), the EU is still allowed to use some export subsidies; for sugar this amounts to 1.3 million tonnes and €500 million. Until recently, the role of indirect export subsidies such as those incorporated in food aid, export credits and cross-subsidization of exports through different internal support mechanisms was rather unclear. In the case of cross-subsidization, in the finding of a WTO dispute settlement on dairy against Canada in 2001, it was announced that cross-subsidization was generally disputable. The WTO case by Brazil against the EU sugar exports went a step further. In April 2005, the Appellate Body of the WTO made it clear that the EU indeed had subsidized exports of up to 4.2 million tonnes of sugar in 2001–02 in different ways: 2.8 million of indirectly subsidized C-sugar and 1.6 million tonnes of ACP sugar (WTO 2005a). At least the exports exceeding the Uruguay commitment must be reformed within 15 months. However, before 2013 all kinds of export subsidies will have to be eliminated, as was agreed during the WTO Ministerial in Hong Kong (December 2005). This requires a substantial reduction of EU sugar production and imports, or an extremely costly and disputed internal disposal or conversion.

Fourthly, under the present CMO, state intervention agencies would theoretically have to purchase all sugar if the sugar price paid to factories fell below the intervention price. In the past, intervention has been extremely rare – it was last used in 1986. This was the result of the very high import protection and additional internal market imperfections. There have been signs of oligopoly market behaviour of the sugar industries (Monti 2003). The rare use of factual intervention is a constitutional and well planned element of the CMO for sugar, since this prevents it from causing EU budget expenditures and thus isolates the CMO from major pressure for policy reform. Instead, a combination of subsidized exports and high import protection kept internal sugar price above intervention price. However, the need to improve market access in the framework of the Doha Round is likely to force the EU to reduce its agricultural tariffs. The price reform scenario would allow reduction of these tariffs by up to 60 per cent; the other scenarios would not permit more than 36 per cent reduction according to EU (2003). It is, of course, not yet clear what the market access negotiations – the most complicated pillar of the WTO agricultural negotiations – will yield. The decisive factor will be how many 'sensitive products' with less ambitious market access improvements will be available for WTO members. If a large number of sensitive products can be selected, many sugar products could be included in the EU sensitive product list; however, if a limited number of sensitive products would be available, this is less probable, since there are products which are politically more sensitive to EU agriculture than sugar, particularly milk and meat products.

In addition, it must be taken into consideration that many products contain sugar. Their tariff reduction will disadvantage the EU sugar-consuming industry vis-à-vis competitors who can use cheap world-market sugar. And as export subsidies on the products of the sugar consuming industry will be phased out, the sugar-consuming industry will suffer twice. This industry is a far larger industry (though with less concentrated interest in the sugar price) than the sugar-producing industry, and it has mobilized its influence to lobby for lower prices (CIUS 2004).

However, it is questionable whether these arguments would have been sufficient to reform the CMO for sugar. In fact, the best shield against reforms has been that, in contrast to most other agricultural market organizations, the transfers are not weighing on the EU budget but are almost entirely financed via (hidden) increases in consumer prices. Even most export subsidies are financed through levies on factories and producers; ultimately, consumers finance these subsidies. The next section will show that the reform agenda of the CMO for sugar was not so much driven by the costs, but rather by the desire of the EU to create more competitiveness in the European sugar sector.

EBA as a Trojan horse

The reform alternatives for the sugar CMO after 2006 were theoretically open, and the European Commission underscored that openness by presenting four different scenarios (EU 2003):

- A continuation without reform including a small 'natural' price reduction of 17 per cent until 2015 (compare Table 10.1).
- Complete liberalization, with a price drop of 42 per cent against the no-reform scenario.
- Price reform with, as a central element, the reduction of the internal white sugar price of 25 per cent.
- Quota reform, with fixed quotas at a level corresponding to the no-reform scenario, that would enable slightly higher EU production and slightly lower imports, assuming that the bulk of the quota reduction would be imposed on LDCs.

After long discussions and consultations, in July 2004 the European Commission proposed a reform with a price reduction of 33 per cent for the institutional (white sugar intervention) price, which would mean beet price reduction of 37 per cent (EU 2004). This proposal was presented before the WTO had declared that a large proportion of EU sugar exports are illegal under the AoA. In order to further reduce supply, the price drop was later increased to 39 per cent (43 per cent sugar beet) in order to further production and imports (EU 2005).

On 24 November 2005 EU agricultural ministers agreed to the reform proposal. This step is seen as the decisive hurdle within the EU reform process. The final shape of the reform is as follows (CTA 2006):

- Reduction of the guaranteed price for white sugar of 36 per cent over four years, beginning in the 2006–07 season.
- Introduction of compensation to sugar beet farmers 'at an average of 64.2 per cent of the price cut', through a 'decoupled' payment linked to 'cross-compliance' which will form part of the 'single farm-payment scheme'.
- Payment of an additional 'coupled payment' equivalent to 30 per cent of the price cut for a transitional period of five years plus the possible payment of

'limited national aid', but only for 'countries which give up more than half of their production quota'.

- Establishment of a 'voluntary restructuring scheme lasting four years for EU sugar factories and isoglucose and inulin producers, consisting of a payment to encourage factory closure and the renunciation of quota'; the aim of the restructuring fund is to 'encourage less competitive producers to leave the industry', to finance social and environmental adjustment costs, and to provide funds for diversification in the most affected regions; payments will be €730 per tonne in the first two years, falling to €625 in year three and €520 in year four.
- Funding of restructuring measures through a special levy placed on remaining quota holders over three years of the transition.
- Introduction of scope to use restructuring funds to compensate beet producers affected by factory closures (reportedly up to 10 per cent of the amount).
- Establishment of a 'diversification fund for member states where the quota taken up is reduced by a minimum amount, with diversification funds increasing the more the quota is renounced'.
- Merging of the A and B quotas.
- Provision for the use of non-quota sugar in the 'chemical and pharmaceutical industries and for the production of bio-ethanol'.
- Allocation of an additional quota of 1.1 million tonnes to 'C' sugar-producing countries against 'a one-off payment corresponding to the amount of restructuring aid per tonne in the first year'.

The detailed modalities for the implementation of the reforms have yet to be fixed. Also tariff reductions are not yet decided upon, they will mainly depend on ongoing WTO negotiations, as argued above. In this context it is interesting that the intervention agency will be maintained during the four-year transition period, followed by 'the introduction of a private storage system as a safety net in case the market price falls below the reference price'.

The list of measures shows that the compensation of European actors will be substantial. According to data from Oxfam the European farmers will in the four-year transitional phase receive annual compensation from the EU of first €900 million which will then increase to approximately €1.5 billion from 2008 (*AgraFacts* 2005). The sugar industry will in the course of the four-year transition period receive a contribution estimated at approximately €6 billion for the deactivation of capacity (*Handelsblatt* 2005). The latter compensation will be borne by consumers. The sugar reform is not as radical as presumed: the sugar price will remain at €404 per tonne, thus most probably at about 100 per cent over the long-term world market price level. Quotas will remain the major instrument for production allocation.

In order to understand the role that EBA has played in pushing and shaping the reform, the context has to be further analysed. EBA was not the only reason, but instrumentally important in pressuring for a reform of the CMO for sugar. Since 2003 the European Commission has argued that the EBA commitments would swamp the market with sugar, which would have to be reduced from EU internal production quotas. Demands for maintaining EBA sugar quotas, together with quotas on EU production, were refused mainly on international credibility over EBA (EU 2003: 18):

> The option of returning to fixed quotas would require the Community to go back on its international commitments like the 'Everything but Arms' initiative, which opens up the Community market to all products from the least developed countries (LDCs). The EBA initiative is one of the pillars of the agricultural proposal on market access in the WTO and other international fora. Reintroducing tariff quotas would exact a high political price and harm the Community's credibility.

The request for continuing EBA quotas was refused, although this was asked by the EU industry and by sugar-producing ACP countries. Even LDCs themselves offered to restrain their preferential exports to the EU to 1.62 million tonnes per year for an extended transition period until 2019, in exchange for maintaining the present price level (LDC sugar group 2004). A new alliance among EU and LDC/ACP sugar producers and their governments emerged, united by the aim of maintaining a high-price quota-based EU sugar regime. Most NGOs supported that proposal (Forum Umwelt und Entwicklung 2004; Oxfam 2005b) although it was contrary to their previous protests against EBA quotas and claims for unrestricted access.

Is it credible that the import quota system was dropped because of a commitment to LDCs against their own expressed position? Most certainly not: that commitment could also have been honoured in other ways. First, EBA imports could have been absorbed by stronger cuts into own production quotas. The EU estimated the additional production between the no-reform and the price reform (minus 39 per cent) scenarios to be about 1.3 million tonnes (Table 10.1). The need for sugar exports and export subsidies could have been prevented via a quota system or via export taxation. In contrast to widespread belief, the WTO has not imposed a certain type of reform, but has only stopped illegal export subsidies: 'the European Communities' obligations to the ACP countries are to *import* certain quantities of ACP sugar, whereas the European Communities' obligations in the present dispute relate to *exports* of the European Communities' own subsidized sugar' (WTO 2005b: 17, original emphasis). Second, a voluntary export restraint of LDCs could have been allowed via a WTO waiver for a very long transition period.[9] If not, a larger cut in EU production would have been necessary – this is the position of most NGOs. Thirdly, in contrast to stated free market access for LDCs, a clause has been introduced in the EBA regulation to 'review' EBA sugar exports to the EU should the exports increase by more than 25 per cent year on year, although it remains to be seen how strictly this safeguard will be applied in practice.[10]

Which arguments have been decisive to make the sugar reform inescapable? The high costs of the present CMO do not really seem to have been an argument for reform: the reform with its manifold compensations is said to be 'budget-neutral' (*Handelsblatt* 2005), thus not saving any money. Some underlying arguments can be deducted from the evolution and final outcome of the reform process in which the European Commission acted against almost all sugar actors involved:

- The present inefficiencies induced by the CMO probably are the most important argument. In effect, the major result of the price reduction and accompanying compensation scheme will be the elimination of high-cost sugar producers and the concentration of sugar production in the most efficient countries (France, Germany and to a lesser extent the Netherlands, Austria, UK, Poland and Slovenia) and regions. This principal aim of competitiveness is underlined by the fact that an additional amount of 1.1 million tonnes plus non-quota industrial sugar will be made available.
- Once sugar production is concentrated in fewer countries, it will be politically easier to introduce additional reforms after 2014. The political process of policy reform in the EU is hampered by the need to find a majority if not unanimity among all member states. In view of the high rents from the extremely high price of sugar that accrue to even marginal producers, it would have been politically more than difficult to push through any meaningful selective production cuts in weak regions in favour of the competitive regions. Uniform reductions would only have served to further undercut the overall international competitiveness of EU sugar.
- The alignment of the sugar market on the CAP trend towards world market prices and decoupled income transfers does not only favour other non-sugar farmers; it also clearly signals that this trend is definite. It discourages attempts to turn the clock back. The 'sacrifice' of northern European countries – they lose more than the southern countries in absolute terms who produce less and at higher cost – will pave the way for the reform of the remaining unreformed markets (olives, cotton, vegetables) where even stronger resistance is to be expected since the southern countries are more dependent on agriculture and have less funds to compensate and restructure farmers and rural areas.
- Europe's room for manoeuvre in the WTO Doha Development Round is clearly enhanced, not only by permitting higher tariff reductions but most probably also by reducing the Amber Box subsidies, since after four years (with the end of the price reduction phase) the intervention mechanism will be given up in favour of a private stockholding scheme.

The impact on developing countries, particularly LDCs

Following the European Commission's prediction (Table 10.1, column 'reform'), the first proposed sugar price reduction of 39 per cent would reduce EBA sugar exports by roughly 1.3 million tonnes or €1.1 billion. Sugar exporters under EBA are by far the most affected group, whereas the ACP countries maintain their exports and EU farmers even increase production.

Similarly, Berkum *et al.* (2005) find that the effect of a 33 per cent sugar price reduction in the EU compared with the present CMO (from €632 to €421 per tonne) is a 49 per cent reduction in exports (from 384,000 tonnes to 196,000 tonnes) under a low substitution hypothesis and a 67 per cent reduction (from 2.7 million tonnes to 0.9 million tonnes) under a high substitution hypothesis, the latter being more realistic in the long run (see above). This is calculated to cause a national income reduction of about US$1 billion.

LMC (2004) predicts that LDC sugar exports to the EU will be reduced by 2.1 million tonnes (from 2.7 million to 0.6 million) when the EU sugar price drop increases from the baseline 20 per cent to 33 per cent at an internal rate of return of 20 per cent required by investors, and a reduction of even 2.8 million tonnes (from 3.9 to 1.1) at an internal rate of return of 10 per cent. Countries that would stop exporting sugar under EBA include the Democratic Republic of Congo, Laos, Madagascar, Nepal and Tanzania, whereas Ethiopia, Malawi, Mozambique, Sudan and Zambia (Pilegaard, Chapter 8 of this volume) would continue to export.

The LMC study, however, also shows that the drop in production is much less severe than the export drop, since in most countries internal prices are very high, as was argued above. Therefore, export revenue losses have fewer consequences than would be the case if a lower price, e.g. the world market price, prevailed. That is most probably the fundamental reason why the advantage of the alternative proposal of the LDC sugar group (LMC 2005) based on a quota of 1.6 million tonnes and a 20 per cent price cut (see above), compared with the EU proposal of no quota and a 33 per cent price reduction, is calculated to be 'only' €290–400 million. (The variance is due to alternative hypotheses on the sugar price development after 2009.)

The indirect effects of the reform of CMO for sugar on world markets and external protection of third countries can have an even larger effect on LDC sugar producers than the direct one. Two opposite effects can be expected. One is that, due to the reduced sugar exports by the EU, world market prices tend to increase. The extent is debated, ranging from 5–40 per cent, depending on the degree of liberalization and assumptions about supply reactions in major exporting countries, notably Brazil (Larson and Borell 2005). The other, partially related, effect is that arguments to heavily protect internal markets will fade away, presumably leading to worldwide tariff reductions with second-round effects on sugar production and consumption. In light of the high levels of current protection, this liberalization effect could clearly outstrip any world market price effect in many countries. The combination of these effects would, in addition to the price level for producers, affect the internal welfare distribution between producers and consumers. These effects of the reform of the CMO, however, are the same for all scenarios involving a halt to EU sugar exports, whether via price or quota reduction.

How the computed income reduction induced by the reform of the CMO for sugar is affecting poor people is a difficult question. LMC (2005) calculates that 122,000 to 146,000 labourers can be directly maintained with the alternative CMO reform, based on quotas. But it seems logical that the level of redistribution will be affected as well. In this chapter it has been argued that the relatively generous remuneration of poor sugar employees and smallholders is partially explained by the existence of rents that sugar estates and factories get from internal and external policy interventions. It is likely that the social benefits supplied by sugar estates will be reduced in order to comply with lower rent margins. Regarding Southern Africa, Todd (2001: 3) supposes that 'the prospect of lower sugar prices . . . implies that these [sugar] companies will find it increasingly difficult to support the same level of social infrastructure, and this will add to governments' budgetary commitments in the region'.

Whatever the exact numbers, it must be taken for granted that the income reduction in sugar-exporting LDCs due to the CMO reform is of the order of US$100 million to US$250 million per year, a substantial reduction. Lower-income groups such as estate workers and small sugar farmers will see their incomes decline as well.

Conclusion: towards compensation for LDCs?

The inclusion of sugar into EBA has had major repercussions for the sugar markets of both the EU and the LDCs. For the EU, EBA threatened to bring in a wave of sugar. Since re-exporting is restricted and will be even more so given recent WTO dispute settlement, these additional sugar imports would have to be completely reduced from EU producer quotas. In addition, EBA extended the vested interest in high sugar prices to more actors outside the EU.

In the end, EBA was an extremely useful argument (a Trojan horse) for the European Commission. It proved to be functional in proposing and imposing drastic price reductions, instead of adapting the quota allocation system. This helped to improve the competitiveness of the EU sugar production and the EU's standing in WTO negotiations. This policy choice is in obvious contradiction to the positions of most other political players involved in the sugar sector: EU sugar producers and industry, member states, most NGOs, sugar-producing ACP and EBA countries and producers. In addition, the reform opens up the battlefield for future reforms after 2014. On the other hand, it may be argued that EBA was an important argument to maintain the fundamental structure of the CMO for sugar and not to liberalize it completely.

If that effect of EBA was actually planned, then the Commission – initially DG Trade, but later obviously also DG Agriculture, see also Chapter 4 in this volume – was very skilful in harmonizing the EBA commitment with the CMO reform schedule. Until now, increased EBA sugar imports have not caused an addition to EU imports (and re-exports) since they were deducted from Special Preferential Sugar imports.

For LDCs, EBA initially promised extremely attractive sugar prices, and an investment and sugar boom followed. It is important to note that, even under the new scheme, LDCs are still guaranteed a very high and stable sugar price with a comfortable time horizon and low risk of export disruption. Important investments of several hundred million US dollars in competitive countries are still expected (LMC 2004; Peltzer 2006). Inclusion of sugar into EBA is still a clear 'development gift'.

However, the agreed price cuts will, compared with the initial promise and with the alternative LDC proposal on a quota solution for the CMO reform, entail adverse impacts on the poorest countries by not guaranteeing the high prices. This will negatively affect the attraction for investments in the sugar sector. LDCs are the only group of countries for which the EU foresees substantial volume changes in addition to the price cut effects.

It is certainly not advisable to induce the creation of non-competitive sugar industries by exaggerated price guarantees, particularly under an international trade regime that strongly pushes for liberalization at least in the medium term. Although investment and rents from exports could be enhanced in the near future, the later social costs of supporting unprofitable sugar industries and eventual breakdown could be extremely expensive. Nevertheless, it is politically and socially disturbing that, in relative terms, the poorest countries are the most important losers from the attempt to bring the CMO for sugar into line with economic rationality, just at the time that they get access to it.

That leads to the question whether there should be 'compensation' for LDC countries. As shown, compensation for European farmers and industry is abundant and will absorb even the funds that hitherto have been used to re-export preferential sugar imports. Compensation for ACP countries is sparse in the short term but probably better in the medium term. The claim for compensation for erosion of deep, bilateral, clearly calculable preferences is almost uncontested, both generally (Tangermann 2002) and specifically for long-standing ACP sugar exporters. For ACP Sugar Protocol countries, the EU committed €40 million for the year 2006 in order to elaborate adjustment plans. The EU has promised further assistance for adjustment via National Action Plans. These plans may include, according to local realities, measures to improve competitiveness of existing sugar industry, promotion of diversification, and measures for general adaptation. Aggregate losses are estimated at about €300 million to €500 million per year by various authors (Mitchell 2004; Gillson *et al.* 2005; Chaplin and Matthews 2006). Compensation of ACP countries for preference erosion in sugar exports to the EU would also address a large part of the general preference erosion that will be the result of multilateral trade liberalization in the Doha Round. It is a stumbling block to the negotiations because such general preference erosion is very diffuse, difficult to calculate and to compensate.[11]

Compensation of EU sugar preference erosion for LDCs, as mentioned, is even more difficult to justify, to calculate and to allocate. In fact, in comparison with ACP Sugar Protocol suppliers, there are no established sugar sectors on which injury will be inflicted, or which have to be reformed or dismantled. The impact of the reform depends heavily on what is the reference scenario. At the time of the introduction of EBA in 2001, there had been discussions about reforming the CMO for sugar for about a decade, since the MacSharry reforms. But the final sugar reform proposal by the European Commission, foreseeing a massive price reduction, was only proposed in June 2005 and adopted by the Council in November 2005. Real export surges of LDC sugar have been prevented by quotas.

Although the claim for compensation of LDCs is not as evident as that of ACP countries, there is a clear reduction in future income. Compensation in this case cannot claim to counteract a real negative variation or injury due to EU action, but to substitute for the initial transfer promise. The amount could be just a fraction of the calculated losses, e.g. 25 per cent or €70 million to €100 million per year. The obvious lack of proportionality between compensation of EU and developing country producers would still persist.

Whether the compensation should consist of a cash fund or of other means depends among other things on several strategic considerations, which are not clear-cut. How is the compensation accounted for in the calculation of Official Development Assistance (ODA), and what about the flexibility and orientation of such compensation compared with other ODA? This is because if, as must realistically be assumed, the compensation funds will be financed out of the EU development budget, the additionality of such a fund over existing ODA is a pertinent demand but hardly obtainable. The EU has promised to increase its ODA to 0.51 per cent of its gross domestic product until 2010 and to 0.7 per cent in 2015. All 'additional' assistance will obviously fall into these ambitious target levels and will most certainly not increase the overall aid. However, if LDCs doubt that the EU promise will hold and that they will be the beneficiaries, or if they want to predefine the way additional ODA will be spent, an additional promise of compensation would be worth while. At worst, these commitments for aid in exchange for preference erosion will shape the sectors to which ODA goes, e.g. to export development and not to health care. At best, consistent and specific cross-sector development programmes linked to (new) export opportunities will emerge that address capacity constraints both internally and through ODA. In contrast, if additionality seems more important, preference erosion should be compensated by non-ODA measures such as additional trade preferences e.g. in the service sector or through clearly improved rules of origin.

If cash compensation seems more reasonable, the way of spending it could be similar to the ACP Action Plans, but a higher degree of flexibility could be applied, e.g. by earmarking a certain share for sugar and another for exports in general, thereby supporting the diversification of EBA export structure. (On the idea of subsidizing exports from LDCs, see Hoekman and Prowse 2005.)

Notes

1 The underlying assumption of this chapter is that major shocks in the international market for sugar are absent (*ceteris paribus* analysis). At the time this book went to press, high energy prices increased demand for biologically produced fuel, particularly in Brazil. This increases world demand for sugar and thus the world market price. This relaxes the transitional phase of the EU reform for both the EU and the preferential suppliers. To the extent that this boom persists, the 'sugar case' is easier to acommodate.

2 It should be noted, however, that at present sugar is of only minor importance for LDCs' exports as a whole: 535,000 tonnes of raw and white sugar or 1.1 per cent of all

LDCs' agricultural exports of US$5.8 billion in 1998, giving it rank 15 at the HS6 level (if including molasses, 1.3 per cent and rank 10 at the HS2 level; Höllinger and Hauser 2002). This puts the EBA initiative into perspective: many export products of LDCs such as crude oil, diamonds, minerals and many tropical products already face low or zero tariffs either on an MFN basis or under general preferential tariff schemes. Other products with high tariff barriers being liberalized in EBA are either not produced in tropical LDCs or face high non-tariff barriers.

3 African members of the LDC sugar group are: Burkina Faso, Burundi, Central African Republic, Chad, Democratic Republic of Congo, Ethiopia, Madagascar, Malawi, Mali, Mozambique, Rwanda, Senegal, Sudan, Tanzania, Togo, Uganda, Zambia. Other countries are: Bangladesh, Haiti, Laos, Myanmar, Nepal.

4 The ACP signatories of the Sugar Protocol are: Barbados, Belize, Côte d'Ivoire, Democratic Republic of Congo, Fiji, Guyana, Jamaica, Kenya, Madagascar, Malawi, Mauritius, St Kitts and Nevis, Suriname, Swaziland, Tanzania, Trinidad and Tobago, Uganda, Zambia, and Zimbabwe. See Appendix 1.1 in Chapter 1.

5 It must be kept in mind that there is a strong degree of uncertainty in the supply response calculations, and both the EU and LMC/LDC sugar exporters could have good reason to exaggerate the 'danger' of EBA exports – the former in order to justify stronger price cuts against the opposition of the EU sugar sector, the latter to convince the EU of its quota model.

6 The price reduction of 11 per cent in Table 10.1 is assumed to eliminate the effect of an assumed equivalent productivity growth in sugar beet production.

7 The positive finding of relative high incomes of estate workers is contrary to some assessments for more advanced developing countries, particularly northern Brazil (Forum Umwelt und Entwicklung 2004).

8 On the size of welfare losses opinions differ because they depend, *ceteris paribus*, on transfer efficiency of the CMO for sugar on which estimations differ (Licht *et al.* 2003).

9 Although it must be stated that voluntary export restraints are illegal under WTO law.

10 Letter of 1 December 2005 by the EU Commissioner for Agriculture to the Chairman of the LDC Sugar Group. Online: available at http://ec.europa.eu/commission_barroso/fischer-boel/speeches/letter1b.pdf (accessed 29 May 2006).

11 Preference erosion and its compensation is a presently hotly debated issue with the ongoing WTO trade talks. Some authors such as Özden and Rheinhardt (2002) doubt that preferences have a positive effect on development, while others find positive results (Mold 2005; see Wainio *et al.* 2005 for reviews). Particularly since the inclusion of preferences into CGE models, a growing body of literature has acknowledged and quantified the costs of preference erosion (IMF 2003; François *et al.* 2005). The overall value amounts to some US$200 million to US$500 million. Tangermann (2002) discusses the different types of preference erosion and the possibilities to compensate them.

References

Achterbosch, T.J., Ben Hammouda, H., Osakwe, P.N. and Tongeren, F.W. van (2004) 'Trade Liberalisation under the Doha Development Agenda. Options and Consequences for Africa', LEI Report 6.04.09, The Hague: LEI.

ACP–EU (2001) 'Resolutions adopted by the ACP–EU Joint Parliamentary Assembly at its second session in Libreville (Gabon) from 19 to 22 March 2001', Libreville, Gabon: ACP–EU Joint Parliamentary Assembly.

Adenäuer, M., Louhichi, K., de Frahan, B.H. and Witzke, H.P. (2005) 'Impact of the "Everything but Arms" initiative on the EU sugar sub-sector', CAPRI Working Paper 05-03, Bonn: Institute of Food and Resource Economics.

AgraFacts (2005) 'Farm Council concludes Historic Sugar Reform Deal'. Available online at http://www.dgroups.org/groups/CoOL/docs[more] (accessed 5 March 2006).

Berkum, S. van, Roza, P. and Tongeren, F.W. van (2005) 'Impacts of the EU sugar policy reforms on developing countries', LEI Report 6.05.09, The Hague: LEI.

Brüntrup, M. (2005) 'Between protectionism, poverty orientation, and market efficiency: reform of the EU sugar market organization', *Analysen und Stellungnahmen*, 8/2005, Bonn: DIE.

Buntzel-Cano, R. (2005) 'Die Zuckermarktordnungsreform in der EU. Auswirkungen auf die Entwicklungsländer in der südlichen Hemisphäre', in Lange (ed.) *Zucker. Markt oder Ordnung?* Loccumer Protokolle 04/05, Loccum: Evangelische Akademie.

Cernat, L. (2005) 'Everything but Arms', *Financial Express*, 23 March. Available online at http://www.financialexpress.com/print.php?content_id=85947 (accessed 3 December 2005).

Cernat, L., Laird, S., Monge-Roffarello, L. and Turrini, A. (2003) 'The EU's Everything but Arms Initiative and the Least-developed Countries', Discussion Paper No. 2003/47, Helsinki: UNU/Wider.

Chaplin, H. and Matthews, A. (2006) 'Coping with the fallout for preference-receiving countries from the EU sugar-reform', *Estey Centre Journal of International Law and Trade Policy*, 7, 1: 15–31.

Chenoweth, F.A. (2000) 'Future Trends in World Sugar Consumption and their Impact on Food Security'. Paper presented at the seventh World Sugar Farmers' Conference, 11–14 September, Durban. Available online at http://prosi.net.mu/mag2000/381 oct/chen381.htm (accessed 6 March 2006).

CIUS (2004) 'Reform of the EU Sugar Regime', Brussels: Committee of Industrial Users of Sugar. Available online at http://www.cius.org/linkdocs/quotas.pdf (accessed 3 December 2005).

Cooksey, B. (2003) 'Marketing reform? The rise and fall of agricultural liberalisation in Tanzania', *Development Policy Review*, 21, 1: 67–91.

CTA (2006) 'The revised sugar regime', Executive Brief, CTA, Brussels: Technical Centre for Agricultural and Rural Cooperation ACP–EU.

EU (2001) 'Chat with Lamy and Nielson'. Available online at http://europa.eu.int/comm/chat/lamy-nielson/lamy-nielson_en.pdf&e=9797 (3 December 2005).

EU (2003) 'Reforming the European Union's Sugar Policy: Summary of Impact Assessment Work', Commission Staff Working Paper, Brussels: Commission of the European Communities.

EU (2004) 'Communication from the Commission to the Council and the European Parliament, accomplishing a sustainable Agricultural Model for Europe through the reformed CAP: Sugar Sector Reform', Communication COM(2004)499final, Brussels: Commission of the European Communities.

EU (2005) 'Reform of the Sugar Sector'. Press release. Available online at http://www.europa.eu.int/comm/agriculture/capreform/sugar/index_en.htm (accessed 3 December 2005).

Forum Umwelt und Entwicklung (2004) 'How we view a Reform of the Sugar Market Order'. Available online at http://www.forum-ue.de (accessed 3 December 2005).

François, J., Hoekman, B. and Manchin, M. (2005) 'Preference Erosion and Multilateral Trade Liberalization', Policy Research Working Paper 3730, Washington DC: World Bank.

Garside, B., Hills, T., Marques, J.C., Seeger, C. and Thiel, V. (2005) 'Who Gains from Sugar Quotas?', ODI-LSE DESTIN DV406 Research Project. Available online at http://www.odi.org.uk/iedg/Projects/EU_banana_sugar_markets (accessed 3 December 2005).

Gillson, I., Hewitt, A. and Page, S. (2005) 'Forthcoming Changes in the EU Banana/Sugar Markets: A Menu of Options for an Effective EU Transitional Package', London: ODI.

Handelsblatt (2005) 'Reform des Zuckermarkts entschärft', 25–27 November.

Hoekman, B. and Prowse, S. (2005) 'Policy Responses to Preference Erosion: From Trade as Aid to Aid for Trade'. Presented at the international symposium 'Preference Erosion: Impacts and Policy Responses', Geneva, 13–14 June.

Höllinger, F. and Hauser, E. (2002) 'Die Agrarexportstrukturen der LDC und probleme des Marktzugangs auf den wichtigsten Exportmärkten. Studie im Rahmen des Sektorvorhabens Agrarhandelsförderung in LDC', Eschborn: GTZ.

Huan-Niemi, E. and Kerkelä, L. (2005) 'Reform in the EU Sugar Regime: Impact on the Global Sugar Markets'. Paper prepared for the ninty-ninth seminar of the European Association of Agricultural Economists, 24–27 August, Copenhagen.

IMF (2003) 'The IMF's Trade Integration Mechanism (TIM): A Factsheet'. Available online at http://www.imf.org/external/np/exr/facts/tim.htm (accessed 6 March 2006).

Josling, T. (2003) 'Domestic Farm Policies and the WTO Negotiations on Domestic Support'. Paper presented at the International Conference 'Agricultural Policy Reform and the WTO: where are we heading?', Capri, Italy, 23–26 June.

Keck, A. and Piermartini, R. (2005) 'The Economic Impact of EPAs in SADC Countries', Staff Working Paper ERSD-2005-04, Geneva: WTO.

Larson, D. and Borrell, B. (2005) 'Sugar Policy and Reform', Policy Research Working Paper No. 2602, Washington DC: World Bank.

LDC sugar group (2004) 'Proposal of the least developed countries of the world to the European Union regarding the adaptation of the EBA initiative in relation to sugar and the role of the LDCs in the future orientation of the EU sugar regime'. Available online at http://www.ldcsugargroup.org (accessed 23 May 2006).

Licht, G., Hussinger, K. and Sofka, W. (2003) 'Wohlfahrtseffekte der EU-Zuckermarktordnung', Mannheim: Centre for European Economic Research.

Lincoln, D. (2005) 'The Historical Geography of the Southern African Development Community's Sugar Protocol'. Available online at http://www.cishsydney2005.org/images/LincolnST13.doc (accessed 14 February 2006).

LMC (2004) 'EU sugar Reform: The Implications for the Development of LDCs'. Report prepared for the Department of International Development (DFID), Oxford: LMC International.

LMC (2005) 'EU Sugar Reform. The LDC Proposal: the Development Dimension'. Report prepared for the LDC Sugar Group, Oxford: LMC International.

Mitchell, D. (2004) 'Sugar Policies: Opportunity for Change', World Bank Policy Research Working Paper No. 3222, Washington DC: World Bank.

Mold, A. (2005) 'Trade Preferences and Africa: The State of Play and the Issues at Stake', African Trade Policy Centre, Work in Progress No. 12, Addis Ababa: Economic Commission for Africa.

Monti, M. (2003) 'The Relationship between CAP and Competition Policy: does EU Competition Law apply to Agriculture?', COGECA Conference, Helsinki Fair Trade, 13 November, speech/03/537. Brussels: Commission of the European Communities.

Oxfam (2000) 'Everything but Arms' *and Sugar?*', *Oxfam Parliamentary Briefing*, No. 13, December.

Oxfam (2004) 'A Sweeter Future? The potential for EU sugar reform to contribute to poverty reduction in southern Africa', Oxfam Briefing Paper No. 70, Oxford: Oxfam International.

Oxfam (2005a) 'Truth or consequences. Why the EU and the USA must reform their subsidies, or pay the price', Oxfam Briefing Paper No. 81, Oxford: Oxfam International.

Oxfam (2005b) 'An end to EU sugar dumping?', Oxfam Briefing Note, 28 April, Oxford: Oxfam International.

Özden, Ç. and Reinhardt, E. (2002) 'The Perversity of Preferences: GSP and Developing Country Trade Policies, 1976–2000', Policy Research Working Paper No. WPS2955, Washington DC: World Bank.

Page, S. (2005) 'Can Special Trade Measures help Development, when Trade Tools are Weak and the Conditions for Development are Uncertain?', London: ODI.

Peltzer, R. (2006) 'Reform des EU-Zuckersektors: kein Geniestreich', *Informationsbrief Weltwirtschaft und Entwicklung*.

Pletziger, S. (2003) 'Die Bedeutung des Zuckersektors für die wirtschaftliche, soziale und regionale Entwicklung in Malawi unter besonderer Berücksichtigung internationaler Handelsvereinbarungen', Master Study, University of Trier.

Tangermann, S. (2002) 'The Future of Preferential Trade Arrangements for Developing Countries and the Current Round of WTO Negotiations on Agriculture', Rome: FAO.

Todd, M. (2001) 'The Sugar Industries of Southern Africa: Challenges and Opportunities', Briefing Paper No. 12, London: Royal Institute of International Affairs.

Tschirley, D. and Benfica, R. (2000) 'Smallholder Agriculture, Wage Labour, and Rural Poverty Alleviation in Mozambique: What does the Evidence tell Us?', Research Report No. 41, Maputo: Directorate of Economics, Ministry of Agriculture and Rural Development.

Wainio, J., Shapouri, S., Trueblood, M. and Gibson, P. (2005) 'Agricultural Trade Preferences and the Developing Countries', Economic Research Report No. (ERR6), Washington DC: United States Department of Agriculture.

WTO (2005a) 'Dispute settlement: Dispute DS266, European Communities – Export Subsidies on Sugar'. Available online at http://www.wto.org/english/tratop_e/dispu_e/cases_e/ds266_e.htm (accessed 3 December 2005).

WTO (2005b) 'Award of the Arbitrator, European Communities. Export Subsidies on Sugar', arb-2005-3/20. Available online at http://www.wto.org/english/tratop_e/dispu_e/265_266_283_arb_e.doc (accessed 3 December 2005).

11 ACP–EU negotiations on Economic Partnership Agreements and EBA

A dual relationship

Sanoussi Bilal

Two regimes for ACP LDCs

The trade policy of the European Union (EU) provides for a number of preferential trade regimes for its partners. One category is composed of countries enjoying free trade with the EU based on free trade agreements (FTAs) and/or deeper forms of integration (customs union, association agreements, specific bilateral agreements, economic area agreements, etc.). These agreements are based on the principle of reciprocity of preferences, where substantially all trade is liberalized among the parties, possibly in an asymmetric way. Such trade agreements are also often complemented by economic, political, strategic and development cooperation dimensions.

The EU has also offered a number of trade preferences on a non-reciprocal basis to favoured partners, because of proximity (e.g. neighbourhood policy) and/or development (and other) concerns. This is the case for former colonies of European countries that belong to the group of African, Caribbean and Pacific (ACP) states. Since 1975, they have benefited from preferential access to EU markets on a non-reciprocal basis, under successive Lomé Conventions, and since 2000 under the Cotonou Agreement. This non-reciprocal regime of preference for the ACP, for which waivers have been obtained at the World Trade Organization (WTO) in 1995 and 2001, will be in place until the end of 2007. Other developing countries can qualify for graduated trade preferences offered by the EU under its Generalized System of Preferences (GSP).

The rest of EU trade takes place under the Most Favoured Nation (MFN) principle enshrined in the multilateral trading system of the General Agreement on Tariffs and Trade (GATT) and the WTO.

With the 'Everything but Arms' (EBA) initiative, formally proposed by the European Commission in September 2000 and adopted by the Council in February 2001, a new layer of preferences has been unilaterally introduced by the EU. This new scheme falls under the framework of the EU's GSP. In essence, under the EBA initiative the EU grants free access to its market in a non-reciprocal way to all products from least developed countries (LDCs), with the exception of arms and, during a period of transition, sugar, rice and bananas.

Although this initiative is intended for all LDCs, it creates a *de facto* dichotomy between the least developed ACP countries, on the one hand, and the non-least developed ACP countries, on the other hand. Indeed, while all ACP countries benefit from preferential market access to the EU under the Cotonou Agreement (at least until 2008), only least developed ACP countries can choose between the Cotonou and EBA trade regimes. The EBA initiative constitutes a nominal improved market access for LDCs compared with the Cotonou trade preferences, although more stringent rules of origin and other custom administration burdens have arguably reduced the attractiveness of EBA over Cotonou (see Brenton 2003).

This special treatment for the LDCs in the ACP group is explicitly foreseen in the Cotonou Agreement. Article 37(9) provides that the EU will offer all LDCs 'duty- free access for essentially all products . . . at the latest in 2005'.[1] The adoption in 2001 by the EU of the EBA initiative providing free access to European markets for all exports 'originating' in LDCs with the exception of arms did exactly that.[2]

Many observers have noted that the European Commission's approach may lead to a split in the ACP group (e.g. Page and Hewitt 2002; and Chapter 2 of this volume). The EBA initiative has *de facto* divided the ACP countries into two distinct categories, the 38 least developed ACP countries, which benefit from the duty-free and quota-free (DFQF) market access to the EU under EBA and the 39 non-least developed ACP countries, which do not (see Appendix 1.1 in Chapter 1). Perhaps more important, the danger is looming that the EBA initiative will further erode the coherence of the ACP group during its negotiations with the EU on Economic Partnership Agreements (EPAs).

The Cotonou Agreement and EPAs

From 1975 to 2000, four successive Lomé Conventions governed the development and trade relations between the ACP countries and the EU. Under this development framework, the EU has granted non-reciprocal trade preferences for ACP exports to its market. This trade regime has been extended under the Cotonou Agreement until the end of 2007. The regime allows most ACP products to enter duty-free on the European market, with the exception of some 'sensitive' agricultural products covered by the EU's Common Agricultural Policy (CAP). Four commodity protocols, annexed to the Lomé Conventions, provide free access for a specified quantity of exports from a selected group of traditional ACP suppliers of bananas, rum, sugar and beef. The Rum Protocol has been abandoned under the Cotonou Agreement.

Despite receiving preference for more than 30 years, ACP exports have, in general, performed poorly. The share of the ACP group in total EU imports from third countries has fallen by more than half, from 8 per cent in 1975 to 2.8 per cent in 2000. Judging from the composition of aggregate ACP exports, trade preferences have in most cases failed to promote diversification. Besides the disappointing results of the Lomé Conventions, pressure has increased on the ACP–EU trade relations to be more consistent with the rules of the multilateral trading system, since the establishment of the WTO.

The Cotonou Agreement, signed in June 2000, contains the basic principles guiding the relations between the EU and the 77 ACP countries for the following

20 years. Both parties agreed to review the ACP–EU trade regime in order to make it compatible with WTO rules and with the main aim of promoting growth, sustainable development and poverty alleviation and helping the ACP countries integrate into the world economy. After more than three decades of non-reciprocal preferential access to the EU market, EPAs are thus meant to replace the existing trade regime by reciprocal agreements that are fully WTO compatible, while providing for differential and asymmetric treatment.

In essence, the EPAs should be essentially enhanced, development-oriented free trade areas between ACP (regional) groupings and the EU. They aim to cover not only trade in goods and agricultural products, but also in services, and should address tariff, non-tariff and technical barriers to trade. As proposed by the European Commission, other trade-related areas would also be covered, including by increased cooperation between the EU and the ACP, such as competition, investment, protection of intellectual property rights, standardization and certi-fication, sanitary and phytosanitary (SPS) measures, trade facilitation, trade and the environment, trade and labour standards, consumer policy regulation and consumer health protection, food security, public procurement, etc.

On 27 September 2002, the ACP and the EU officially launched negotiations on EPAs. For the period of negotiations, foreseen until the end of 2007, the current preferential trade regime is extended. The EPA negotiations have been structured around two main phases. The first phase of the negotiations, extending until September 2003, took place between the European Commission and the ACP group as a whole. The objectives were to define the format, structure and principles for the negotiations. After this initial phase of negotiations (consisting mainly in exchange of views and clarifications from both parties) at the all ACP group level with the EU, a second phase of negotiations started at the regional level, in view of concluding regional EPAs. Each of the main ACP regional groupings has thus entered into bilateral negotiations with the EU: Central Africa (CEMAC-plus) and West Africa (ECOWAS-plus) in October 2003, East and Southern Africa (COMESA) in February 2004, the Caribbean (CARIFORUM) in May 2004, Southern Africa (SADC-minus) in July 2004, and Pacific in September 2004. These negotiations are thus intended to build on and foster the regional integration process of the ACP groupings. While the negotiations should be completed by the end of 2007 for EPAs to enter into force by 2008, the transition period for the full implementation of these EPAs may take well over a decade.

It is important to note that there is no obligation to sign an EPA. ACP countries that would decide not to join an EPA shall be provided with alternative arrangements.

Coherence between EPAs and EBA?

In the context of the EPA negotiations, the key issues relate to

- The incentive that least developed ACP countries would have to conclude an EPA.
- Consistency between EPA and EBA in terms of market access.

Incentives for least developed ACP countries to conclude an EPA?

One of the recurrent questions about EPA negotiations is: why should an LDC in an ACP region sign an EPA with the EU? Officials and diplomats from ACP countries and EU member states, many civil society representatives and NGOs, as well as several other observers, have frequently raised this question.

Indeed, least developed ACP countries already benefit from WTO-compatible free market access to the EU for all their products, without any restriction (except arms) from 2009. Unlike other ACP countries, they do not risk losing their preferential access to the EU under the Lomé/Cotonou regime should they fail to conclude an EPA. Why then should they open up their markets on a reciprocal basis to EU products when they can freely export their products to the EU under EBA?

Addressing uncertainty

From a formal perspective, it is worth stressing that EBA is a unilateral initiative by the EU, with no contractual obligation. As such, it could be repealed at will by the EU, notably during one of its regular revisions of its GSP regime. So, while it is true that ACP LDCs can currently export to the EU under the EBA regime, this may not be the case in the future. Should the EU decide to end its EBA regime some time in the future, the least developed ACP countries that had not entered into an EPA would lose their current level of preferences. With the end of the WTO waiver for Lomé/Cotonou-type of preferences at the end of 2007 and the unwillingness of the EU to seek to prolong this regime, the ACP countries that would not be covered by an EPA would thus have to export to the EU under the GSP, the level of preference of which is unilaterally determined by the EU and which is currently less advantageous. In the worst-case scenario, were the EU to also abolish its GSP, non-EPA ACP countries would lose all preferences, having to trade on an MFN basis with the EU.

As a consequence, ACP LDCs may see the signing of an EPA with the EU as the only viable option to guarantee preferential market access to the EU over time. By entering into a contractual agreement with the EU in the form of an EPA, ACP countries can ensure legal certainty with regard to their access to the EU market.

From a political perspective, it is doubtful whether the EU will ever protect its market against LDC products. In the current Doha Development Agenda the EU has attempted, with mixed results, to multilateralize its DFQF market access for LDCs, proposing that all developed countries, as well as more advanced developing countries, offer similar concessions to all LDCs, under WTO binding commitments.[3] The EU will also have difficulty justifying a reversal of its policy in favour of LDCs, should it repeal EBA. None the less, although EBA appears to be here to stay, a policy shift can never be ruled out. The assessment of the likelihood of this risk that least developed ACP countries make may affect their negotiating strategy with the EU in the context of an EPA.

Potential effects

Whether or not an EPA can be more advantageous for least developed ACP countries than EBA treatment will ultimately depend on the nature and specific content of an EPA (as well as possible accompanying measures). Since EPAs are currently under negotiation, their specific shape is not yet known. At this stage, it seems thus more relevant to refer to the *potential* benefit of an EPA over EBA.

In terms of market access, EBA covers trade in goods only. However, trade in services has become increasingly relevant for most developing countries. As illustrated in Figure 11.1, during the 1980–99 period service exports have about tripled in the Caribbean and increased fourfold in the Pacific, accounting respectively for half of the Caribbean trade and one-quarter of the Pacific trade by the end of the 1990s. While African service exports have not followed the same trend, the potential remains high in this sector. The EU constitutes already a major market for ACP services exports, accounting for over half of ACP trade in services. Should the EU agree to further open its market in the context of an EPA to services imports where ACP countries have a comparative advantage (notably in Mode 4, the temporary movement of natural persons), EPAs would provide least developed ACP countries with potential exporting opportunities beyond the reach of EBA. However, to be of additional value, an EPA will have to entail provisions on services in the interest of the ACP countries concerned that go beyond those granted under the General Agreement on Trade in Services, as currently negotiated under the Doha Development Round.

Besides, nowadays impediments to trade take various forms, reaching far beyond the simple imposition of tariffs and quotas addressed under EBA. First, rules of origin are an important factor in the restrictiveness of any preferential trade regime (e.g. Augier *et al.* 2005; Cadot *et al.* 2006; Lanchovichina *et al.* 2001; Brenton and Özden in Chapter 7 of this volume). In particular, the rules of origin under the EBA initiative (which are those of the EU GSP) are less generous than the ones

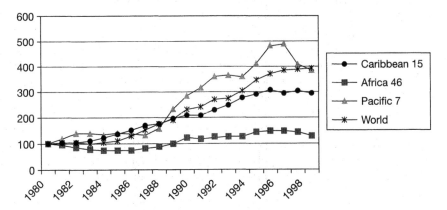

Figure 11.1 Evolution of service exports by region since 1980 (1980 = 100).

Source: UNCTAD (2002)

prevailing under the Cotonou trade regime (notably with regard to cumulation), which could explain the low rate of utilization of EBA by least developed ACP countries (see also Brenton 2003; Brenton and Manchin 2003; Candau *et al.* 2004; Candau and Jean 2005; Manchin 2005; Sandrey 2005). In the context of an EPA, the EU is committed, in line with the Cotonou Agreement, to simplify its rules of origin towards the ACP. This opportunity to negotiate more favourable rules of origin under an EPA could thus significantly increase the effective market access to the EU of ACP products, and hence the value of the preferences granted under an EPA as opposed to EBA.

Second, technical barriers to trade (TBT) and SPS measures, although difficult to quantify, *de facto* also play an important role in restricting trade flows, thus reducing the value of preferences (see Beghin and Bureau 2001; Maskus and Wilson 2001; as well as Vancauteren 2002, in the context of the EU). EBA removes duties, levies and quotas only, not other barriers to trade. Nominal free access to the EU market is thus not translated into effective free access. As a possible remedy, EPAs aim to address SPS and TBT. They have the potential to cut red tape, simplify administrative procedures, promote the timely exchange of information and facilitate compliance with standards, notably by strengthening the capacity (including at the institutional level) of the ACP countries (e.g. Doherty 2005; Rudloff and Simons 2004).

In the same vein, EPAs have the potential to address 'beyond the border' regulatory frameworks that affect trade flows. The objective would not simply be to promote trade, but more significantly to create the economic and regulatory conditions favourable to an environment conducive to business activities and to sustainable development. The inclusion in an EPA of trade-related provisions on issues such as trade facilitation, competition policy, investment, government procurement, intellectual property rights, trade and environment, labour standards, etc., could have a significant impact on the trade, economic and development potential of an ACP country or region. According to the European Commission, EPAs could thus stimulate the development of attractive regional markets that will foster investment and facilitate the integration of ACP countries into the world economy (see European Commission 2005a).

Such ambits clearly go beyond the scope and intent of EBA, which provides only DFQF market access to the EU.

The European Commission also doubts the ultimate contribution to development that can be derived from preferential access to its market, arguing that ACP countries mostly fail to effectively take advantage and develop under the 30-year-long Lomé/Cotonou non-reciprocal regime of preferences. As a consequence, the EU has encouraged developing countries to enter into more comprehensive economic agreements, to stimulate domestic reforms necessary to foster growth and development. In the words of the EU Trade Commissioner Peter Mandelson (European Commission 2005a: 2–3),

> [EU] preferences are generous and they are being used. We will try to improve our record even further, but we should be aware of the limits that are intrinsic

to any preferential system. Trade preferences offer opportunities for developing countries. There is no guarantee that preferences will be translated into practical economic gains. Those opportunities will have to be seized and for this to happen it requires a combination of factors. Experience shows in fact that preferences alone are not sufficient to promote growth, economic development and poverty reduction. Supply side and productivity bottlenecks are crucial and thus complementary reforms and investments are needed to stimulate the desired supply side response especially by the private sector and allowing households to take full advantage of preferential market access.

Here perhaps lies the crux of the EPA versus EBA debate. EBA offers the best nominal market access to the EU for least developed ACP countries. To improve on their effective market access to the EU, for trade in goods but also services, least developed ACP countries must consider EPAs that alone offer the potential to address technical and trade-related barriers to trade. However, the extent to which such opportunities will materialize will critically depend on the specific content of the provisions contained in an EPA. More important, to be of benefit to an ACP country and region, an EPA must build on and support reforms that are initiated at the domestic level. In particular, numerous capacity constraints, in terms of institutional development, infrastructure, production capacity, as well as human and resources constraints, have prevented ACP countries to take advantage of new trade opportunities and to pursue policies conducive to their sustainable development. A new trade framework, as envisaged in an EPA, can thus offer renewed perspectives for development only if it is enshrined in endogenously owned domestic reforms and is accompanied by appropriate accompanying measures.

The scope of an EPA should thus be intrinsically linked with the scope of domestic reforms envisaged. Should a least developed ACP country not be willing to engage in substantive reforms, the attractiveness of an EPA over the EBA market access regime would be reduced.

In addition, even in the positive event that the potential benefits of an EPA will materialize, they will require significant adjustment costs, in terms of reforms to be undertaken and accompanying policies, infrastructure and social measures to put in place. For instance, the reduced collection of import duties that results from import liberalization affects government revenues, and increased competition from foreign producers may cause disruption in domestic economic sectors. An EPA may thus be accompanied by temporary adjustment funds and fiscal reforms. Similarly, 'supply-side constraints' such as poor economic infrastructure, inadequate production facilities, unfavourable investment climate, weak institutions and lack of a trained work force may require significant investment, regulatory reforms, provision for social safety needs, retraining, etc., so as to allow the country to take advantage of new export opportunities created by the market opening compatible with sustainable development and poverty alleviation objectives. Without adequate support for policy reforms and sufficient resources to adjust and foster the necessary economic transformation and to produce and market their goods competitively,

ACP countries are unlikely to fully benefit from new free trade arrangements with the EU.

Whether or not the potential benefits of EPAs (to be expected mainly in the longer run) will compensate for the perhaps necessary but certainly costly adjustment process (whose impacts are felt on the short term) remains an open question. In this regard, the attractiveness of an EPA over the EBA initiative will depend on the scope and specific contents of an EPA, the undertaking of domestic reforms and the provision of appropriate accompanying measures, for which substantial support will have to be provided by the EU as part of an EPA.

EPA market access and EBA

One of the pending questions is whether products from least developed ACP countries would have a less preferential access to the EU market under an EPA than they would enjoy under the EBA regime. The EU, in line with the Cotonou Agreement, agreed that ACP countries should at least keep, and preferably be improved on, their level of preferences to the EU market. 96.5 per cent of all imports (all industrial products and 80 per cent of agricultural products) from the ACP already enter the EU duty-free (European Commission 2005b; Maerten 2004). This is commonly interpreted as meaning that an EPA should provide market access to the EU for ACP products no worse than the Lomé/Cotonou regime of preferences.

The European Commission has pledged to further open the EU market to ACP products under EPAs, improving on the current level of preferences. However, the EU's commitment to at least maintain its current openness to ACP exports would imply that, for the least developed ACP countries, an EPA should provide for market access identical to EBA, i.e. DFQF. In this respect, it is worth remembering that in drafting the European Commission negotiating directives on EPAs (i.e. the negotiating mandate of the EU member states to the Commission), DG Trade initially proposed to grant EBA equivalent market access to all ACP. This potential offer was however withdrawn a couple of months later in the final version of the mandate as approved in June 2002, allegedly because of opposition by DG Agriculture.[4]

Three main lessons can be identified from this. First, it would indeed make sense for the EU to abolish all remaining duty and quota restrictions on ACP products, so as to grant them EBA equivalent market access, in order to avoid any undue erosion of preferences for least developed ACP countries following the implementation of an EPA. In theory, such an EBA equivalent treatment could be granted to least developed ACP countries only. In practice, however, such differential treatment among ACP countries, including within one region, would create discrimination that might be difficult to reconcile with the regional dimension of an EPA advocated by the EU (see also discussion in the final section of this chapter). Hence, the need for coherence would suggest that EBA equivalent market access should be granted to all ACP countries, least developed and non-least developed alike.

Second, DG Trade is in principle willing to grant such free market access to all ACP countries under an EPA. While this is not yet the official position of the European Commission, EU trade negotiators are likely to favour such an offer to the ACP states.

Third, resistance to the extension of EBA-equivalent treatment to all ACP countries within the context of an EPA is likely to arise within the European Commission and some EU member states; this opposition is likely to focus on a limited number of agricultural products originating from some ACP countries (non-LDCs) and that could compete with EU production or other sources of preferred import.

In order to diffuse possible tensions on the issue of market access, in particular at the time of the conclusion of the EPAs, it would be useful for both the EU and the ACP to promptly identify the specific products and their origins that could cause problems. The adoption of appropriate safeguard measures might also facilitate a complete opening up of EU market for all ACP products, equivalent to EBA.

In the event the EU would maintain some tariffs or quantitative restrictions on some ACP products in the context of an EPA, several questions would arise. First, were such restrictions to affect products from least developed ACP countries in a collective agreement, i.e. a regional EPA, could such products be exported by the concerned LDCs under EBA? In other words, would a least developed ACP country forfeit its preferential treatment under EBA should it join an EPA? Second, were the least developed ACP countries to maintain their EBA equivalent market access, how would the appropriate rules of origin and other administrative procedures affect the functioning of a regional EPA, and more broadly the regional integration process on which each EPA is supposed to build? Surely, differential treatment between LDCs and non-LDCs within one EPA region would have negative consequences on regional integration, including intra-regional trade? (See also the final section of this chapter.)

Another issue relates to the treatment of products currently covered by the commodity protocols (banana, sugar and beef and veal), whereby these products benefit under the Cotonou Agreement from a price and quantitative regime derived from the EU CAP. These commodities, part of the CAP reform agenda, have a significant impact on some least developed ACP countries. Besides, their compatibility with the WTO rules has become questionable as a result of panel outcomes in the WTO on the EU banana and sugar regimes.

EBA has arguably contributed to the erosion of the preferences available to all ACP countries under these protocols (e.g. see Chapter 10 on sugar in this volume). The way the commodity protocols will feature in an EPA, if at all, remains to be determined. As stand-alone agreements simply annexed to the Cotonou Agreement, they do not have to be explicitly integrated into an EPA, in which case the issue of coherence between an EPA and EBA for the commodities covered by the protocols does not explicitly arise. In the case the commodity protocols are 'imported' into an EPA, provisions will have to be made to accommodate the different interests of ACP countries within one region, and their differential access to the EU market, in particular for least developed ACP countries. Obviously, the future of the commodity protocols as such would be called into question, and a reviewed framework could be envisaged. Such considerations, however, fall beyond the scope of this paper.

The EBA-plus concept: EPA principle or alternative to EPAs?

Even though the EU has pledged to improve market access for ACP products under EPAs as discussed above, many observers fear that least developed ACP countries will lose their guaranteed DFQF market access to the EU if they decide to enter into an EPA. EU Trade Commissioner Peter Mandelson dismissed such a hypothesis, indicating during a hearing of the UK House of Commons that 'ACP countries will be no worse off once the EPAs kick in, from 'Everything but Arms'. [.] We are asking for EBA plus not EBA minus' (House of Commons 2005: 18). In its report, the International Development Committee of the House of Commons understood this remark as implying that EBA-plus means that 'LDCs who choose to sign an EPA will not have to offer the EU reciprocal market access', a position that they endorsed in their recommendations. An EBA plus would thus be an EPA where least developed ACP countries would keep an EBA equivalent market access to the EU, with no requirement to open their market on a reciprocal basis, while stressing the development element (to be determined) of such agreement.

   Although such an EBA plus is obviously not compatible with the current rules at the WTO, notably GATT Article XXIV, the Southern African Development Community (SADC) EPA region has proposed such an option to the European Commission, whereby SADC countries would sign an EPA which would entail reciprocity only for non-LDC countries (i.e. Botswana, Namibia, Swaziland), whereas the SADC LDCs (i.e. Angola, Lesotho, Mozambique and Tanzania) would be able to keep their EBA preferences without opening their market to EU products. Box 11.1 gives more information on the role of EBA in the EU SADC negotiations on an EPA.

   However, Commissioner Mandelson never mentioned such a non-reciprocal option. As suggested by the comments of the British government,[5] an EBA-plus probably means that, under an EPA, all ACP countries (LDCs and non-LDCs) would have EBA market access equivalent, while the plus would be the other claimed advantages of an EPA (tackling technical and trade-related barriers, simplified rules of origin, strengthening of regional markets, etc.). Such an EBA-plus would constitute not an alternative to EPAs but a market opening offer by the EU in the context of EPA negotiations (see previous section).

EBA as an alternative to EPAs

As indicated above, while all ACP countries are engaged in EPA negotiations, they are under no obligation to conclude such an agreement. For least developed ACP countries, the DFQF EU market access offered under EBA constitutes the alternative trade regime, improving on the current Lomé/Cotonou regime of

---

BOX 11.1 EBA AND EPA IN SOUTHERN AFRICA[a]

The case of Southern Africa illustrates the complexity of cross-cutting EBA, EPA and other trade schemes. Although South Africa became a member of the ACP group, it concluded a Trade Development and Cooperation Agreement (TDCA) with the EU instead of joining the Lomé trade regime in 1999. The TDCA can thus be seen as a guinea pig for the future EPA negotiations (Holland 1998: 225–6).

However, South Africa is a member of the Southern African Customs Union (SACU). The other member states are Botswana, Lesotho, Namibia and Swaziland (BLNS). This customs union dates back to 1910. There is free internal trade, a common customs policy and a mechanism to share the customs revenues collected by South Africa. The TDCA gives the EU preferential market access in the SACU area. Thus Lesotho, being the only LDC in SACU, has a reciprocal preferential trading arrangement with the EU, despite its LDC status.

In 2004 the EU started EPA negotiations under the configuration of the Southern African Development Community (SADC), including the BNLS countries as well as the three LDCs of the MAT (Mozambique, Angola and Tanzania).[b] It was agreed that South Africa would participate in an observatory and supportive capacity. But since the TDCA between the EU and South Africa foresees a review after five years, this intermeshes with the ongoing EPA negotiations. Therefore, at the insistence of the EU, South Africa became an active participant in the EPA negotiations.

The SADC countries have suggested a 'variable geometry' approach. On the one hand, the EPA would maintain the current preferential access of the EU to the SACU, while taking into account the 'sensitivities' of BNLS countries, such as tariff revenues. Given that these countries are part of the SACU, South Africa would formally be associated with this EPA. On the other hand, the MAT countries would continue to get non-reciprocal EBA access to the EU. Legitimized by the Enabling Clause, these LDCs would be allowed to keep their national trade policies with respect to imports from the EU. This EBA status should also be extended to Lesotho, an LDC member of the BLNS. This would create the risk of trade deflection: third-country firms would sell to the MAT countries through the SACU. Regarding the offensive side of the negotiations, viz. the treatment of exports to the EU market, the Southern African countries ask for EBA-equivalent status in 2008. In terms of access to the European market, this implies an extension of EBA to non-LDC countries, including South Africa.

The main problem of these proposals is that the preferred EBA status (non-reciprocal, unilateral preferences) of the MAT is not compatible with an EPA: being a member of a free trade area (FTA) with the EU makes it

continued

impossible to maintain the existing trade barriers with respect to the imports of one member state of the FTA (viz. the EU). In the end, EBA and EPA are non-compatible options. On the same arguments, Lesotho, will not be able to maintain a claim on EBA status and remain in SACU and become a member of a SADC-EU EPA.

A different issue is whether the MAT and Lesotho have to give up their claim of DFQF access to the EU. Offering these countries such access and promoting regional integration in Southern Africa are possible by offering all Southern African members DFQF access. Olympio *et al.* (2006) argue that the cost to the EU of DF access would be minimal.

Sources: *Trade Negotiation Insights*, March–April 2006, p. 6 (Melissa Julian, ECDPM); C. Stevens, 'The EU, Africa and Economic Partnership Agreements: unintended consequences of policy leverage' *Journal of Modern African Studies*, 44, 3 (2006), 1–18.

Notes:
a Box written by the editors.
b Other SADC countries (such as Zambia, see Chapter 8 in this volume) are negotiating an EPA with the EU as part of the Eastern and Southern Africa (ESA) configuration.

preferences and fully compatible with WTO rules (in this case the Enabling Clause which explicitly allows for trade preferences in favour of LDCs; see the introductory chapter in this volume).

The situation is more complicated for non-least developed ACP countries, for which no more favourable regime of preference is readily available, should they reject an EPA. However, Article 37(6) of the Cotonou Agreement provides for a mechanism to reach an alternative trading arrangement for the non-LDC ACP countries that do not wish to enter into an EPA:

> In 2004, the Community will assess the situation of the non-LDC which, after consultations with the Community decide that they are not in a position to enter into economic partnership agreements and will examine all alternative possibilities, in order to provide these countries with a new framework for trade which is equivalent to their existing situation and in conformity with WTO rules.

The main alternative to an EPA available to the non-LDCs among the ACP countries arguably lies in the realm of the EU GSP (see Bilal and Rampa 2006). In relation to EBA, two types of scenarios can be envisaged. First, some of these non-LDCs may choose not to sign an EPA. Second, EBA may be extended to some non-LDCs so as to cover non-LDCs in the ACP group as an alternative to EPA. Both scenarios will respectively be examined in the following two sections.

EPAs for non-LDCs and EBA for LDCs in the ACP group

This scenario focuses mainly on the issue of WTO compatibility, the principle that no ACP country should be worse off under the new ACP-EU trading arrangements and the negative effects of reciprocal trade liberalization, in particular for the poor countries. As ACP countries that are LDCs already benefit from the EBA initiative under the EU GSP, there is no need for them to provide reciprocity to maintain their preferential access to the EU market. In addition, poorer countries, having generally weaker (production, institutional and infrastructure development) capacities, are less able to compete and adjust in a market open to EU imports, and thus are more likely to be negatively affected by the introduction of a reciprocal free trade agreement. Many NGOs argue for instance that, since ACP LDCs will gain little benefits from signing an EPA in return for undertaking a lot of obligations, they should better say no to an EPA.

Thus, only non-LDC ACP countries need to find an alternative trade regime to the current Lomé/Cotonou preferences, whereas LDC ACP countries can keep their preferential EBA access. Assuming that the EU GSP or any other alternative does not offer a market access as advantageous as the current regime, the only option for ACP non-LDCs to maintain or improve on their level of preferences to the EU market would be to enter into an EPA.

While this option would not address potential concerns about reciprocity of ACP non-LDCs, it would allow two-thirds of the ACP countries (i.e. the LDCs) to avoid granting free market access to EU products.

A major drawback of this option, apart from the fact that two-thirds of the ACP countries would renounce the potential benefits entailed in an EPA, is that it would *de facto* seriously undermine the ACP regional integration process, splitting each region between the (non-LDC) countries that enter an FTA/EPA with the EU and those (the LDCs) that maintain their trade barriers against the EU. It would be difficult under these conditions to imagine any ACP region effectively implementing its regional integration programme. In its report on the EU's trade agreements with ACP countries, the UK House of Commons International Development Committee noted (House of Commons 2005: 16, para.38; see also UK Government 2005: 5, para. 11):

> DFID's view is that if the LDCs choose not to negotiate an EPA – that really makes things very, very complicated in terms of integrating into a region. We do not think that things should be made complicated for the LDCs. The EBA should be a real option for LDCs. And they should not have to offer reciprocal market access to the EU until they have graduated from LDC status. The EBA should not conflict with regional integration initiatives in the ACP, especially given the emphasis that DG Trade is placing on the importance of regional integration.

For instance, customs unions would not be compatible with such an option, as all regional members need to abide by the same common external tariff.

Differentiating duties for EU imports depending on their destination would *de facto* require specific rules of origin and border controls within the region, hence negating the principle of the customs union. In practice, this is however not impossible, although highly undesirable, as illustrated by the case of Southern African Customs Union (SACU), with South Africa having entered an FTA with the EU whereas Botswana, Lesotho, Namibia and Swaziland (the BLNS), although part of SACU, enjoy preferential market access to the EU under the Cotonou Agreement and are negotiating an EPA within the SADC context (see Box 11.1).

In addition, the EBA rules of origin are less generous than the one prevailing under the Cotonou trade regime and EBA is a unilateral initiative by the EU, as part of its GSP, which can be revoked at the will of the EU will, thus creating unwarranted uncertainty (as discussed above).

EBA for all

In terms of nominal market access to the EU, the EBA initiative offers the best trading framework: beneficiaries enjoy a DFQF market access to the EU, whereas no element of reciprocity is required from them. Instead of limiting such a scheme to LDCs, possible scenarios would consist in extending it to

*   All ACP countries (including non-LDCs).
*   The group of poorer countries (G-90).
*   All developing countries.

For all ACP countries

To give EBA treatment without reciprocity to all ACP, including non-LDCs, would contravene the existing WTO rules: it would artificially discriminate among developing countries, in contradiction to the Enabling Clause, and it would not cover the elimination of trade barriers on 'substantially all trade' among the parties, in contradiction to GATT Article XXIV. The only solution would thus be a WTO waiver or a change of WTO rules.

For all G-90

A priori, the compatibility with WTO rules would also arise should EBA be extended to all G-90 members. However, should this group of poorer developing countries be officially recognized under WTO rules, as a result of the negotiations on the Doha Work Programme, an EBA for all G-90 could be compatible with the Enabling Clause.

Such an approach would also seem to be consistent with the EU proposal of a 'Round for Free' offered to the G-90. In the letter by the European Commissioners Pascal Lamy (DG Trade) and Franz Fischler (DG Agriculture) sent on 9 May 2004 to all WTO members, the European Commission outlined its proposals for the continuation of the Doha Round, proposing, among other things, that less developed countries (G-90) should not be required to lower their trade barriers and should be granted better access to the markets of developed and more advanced (G-20?) developing countries, thus offering the G-90 what the EU calls a 'Round for free'.[6]

For all developing countries

Proposing EBA to all developing countries would amount to nothing less than completely replacing the GSP regime of the EU by the EBA provisions. This would of course be compatible with the existing Enabling Clause. It would, however, open the EU market to large, highly competitive, exporters, such as Brazil, China and India, among others, and is therefore a very unrealistic outcome.

The regional dimension

A common characteristic of all six regional EPA negotiations is the focus on their respective regional integration processes. Indeed, a basic principle of EPAs contained in the Cotonou Agreement is that they should build on and reinforce the regional integration process of the ACP. Article 37(5) of the Cotonou Agreement states that the negotiations of EPAs shall 'take into account regional integration process within the ACP'. The reference to ACP regional integration processes is a recurrent theme in the Cotonou Agreement and appears in numerous articles.[7] According to the European Commission, by building on larger well integrated regional markets, regional EPAs should contribute to foster the integration of the ACP in the world economy, provide for economies of scale, stimulate investment and contribute to lock in the necessary trade reforms. This is also reflected in structure of the EPA negotiations. During the first regional phase, the European Commission has undertaken to review, with its ACP regional partners, the state of regional integration in all six ACP regions and their future agenda, so as to better anchor an EPA into its regional dimension (see Bilal 2005).

However, the dichotomy between LDCs and non-LDCs cut through all ACP regions negotiating an EPA, as illustrated in Table 11.1. This may create tensions in the respective regional integration processes, as LDCs in ACP regions may have interests in EPAs that differ from non-LDC members. According to some NGOs, EPAs in their current form will undermine the regional integration efforts of the ACP regions, since it puts the LDCs, which already benefit from generous trade preferences under EBA, in a dilemma vis-à-vis the non-LDCs countries in the region. Joining an EPA would mean that the LDC members open up their market to EU products on a reciprocal basis, which they may not wish to do.

Opting out of an EPA, as outlined above, would require different treatment within one regional grouping between LDCs, which would protect their market against EU imports, and non-LDCs that will open up within the context of an EPA. This would be incompatible with deep integration agenda, as in the case of custom unions that require members to adopt a common external trade policy. Even in the context of an FTA, stringent border control would have to take place within

Table 11.1 EPA negotiating groupings and LDCs

Grouping	Members	LDCs
ECOWAS	16	12
CEMAC	8	5
ESA	15	11
SADC	7	4
Pacific	14	5
CARIFORUM	16	1

an ACP region to avoid trade deflection (such as undue transit trade). Such measures would *de facto* limit intra-regional trade and erode the regional integration agenda. Box 11.1 shows that this situation may arise in the SADC region. Paradoxically, an ACP LDC may prefer to remain within an EPA against its will simply to avoid undermining regional integration ambitions or prevent its own exclusion from the regional integration process. Indeed, as Jess Pilegaard shows in Chapter 8, the preference for regional integration appears to be one of the prime motives for Zambia to participate in EPA negotiations between the EU and COMESA.

Hence, as an arguably unintended consequence, the EU, by offering two – somewhat competing – preferential trade regimes to ACP LDCs, EBA or an EPA, may generate tensions between LDC and non-LDC members of one region, which may ultimately weaken the regional integration process that EPAs are supposed to foster and build upon.

Notes

1   Article 37(9) of the Cotonou Agreement states that: 'The Community will start by the year 2000, a process which by the end of multilateral trade negotiations and at the latest 2005 will allow duty-free access for essentially all products from all LDCs building on the level of the existing trade provisions of the Fourth ACP–EC Convention and which will simplify and review the rules of origin, including cumulation provisions, that apply to their exports.'

2   The Cotonou Agreement, however, also foresees that any change to the regime applied to the ACP should be made in consultation with the ACP, which has not been the case for EBA, the EU having omitted to engage with the ACP group on this issue (see Carbone in Chapter 3 of this volume).

3   Chapter 12 of this volume discusses the issue of EBA and the WTO more in depth.

4   The two texts are available online at http://www.epawatch.net/general/text.php?itemID=71&menuID=24 (accessed 23 June 2006).

5   See UK Government (2005: 6, para. 12).

6   Available online at http://europa.eu.int/comm/trade/issues/newround/ pr100504_en.htm (accessed 23 June 2006).

7   Article 1(4) states that 'Regional and sub-regional integration processes which foster the integration of the ACP countries into the world economy in terms of trade and private investment shall be encouraged and supported'. Article 2 mentions regionalization as one of the fundamental principles, noting that 'Particular emphasis shall be placed on the regional dimension'. This can be found in many aspects of the Cotonou

Agreement not directly related to the negotiation of EPAs. With respect to economic and trade cooperation, Article 35(2) stipulates that 'Economic and trade cooperation shall build on regional integration initiatives of ACP States, bearing in mind that regional integration is a key instrument for the integration of ACP countries into the world economy'.

References

Augier, P., Gasiorek, M. and Lai Tong, C. (2005) 'The impact of rules of origin on trade flows', *Economic Policy*, 20, 43: 567–624.

Beghin, J.C. and Bureau, J.C. (2001) 'Quantification of Sanitary, Phytosanitary, and Technical Barriers to Trade for Trade Policy Analysis', Working Paper 01-WP 291, Center for Agricultural and Rural Development, Iowa State University, December. Available online at http://www.card.iastate.edu/publications/DBS/PDFFiles/01wp 291. pdf (accessed 22 June 2006).

Bilal, S. (2005) 'Economic partnership agreements (EPAs): the ACP regions and their relations with the EU', Paper presented at the third ECPR conference, Budapest, 8–10 September.

Bilal, S. and Rampa, F. (2006) 'Alternative (to) EPAs: Possible scenarios for the future ACP trade relations with the EU', Policy Management Report 11, Maastricht: ECDPM.

Brenton, P. (2003) 'Integrating the Least Developed Countries into the World Trading System: The Current Impact of EU Preferences under 'Everything but Arms', Policy Research Working Paper No. 3018, Washington DC: World Bank.

Brenton, P. and Manchin, M. (2003) 'Making EU trade agreements work: the role of rules of origin', *World Economy*, 26, 5: 755–69.

Cadot, O., Estavadeoral, A., Eisenmann, A.S. and Verdier, T. (eds) (2006) *The Origin of Goods: Rules of Origin in Regional Trade Agreements*, Oxford: Oxford University Press.

Candau, F. and Jean, S. (2005) 'What are EU Trade Preferences worth for sub-Saharan Africa and other Developing Countries?', CEPII Working Paper No. 2005–19, Paris: CEPII. Available online at http://www.cepii.fr/anglaisgraph/workpap/pdf/2005/wp 05-19.pdf (accessed 22 June 2006).

Candau, F., Fontagne, L. and Jean, S. (2004) 'The Utilisation Rate of Preferences in the EU'. Preliminary draft presented at the seventh Global Economic Analysis Conference, Washington DC, 17–19 June. Available online at http://www.uneca.org/eca_ programmes/trade_and_regional_integration/meetings/TunisNovember2004/FC_L F_SJ_08-05-04.pdf (accessed 22 June 2006).

Doherty, M. (2005) 'ACP–EU Economic Partnership Agreements Sanitary and Phytosanitary Measures', ECDPM Discussion Paper No. 68 with CTA, Maastricht: ECDPM. Available online at www.ecdpm.org/dp68 (accessed 22 June 2006).

European Commission (2005a) 'The Trade and Development Aspects of EPA Negotiations', Commission Staff Working Document SEC(2005)1459, 9 November, Brussels: Commission of the European Communities.

European Commission (2005b) 'Opening the Door to Development: Developing Country Access to EU Markets, 1999–2003', White Paper, Directorate General for Trade, 17 May, Brussels: Commission of the European Communities.

Holland, M. (1998) 'Europe's foreign policy and South Africa, 1977–1997', *European Foreign Affairs Review*, 3: 215–32.

House of Commons (2005) 'Fair Trade? The European Union's trade agreements with

African, Caribbean and Pacific countries', report by the International Development Select Committee of the House of Commons, Session 2005–06, London: House of Commons.

Lanchovichina, E., Mattoo, A. and Olarreaga, M. (2001) 'Unrestricted Market Access for sub-Saharan Africa: How Much is it Worth and Who Pays?', World Bank Policy Research Working Paper No. 2595. Washington DC: World Bank. Available online at http://econ.worldbank.org/files/1715_wps2595.pdf (accessed 22 June 2006).

Maerten, C. (2004) 'Economic partnership agreements: a new approach to ACP–EU economic and trade cooperation'. Presentation at the TRALAC Annual International Trade Law Conference, Stellenbosch, South Africa, 11 November. Available online at http://www.tralac.org/pdf/04-11-09_EPA_(TRALAC-1).ppt (accessed 22 June 2006).

Manchin, M. (2005) 'Preference utilization and tariff reduction in European Union imports from African, Caribbean, and Pacific countries', World Bank Policy Research Working Paper No. 3688, Washington DC: World Bank. Available online at http://www-wds.worldbank.org/servlet/WDS_IBank_Servlet?pcont=details&eid=000016406_200 50819124920 (accessed 22 June 2006).

Maskus, K.E. and Wilson, J.S. (eds) (2001) *Quantifying the Impact of Technical Barriers to Trade: Can it be Done?*, Ann Arbor MI: University of Michigan Press.

Olympio, J., Robinson, P. and Cocks, M. (2006) 'A Study to assess the likely Impacts on Southern African and EU Producers of further liberalising the Trade Development and Cooperation Agreement (TDCA) by granting South Africa Duty-Free Access to the EU', Trowbridge: Landell Mills.

Page, S. and Hewitt, A. (2002) 'The New European Trade Preferences: does 'Everything but Arms' (EBA) help the Poor?', *Development Policy Review*, 20, 1: 91–102.

Rudloff, B. and Simons, J. (2004) 'Comparing EU Free-Trade Agreements: Sanitary and Phytosanitary Standards', ECDPM InBrief 6B, Maastricht: ECDPM with CTA – the Technical Centre for Agriculture and Rural Cooperation ACP–EU. Available online at www.ecdpm.org/ftainbriefs (accessed 22 June 2006).

Sandrey, R. (2005) 'Trade after Preferences: a New Adjustment Partnership?', Tralac Trade Brief No. 1, May. Available online at http://www.tralac.org/pdf/TB1_trade_after_preferences.pdf (accessed 22 June 2006).

UK Government (2005) 'UK government's response to International Development Committee's Sixth Report of session 2004–05', London: HMSO.

UNCTAD (2002) 'Participation of the African, Caribbean and Pacific Group of States in International Trade', UNCTAD/DITC/TNCD/Misc.27, Report by the UNCTAD Secretariat to the Third Summit of ACP Heads of State and Government, 18–19 July, Fiji.

Vancauteren, M. (2002) 'The Impact of Technical Barriers to Trade on Home Bias: An Application to EU data', IRES Discussion Paper No. 2002–32, Université Catholique de Louvain, Belgium. Available online at http://www.ires.ucl.ac.be/DP/IRES_DP/2002-32.pdf (accessed 22 June 2006).

12 'Everything but Arms' or all about nothing?

Jan Orbie and Gerrit Faber

At first sight 'Everything but Arms' (EBA) seems a limited initiative. It liberalizes only 919 (out of 10,200) tariff lines, specifically targeted at imports from the poorest countries, and stretched out between 2001 and 2009 for their most important products. However, when the European Commission launched the EBA proposal in 2000, it was broadly welcomed as a positive step towards a more development-friendly trade policy. More than five years after its inception, this book attempts to evaluate the importance of EBA.

The main conclusion reads that EBA is not 'all about nothing'. It has had a significant impact. Most chapters illustrate that the EBA regulation has influenced upon several policy domains of the European Union (EU), and that some of its effects have only started to materialize. The other chapters, however, highlight the one dimension where the relevance of EBA is questionable: development of the least developed countries (LDCs). The *leitmotiv* through the chapters thus reads that EBA has considerable consequences, both within the EU and on the international scene. All contributions confirm the basic hypothesis that, although EBA is limited in terms of trade flows, this initiative has important 'multiplier effects' in several areas beyond the area of application – the export promotion of the poorest countries in the world.

The first section elaborates on this conclusion, summarizing the main findings of the book chapters. Subsequently it is argued why EBA continues to be relevant for the European and multilateral trade policy agenda.

Everything but development

EBA and economic development of LDCs

Thus the importance of EBA cannot be underestimated – except perhaps for its impact on LDC export figures to the European market. These limited economic results did not really come as a surprise. During past years a number of studies (e.g. Cernat *et al.* 2003; Achterbosch *et al.* 2003; Brenton 2003; UNCTAD 2003a; Yu and Jensen 2005) showed that EBA hardly increases LDC exports. The economic assessments of this volume basically confirm these results. But they also add a number of interesting variables, such as the role of geography, market size and institutions (Chapter 6), and of the rules of origin (Chapter 7). These two contributions also make interesting comparisons between EBA and US trade policy vis-à-vis LDCs. They are complemented with a 'bottom up' perspective from Zambia by Jess Pilegaard (Chapter 8).

Focussing on sub-Saharan Africa (SSA), Olufemi Babarinde and Gerrit Faber (Chapter 6) find that EBA does not have an observable effect on exports. But they also reject the hypothesis that the US African Growth and Opportunity Act (AGOA) is more effective on *LDC* exports than EBA. On further consideration, AGOA's larger success is related to exports of *non-LDC* beneficiaries. This indicates the incomparability of AGOA and EBA style preferences. Thus, the performance of AGOA is better compared with the Lomé/Cotonou trade regime than with EBA. In fact, it appears that even ACP LDCs continue to export to the European market under the Cotonou regime, instead of the EBA preferences. This finding underlines the limited relevance of EBA for ACP LDCs, at least for the year 2002. It also suggests that these sub-Saharan countries will prefer to enter Economic Partnership Agreements (EPAs) with the EU, rather than exporting under EBA (see below).

Babarinde and Faber also point to the importance of geographical factors for LDC export performance. In this respect the distance from a seaport in the exporting SSA country proves to be particularly important. This finding corresponds with Pilegaard's account about Zambia in Chapter 8. Here it is argued that market access is not the major constraint facing Zambian exporters. Besides transport costs, he points to difficulties in customs administration, quality and safety standards, and the business environment in general.

But there is one caveat. The impact of EBA may be higher for the non-African (mostly Asian) LDC beneficiaries such as Afghanistan, Bangladesh, Bhutan, Cambodia, Laos, Maldives, Nepal and Yemen (see Appendix 1.1 in Chapter 1). These countries traditionally occupied a lower place on the European 'pyramid of preferences' than the former colonies of the ACP group (Africa, Caribbean and Pacific countries). Most economic assessments of EBA do not specifically look at these countries. Yet there are several reasons that justify a specific focus on their exports to the European market since 1998. First, in Chapter 2 it was revealed that Europe had already improved its Generalized System of Preferences (GSP) market access for these countries since January 1998. This 'EBA *avant la lettre*' initiative granted Lomé/ACP equivalent access to these non-ACP countries. This raises the question: do the limited improvements in LDC market access since EBA hide some more substantial export rises since 1998? Second, Chapter 6 came to the conclusion that African LDCs continue to export under the Lomé/Cotonou regime, rather than making use of the new EBA scheme, which partly explains the limited success of EBA. But this consideration cannot apply to the non-ACP LDCs, for which the only avenue to export to the European market at a preferential tariff is the GSP/EBA.

Figure 12.1[1] suggests that there were no considerable shifts in export performances to the European market since 1998. Two non-ACP LDCs (Laos and Maldives) show improved exports, although the effect seems to be mitigated afterwards.

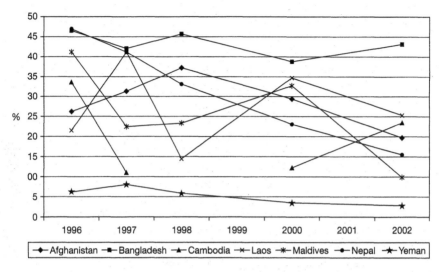

Figure 12.1 The impact of EBA *avant la lettre*: share of the EU in exports as a percentage of total exports, 1996–2002

The comparative advantage of these Asian LDCs is mainly in textiles and clothing. These are precisely the sectors that are most affected by Europe's rules of origin. Focusing on the apparel sector, Paul Brenton and Çağlar Özden (Chapter 7) exemplify that these rules are a considerable impediment to effective and potential LDC exports to the European market. EU rules of origin aim to avoid trade deflection, ensuring that a substantial part of their export value is effectively created in LDCs. However, they prove to be more restrictive than necessary for meeting this objective. Despite initiatives to adjust EU rules of origin, they continue to be the main culprit for limited export performances under EBA. In order to be able to export at a profit in this highly competitive world market, in particularly after the abolition of the Multifibre Arrangement and China's accession to the World Trade Organization (WTO), small LDCs should be able to source their inputs from suppliers at the lowest cost.

Rules of origin are discussed in the Doha Development Round of the WTO. In the Hong Kong Declaration (December 2005) WTO members resolved to apply 'simplified and transparent rules of origin so as to facilitate exports from LDCs'. They also decided to multilateralize EBA, holding out the prospect of duty-free and quota-free (DFQF) access for LDC products to the markets of the developed and developing countries 'declaring themselves in a position to do so'. Such a 'global EBA' would substantially increase LDC export opportunities and their benefits from a Doha Package. In a model study, IFPRI (2006) calculates that the LDC welfare gain from a non-ambitious Doha Package would be only US$1 billion. This gain would increase to US$7 billion in case all OECD countries would grant full DFQF treatment to LDC exports. It would in particular be meaningful for countries like Bangladesh (textiles and apparel), some developing countries in

Asia (rice) and sub-Saharan African LDCs such as Malawi (other agricultural products). However, the success of these commitments depends on the outcome of the Doha Round and on the agreement of a clear timetable for liberalization of the remaining 3 per cent. As explained below, the 3 per cent would enable importing countries to exclude most of the products that LDCs can supply competitively, such as clothing and a number of agricultural products, and would severely reduce the gains for the countries concerned.

It is a commonplace to argue that market access as such will not be sufficient. Initiatives *à la* EBA can be effective only if they are embedded in a wide range of other national and international policy measures. However, one remarkable conclusion with regard to EBA is that complete DFQF market access may in fact deteriorate LDC development in the short run. This rather paradoxical finding applies to the case of sugar – the most important (if not the only relevant) agricultural product under EBA. Michael Brüntrup (Chapter 10) shows that the quota regime under the current European sugar market organization allows for relatively high sugar prices for LDC exporters, such as Ethiopia, Malawi, Myanmar, Sudan, Zambia and Angola. In Mozambique and Tanzania production capacity is rehabilitated in order to profit from the EBA opportunities. Some of the exporters need these high prices to cover high production and/or transport costs. The phasing out of sugar quotas by 2009 and the sugar market reform based on price reductions would lead to lower benefits for EBA countries. LDCs vainly asked the EU to keep its stable and remunerative prices for LDC sugar exports – even if this would imply the continuation of sugar quotas and thus less than 'Everything but Arms'. Brüntrup warns that negative long-term consequences of EBA for LDC sugar producers may have broader repercussions for the worldwide liberalization process, 'making a precedent case that liberalization negatively affects the poorest countries in particular'. He therefore argues that LDCs affected by the sugar market liberalization should receive some kind of compensation, in line with restructuring funds for EU and (to a smaller extent) ACP producers. In any case, the sugar dossier confronts us with a paradox: the more we move towards the actual implementation of 'Everything but Arms' the less clear-cut are its developmental effects.

These conclusions somehow qualify the conventional evaluation of EBA, which focuses on lack of export capacity (on the LDC side) and delayed transition periods for sensitive agricultural products (on the EU side). Besides domestic factors, these findings point to difficulties that continue to exist after the phasing out of the transition period for bananas, rice and sugar. These obstacles relate to deliberate EU policy choices, rather than LDC characteristics: the restrictiveness of Europe's rules of origin and the organization of Europe's sugar market.

An UNCTAD report adds a different contribution of EBA. Despite the small commercial value added to LDC producers, it 'has had an immense impact in terms of stimulating discussion of practical and innovative ways to increase market access for LDCs' (UNCTAD 2004: 249). Yet several questions beyond the area of market access remain unanswered. The 'Aid for Trade' issue is a case in point. EU policy makers have never simply presented EBA as a panacea for all distress of

LDCs, and they have always stressed the importance of aid in fostering LDC exports. Today the Aid for Trade agenda constitutes an important element of the WTO Development Agenda. In this context, Europe announced an increase in its annual trade-related assistance by 2010 to €1 billion by the member states and €1 billion by the Community.[2] This fits in with Europe's commitment to step up its development aid figures and reach the United Nations (UN) Millennium Development Goals. In the EPA negotiations, there is also a growing emphasis on flanking measures such as development aid (Goodison 2005: 299). Further research should investigate Europe's Aid for Trade policy vis-à-vis LDCs, a topic that has not been dealt with in this book. Several questions emerge, e.g. is there a coherent European development policy in this domain of shared competences; how effective are Europe's Aid for Trade disbursements; does it concern an added value or merely a repackaging of previous EU aid commitments?

Another, but related, question for further research has been touched upon in Chapter 2. Everyone agrees that market access is not sufficient to stimulate development. There is also a growing consensus that institutions are vitally important (cf. Chapter 6). But what about more interventionist commodity schemes, inspired by the demands for a New International Economic Order (NIEO) in the 1970s? In recent years the debate on international commodity regulation (including supply management) has somewhat resurfaced (see e.g. Robbins 2003; Gibbon 2004). On the one hand this stems from the sharply declined commodity prices of some developing country products; on the other hand it illustrates the growing legitimacy crisis of neo-liberal trade recipes. French President Jacques Chirac's call to end the 'conspiracy of silence' around commodities stimulated renewed calls for interventionist commodity arrangements (see UNCTAD 2003b). Are the NIEO ideas still helpful in the establishment of a more equitable trading system? What is Europe's policy in the commodity debate, and how does it react to the renewed calls for interventionism? As indicated in Chapter 11, it also remains to be seen if and how the commodity procolos on banana, sugar, beef and veal – currently stand-alone agreements annexed to Cotonou – will be integrated in EPAs.

EBA in the broader picture

In spite of disappointing economic effects on LDC exports, EBA has played an interesting role in a number of other domains. Several chapters analysed how EBA intermeshes with internal and external policies of the EU, in line with the internal/external and realization/impact matrix in Chapter 1 (Table 1.1). They examined if and how EBA has affected upon broader evolutions in Europe's political and economic affairs. This proved to be a complex undertaking. EBA did obviously not result from a deliberate attempt to induce EU policy reforms in a particular direction. The EBA regulation as it was agreed in February 2001 stemmed from different considerations and objectives of different actors at different levels in the complex EU policy making process.

Indeed, even in trade there are various preferences behind the 'single voice' of the EU (cf. Meunier 2005). The contributions by Maurizio Carbone (Chapter 3) and Adrian van den Hoven (Chapter 4) give a detailed account of intra-European divergences on the EBA case. Carbone reminds us of the continuing north–south gap within the European Council of Ministers, whereas Van den Hoven empha- sizes conflicting bureaucratic strategies within the European Commission. The need for WTO compatibility also imposes external restrictions on Europe's capacity to act in trade policy. In short, one must be paranoid to see EBA as the instigator of all trade-related changes in EU policies over the past five years, conciously designed by EU policy makers.

Nevertheless, policy choices do not happen in splendid isolation. The design of a concrete trade initiative such as EBA reflects the power relations within the European Union. In this sense EBA provides an interesting case study to analyse the role of interests, ideologies and institutions in EU trade. Several chapters illustrate that the significance of EBA goes beyond merely reflecting EU policy choices. For being a relatively small initiative, it plays a remarkable catalyzing role in the formulation and implementation of several European policies. Thus without identifying EBA as the ultimate 'smoking gun', this conclusion posits that it proves instrumental for some EU policy actors to steer a number of policy choices. Generally speaking, these actors can be situated in the northern member states (within the Council) and in DG Trade (within the Commission) – although the picture often proves to be more complex.

Starting with intra-European policies, the situation of Europe's Common Agricultural Policy (CAP) is the most obvious example. It is no coincidence that the debate over the Commission's EBA proposal mainly concerned European 'sensitive' products such as rice, bananas and sugar. The Council's decision to introduce a transition period for these agricultural products gave rise to the cynical label of 'Everything But Farms'. But how and to what extent does EBA impact upon Europe's agricultural market?

Alan Matthews and Jacques Gallezot tackle this question in Chapter 9 and conclude that EBA has not played a significant role in the evolution of CAP reform, except for rice and sugar. In the case of bananas, the phasing-out deadline of 2006 merely reflected the previously agreed timetable for the introduction of a tariff- only regime. The (potential) impact of EBA was not a factor in the European banana reform, and with hindsight the phasing-out period for LDC banana imports was overly cautious. As for rice and sugar, however, a clear link can be made between the EU reform process (2002–03 for rice; 2003–05 for sugar) and concerns about the impact of additional EBA imports. Again the sugar case is most compelling. Expectations of increased sugar imports under EBA turned out to be a useful argument for proponents (initially DG Trade, and later also DG Agriculture) of an ambitious EU sugar market reform. In Chapter 10 Brüntrup describes how the EBA initiative served as a 'Trojan horse'. And although the tenor of the new sugar regime (price reductions) went contrary to the LDC sugar proposals (higher price under fixed quotas), the credibility of Europe's commit- ments under EBA was cited among the reasons for reform. Brüntrup argues that the main rationale behind this reform was to improve the competitiveness of EU sugar production and the standing of the EU in the WTO negotiations.

This is closely connected with another international dimension of EBA: its consequences for the sustainability of the EU–ACP Sugar Protocol. In Chapter 2 Jan Orbie describes how the establishment of EBA reflects the ideological shift from a more interventionist to a more neo-liberally inspired trade regime vis-à-vis the ACP. Moreover, Orbie argues that EBA plays a catalyzing role in the abandonment of the Sugar Protocol. It constitutes one of the factors that put pressure on the functioning of this sugar arrangement – not least in EU policy makers' discourse. From an economic point of view, Matthews and Gallezot also mention the problems that could arise after 2009, when EBA quotas disappear and with them the ability of the EU to insist that the refiners pay a minimum price for EBA sugar. Under the protocol Europe would be obliged to purchase ACP sugar at the EU reference price, whereas EU sugar refineries would buy cheaper EBA sugar.

By and large, the Sugar Protocol seems to meet the same fate as many other international commodity agreements that were conceived in the 1970s: although officially they continue to exist, their capacity to regulate commodity markets is effectively being eroded. This conclusion corresponds with Arts and Dickson's (2004) thesis that EU development cooperation has evolved 'from model to symbol'.

Dries Lesage and Bart Kerremans (Chapter 5) also pay attention to the ideological underpinnings of EU trade policy vis-à-vis the LDCs. They argue that Europe is much keener to promote reciprocal free trade with sub-Saharan Africa than the US. One reason lies in the political economy of Free Trade Agreements (FTAs) in the US, where Congress is reluctant to establish an 'FTA legacy' with binding commitments. In addition, LDCs are so small that incentives for business mobilization in favour of an FTA do not outweigh opposition from import-competing interests in the US. And in contrast to some countries in the Middle East, there are no clear-cut strategic and security reasons that tilt the balance in favour of support for FTAs with LDCs. According to Lesage and Kerremans, their different institutional settings help to explain transatlantic divergence on reciprocal FTAs with sub-Saharan countries. Because of the less politicized trade policy making process, EU officials meet less internal opposition against binding FTA commitments.

Europe's active pursuit of reciprocity with ACP countries has important consequences for the LDCs among them. Today they are confronted with a dilemma: opening their markets under EU-EPA schemes, or receiving EBA preferences from a rather isolated position? As Lesage and Kerremans point out, a refusal by ACP LDCs to join the EPAs would be seen as a setback by the EU. Because of asymmetric power relations between the EU and LDCs, the possibility of additional development aid, and the incentive for regional integration, LDCs will probably take part of the EPA schemes. This fits in with the conclusions of Babarinde and Faber (2004) and with Pilegaard's findings about Zambia's decision to participate in EU–COMESA negotiations (Chapter 8). However, there is no guarantee that all ACP LDCs will smoothly integrate in reciprocal free trade arrangements. Sanoussi Bilal (Chapter 11) scrutinizes the links between the ongoing EPA negotiations and EBA. He argues that the EU, by offering two preferential trade regimes to ACP LDCs, runs the risk of generating tensions between LDC and non-LDC members of one region, which may ultimately weaken the regional integration process that EPAs are supposed to foster and build upon. These tensions have two aspects. First, LDCs have DFQF access to the EU market. Will the EPA of which they may become a member provide them with the same access conditions? This will be the case only if all ACP EPA members get DFQF access to the EU. We return to this issue in the next section. Second, EPAs are constructed between an integrated ACP region and the EU. Thus, the ACP region will have to grant free access to 'substantially all' EU imports, in order to make the EPA reciprocal and WTO compatible. It will be impossible for the LDC members of EPAs to save the non-reciprocal nature of EBA. The example of the EU/SADC negotiations (Chapter 11, Box 11.1) shows that this aspect may turn out to be a major stumbling block on the road to EPAs.

The EPA negotiations provide an interesting subject for researchers on EU trade and development policies. Regional integration among developing countries constitutes an important factor for development through trade. In fact, the figures in Table 8.1 suggest that Zambia's international trade is already increasingly focused on the South African region. Further research should examine the role of the EU in fostering South–South trade, and the possible contribution of EPAs.[3]

Besides the EU–ACP trade agenda, there is another international dimension where EBA played a role: the Doha Development Round. Towards the end of the 1990s the EU showed itself the most ardent supporter of a new and comprehensive round of WTO trade negotiations. After the failure to launch the Millennium Round in Seattle in 1999, several trade policy measures were elaborated in order to take developing countries on board in Doha in 2001 (cf. Kerremans 2004). The approval of EBA in early 2001 constituted only one (but a very symbolic) trade-and-development initiative in the run-up to the UN Third LDC Conference (May 2001) and the Doha WTO summit (November 2001). It showed Europe's goodwill towards the LDCs and its intention to pursue a development agenda within the WTO. It allowed the EU to hold the high moral ground, encouraging other WTO members to follow Europe's lead.

But the construction of a development discourse – with EBA figuring as Europe's showpiece – also served intra-European purposes. In the course of the 1990s we have witnessed a politicization of EU trade policy. Political actors and civil society groups have become more engaged in this policy domain. The politicization of trade is not merely an EU phenomenon: anti-globalist protests since Seattle illustrate the increasingly contested legitimacy of the international trade regime. But in the EU the shift from a relatively technocratic trade policy style to a larger engagement of political and civil society actors has occurred relatively recently (cf. Smith and Woolcock 1999). During the EU negotiations on the Treaty of Nice in 2000, development NGOs castigated Europe's common commercial policy. Campaigns against 'Article 133' argued that EU trade policy making is undemocratic and that it pays insufficient attention to sustainable development objectives. In response, by the end of the 1990s the Commission intensified and formalized its consultations with civil society groups (Young 2004: 207).

A few years before, EU development aid policy had also been attacked for its slow disbursements, incoherence, donor duplication, personnel shortages and financial irregularities. In response, the Prodi Commission radically reformed EU development policies in 2000. With the overall aim of more coherence, the EU decided on the decentralization of aid management, the introduction of Country Strategy Papers, the creation of EuropeAid, etc. (cf. Holland 2002: 89–100). An OECD report welcomed these measures, and it highlighted 'Everything but Arms' as an important example of coherence in the new architecture of EU external policies (OECD 2002: 62, 149).

Thus, at the beginning of this millennium, the EU experienced a legitimacy crisis in its external trade and development nexus. EBA constituted an attractive response in this difficult context. Confronted with the traditional critique against EU import barriers for developing countries, EU officials and policy makers conveniently pushed forward the EBA initiative. Critics had to admit that this constituted, at least, a step in the right direction. This strategy relates to the second level in Van den Hoven's two-level games model, where it was argued that EBA also serves to gain the support of development NGOs and the broader development community for EU trade policy (see Chapter 4). As pointed out in the introductory chapter, EBA was very successful in this respect.

Europe's successful engagement in global affairs may also serve as a form of 'cement' for the European project more generally. Europe's pursuit of international objectives may indeed compensate for the internal legitimacy crisis of the EU (cf. Smith 2006: 11). In any case, public opinion in European countries generally favours a larger EU role in the world – in contrast to a more sceptical attitude about internal EU politics. Although it is less clear how this EU role is exactly conceived, Europe's public opinion seems to support a more ambitious EU in the domain of development policy. One typical ingredient in the construction of a distinctive EU world role, characterized by a development-friendly image, is the contrast with Europe's 'significant other', the US (cf. Orbie 2003). EBA is a textbook case of this well tried strategy. It placed Europe in the driving seat of a pro-development trade round, in contrast to other developed countries such as the US.

Yet this book comes to a more qualified conclusion. Chapters 6 and 7 make it clear that, in terms of economic impact, EBA is not much more generous than US trade policy towards LDCs. In fact, EBA and AGOA do not address the same groups of countries. A comparison between 'Lomé-style' preferences and AGOA is more apt, and shows that both systems are effective, while controlling for geography, market size and institutions. The US experience with AGOA shows that a bold approach to rules of origin can provoke substantial supply responses from developing countries and help them build a more diversified export base. The EU should take this into account when reforming its rules of origin for preferential systems. Examining the political dynamics behind EBA and AGOA, Lesage and Kerremans (Chapter 5) also put apparent divergences between EU and US trade policies into perspective. EBA and AGOA stem from different idiosyncratic trade and development policy making processes, but divergences between both regimes are smaller than appears at first glance.

The 'internal consumption' of EBA could also extend to the agricultural sector. First, as mentioned by Van den Hoven, Matthews and Gallezot, and Brüntrup (Chapters 4, 9, 10 respectively), EBA gives the LDCs a stake in Europe's protected agricultural market. To some extent it creates a coalition between EU agricultural interests and developing-country producers. Since the creation of EBA, LDC producers indeed have an interest in high European prices. They also side with Europe's reluctance about agricultural tariff reductions in the WTO negotiations, for fear of preference erosion vis-à-vis non-LDCs. Again, this particularly applies to the sugar case. The convergence of interests between Northern and Southern producers even provoked joint demonstrations of European farmers and development NGOs against the sugar market reform.

Attempts to find allies among developing countries for WTO agricultural negotiations are not a new phenomenon. Europe's preferential trade relationship with the ACP is an obvious illustration. Commodity arrangements for products such as bananas created an ACP–EU alliance in favour of a protected European agricultural market. And their preferential market access explains the ACP countries' reluctant attitude to further liberalization of European tariffs. More recently, the EU attempts to build an alliance with the G-33 around the idea of multifunctionality in agriculture. EU discourse in the Doha Round consistently emphasizes objective conflicts of interests between smaller (G-33/G-90/LDC) and larger (G-20) developing-country producers (cf. Van Dijck and Faber 2006). In fact, the EBA dossier also exemplifies this strategy. Europe's call to follow its lead in granting DFQF market access to LDCs is not only directed to developed countries: it explicitly targets the 'advanced developing countries' as well.

Second, the EBA initiative gives the EU agricultural sector an appealing argument that Europe has done its homework. EBA shows Europe's willingness to sacrifice its agricultural interests for the benefit of the South. However, this development initiative is targeted at the neediest countries – the LDCs, which do not have a large supply capacity – and not at export-competitive producers (the G-20). As one European sugar industry representative put it: we opened the door for agriculture and we gave the key to the poorest countries.[4]

There is another implication of EBA. The focus on the group of LDCs as an objective category heralded a radical departure from Europe's trade relations. During the past five decades the European Community has constructed a complex 'spaghetti bowl' (Bhagwati 2002: 112–14) of preferential trade arrangements. The result is that only a small number of developed countries (US, Canada, Australia, New Zealand, Japan, Taiwan, Hong Kong, Singapore) actually enjoy Most Favoured Nation (MFN) treatment. All other countries find themselves in a higher layer of Europe's pyramid of preferences. These exceptions from the MFN rule are legitimized under various WTO provisions: Article XXIV on FTAs and customs unions, the Enabling Clause about the GSP, and waivers for other unilateral preferences.

To date, the dominant approach of EU trade policy has been a geographical one. Until recently the ACP and southern Mediterranean countries appeared at the apex of the preferential pyramid, by means of temporary waivers. EU regional integration and enlargements are justified under Article XXIV. Since 1995 EU trade policy vis-à-vis developing countries aims for reciprocal FTAs: it signed such agreements with southern Mediterranean countries, Mexico, Chile and South Africa; negotiations with MERCOSUR and the Gulf Cooperation Council are pending. ACP regions are also involved in FTA negotiations. More recently, the EU suggested negotiating an FTA with ASEAN, India, South Korea and with Russia (after WTO accession). Departing from this geographical rationale, the GSP regime has always been a residual category for those developing countries outside the ACP group, the Mediterranean region and (more recently) the countries having an FTA with the EU. Developing countries exporting under Europe's GSP have done this, in a sense, for want of anything better.

EBA runs counter to the geographical approach, catapulting a multilateral category, the LDCs, to the top of the preferential pyramid. As explained by Orbie in Chapter 2, this decision goes back to 1997, when the EU agreed to grant LDCs the same market access as ACP countries. This ostensibly limited decision set off a path-dependent process that almost inevitably led to further differentiation between Europe's trade relations with *all* LDCs (including ACP LDCs) on the one hand and the other ACP countries on the other. The 1997 decision about 'EBA *avant la lettre*' proved to be functional in the post-Lomé reform process, where Europe aimed at the break-up of the ACP group. Carbone argues that the lack of consultation of the ACP group can be seen as part of a consistent strategy inside the EU that has gradually undermined the traditional partnership approach of the Lomé Convention (Chapter 3 of this volume). He also states that EBA 'may have made a terminal contribution to the ACP unity and its privileged relationship with the EU'. The promotion of LDCs provided a legitimate reason to discard the ACP group as a dinosaurian category in Europe's trade policy network.

But today, this hybrid status among ACP members aggravates the pursuit of Europe's free trade agenda with these countries. LDCs that form part of an ACP region are faced with a dilemma: joining a reciprocal EPA with the EU, or continuing to receive unilateral preferences under EBA? In Chapter 8 Pilegaard suggests a number of reasons why Zambia ultimately decided to participate in EPA negotiations – despite fear of increased competition from the EU, and tariff revenue losses at its borders. He mentions Zambia's eagerness to engage in regional economic integration under COMESA, the hope that long asymmetric liberalization periods and special and differential treatment provisions for LDCs will be foreseen, and the prospect of increased development aid. As mentioned above, LDCs may also find it difficult not to join EPAs because of asymmetric power relations with the EU, which has actively promoted reciprocal FTAs with all ACP countries.

This EPA/EBA confusion is exemplary of a more general conclusion. Although the EBA initiative has proved to be functional for a number of EU policy makers in a number of different intra-European and international issues, there is no 'grand design' hiding behind it. As mentioned in Van den Hoven's conclusion (Chapter 4), the formulation and implementation of EBA seem to have been driven by, at times, very contradictory strategies.

The future of 'Everything but Arms': a regional and multilateral benchmark

This is not a history book. One reason for the continued significance of EBA is explained above: it has wide-ranging ramifications on several policy domains, some of which have only started to materialize. Some of these implications may not have been anticipated by a number of political actors in Europe. But anyhow, EBA is here to stay. Although EBA could so to speak be amended with almost one stroke of the pen – as a unilateral GSP regulation by qualified majority vote in the Council and without involvement of the European Parliament – it is politically unfeasible to reverse or substantially revise this highly symbolic initiative.

The other reason is that at present the issue of DFQF market access occupies centre stage on the international trade agenda. More specifically, market access preferences *à la* EBA serve as an explicit benchmark for regional as well as multilateral trade negotiations with developing countries – and not just the least developed. Granting DFQF market access to LDCs has set a precedent. For LDCs it remains an important demand towards other WTO member states. For non-LDC ACP countries it constitutes a yardstick to evaluate Europe's generosity in the ongoing EPA negotiations.

The international diffusion of EBA

As stated above, the development gains for LDCs from the Doha Round would substantially increase if all OECD countries would grant them full DFQF treatment. The EU has partly succeeded in its demand for a 'global EBA' within the WTO. As explained in Chapter 2, in 1997 Europe had already posited the proposal of a multilateralized DFQF market access scheme, as a long-term objective of its 'LDC strategy'. Since then, and consistent with its 'leading by example' discourse, EU policy makers have never failed to urge other WTO members to grant completely free market access to LDCs. Similarly, the LDCs themselves have made DFQF market access their single most important issue in the Doha Round. Even though the EBA experience makes it clear that complete market access is far from the most important barrier for LDC exports, LDCs are asking for more of the same. In Chapter 8 Pilegaard provides some interesting explanations for 'the attractiveness of a strategy that does not work'. Looking at the character of the LDC group as an international negotiator, he clarifies that the DFQF market access agenda has more to do with the internal politics of LDC negotiations than with immediate economic utility.

Until 1999 Europe's 'leading by example' campaign did not seem to be very fruitful: conclusions of the WTO (May 1998), G-7/G-8 (May 1998, June 1999) and Quad (May 1997, April 1998, May 1999) meetings do not go further than the Singapore Declaration's 1996 commitment about increased market access. The EU attempted to put a commitment for DFQF market access in the declaration of the WTO summit in Seattle (1999), where a new trade round was to be launched. But according to the then Commissioner Lamy, the US and Canada had problems with the European LDC proposal (*Agence Europe* 1999a, b). Later WTO Director

General Moore declared that there was almost agreement on an 'LDC market access and technical assistance package' in Seattle (Watal 2000: 81), although a Bangladesh representative said that in the latest version of the text that was under discussion at Seattle on action in favour of LDCs the entire paragraph on market access had been missing.[5]

Seattle nevertheless led to a radicalization of market access initiatives favouring LDCs. Since 2000 several countries including the Quad members have elaborated on schemes envisaging improved (possibly DFQF) access for LDC products. Canada extended the coverage of its GSP for the LDCs in 2001 and made further improvements in 2003. Japan added new products to its special GSP for LDCs in the fiscal year 2001/02. In 2003 the country added a number of agricultural and fish products to the scheme. The US and the EU introduced AGOA and EBA in 2001 (UNCTAD 2003a) and expanded free market access in subsequent years. Still Europe's EBA remains the most ambitious initiative in terms of LDC market access. And in Doha it became clear that other WTO member states were not willing to engage in firm multilateral DFQF commitments. The Doha Declaration states that 'we welcome the significant market access improvements by WTO members . . . We further commit ourselves to consider additional measures for progressive improvements in market access for LDCs'. Two years later, the Cancun draft Ministerial Declaration (Annex A) was only slightly more ambitious: 'Developed countries [should] [shall] provide duty-free and quota-free market access for products originating from least developed countries.'

Therefore the Hong Kong Declaration of end 2005 looks like a breakthrough. Paragraph 47 on LDCs states that 'developed-country Members, and developing-country Members declaring themselves in a position to do so, agree to implement duty-free and quota-free market access for products originating from LDCs as provided for in Annex F to this document'. This seemingly firm commitment is somewhat nuanced by a reading of the annexes. Annex A on agriculture also makes clear that this DFQF commitment 'is not at this point concretely operational for all Members'. In other words, it should be implemented only as part of the successful conclusion of the Doha Round as a single undertaking. Annex F on LDCs gives a timetable, namely '2008 or no later than the start of the implementation period'. But it also introduces an important qualification:

> Members facing difficulties at this time to provide market access as set out above shall provide duty-free and quota-free market access *for at least 97 per cent of products originating from LDCs* . . . In addition, these Members shall take steps to progressively achieve compliance with the obligations set out above, taking into account the impact on other developing countries at similar levels of development . . .

There is thus no firm timetable for the progressive liberalization of the remaining 3 per cent. This allows the US to exclude a broad range of sensitive products among which most probably textiles and clothing (see Chapter 5). As regards sensitive agricultural products, it could allow Japan to exclude rice, the US to take sugar out of the preferences, Canada to exclude poultry meat (see Chapter 9). In May 2006 the US suggested using the ability to exempt 3 per cent of tariff lines, which is about 330 tariff lines (or products), or, potentially, all current LDC exports (Rangaswami 2006: 8).

But even though the commitment to LDCs is still ambiguous,[6] the DFQF issue constituted one of the few concrete decisions of the Hong Kong summit. It shows that the idea of EBA continues to hold a remarkable power of persuasion within the WTO. Thus Europe's EBA did not only stimulate the *launching* of the Doha Round in 2001; the 'multilateralization' of EBA potentially plays a role in the Round's successful *conclusion as a development agenda*. A clear decision on the 3 per cent timetable, going beyond the Hong Kong text, may emerge as one of the crucial elements of a final package deal.[7]

Polaski (2006: 72) comes up with an even more ambitious proposal for the Doha Development Agenda: extending the DFQF commitment to a number of middle-income developing countries. This is precisely what some of these non-LDCs expect from the EU, particularly in the context of the EPA negotiations.

EBA as a benchmark for EPA

Besides its international diffusion, the existence of EBA also influences the ongoing regional trade negotiations with ACP countries on EPAs. As explained in Chapter 11 by Bilal, this new EU–ACP trade architecture should guarantee compatibility with WTO rules (Article XXIV) and foster regional integration between ACP countries. The ACP countries and the development community in the EU have expressed their concern about possible negative side effects of these EPAs. For one thing, reciprocal tariff liberalization implies a loss of tariff revenues, which constitutes an important part of their government budgets. Facilitating imports from more competitive European producers, it could also hurt non-competitive sectors in ACP countries. Another stumbling block is Europe's demand to insert 'WTO-plus' provisions (e.g. about investment, competition, intellectual property) in the EPAs.

It is safe to say that the EU will have to make a number of concessions vis-à-vis EPA members. Longer transition periods for ACP tariff reductions, asymmetrical liberalization and increased financial assistance to compensate for this liberalization (Aid for Trade) will undoubtedly be part of the deal. But in addition to this, ACP countries are looking for concessions at the EU border as well. It takes two to tango, and liberalization under an FTA must come from both sides. For ACP negotiators, EBA forms the obvious benchmark in their plea for improved access to the European market. After all, this is the treatment that LDCs receive, which are often part of the same regional integration scheme. Therefore it would also solve part of the EPA/EBA confusion. There are a number of additional reasons why the DFQF demand is an attractive option for ACP negotiators, analogous with Pilegaard's explanation of the LDC stance on this topic in the WTO (see Chapter 8): it is an easy message, it will receive support from European development communities, and it puts the EU on the defensive.

EBA thus clearly functions as a benchmark. For ACP countries that do not belong to the LDC group, EBA treatment is the ultimate touchstone to evaluate any European tariff concessions. For example, Southern African countries, including South Africa, demand EBA equivalent market access in 2008 (see Box 11.1 in Chapter 11). But is extended EBA market access for the ACP countries a feasible option? For LDCs this is an unattractive alternative: on the one hand they open their own markets, on the other they have to share their preferential margin to the European market with other ACP countries which implies more competition. This option would thus meet disagreement between ACP countries. The EU for its part is unlikely to agree with a generalized DFQF offer to ACP regions. During the Cotonou negotiations, the EU even refused to include small and vulnerable non-LDCs (i.e. landlocked and island states such as St Kitts and Nevis) in the future EBA. Despite the insistence of ACP negotiators to broaden the application of EBA, Europe restricted DFQF treatment to the official UN list of LDCs. Today Europe may be more willing to grant these countries equivalent market access as LDCs. DG Trade's initial negotiating proposal even suggested DFQF access for all EPA members (Chapter 11). However, as in the EBA dossier, and in line with Van den Hoven's emphasis on bureaucratic divisions in EU trade policy (Chapter 4), DG Agriculture was opposed to this ambitious offer. This resistance is not surprising. As explained by Matthews and Gallezot (Chapter 9), the implications of a DFQF EPA scenario on Europe's agriculture would be much more far-reaching than the current impact of EBA. Thus, it is plausible that EPAs will contain important exceptions for agricultural products. The EU–South Africa Trade Cooperation and Development Agreement, concluded in 1999, already illustrates that the WTO requirement under Article XXIV to liberalize 'substantially all' trade allows for a relatively flexible interpretation. Important European agricultural products such as sugar and beef continue to be protected from South African competition (cf. Holland 1998: 225; Hurt 2004: 163). Olympio *et al.* (2006) argue that the supply response by South African exporters on the introduction of DFQF access to the EU market will be minimal. Sugar and beef are the main exceptions, for which the commodity protocols should be maintained in order to make a unified SADC/EU EPA feasible. Thus, complete DFQF market access will be difficult to realize for all EPA members. The EU is unlikely to extend EBA treatment to other ACP countries (or to other trading partners such as the MERCOSUR) in the near future. At the same time, the EU will feel strong pressure to discriminate between LDC and non-LDC EPA members in order to continue DFQF market access for the LDCs, which is distorting the FTAs that underpin EPAs.

This discussion makes it clear that EBA complicates the EPA negotiations as far as market access to the EU is concerned. In the last section we argued that the same applies for the loss of national trade policy space (reciprocity) that the shift from EBA to EPA implies for the LDCs concerned. Although a vast number of alternative EPAs may, and will be, discussed in the negotiations (Bilal and Rampa 2006 give an overview), in the end LDCs can be accommodated in EPAs only if they derive sufficient benefits compared with their EBA fall-back position. These benefits may be sought in the contractual nature of EPAs, much improved rules of origin and support for trade capacity development. If this would be the result, EBA has been used as a lever by the ACP LDCs to get a better deal. The policy makers who introduced EBA will not have foreseen this function.

EBA and LDCs in EU discourse: fading away?

As explained in the introductory chapter, EBA has often been presented as the best example of 'normative power Europe' through trade. The initiative takes a central position in Europe's trade and development discourse. Yet recently EU policy makers seem to put somewhat less emphasis on (1) the 'Everything but Arms' label and on (2) the LDC group as a relevant trade category.

Europe continues to stress its DFQF treatment for LDC imports, and to insist on other WTO members following its lead. But a cursory reading of some policy documents suggests that 'EBA' appears less prominently as a catchword in European discourse.[8] This wearing away of the EBA motto relates to the adoption of similar arrangements by other trading powers – and thus to EBA's successful international diffusion – but also to the fact that its limited effect in terms of LDC development has become clear. At the time of its inception, EBA served as a prime illustration of Europe's offensive and self-confident stance in the Doha Development Round. Even though its export subsidies in agriculture were the butt of criticism, at least the EU had taken the lead in the area of agricultural market access. Meanwhile, market access in agriculture has resurfaced as one of the main bones of contention in the Doha negotiations, and notwithstanding EBA, the EU is on the defensive. More powerful developing coutries, supported by the US, are insisting on deeper tariff cuts at the EU borders. Matthews and Gallezot made a similar point about Europe's position at the Hong Kong summit (see Chapter 9): 'EBA appears to have been interpreted more as a fig leaf designed to disguise its reluctance to make an offer that was deemed adequate particularly by the major developing country players in the G-20.' There is some irony in these observations: now that we finally approach 'everything' but arms – including rice, bananas and finally sugar in 2009 – its appeal seems to be fading away, and so does its prominence in EU discourse.

A similar observation may be noticed with regard to the LDC category. As explained above, this group of countries gained relevance in EU trade politics from 1997. It characterized the globalization of EU trade policies. But today the emphasis on LDCs appears to be less outspoken. On the bilateral trade front, it is now clear that different treatments of non-LDC ACP countries and LDC ACP countries make the EPA negotiations boundlessly complicated. The EU insists on LDC participation in EPA trade schemes.[9] With regard to the multilateral trade negotiations, Van den Hoven (Chapter 4) points out that Europe's 'policy towards differentiation' is not limited to the LDC criterion. EU proposals to provide a 'G-90 round for free' indicate that Europe attempts to build an 'everything but G-20' coalition. This includes the group of LDCs, but also other weak and vulnerable developing countries. The main message is that emerging countries with competitive export industries, such as Brazil, China or India, do not require special treatment under WTO rules. It should also be noticed that these G-20 countries – rather than the LDCs, which have a less persistent negotiating stance – are key to the succesful conclusion of the Doha Development Round. In its unilateral GSP system, the EU has recently introduced a special GSP regime for 'sustainable development and good governance'. The GSP regulation defines a new category of 'vulnerable' countries.[10] If these vulnerable countries comply with a number of international conventions, they receive a tariff reduction from the GSP scheme that comes close to EBA treatment for LDCs. Since 2006 Bolivia, Colombia, Costa Rica, Ecuador, Georgia, Guatemala, Honduras, Sri Lanka, Moldova, Mongolia, Nicaragua, Panama, Peru, El Salvador and Venezuela benefit from the 'GSP-plus' regime (cf. Orbie 2007).

In conclusion, Europe's trade policy towards developing countries remains to a large extent focused on geographical factors (EPAs with ACP regions, FTAs with other countries and regions), and to the extent that other criteria are used in Europe's unilateral, bilateral and multilateral trade policies the LDC group is far from the only relevant category.

Final conclusion

The various chapters of this volume make it perfectly clear that although EBA may have had a very modest impact on the export performance and development of the LDCs, its influence on various fields of policy making in the EU and on Europe's external relations have far outweighed its original intentions as a development tool. EBA has been functional for a number of EU policy makers in a number of different intra-European and international issues. However, there is no hidden agenda or master design in the background. In fact, with hindsight, EBA entailed a number of paradoxical evolutions: facilitating the launching of a new WTO trade round, but at the same time reducing the stake of LDCs in further liberalization; contributing to the breaking up of interventionist commodity arrangements and to the splitting of the ACP group, but at the same time hindering the reciprocal EPA process; pressurizing the European sugar market reform, but at the same time creating a coalition between LDC and European sugar producers; supporting Europe's legitimacy with public opinion and the development community, but at the same time provoking cynical reactions about 'Everything But Farms' . . .

The bottom line of this is a lack of consistency. The establishment of EBA has been driven by very contradictory strategies. EBA obviously had a strategic value, serving specific EU agendas at specific times, with ramifications that are much broader than one would expect from such a limited initiative. Nevertheless, the overall picture is less univocal.

In Chapter 1 we asked the question 'Is EBA all about nothing, or has it somehow a political and economic relevance?' The answer is clear. The relevance of EBA has been widespread in the six years after its inception, and, although its prominence in EU trade and development discourse may now be fading away, more is to be expected in the coming years.

Notes

1 The data come from the subsequent UNCTAD LDC reports (available online at http://www.unctad.org). There were no data available for Bhutan, or for Cambodia in 1998; Myanmar/Burma is excluded from EU trade preferences.
2 For comparison, between 2001 and 2004 the average annual amount was €300 million by member states and €800 million by the Community (EU 2006: 15).
3 Recent research by Stevens (2006) suggests that EPAs will weaken regionalism, rather than meeting the stated objective of regional integration.
4 Debate on 'WTO: blessing or threat for agriculture', Faculty of Bioscience Engineering, Ghent University, 8 February 2006.
5 Minutes GC WTO 7–8 February 2000, WT/GC/M/53 (available on line at http://www.wto.org).
6 This is also the case for the addition that the 'impact on other developing countries at similar levels of development' will be taken into account. This phrase seems to suggest that DFQF market access should not be implemented when the accompanying preference erosion has a negative impact on small and vulnerable countries (e.g. landlocked and island states).
7 Inversely, when the Doha Round is in a deadlock, advocates of the WTO negotiations point to the DFQF commitment as one of the main losses for developing countries.
8 This is still a tentative observation. Yet see e.g. the following three documents of December 2005: the EU Strategy for Africa adopted by the European Council (EU 2005a: 5), the 'European consensus on development' adopted by the Council, the Parliament and the Commission (EU 2005b: 11), and the statement of Commissioner Mandelson at the Hong Kong summit (EU 2005c: 2). Each time the EU mentions the 'DFQF' issue, but it does not literally speak of 'EBA'.
9 Another example specifically relates to 'Flex', the export stabilization scheme, which succeeded the STABEX mechanism under the Cotonou agreement. Initially the eligibility requirements for Flex disbursements were more flexible for LDCs: 2 per cent loss in export earnings instead of 10 per cent. But this LDC clause was subsequently amended to include two other categories of ACP countries: 'landlocked countries and island states' and 'post-conflict and post-natural disaster states'.
10 A vulnerable country is defined by means of two criteria: a country (1) that is not classified by the World Bank as a high-income country during three consecutive years, and whose five largest sections of its GSP-covered imports to the Community represent more than 75 per cent in value of its total GSP-covered imports, and (2) whose GSP-covered imports to the Community represent less than 1 per cent in value of total GSP-covered imports to the Community. See Article 9(3) of Council Regulation 980/2005, 27 June 2005, OJ L169.

References

Achterbosch, T., Van Tongeren, F. and De Bruin, S. (2003) 'Trade Preferences for Developing Countries', The Hague: Agricultural Economics Research Institute (LEI), May.

Agence Europe (1999a), No. 7607, 4 December.

Agence Europe (1999b), No. 7608, 6–7 December.

Arts, K. and Dickson, A.K. (eds) (2004) *EU Development Cooperation: from Model to Symbol?*, Manchester: Manchester University Press.

Barbarinde, O. and Faber, G. (2004) 'From Lomé to Cotonou: business as usual?', *European Foreign Affairs Review*, 9: 27–47.

Bhagwati, J. (2002) *Free Trade Today*, Princeton NJ: Princeton University Press.

Bilal, S. and Rampa, F. (2006) *Alternative (to) EPAs: Possible Scenarios for the Future ACP Trade Relations with the EU*, Maastricht: ECDPM.

Brenton, P. (2003) 'Integrating the Least Developed Countries into the World Trading System: The Current Impact of EU Preferences under Everything but Arms', Policy Research Working Paper No. 3018, Washington DC: World Bank.

Cernat, L., Laird, S., Monge-Roffarello, L. and Turrini, A. (2003) 'The EU's Everything but Arms Initiative and the Least-developed Countries', Discussion Paper No. 2003/47, Wider, United Nations University. Available at http://www.wider.unu.edu/publications/dps/dps2003/dp2003-047.pdf (accessed 8 May 2006).

Dijck, P. van, and Faber, G. (2006) 'How to save the Doha Round: a European perspective', *European Foreign Affairs Review*, 11, 3: 291–309.

EU (2005a) 'The EU and Africa: towards a strategic partnership', Brussels: Council of the European Union, 19 December.

EU (2005b) The European Consensus on Development, Joint statement by the Council and the representatives of the governments of the Member States meeting within the Council, the European Parliament and the Commission, Brussels, 20 December.

EU (2005c) European Communities Statement by Right Honourable Peter Mandelson, Commissioner for Trade, Hong Kong: WTO Ministerial Conference, 14 December.

EU (2006) 'Report on the EU action plan on agricultural commodities: EU–Africa partnership on cotton', Brussels: European Commission, 3 April.

Gibbon, P. (2004) *The Commodity Question: New Thinking on Old Problems*, Copenhagen: Danish Institute of International Studies.

Goodison, P. (2005) 'Six months on: what shift is there in the EU approach to EPA negotiations?', *Review of African Political Economy*, 32, 104–5: 295–308.

Holland, M. (1998) 'Europe's foreign policy and South Africa, 1977–1997', *European Foreign Affairs Review*, 3, 2: 215–32.

Holland, M. (2002) *The European Union and the Third World*, Basingstoke: Palgrave.

Hurt, S. (2004) 'The European Union's external relations with Africa after the Cold War: aspects of continuity and change', in I. Taylor and P. Williams (eds) *Africa in International Politics: External Involvement on the Continent*, London: Routledge.

IFPRI (2006) 'Two Opportunities to Deliver on the Doha Development Package', second IFPRI Assessment Brief on a Doha Round Conclusion, Draft, 18 June, by A. Bonet, S. Mevel and D. Orden, Washington DC: International Food Policy Research Centre.

Kerremans, B. (2004) 'What went wrong in Cancun? A principal–agent view on the EU's rationale towards the Doha Development Round', *European Foreign Affairs Review*, 9, 3: 363–93.

Meunier, S. (2005) *Trading Voices: The European Union in International Commercial Negotiations*, Princeton NJ and Oxford: Princeton University Press.

OECD (2002) *European Community Development Co-operation Review*, Paris: Development Assistance Committee, OECD.

Olympio, J., Robinson, P. and Cocks, M. (2006) 'A Study to Assess the likely Impacts on Southern African and EU Producers of further liberalising the Trade Development and Cooperation Agreement (TDCA) by granting South Africa Duty-free Access to the EU', Trowbridge: Landell Mills.

Orbie, J. (2003) 'EU development policy integration and the Monterrey process: a leading and benevolent identity?', *European Foreign Affairs Review*, 8, 3: 395–415.

Orbie, J. (2007) 'Core labour standards in trade policy; the GSP regime of the European Union', in C. Fenwick and T. Novitz (eds) *Legal Protection of Workers' Human Rights: Regulatory Changes and Challenges*, Oxford: Hart Publishing (forthcoming).

Polaski, S. (2006) 'Winners and Losers: Impact of the Doha Round on Developing Countries', Carnegie Endowment report, February.

Rangaswami, V. (2006) 'Nickel-and-diming the Poor: US Implementation of the LDC Initiative', Washington DC: Carnegie Endowment for International Peace, Policy Outlook, July.

Robbins, P. (2003) *Stolen Fruit: The Tropical Commodities Disaster*, London: Zed Books.

Smith, M.H. (2006) 'The European Union and International Order: European and Global Aspects'. Paper presented at the workshop 'EU Foreign/Security/Defense Policy: Current Challenges, Future Prospects', Washington DC: Maxwell EU Center (Syracuse University) and 'EU as a Global Actor' interest section (EUSA), 3 April.

Smith, M. and Woolcock, S. (1999) 'European commercial policy: a leadership role in the new millennium?', *European Foreign Affairs Review*, 4, 4: 439–62.

Stevens, C. (2006) 'The EU, Africa and Economic Partnership Agreements: unintended consequences of policy leverage', *Journal of Modern African Studies*, 44, 3, 441–58.

UNCTAD (2003a) 'Main Recent Initiatives in Favour of Least Developed Countries in the Area of Preferential Market Access: Preliminary Impact Assessment', TD/B/50/5, Geneva: UNCTAD.

UNCTAD (2003b) 'Economic development in Africa: Trade Performance and Commodity Dependence', New York and Geneva: UN.

UNCTAD (2004) *The Least Developed Countries Report 2004*, New York/Geneva: UN.

Watal, J. (2000) 'Developing countries' interests in a "Development Round"', in J.J. Schott (ed.) *The WTO after Seattle*, Washington DC: Institute for International Economics.

Young, A.R. (2004) 'The EU and world trade: Doha and beyond', in M. Green Cowles and D. Dinan (eds) *Developments in the European Union 2*, Basingstoke: Palgrave Macmillan.

Yu, W. and Jensen, T.V. (2005) 'Trade preferences, WTO negotiations and the LDCs: the case of the "Everything but Arms" initiative', *Journal of World Trade*, 43: 375–405.

Index

Page numbers referring to figures/tables are in **bold** type